Intranet ... For Du...

Key Intranet Publishing Abbreviations

CGI (Common Gateway Interface). A standardized method for a web server to pass instructions and data along to an external program, and for that program to return information to the user.

FAQ (Frequently Asked Questions). A document, such as an intranet web page, featuring a list of common questions and their answers.

FTP (File Transfer Protocol). A TCP/IP application designed for copying files of various types between computers.

GIF (Graphics Interchange Format). A compressed graphics file format developed by CompuServe and characterized by small file sizes and a maximum palette of 256 colors.

HTML (HyperText Markup Language). The most popular coding method for defining documents on intranets, HTML permits the web page author to specify approximately where text, graphics, and links should appear, and what they should do (if anything).

HTTP (HyperText Transfer Protocol). The client/server protocol that manages links between pages on a web server. Intranet servers and browsers "speak" HTTP, which underpins the World Wide Web and corporate intranets.

IBT (Intranet-Based Training). Computer-based training designed for distribution on an intranet.

JPEG (Joint Photographic Experts Group). A graphic file type featuring adjustable compression and the ability to display millions of colors. Best suited for compressing photorealistic images rather than images with precise lines and curves.

LAN (Local Area Network). A network containing servers, workstations, cable and software all connected together within a relatively small geographical area.

OCR (Optical Character Recognition). The process of converting a scanned document from a collection of tiny dots into a text document that a computer word processor or editor can understand.

ODBC (Open DataBase Connectivity). The most widely supported standard for open database software, initially developed by Microsoft. All major relational Data Base Management Systems (DBMSs) support ODBC — DBMS vendors supply their own ODBC software.

PDF (Portable Document Format). Adobe's file format standard for document interchange, and one of the more popular document formats on the Internet and intranets.

PERL (Practical Extraction and Report Language). A programming language used frequently in CGI scripts. PERL contains several commands for handling text, making it suitable for processing HTML forms.

SGML (Standard Generalized Markup Language). A document design system used in high-end publishing applications, and the parent of HTML. SGML imposes a stricter separation of form and content than HTML.

SSL (Secure Sockets Layer). A standard method of providing encrypted data transmission between an intranet browser and web server.

TCP/IP (Transmission Control Protocol/Internet Protocol). A set of network protocols (languages) that intranets use for file transfer, network management, and messaging.

URL (Uniform Resource Locator). The address that points users to a specific intranet service (usually HTTP or FTP) and location (web page, file to download). Every link on a web page has an associated URL.

WAN (Wide Area Network). Local Area Networks (LANs) connected across large distances, usually via communications protocols running on satellite, microwave or Internet links.

WWW (World Wide Web). Born in 1993, the multimedia face of the Internet. Web pages can include color graphics and even sound and video. They can also include convenient and automatic links to other Web pages.

...For Dummies: #1 Computer Book Series for Beginners

Intranet Publishing For Dummies®

Cheat Sheet

Ways to Publish Documents on an Intranet

Publishing Format	Concerns, Problems, and Particulars
Native Format	Okay if browser supports the format (e.g. text, GIF, JPEG, etc.)
Native Format, with browser plug-in	Plug-in runs in browser's memory space and adds viewing capabilities for native format documents
Native Format, with helper program	Helper program runs in its own memory space, can be called by browser to display the document in its native format
Convert to HTML/Java, retain exact formatting	Java-based programs such as Net-It Now! retain exact text and graphics layout as you have in the unconverted document
Convert to HTML, web-style formatting	Conversion tools such as HTML Transit reformat document to web conventions, don't require Java, don't always look exactly like the original
Convert to HTML using original	HTML export feature of original program may be built-in or an application add-in to the original program — converted document doesn't always look exactly like the original
Scan, convert to editable text using OCR, and save as HTML	For paper-based documents — use software that can do all three in one program
Convert to portable document format	Requires a browser plug-in or helper program, such as Adobe Acrobat Reader
Convert to specialized database format	Create a document database (such as a Folio infobase) for fast and standardized search and retrieval
Convert to Open Database (ODBC) format	Store documents as ODBC database records and use database connectivity products to view and update them
Publish as binary file	Create a download page for software upgrades, computer-based presentations, and so on using FTP or HTTP
Publish as push document	Create channels for automatic distribution to users who specify preferences, distributes documents to users automatically

Copyright © 1997 IDG Books Worldwide, Inc. All rights reserved.
Cheat Sheet $2.95 value. Item 222-0.
For more information about IDG Books, call 1-800-762-2974.

...For Dummies: #1 Computer Book Series for Beginners

References for the Rest of Us!®

COMPUTER BOOK SERIES FROM IDG

Are you intimidated and confused by computers? Do you find that traditional manuals are overloaded with technical details you'll never use? Do your friends and family always call you to fix simple problems on their PCs? Then the *...For Dummies*® computer book series from IDG Books Worldwide is for you.

...For Dummies books are written for those frustrated computer users who know they aren't really dumb but find that PC hardware, software, and indeed the unique vocabulary of computing make them feel helpless. *...For Dummies* books use a lighthearted approach, a down-to-earth style, and even cartoons and humorous icons to diffuse computer novices' fears and build their confidence. Lighthearted but not lightweight, these books are a perfect survival guide for anyone forced to use a computer.

> *"I like my copy so much I told friends; now they bought copies."*
> — Irene C., Orwell, Ohio

> *"Quick, concise, nontechnical, and humorous."*
> — Jay A., Elburn, Illinois

> *"Thanks, I needed this book. Now I can sleep at night."*
> — Robin F., British Columbia, Canada

Already, millions of satisfied readers agree. They have made *...For Dummies* books the #1 introductory level computer book series and have written asking for more. So, if you're looking for the most fun and easy way to learn about computers, look to *...For Dummies* books to give you a helping hand.

by Glenn Weadock

Illustrated by Emily Weadock

IDG Books Worldwide, Inc.
An International Data Group Company

Foster City, CA ♦ Chicago, IL ♦ Indianapolis, IN ♦ Southlake, TX

Intranet Publishing For Dummies ®

Published by
IDG Books Worldwide, Inc.
An International Data Group Company
919 E. Hillsdale Blvd.
Suite 400
Foster City, CA 94404
www.idgbooks.com (IDG Books Worldwide Web site)
www.dummies.com (Dummies Press Web site)

Copyright © 1997 IDG Books Worldwide, Inc. All rights reserved. No part of this book, including interior design, cover design, and icons, may be reproduced or transmitted in any form, by any means (electronic, photocopying, recording, or otherwise) without the prior written permission of the publisher.

Library of Congress Catalog Card No.: 97-80213

ISBN: 0-7645-0222-0

Printed in the United States of America

10 9 8 7 6 5 4 3 2 1

1O/SS/QZ/ZX/IN

Distributed in the United States by IDG Books Worldwide, Inc.

Distributed by Macmillan Canada for Canada; by Transworld Publishers Limited in the United Kingdom; by IDG Norge Books for Norway; by IDG Sweden Books for Sweden; by Woodslane Pty. Ltd. for Australia; by Woodslane Enterprises Ltd. for New Zealand; by Longman Singapore Publishers Ltd. for Singapore, Malaysia, Thailand, and Indonesia; by Simron Pty. Ltd. for South Africa; by Toppan Company Ltd. for Japan; by Distribuidora Cuspide for Argentina; by Livraria Cultura for Brazil; by Ediciencia S.A. for Ecuador; by Addison-Wesley Publishing Company for Korea; by Ediciones ZETA S.C.R. Ltda. for Peru; by WS Computer Publishing Corporation, Inc., for the Philippines; by Unalis Corporation for Taiwan; by Contemporanea de Ediciones for Venezuela; by Computer Book & Magazine Store for Puerto Rico; by Express Computer Distributors for the Caribbean and West Indies. Authorized Sales Agent: Anthony Rudkin Associates for the Middle East and North Africa.

For general information on IDG Books Worldwide's books in the U.S., please call our Consumer Customer Service department at 800-762-2974. For reseller information, including discounts and premium sales, please call our Reseller Customer Service department at 800-434-3422.

For information on where to purchase IDG Books Worldwide's books outside the U.S., please contact our International Sales department at 415-655-3200 or fax 415-655-3295.

For information on foreign language translations, please contact our Foreign & Subsidiary Rights department at 415-655-3021 or fax 415-655-3281.

For sales inquiries and special prices for bulk quantities, please contact our Sales department at 415-655-3200 or write to the address above.

For information on using IDG Books Worldwide's books in the classroom or for ordering examination copies, please contact our Educational Sales department at 800-434-2086 or fax 817-251-8174.

For press review copies, author interviews, or other publicity information, please contact our Public Relations department at 415-655-3000 or fax 415-655-3299.

For authorization to photocopy items for corporate, personal, or educational use, please contact Copyright Clearance Center, 222 Rosewood Drive, Danvers, MA 01923, or fax 508-750-4470.

LIMIT OF LIABILITY/DISCLAIMER OF WARRANTY: AUTHOR AND PUBLISHER HAVE USED THEIR BEST EFFORTS IN PREPARING THIS BOOK. IDG BOOKS WORLDWIDE, INC., AND AUTHOR MAKE NO REPRESENTATIONS OR WARRANTIES WITH RESPECT TO THE ACCURACY OR COMPLETENESS OF THE CONTENTS OF THIS BOOK AND SPECIFICALLY DISCLAIM ANY IMPLIED WARRANTIES OF MERCHANTABILITY OR FITNESS FOR A PARTICULAR PURPOSE. THERE ARE NO WARRANTIES WHICH EXTEND BEYOND THE DESCRIPTIONS CONTAINED IN THIS PARAGRAPH. NO WARRANTY MAY BE CREATED OR EXTENDED BY SALES REPRESENTATIVES OR WRITTEN SALES MATERIALS. THE ACCURACY AND COMPLETENESS OF THE INFORMATION PROVIDED HEREIN AND THE OPINIONS STATED HEREIN ARE NOT GUARANTEED OR WARRANTED TO PRODUCE ANY PARTICULAR RESULTS, AND THE ADVICE AND STRATEGIES CONTAINED HEREIN MAY NOT BE SUITABLE FOR EVERY INDIVIDUAL. NEITHER IDG BOOKS WORLDWIDE, INC., NOR AUTHOR SHALL BE LIABLE FOR ANY LOSS OF PROFIT OR ANY OTHER COMMERCIAL DAMAGES, INCLUDING BUT NOT LIMITED TO SPECIAL, INCIDENTAL, CONSEQUENTIAL, OR OTHER DAMAGES. FULFILLMENT OF EACH COUPON OFFER IS THE RESPONSIBILITY OF THE OFFEROR.

Trademarks: All brand names and product names used in this book are trade names, service marks, trademarks, or registered trademarks of their respective owners. IDG Books Worldwide is not associated with any product or vendor mentioned in this book.

 is a trademark under exclusive license to IDG Books Worldwide, Inc., from International Data Group, Inc.

About the Author

Glenn E. Weadock is president of Independent Software, Inc., a Colorado-based consulting firm he founded in 1982 after graduating from Stanford University's engineering school. One of the country's most popular technical trainers, Glenn has taught networking topics to thousands of students in the United States, United Kingdom, and Canada in more than 160 seminars since 1988. He has written six intensive two-day seminars for Data-Tech Institute, and has presented eight Data-Tech computer videos, including *Internet Security Solutions* and *Understanding, Configuring, and Optimizing TCP/IP*.

Glenn is the author of *Exploding the Computer Myth,* which Jerry Pournelle of *Byte* magazine called "the business computer book of the decade." He has also written *Bulletproofing Client/Server Systems, Bulletproofing NetWare, Bulletproofing Windows 95* and *Bulletproof Your PC Network* for McGraw-Hill. Glenn is a Microsoft Certified Professional and member of the Association for Computing Machinery, Independent Computer Consultants Association, and American Society for Training and Development.

About the Illustrator

Emily Sherrill Weadock is the Director of Independent Software's Digital Art Studio. An award-winning computer artist whose work has been featured in international magazines, Emily's talent ranges from technical illustration to broadcast-quality 3D animation and multimedia development. She has illustrated seven books to date, and is the co-author of *Creating Cool PowerPoint 97 Presentations*. Before trading brushes for mice, Emily enjoyed success as a mixed-media construction artist, and studied art at SMU and Baylor University.

ABOUT IDG BOOKS WORLDWIDE

Welcome to the world of IDG Books Worldwide.

IDG Books Worldwide, Inc., is a subsidiary of International Data Group, the world's largest publisher of computer-related information and the leading global provider of information services on information technology. IDG was founded more than 25 years ago and now employs more than 8,500 people worldwide. IDG publishes more than 275 computer publications in over 75 countries (see listing below). More than 60 million people read one or more IDG publications each month.

Launched in 1990, IDG Books Worldwide is today the #1 publisher of best-selling computer books in the United States. We are proud to have received eight awards from the Computer Press Association in recognition of editorial excellence and three from *Computer Currents'* First Annual Readers' Choice Awards. Our best-selling *...For Dummies*® series has more than 30 million copies in print with translations in 30 languages. IDG Books Worldwide, through a joint venture with IDG's Hi-Tech Beijing, became the first U.S. publisher to publish a computer book in the People's Republic of China. In record time, IDG Books Worldwide has become the first choice for millions of readers around the world who want to learn how to better manage their businesses.

Our mission is simple: Every one of our books is designed to bring extra value and skill-building instructions to the reader. Our books are written by experts who understand and care about our readers. The knowledge base of our editorial staff comes from years of experience in publishing, education, and journalism — experience we use to produce books for the '90s. In short, we care about books, so we attract the best people. We devote special attention to details such as audience, interior design, use of icons, and illustrations. And because we use an efficient process of authoring, editing, and desktop publishing our books electronically, we can spend more time ensuring superior content and spend less time on the technicalities of making books.

You can count on our commitment to deliver high-quality books at competitive prices on topics you want to read about. At IDG Books Worldwide, we continue in the IDG tradition of delivering quality for more than 25 years. You'll find no better book on a subject than one from IDG Books Worldwide.

John Kilcullen
CEO
IDG Books Worldwide, Inc.

Steven Berkowitz
President and Publisher
IDG Books Worldwide, Inc.

Eighth Annual Computer Press Awards ≥ 1992

Ninth Annual Computer Press Awards ≥ 1993

Tenth Annual Computer Press Awards ≥ 1994

Eleventh Annual Computer Press Awards ≥ 1995

IDG Books Worldwide, Inc., is a subsidiary of International Data Group, the world's largest publisher of computer-related information and the leading global provider of information services on information technology. International Data Group publishes over 275 computer publications in over 75 countries. Sixty million people read one or more International Data Group publications each month. International Data Group's publications include: **ARGENTINA:** Buyer's Guide, Computerworld Argentina, PC World Argentina; **AUSTRALIA:** Australian Macworld, Australian PC World, Australian Reseller News, Computerworld, IT Casebook, Network World, Publish, Webmaster; **AUSTRIA:** Computerwelt Osterreich, Networks Austria, PC Tip Austria; **BANGLADESH:** PC World Bangladesh; **BELARUS:** PC World Belarus; **BELGIUM:** Data News; **BRAZIL:** Annuário de Informática, Computerworld, Connections, Macworld, PC Player, PC World, Publish, Reseller News, Supergamepower; **BULGARIA:** Computerworld Bulgaria, Network World Bulgaria, PC & MacWorld Bulgaria; **CANADA:** CIO Canada, Client/Server World, ComputerWorld Canada, InfoWorld Canada, NetworkWorld Canada, WebWorld; **CHILE:** Computerworld Chile, PC World Chile; **COLOMBIA:** Computerworld Colombia, PC World Colombia; **COSTA RICA:** PC World Centro America; **THE CZECH AND SLOVAK REPUBLICS:** Computerworld Czechoslovakia, Macworld Czech Republic, PC World Czechoslovakia; **DENMARK:** Communications World Danmark, Computerworld Danmark, Macworld Danmark, PC World Danmark, Techworld Denmark; **DOMINICAN REPUBLIC:** PC World Republica Dominicana; **ECUADOR:** PC World Ecuador; **EGYPT:** Computerworld Middle East; **EL SALVADOR:** PC World Centro America; **FINLAND:** MikroPC, Tietoverkko, Tietoviikko; **FRANCE:** Distributique, Hebdo, Info PC, Le Monde Informatique, Macworld, Reseaux & Telecoms, WebMaster France; **GERMANY:** Computer Partner, Computerwoche, Computerwoche Extra, Computerwoche FOCUS, Global Online, Macwelt, PC Welt; **GREECE:** Amiga Computing, GamePro Greece, Multimedia World; **GUATEMALA:** PC World Centro America; **HONDURAS:** PC World Centro America; **HONG KONG:** Computerworld Hong Kong, PC World Hong Kong, Publish in Asia; **HUNGARY:** ABCD CD-ROM, Computerworld Szamitastechnika, Internetto online Magazine, PC World Hungary, PC-X Magazin Hungary; **ICELAND:** Tolvuheimur PC World Island; **INDIA:** Information Communications World, Information Systems Computerworld, PC World India, Publish in Asia; **INDONESIA:** InfoKomputer PC World, Komputek Computerworld, Publish in Asia; **IRELAND:** ComputerScope, PC Live!; **ISRAEL:** Macworld Israel, People & Computers/Computerworld; **ITALY:** Computerworld Italia, Macworld Italia, Networking Italia, PC World Italia; **JAPAN:** DTP World, Macworld Japan, Nikkei Personal Computing, OS/2 World Japan, SunWorld Japan, Windows NT World, Windows World Japan; **KENYA:** PC World East African; **KOREA:** Hi-Tech Information, Macworld Korea, PC World Korea; **MACEDONIA:** PC World Macedonia; **MALAYSIA:** Computerworld Malaysia, PC World Malaysia, Publish in Asia; **MALTA:** PC World Malta; **MEXICO:** Computerworld Mexico, PC World Mexico; **MYANMAR:** PC World Myanmar; **NETHERLANDS:** Computer! Totaal, LAN Internetworking Magazine, LAN World Buyers Guide, Macworld Netherlands, Net, WebWereld; **NEW ZEALAND:** Absolute Beginners Guide and Plain & Simple Series, Computer Buyer, Computer Industry Directory, Computerworld New Zealand, MTB, Network World, PC World New Zealand; **NICARAGUA:** PC World Centro America; **NORWAY:** Computerworld Norge, CW Rapport, Datamagasinet, Financial Rapport, Kursguide Norge, Macworld Norge, Multimediaworld Norge, PC World Ekspress Norge, PC World Nettverk, PC World Norge, PC World ProduktGuide Norge; **PAKISTAN:** Computerworld Pakistan; **PANAMA:** PC World Panama; **PEOPLE'S REPUBLIC OF CHINA:** China Computer Users, China Computerworld, China InfoWorld, China Telecom World Weekly, Computer & Communication, Electronic Design China, Electronics Today, Electronics Weekly, Game Software, PC World China, Popular Computer Week, Software Weekly, Software World, Telecom World; **PERU:** Computerworld Peru, PC World Profesional Peru, PC World SoHo Peru; **PHILIPPINES:** Click!, Computerworld Philippines, PC World Philippines, Publish in Asia; **POLAND:** Computerworld Poland, Computerworld Special Report Poland, Cyber, Macworld Poland, Networld Poland, PC World Komputer; **PORTUGAL:** Cerebro/PC World, Computerworld/Correio Informático, Dealer World Portugal, Mac*In/PC*In Portugal, Multimedia World; **PUERTO RICO:** PC World Puerto Rico; **ROMANIA:** Computerworld Romania, PC World Romania, Telecom Romania; **RUSSIA:** Computerworld Russia, Mir PK, Publish, Seti; **SINGAPORE:** Computerworld Singapore, PC World Singapore, Publish in Asia; **SLOVENIA:** Monitor; **SOUTH AFRICA:** Computing SA, Network World SA, Software World SA; **SPAIN:** Communicaciones World España, Computerworld España, Dealer World España, Macworld España, PC World España; **SRI LANKA:** Infolink PC World; **SWEDEN:** CAP&Design, Computer Sweden, Corporate Computing Sweden, Internetworld Sweden, it.branschen, Macworld Sweden, MaxiData Sweden, MikroDatorn, Natverk & Kommunikation, PC World Sweden, PCaktiv, Windows World Sweden; **SWITZERLAND:** Computerworld Schweiz, Macworld Schweiz, PCtip; **TAIWAN:** Computerworld Taiwan, Macworld Taiwan, NEW ViSiON/Publish, PC World Taiwan, Windows World Taiwan; **THAILAND:** Publish in Asia, Thai Computerworld; **TURKEY:** Computerworld Turkiye, Macworld Turkiye, Network World Turkiye, PC World Turkiye; **UKRAINE:** Computerworld Kiev, Multimedia World Ukraine, PC World Ukraine; **UNITED KINGDOM:** Acorn User UK, Amiga Action UK, Amiga Computing UK, Apple Talk UK, Computing, Macworld, Parents and Computers UK, PC Advisor, PC Home, PSX Pro, The WEB; **UNITED STATES:** Cable in the Classroom, CIO Magazine, Computerworld, DOS World, Federal Computer Week, GamePro Magazine, InfoWorld, I-Way, Macworld, Network World, PC Games, PC World, Publish, Video Event, THE WEB Magazine, and WebMaster; online webzines: JavaWorld, NetscapeWorld, and SunWorld Online; **URUGUAY:** InfoWorld Uruguay; **VENEZUELA:** Computerworld Venezuela, PC World Venezuela; and **VIETNAM:** PC World Vietnam. 3/24/97

Dedication

To Emily, Carina, and Cecily, *sine qua non*.

Author's Acknowledgments

An unusually large number of people contributed time and energy to this project. My thanks go to Gareth Hancock, John Kaufeld, and Mike Snell for making my first *Dummies* book possible. Thanks also to the helpful and professional folks at IDG Books, including my project editor, Clark Scheffy, and (in alphabetical order) Jill Brummett, Heather Dismore, Angie Hunckler, and Joyce Pepple, as well as to the other IDG employees whom I don't know but who helped with the project. Thanks to Paul Summitt for the technical review. To the software vendors who helped me learn more about their products, my thanks (again alphabetically) to Suzanne Anthony of Netscape, Ann Bagley of Asymetrix, Gillian Brouse of Fulcrum, Susan Breuer of the Weber Group, Kathleen Burnham of Folio, Teri Campbell of MetaCreations, David Conti of Aimtech, Mark Craemer of InfoAccess, Patrick Crisp of Caere, Veronica Duran of Adobe, Laura Edens of Net-It Software, Sabrina Ellison of Microsoft, Michelle Glau of Waggener-Edstrom, Linda Hazzan of SoftQuad, Laura Krawec of Net-It Software, Leona Lapez of Macromedia, Steve Lurie of Microsoft, Steve McConaughey of Hummingbird Communications, Bea McKinney of askSam Systems, Jonathan Moore of Waggener-Edstrom, Jennifer Penunuri of Netscape, Alison Topham of Blue Sky Software, Daria Winter of Randomnoise, and Jennifer Willson of Design Intelligence.

Publisher's Acknowledgments

We're proud of this book; please send us your comments about it by using the IDG Books Worldwide Registration Card at the back of the book or by e-mailing us at feedback/dummies@idgbooks.com. Some of the people who helped bring this book to market include the following:

Acquisitions, Development, and Editorial

Project Editor: Clark Scheffy

Acquisitions Editor: Gareth Hancock

Media Development Manager: Joyce Pepple

Associate Permissions Editor: Heather H. Dismore

Copy Editor: Jill Brummett

Technical Editor: Paul M. Summit

Associate Technical Editor: Kevin Spencer

Editorial Manager: Mary Corder

Editorial Assistant: Michael Sullivan

Production

Project Coordinator: Valery Bourke

Layout and Graphics: Steve Arany, Angela Bush-Sisson, Maridee V. Ennis, Sherry Gomoll, Todd Klemme, Jane Martin, Anna Rohrer, Kate Snell, Michael A. Sullivan M. Anne Sipahimalani, Deirdre Smith

Proofreaders: Jennifer K. Overmyer, Christine Berman, Kelli Botta, Joel K. Draper, Rachel Garvey, Rebecca Senninger, Carrie Voorhis, Janet Withers

Indexer: Richard Shrout

Special Help

Tammy Castleman, Senior Copy Editor; Linda Stark, Copy Editor; Mary Bednarek, Product Development Editor; Michael De Oliveira, IDG Books Indianapolis LAN Site Manager; Elizabeth Kuball, Copy Editor; Stephanie Koutek, Proof Editor; Christine Meloy Beck, Senior Copy Editor; Kyle Looper, Project Editor; Constance Carlisle, Copy Editor; Mary Corder, Editorial Manager

---

General and Administrative

IDG Books Worldwide, Inc.: John Kilcullen, CEO; Steven Berkowitz, President and Publisher

IDG Books Technology Publishing: Brenda McLaughlin, Senior Vice President and Group Publisher

Dummies Technology Press and Dummies Editorial: Diane Graves Steele, Vice President and Associate Publisher; Kristin A. Cocks, Editorial Director; Mary Bednarek, Acquisitions and Product Development Director

Dummies Trade Press: Kathleen A. Welton, Vice President and Publisher

IDG Books Production for Dummies Press: Beth Jenkins, Production Director; Cindy L. Phipps, Manager of Project Coordination, Production Proofreading, and Indexing; Kathie S. Schutte, Supervisor of Page Layout; Shelley Lea, Supervisor of Graphics and Design; Debbie J. Gates, Production Systems Specialist; Robert Springer, Supervisor of Proofreading; Debbie Stailey, Special Projects Coordinator; Tony Augsburger, Supervisor of Reprints and Bluelines; Leslie Popplewell, Media Archive Coordinator

Dummies Packaging and Book Design: Patti Sandez, Packaging Specialist; Lance Kayser, Packaging Assistant; Kavish + Kavish, Cover Design

♦

The publisher would like to give special thanks to Patrick J. McGovern, without whom this book would not have been possible.

♦

Contents at a Glance

Introduction 1

Part I: Welcome to the Revolution! 19
Chapter 1 : What's Intranet Publishing? 21
Chapter 2 : Assessing Costs and Risks: Diving in with your eyes open 41

Part II: Intranet Publishing Applications 55
Chapter 3 : Choosing Your Project (Choose with Care!) 57
Chapter 4 : Company Information 73
Chapter 5: Procedural Support: Streamlining the Routine 87
Chapter 6: Sales Support: Getting and Keeping Customers 107
Chapter 7: Technical Support: Making Your Technology Work Better 117
Chapter 8: Intranet-Based Training (IBT) 139

Part III: Strategies, Techniques, and Tools 153
Chapter 9: Plan Your Work and Work Your Plan 155
Chapter 10: Formatting Data for Your Intranet 171
Chapter 11: Adding Structure to Your Substance 191
Chapter 12: Spinning Your Web 207

Part IV: Intranet Care and Feeding 229
Chapter 13: Webmasters and Beyond: Maintaining an Intranet 231
Chapter 14: High-Octane Performance 249
Chapter 15: Intranet Security 267
Chapter 16: Publicity and Promotion 291

Part V: The Part of Tens 303
Chapter 17: Ten Ps of Intranet Publishing Success 305
Chapter 18: Ten Standards to Watch 313

Part VI: Appendixes 325
Appendix A: Glossary 327
Appendix B: References & Resources 343
Appendix C: About the CD-ROM 355

Index 365

Java™ Development Kit Version 1.1.3 Binary Code License 382

IDG Books Worldwide, Inc., End-User License Agreement 384

Installation Instructions 386

IDG Books Worldwide Registration Card .... Back of Book

Cartoons at a Glance

By Rich Tennant

page 303

page 229

page 153

page 19

page 55

page 325

Fax: 508-546-7747 • **E-mail:** the5wave@tiac.net

Table of Contents

Introduction 1
   About this Book 1
   How This Book Is Organized 3
      Part I: Welcome to the Revolution! 3
      Part II: Intranet Publishing Applications 3
      Part III: Strategies, Techniques, and Tools 4
      Part IV: Intranet Care and Feeding 4
      Part V: The Part of Tens 4
      Part VI: Appendixes 4
   Who Can Skip What 5
   Icons Used in This Book 5
   Intrawhats? 6
      Big I versus little i 6
      The company-wide web 10
         Intranets versus traditional networks 12
         Intranets as client/server systems 13
      The main intranet flavors 15
         Document publishing 15
         Database publishing 15
         Groupware and collaboration tools 16
         Extranets (involving customers and vendors) 16
      Curing Mad Internet Disease 16
         What makes your business tick? 16
         Revenues and costs — asking the right questions 17

Part I: Welcome to the Revolution! 19

Chapter 1: What's Intranet Publishing? 21
   Zeroing in on a Concise Definition 21
   Benefits of Publishing on an Intranet 23
      Accessibility 23
      Manageability 24
      Development speed 24
      Distribution speed 25
      Navigability 25
      Integration 28
      Familiar, standardized user interface 28
      Compatibility with client workstations 30
      (Relative) Ease of development 31
      (Also relative) Ease of upsizing 32
      Ability to publish many types of documents 32
      Cheaper than paper publishing 33

Intranet Publishing For Dummies

When to Publish with an Intranet — Not! 34
Intranet Publishing and the Enterprise 35
    What happens if intranet publishing takes off? 35
    What happens to all our existing systems? 36
    Intranets and Network PCs 37
        Network PC pros and cons 37
        How intranets fit in 39
    Intranets as competitive weapons 40

Chapter 2: Assessing Costs and Risks: Diving In with Your Eyes Open 41

Intranet Publishing Costs 41
    Software 42
        Basic software 43
        Site development tools 43
        Publishing applications 44
    Hardware 45
    Infrastructure 46
    People costs 46
        Warm bodies (wetware) 47
        Training 47
        System management 48
    Other indirect costs 48
Intranet Publishing Risks 48
    Department of Redundancy Department 49
    Inconsistent user interfaces 49
    Overcentralizing development 51
    Dangerous dilettantes 51
    Printing pitfalls 52
    Electronic lies 53
    Resistance to change 53

Part II: Intranet Publishing Applications 55

Chapter 3: Choosing Your Project (Choose with Care!) 57

Start Simple 57
    Simple data 58
    Simple data flows 58
    Simple technology 60
User Needs 61
    The user survey 61
    The manager survey 62
    Conditioning expectations 62
Technology Fit 63
    What can your servers handle? 63
        Industrial servers 64
        Casual servers 66

Table of Contents

xv

What can your clients handle? 67
        Netscape and Microsoft clients 68
        Client performance bottlenecks 69
What can your infrastructure handle? 70
Can You Measure Success? 70
Do You Own the Data? 71
    Copyrights 71
    Trademarks 71
    Trade secrets 72

Chapter 4: Company Information 73

HTML Tables 73
    Tabular data and HTML 73
    Grid and bear it 75
Sample Applications 75
    Employee directory 76
    Organizational charts 77
    Policies and procedures 78
    Benefits 80
        Insurance plan data 80
        Retirement plan data 81
        Stock purchase plan data 81
    Career management 81
        Job board 82
        Educational opportunities 82
    Newsletters and periodicals 82
    Government regulations 84
    Schedules 84
    Emergency and disaster plans 85
    Pages of useful links 86

Chapter 5: Procedural Support: Streamlining the Routine 87

Formfitting HTML 88
    Standard HTML forms 88
    Fancy forms 90
Data Processing, Intranet Style 91
    Common Gateway Interface (CGI) 91
    Web server Application Program Interfaces (APIs) 94
    Java, east of Krakatoa 95
Sample Applications 96
    Purchase requisitions 96
    Expense reports 97
    Budgeting 98
    Document editing 98
    Travel information 100
    Design and manufacturing.. 100
    User surveys 102
    New hire information 103
    Obtaining technical support 104

Reengineering Opportunities 104
    Basics of business process reengineering 104
    Can your intranet project implement a process change? 105

Chapter 6: Sales Support: Getting and Keeping Customers 107

Product Information 108
    Spec sheets and configuration data 108
    Diagrams and illustrations 109
    Price lists 110
    Computer-based presentations 111
    Testimonials and references 111
    Competitive analyses 112
    Sales and marketing bulletins 113
Customer Information 113
General Sales Support 115

Chapter 7: Technical Support: Making Your Technology Work Better 117

Systems for Internal Help Desk Use 118
    Internet access 118
    Inventory and configuration data 119
    User information 120
    Network maps 121
    Knowledge bases 121
Intranet Publishing for Call Support 123
    Software distribution 123
        Pull systems 124
        Push systems 128
    Publishing the troubleshooting hit parade 129
        Frequently Asked Questions 129
    Searchable documentation 130
        Publishing documentation for hardware and
            commercial software 132
        Publishing documentation for custom software 133
    User knowledge bases 134
    Problem reports and HTML forms 134
    Technical videos 135
The Tool that Explains Its Own Use 137

Chapter 8: Intranet-Based Training (IBT) 139

Training Topics 140
    Good prospects 140
    Not-so-good prospects 141
Delivery Techniques 142
    Making text-based training materials available
        on your intranet 142

Publishing computer-based training materials
    on your intranet 142
  Publishing courseware designed for the intranet 145
IBT Design Guidelines 146
  Navigation 147
  Interactivity 148
  Modularity 150
  Multimedia 151
Keys to Successful IBT Publishing 152

Part III: Strategies, Techniques, and Tools 153

Chapter 9: Plan Your Work and Work Your Plan 155

Building Consensus 155
  Top-down, bottom-up, or all together? 156
    A message to business managers 158
    A message to project leaders 159
    A message to content providers 159
    A message to key users 160
The First Project 161
  Prototype or pilot? 161
  Track and learn 162
Who Does the Design? 163
  Outsourcing 163
  Partnering 164
  Consulting 164
Thinking Ahead 165
  Who may and may not publish? 166
  Domain name and IP address registration 167
Measuring Success One User at a Time 168
  Why it's important 169
  How to do it 169
    Number of users 169
    Number of hits 169
    Number of satisfied customers 170
    Cost savings 170
    Success stories 170

Chapter 10: Formatting Data for Your Intranet 171

Two Publishing Strategies 172
  Intranet only 172
  Intranet plus 173
Three Delivery Strategies 175
  Stock HTML 175
  Custom HTML 177
  Pure Java 179

Four Data Sources 181
   Paper 181
   Word processing and desktop publishing programs 183
   Graphics 185
   Databases 186
One Popular Standard: Acrobat 188

Chapter 11: Adding Structure to Your Substance 191

Organizing Your Site for Easy Navigation 192
   What Puerto Rico and intranets have in common 192
   Hyperlinks to the rescue 193
   There's no place like home (page) 194
   Image maps 196
   Bookmarks 197
   Frames 197
   Product-specific navigation 198
Search Engines 200
   An alternative to hyperlink navigation 200
   Evaluation criteria 201
      Indexable data types 201
      Search method flexibility 201
      Balance between thoroughness and selectivity 202
      Ease of whittling 202
      Platform support 202
      Ability to crawl 203
      Automatic indexing 203
      Remote administration 203
   Product choices 203
Getting Pushy 205
   Concepts 205
   Products 206

Chapter 12: Spinning Your Web 207

Site Design Principles 207
   A screen is not a page! 208
      Smaller 208
      Resizable 208
      More hidden 208
      More independent 209
      More cosmopolitan 209
   How not to be boring 210
      Text formatting 210
      Backgrounds 211
      Funny bits 212
The Web and Multimedia 212
   Graphics 213
      Graphics Interchange Format (GIF) 214
      Joint Photographic Experts Group (JPEG) 214

Sound 215
Animation 216
   Animate your GIFs 217
   A Flash in the pan 218
   What I really want to do is direct 219
Video 219
Interactivity 220
   Java: a client programming language 220
   ActiveX: making use of Microsoft programs 222
   Scripting: JavaScript and VBScript 223
Page and Site Design Tools 224
   FrontPage 224
   HoTMetaL intranet Publisher (H.i.P.) 225
   PageMill 227
   Backstage Internet Studio 227

Part IV: Intranet Care and Feeding 229

Chapter 13: Webmasters and Beyond: Maintaining an Intranet 231

People Issues 232
   Intranet advisory board 232
   Hiring and training webmasters 232
   Publishing policies 234
   User support 234
Designing for Maintenance 235
   Hardware and software guidelines 235
   IP addressing control 236
   Portability 238
   Case sensitivity 239
   Documentation 239
Maintaining Applications 240
   The case of the missing links 241
   Freshness dating 242
Maintaining the System 243
   The network 243
   The server 245
      Web server log files 245
      LAN-based reporting tools 247
   The client (apologies to John Grisham) 247

Chapter 14: High-Octane Performance 249

Giving the Network a Tune-Up 250
   Server tuning 251
      Processor 252
      Memory 252
      Disk 253
      Communications 253
      Load balancing: dividing the labor 253

Infrastructure tuning 254
    How important is infrastructure tuning? 255
Client tuning 256
    Network software 256
    Memory 256
    Caching 256
    Communications 258
Designing for the Best Performance 258
    Search engines 259
    Link pages versus content pages 259
    Long pages versus new pages 259
    Graphics optimization 260
    Intranet advertisements 261
    Back-end technologies 262
    File distribution 262
    Standard templates and central sites 263
Performance Monitoring 263
    Network management systems 263
    Wide Area Network monitoring 264
    Operating system tools 265
    Web server tools 265

Chapter 15: Intranet Security 267

Security? We Don't Need No Stinking Security 267
    Yes, we're Internetted 268
    No, we're not Internetted 268
Physical Security 269
LAN-Based Security 269
Application-Level Security 271
    Web server-specific programs 271
    Product-specific 274
    Java versus ActiveX security 275
Remote Access Security 276
    Airwalls and firewalls 276
    Dial-up security 278
Communications Security 280
    Secure HyperText Transfer Protocol 281
    Secure Sockets Layer (SSL) 281
    Point-to-Point Tunneling Protocol 282
Uptime Security 283
    Intranet fault tolerance 284
        Power backup 284
        Server mirroring and clustering 285
        Antivirus technology 286
        Antivirus policies 287
    Intranet fault resilience 287
        Data backup 287
        Disaster recovery 289

Chapter 16: Publicity and Promotion 291
Nothing Sells Itself 291
Eight Ways to Promote Your Project 292
    Pick an easy intranet address and name 292
    Use existing communications vehicles 293
        Print and electronic newsletters 294
        Real and virtual bulletin boards 294
        Get into the new-hire book 295
    Place links everywhere 295
        On the desktop 296
        Within other documents 296
    Provide a demo 297
    Make continuous improvement 298
        A true story 298
        User suggestion box 299
        Continuing education 299
    Trumpet your success 300
    Cultivate key users 301
    Don't forget the managers! 301

Part V: The Part of Tens 303

Chapter 17: Ten Ps of Intranet Publishing Success 305
Pick Your Projects 305
Play with Possibilities 306
Plan for Success 307
Pinclude Everyone 308
Put Performance on a Pedestal 309
Put Productivity on a Higher Pedestal 309
Publish for the Screen 310
Promote the Site 311
Prepare for the Future 311
Prove the Value 312

Chapter 18: Ten Standards to Watch 313
HTML and Dynamic HTML 314
Cascading Style Sheets 316
eXtensible Markup Language (XML) 317
Java 318
ActiveX 318
PostScript Level 3 319
OpenType and TrueDoc 321
RealAudio 322
Object-Relational DBMS 323
Gigabit Ethernet 324

Part VI: Appendixes 325

Appendix A: Glossary 327

Appendix B: References & Resources 343
Companies Mentioned in This Book 343
Books 350
Magazines 351
CD-ROMs 353
Useful Links 353

Appendix C: About the CD-ROM 355
System Requirements 355
What You'll Find 355
Document Publishing Applications 356
Document Viewers and Utilities 358
Graphic Images and Utilities 360
Multimedia Utilities 360
Templates 361
Web Browsers 361
Web Page Design Programs 362
Web Sites 362
Miscellany 362
If You've Got Problems (Of the CD Kind) 363

Index 365

Java™ Development Kit Version 1.1.3 Binary Code License 382

IDG Books Worldwide, Inc., End-User License Agreement 384

Installation Instructions 386

IDG Books Worldwide Registration Card .... Back of Book

Introduction

Welcome to *Intranet Publishing For Dummies!* If you want a quick and to-the-point introduction to publishing documents on an internal web-type network, or *intranet* as they're called, you're in the right place.

This introductory section presents the book's purpose, intended readership, and organization, along with a description of the icons used. If you're not only new to intranet publishing but also new to intranets, this section presents a short intranet technology primer.

About This Book

Although many applications exist for intranets, using them to publish valuable information is the easiest, simplest, and smartest place to start. This book presents the essentials of intranet publishing concisely, conversationally, and clearly. The chapters are designed to quickly bring you up to speed on the key things you need to know to help create a successful intranet publishing project.

Intranet Publishing For Dummies may be the only book you want to read on the subject if you only need an overview to understand the key issues involved, or to be up to speed in meetings. If you're going to be directly involved with project design (choosing software, for example), this book is a great place to start.

This book is written for anyone involved in, about to be involved in, or just considering an intranet publishing project at any organizational level. If you find yourself in any of the following groups, this book is for you:

- **General managers:** who understand that a revolution is underway, and who want to understand it so that they can take advantage of it
- **Project leaders:** who are responsible for rolling out an intranet publishing system
- **Department heads:** who want to know more about how intranet publishing can improve information sharing
- **Team leaders:** who need to make project-related documents available to team members
- **Novice intranet designers:** who will help construct a publishing system

- **Intranet *lead users:*** who provide input for intranet designers or act as user representatives on intranet design committees
- **Consultants:** who have clients using or thinking about using intranets
- **Information system professionals:** who have experience with traditional networks but who are just getting into intranets

You may also find this book very helpful if you've heard some of the hoopla about intranet publishing, and want to find out if it can be applied to meet business needs in *your* organization.

This book makes a few assumptions:

- **You're working in, or with, an organization that actually needs an intranet.** Generally one having 15 to 20 employees minimum, and perhaps at multiple locations. Your organization also has a geographically distributed customer base, and at least a few different computer applications.
- **You're fairly new to the subject and want to get up to speed quickly.** This book assumes no prior expertise with intranets, which is a good thing, because they've only been around since 1995. If you've spent a bit of time using the Internet and the World Wide Web, you'll be pleased, because intranets borrow almost all their technological bits and pieces from the Internet.
- **Your main interest is in document publishing.** That is, you want to use your intranet to supplement and perhaps replace some of the paper your organization slings around.
- **You plan to use mostly World Wide Web-type servers for your publishing project or projects.** If you're not exactly sure what this means, read the "Intrawhats?" section later in this introduction.
- **You're not looking for a lot of detailed information on how to build a general-purpose intranet from scratch in the first place.** That's the focus of *Building an Intranet For Dummies* by John Fronckowiak (IDG Books Worldwide, Inc.) — plug, plug.
- **You're not *really* a *dummy*.** You just need the basics on the subject — in a hurry.

Finally, this book's focus is on business applications first, and the supporting technology second. The book identifies what a company can profitably do with intranet publishing inside its own organization, and then gives examples of enabling technologies, with references to specific products to make the discussions *real*.

I should say in passing that just because this book mentions a particular product, or even includes a screen snapshot or two of the product in action, doesn't necessarily mean I think it's a great product that you need to buy *right now.* Nor does the product reference mean that the vendor flew me to Maui for a few days to demo the product over Mai Tais (I'm a consultant, not a politician). It just means that the product is popular or interesting, and that you may want to investigate it further for yourself. *Caveat intranetter.*

How This Book Is Organized

As with most *Dummies* books, this one's designed so that you can dip in and out of specific chapters according to where you are in your project, what your responsibilities and interests are, and what level of knowledge you already have about particular subjects. You certainly can read this book cover to cover, but each chapter is designed to stand alone.

The overall organization follows a logical order: concepts, applications, implementation, and management.

Part I: Welcome to the Revolution!

This part presents intranet publishing *concepts*. It presents a definition of the subject, the main benefits of the technology, and, to be evenhanded, a treatment of the costs and risks involved. Just about everyone can find something of interest in this part.

Part II: Intranet Publishing Applications

Here's where I look at specific *applications* for intranet publishing — the *what* of the book. The focus in this part is on the many creative ways you can use an intranet intelligently, appropriately, and effectively to meet business goals by publishing certain types of information. This part also explores what that information may be: policy and procedure manuals, online training, parts catalogs, and so on.

Part II begins with a very important chapter on project selection, and then proceeds to examine applications in the categories of company information, procedural support, sales support, technical support, and Intranet-Based Training (IBT). These applications aren't the only possibilities, but they're the ones in common use, or that have the greatest potential for cost savings, or improving your productivity.

If you don't already know how you want to use intranet publishing, this part is a great way to jump-start your brain. If you do have a specific application in mind, this part suggests ideas and products you can use to get it going.

Part III: Strategies, Techniques, and Tools

Part III deals with the *how* of intranet publishing: *implementation* issues. I include a chapter on project planning, a chapter on formatting documents for your intranet, a chapter on structuring your intranet for ease of use and management, and a chapter covering essential intranet web site design principles.

Part IV: Intranet Care and Feeding

Intranet publishing success depends on following through and *managing* the project after you roll it out to users. Part IV is very important, for two reasons:

- Intranets, more than most other kinds of information systems, depend on continuous refinement; and
- Intranets have a tendency to grow rapidly, especially if the application is truly useful, and the execution is competent (both of which will surely be true when you're done with this book!).

The chapters in Part IV deal with project maintenance, system performance, security, and publicity and promotion.

Part V: The Part of Tens

"The Part of Tens" is a standard part of *Dummies* books, and this one's no exception. If you want a super-fast overview of the book's key points, or a reminder of things covered elsewhere in the book, cruise to "The Part of Tens," and read the ten P's of intranet publishing success. I also throw in a list of ten standards to keep an eye on, for two reasons: they're evolving very rapidly; and the closer you can adhere to them, the easier you can maintain and expand your project over time.

Part VI: Appendixes

This book has three appendixes:

- **Appendix A *(Glossary):*** Contains concise definitions of terms used in the book
- **Appendix B *(References & Resources):*** Provides details on companies and products mentioned in the book, books, magazines, CD-ROMs, and interesting intranet-related Internet sites

Introduction

✔ **Appendix C *(About the CD-ROM):*** Describes the enclosed CD-ROM, which contains many goodies to assist you in your intranet publishing projects, from program demos, to functioning utilities and sample web templates

Who Can Skip What

You do *not* have to read everything in this book. In fact, you *shouldn't* read everything in this book. You can usually tell from the "In This Chapter" section at the beginning of each chapter whether you need the information the chapter contains. Here are a few additional guidelines:

- ✔ If you're already in the middle of a big intranet publishing project, don't spend a lot of time in Part I; just read the chapters of Part II that pertain to your situation.
- ✔ If you aren't involved in the actual implementation details, you can skip over much of the techie stuff in Part III.
- ✔ If you're only developing a *show-and-tell* pilot project to sell the intranet publishing concept to higher-ups or colleagues, you don't need to spend much time reading Part IV.

Icons Used in This Book

In the spirit of making this book suitable for high-speed consumption, eight graphical icons separate out certain kinds of material:

Here's a *gotcha* you may want to know about in order to avoid a common trap or pitfall. Sure, intranet publishing is new, but enough people have made enough of the same mistakes that I can flag some of them with this icon.

This book is more useful to you if you get actively involved with it at key points. This icon prompts you to answer a question about your organization so that you can define and implement your intranet publishing project. The more thought you put into these little Q&As, the more you get out of them.

This icon suggests that you hop over to other sections of the book where you can find more information relative to the topic at hand. It's not a Web-page hyperlink (the book's printed on paper, after all!), but the idea's the same. Chapter references made in the text, without this icon, also exist; they just aren't quite as critical for your understanding.

When you see this icon, it means that I succumbed to the temptation to editorialize a little bit. These rants and exhortations are highly opinionated, and other knowledgeable people may disagree with them. They *are,* however, based on experience. Besides, a few opinions liven up a book.

This icon points out notable tidbits of juicy information that are worth committing to your long-term memory.

Technical points that fall into the category of *isn't that interesting?* If you have a technical inclination or background, and *boring as all get-out,* if you don't. You can skip these points, and still get what you need from this book.

Short suggestions and hints appear next to this icon. These hints are usually based on real-life experience at various companies, and can help make your intranet publishing project even cooler.

When a new and important term comes up that requires a paragraph or so to define it, I point it out with this icon. You can also refer to the glossary at the back of the book for definitions that don't appear in the main text.

This icon points out a discussion of a software program that comes on this book's CD-ROM.

Intrawhats?

If you're new to the intranet concept and you aren't quite sure how to pronounce the word, this section is for you. On the subject of pronunciation, I've found it helpful to emphasize the second syllable slightly, just to make sure that people know you're not talking about the *IntERnet.*

If, on the other hand, you're up to speed on what an intranet is, jump to Part I.

Big I versus little i

Q: *What, exactly, is the Internet?*

A: The Internet is a worldwide network of university, government, business, and private computer systems.

Q: *Who runs it?*

A: A 13-year-old named Jason.

– Dave Barry, *Dave Barry in Cyberspace* (Crown, 1996)

Any introduction to intranets (with a lowercase *i*) has to start with the *Internet* (or, as some refer to it, the *Big I Internet*). The Internet is that sprawling collection of literally millions of computers, linked in a global network, that nobody had ever heard of a few years ago, and that is now the biggest thing since sliced bread (see Figure I-1).

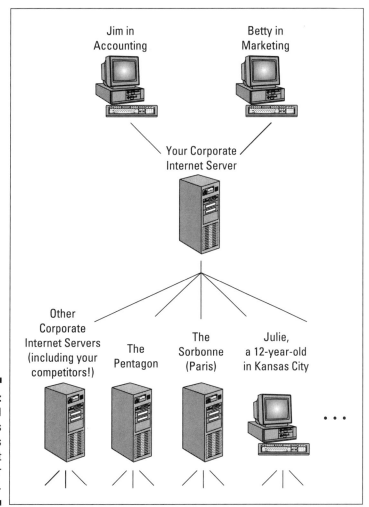

Figure I-1: The Big I Internet is Earth's largest computer network.

Also known as the information superhighway, or more accurately, the *information ball of yarn,* the Internet was originally just for military and academic use but has now grown to include all manner of private, public, and commercial uses. Whether you want to find out how to install a memory upgrade into a particular make and model of PC, check the weather in Vail before you hop a plane for a ski vacation, or read some of the enlightened wisdom supermodels are willing to share with the rest of the world, chances are good that the information's out there somewhere on the Internet.

Physically, the Internet is a collection of computers that each has its own unique network address to identify it to other computers, and that each speak the same basic communications language: TCP/IP (see the sidebar, "What the heck is TCP/IP?"). These computers connect to each other via a complex network of communication links (some fast and some slow), managed by computerized traffic *routers* (kind of like information traffic cops), for the purpose of exchanging information.

An Internet-connected computer that makes information available for others to access is called a *server,* and a computer that reads that information is called a *client.* Because of the way the Internet is set up, any computer connected to the Internet can be a server, a client, or both.

As with any network, the software that runs on all those computers is what enables you to do useful things with it. Internet software has evolved over time, and there are many different Internet applications and protocols (a *protocol* is just a communications standard) — some used much more than others:

- **File Transfer Protocol (FTP):** An Internet application that enables you to send an electronic file from point A to point B. You probably use FTP to move document files from a client workstation onto an intranet server.

- **Simple Mail Transfer Protocol (SMTP):** An Internet e-mail application that enables users to send and receive electronic messages across the Internet or an intranet.

- **Gopher:** An information search-and-retrieval application that started at the University of Minnesota. Gopher servers around the world (usually at academic institutions) help Internet users find data they need, but it's a text-only service (no graphics).

- **Archie:** A file-locating service that can help you find a specific file on a FTP site somewhere — as long as you know the exact file name, which you almost never do.

- **Veronica:** Another Internet search service. Veronica stands for *Very Easy Rodent-Oriented Net-wide Index to Computer Archives.* I'm not kidding.

- **Wide Area Information Services (WAIS):** Pronounced *ways,* this is an Internet application for locating documents with key words, usually a more convenient way than Gopher.

✓ **HyperText Transfer Protocol:** HTTP is the cornerstone of the World Wide Web (or the *Web,* for short), and it is the Internet technology that intranet publishers are most interested in. The Web, born in 1993, is the multimedia face of the Internet — Web pages can include color graphics, and even sound and video. They can also include convenient and automatic links to other Web pages. These links are usually underlined words that show up in a different color than regular text. For these reasons, the Web is the Internet application most users already know, and it certainly receives most of the industry's attention. Users view Web pages with software called *browsers.*

Web servers are computers that host Web pages, and they generally run some flavor of UNIX, or Microsoft Windows NT Server operating system. These days, many network operating systems come packaged with a Web server. For example, Windows NT Server 4.0 comes with Microsoft's Internet Information Server (IIS). You can even get *personal* Web server software for workstations — an example is Microsoft Personal Web Server for Windows 95.

Web servers and browsers speak a special Internet language called *HyperText Transfer Protocol (HTTP).* If you've done any Web surfing yourself, you've no doubt seen Web server addresses, or *Uniform Resource Locators (URLs)* as they are more formally called, that begin with `http://`. HTTP is just the protocol that allows Web servers to know how to jump to the right place when the user clicks on a link — and that's probably all you need to know about HTTP!

Web browsers know that URLs begin with `http://`, and are happy to jump to a page without the `http://` prefix. The web addresses listed in this book, therefore, appear without the `http://`.

Computers can connect to the Internet several ways. A company may have a direct *leased line* connection to the Internet, which is preferable for speed reasons. Or an individual may get a dial-up modem connection to the Internet through an online service (such as America Online or CompuServe) or through an Internet Service Provider (ISP). ISPs are companies like PSINet and AT&T WorldNet that offer Internet connections as their main business. ISPs also offer Web hosting services for organizations that don't want to maintain their own Web servers in-house.

Since the Internet mutated from its role as strictly an academic and military network, businesses have been grappling with the problem of how to take advantage of its exploding popularity, and use Earth's largest computer network to meet business needs. Many companies use the Internet for advertising, customer support, and even for *virtual private networks* (they connect their own computers using the Internet and encryption technology to keep information secret while it cruises around the world) to back up their existing Wide Area Networks (WANs).

Many other businesses, however, have hesitated to put big projects on the Internet because of its traffic congestion, occasional outages, and lack of ironclad security. It's like using an interstate highway as opposed to a private road — you may have to put up with the occasional data traffic jams that the explosive growth of the Internet has created. The infrastructure that handles traffic routing isn't immune to outages either, and if and when they occur, they're outside your company's control. Although the Internet is becoming a safer place to do business, the fact remains that it's a publicly accessible network that evil-minded geniuses worldwide take special and perverse pleasure in invading and disturbing.

The company-wide web

In 1995, the corporate world had a collective brainstorm: What if we built a mini-Internet *inside* our company? Could we take the bits and pieces that make the Internet such an interesting, dynamic, and accessible place, and put them to work on internal corporate networks?

A *private Internet* could run faster, more reliably, and more securely than any system on the congested and hacker-prone Internet (see Figure I-2). Practically any computer could connect to it, it would require almost no user workstation setup and management, and it would use *open standards* that no single vendor dominates. It could help businesses approach the goal of the paperless office, which previous computer revolutions have hindered rather than advanced (the PC and LAN revolutions were the two biggest windfalls for the paper industry since movable type). The private Internet sounds like the Holy Grail of distributed computing — but is it, in business lingo, *doable?*

You betcha. For most organizations, the technological bits and pieces are already in place. Thanks to Internet frenzy, one can now literally buy a web server in a box — web server software also comes bundled with all major LANs. The *intranet* has fallen, practically full-grown, into corporate America's virtual lap. Since *Business Week* ran a cover story on intranets in February 1996, nearly every Fortune 500 company has rolled out at least one — some have dozens — and the trend is gaining momentum.

Here are some statistics you can quote, if you're trying to convince your boss (or consulting client) that intranetting is in line with current trends:

- In a survey of 400 Fortune 1000 companies, 90 percent are either using or evaluating intranets. (Delphi Consulting Group, Boston, quoted in *Datamation,* December 1996)

- The installed base of intranet servers grew from 50,000 in 1995 to more than 200,000 in 1996, and is projected to hit 4.5 million by the year 2000 — which is ten times the projected number of 440,000 public Internet servers in that year! (Zona Research and International Data Corporation, quoted in *Communications News,* November 1996, and *Computer Reseller News,* November 1996)

What the heck is TCP/IP?

Transmission Control Protocol/Internet Protocol (TCP/IP) — don't pronounce the slash — is the basic communication language of the Internet and, therefore, of intranets. TCP/IP is a set of rules that computers agree upon to be able to send, receive, and understand each other's messages.

The TCP/IP rules govern *addressing*, routing information from one computer to another, breaking data into small chunks (or *packets*) for transmission, reassembling those packets at the receiving end, and checking for transmission reliability.

One of the big deals with TCP/IP is assigning unique addresses to each computer. Just as the postal service can't deliver mail to a house without an address, every computer in the network has to have an electronic address, called an *Internet Protocol (IP)* address. Just as physical business or residential postal addresses must be unique, IP addresses must be unique (at least if the computers using them will connect to the Internet). You can imagine that IP address assignment is a major concern. On the Internet, a central authority called the InterNIC, in Virginia, assigns IP addresses to Internet servers.

TCP/IP isn't just used for the Internet: A lot of companies use TCP/IP for their internal computer networks. One reason is that as those networks grow, perhaps to include wide-area links between cities or even countries, TCP/IP can grow with them — unlike some other network protocols that don't permit communication across *routers* (the traffic cops that connect pieces of large networks to each other).

Other popular network communication languages exist besides TCP/IP. Internet Package eXchange (IPX), for example, is very popular, largely because of the market success of Novell NetWare. NetWare is used in something like 60 percent of all *Local Area Networks* (*LANs*, which are networks in a limited geographical area, such as an office building). Are you up the creek if you have an IPX network? Not necessarily. You may be able to use a *gateway* product, such as Novell IPX-to-IP gateway, to allow computer users running IPX to connect to an intranet server running TCP/IP. Setting up your intranet is much easier, though, if your organization's networks already run TCP/IP.

> ✓ In terms of cold, hard cash, the intranet market was $6 billion in 1996 and expected to hit $28 billion by 1999. (Zona Research, quoted in *Telecommunications,* January 1997, and *Computer Reseller News,* March 3, 1997)

In a word: Wow.

An internal intranet doesn't *have* to be completely separate from the public Internet. As a matter of fact, over time, most intranets can link to the Internet in some form or fashion. The point is that to do intranets, you don't have to expose your networks to the dark alleyways of the public Internet, and you don't have to rely on the Internet to move data and programs

12 Intranet Publishing For Dummies

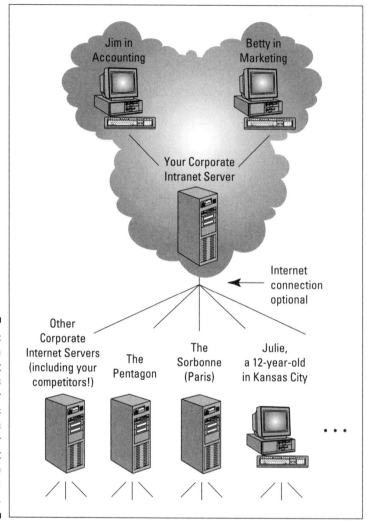

Figure I-2: A private intranet resides within your organization's boundaries and may or may not connect to the public Internet.

around. An intranet can leverage all the cool technology developed for the Internet, without incurring the security risks and traffic problems that beset the information superhighway.

Intranets versus traditional networks

What's different about an intranet compared to a *traditional* computer network, like Novell's NetWare or Microsoft's Windows NT Server? Here are some key distinctions:

- ✓ **Open architecture:** Intranets, for the most part, use *open standards* (public, not controlled by a single company) for their operation, such as the TCP/IP network communication language. Traditional networks often use *proprietary* (private — controlled entirely or primarily by one vendor) standards, such as Novell IPX network communication language. Traditional networks are moving toward open standards, and it's safe to say that the intranet phenomenon has nudged them strongly in that direction.

- ✓ **Web publishing:** Until recently, traditional LAN operating systems haven't offered the tools to create a web server. Novell, for example, recently added a web server in its IntraNetware product.

- ✓ **Platform independence:** Intranets generally work with any platform that works with the Internet. Intranet web servers, for example, can automatically support PC, Macintosh, and UNIX workstations. Traditional networks are more limited and typically do not support a wide variety of workstations "out of the box," and when they do, administrators often have to contend with compatibility problems, such as providing different *name spaces* for computers that use different file naming systems (*ipingw.doc, Glenn's Book Introduction*).

- ✓ **Poorer print support:** Internet technologies have never been too concerned with printing. They were designed primarily for on-screen use. Traditional networks arose in the first place largely so that users could share expensive printers (laser printers used to cost $100,000!), so their printing support is stronger and more mature than what you find with an intranet.

- ✓ **Weaker security:** The Internet, where intranet networking technology developed, is a public place for information sharing. Traditional networks, such as Novell NetWare and Windows NT, are built for companies that need to protect their data from within and without, and have extensive security systems in place to restrict what data users can access and what they can do with that data.

Intranets as client/server systems

Understanding intranets is easier if you think of them as a special kind of *client/server system*. You've probably heard a lot about client/server systems if you've been involved with information technology in recent years. Here's a concise definition:

A *client/server system* is a computing environment in which a client computer (typically, a user workstation) runs part of a program and a server computer (such as a database or file server) runs another part, typically with various software and hardware in between to help manage the communication between the two parts.

Client/server systems are, therefore, cooperative processing systems that split the computing chores up between multiple computers. For example, the client part may put a pretty, user-friendly screen up on the user's computer and provide a way for the user to ask a question ("How many Thighmasters did we sell in April?"). The server part may do the grunt work behind the scenes to go get the numbers, add them up, and send the total back to the user.

Client/server systems are very different from mainframe systems, which do all the processing work in a single central location. Mainframes were great when computers were expensive and people were cheap. Today, however, you can get a great computer for relatively little dough, while at the same time, human resources costs are increasing. The result is that more and more companies are moving to client/server computing. Client/server computing systems are not the be-all and end-all of information processing, though. They have great flexibility and power, but because the computing chores are distributed, they may be more challenging to design, budget, schedule, monitor, manage, and secure.

Intranets are really a special form of client/server system, although industry journals rarely refer to them this way. The client in an intranet is usually a workstation running a web browser program, which communicates with a web server to request information. The web server spits out the requested information and then the browser displays it. Sometimes the workstation runs programs *inside* the web browser, too, and the web server may hand over certain programming chores to another server on the same network. If that isn't distributed, cooperative, client/server processing, my name's Mel Gibson. My wife can confirm that this is *not* the case, although I maintain there are many remarkable similarities.

Although intranets are in many ways better than traditional client/server LAN setups, for example, because of their use of open versus proprietary standards, they also come with a unique set of features and limitations. Intranets didn't exist until the mid-1990s, so few businesses have any experience with them. Intranets are also evolving the same way LANs did, from the bottom up: Divisions, departments, even project teams are setting up their own intranets because it's fairly easy to do. All this means that the intranet phenomenon could spread out of control like North Carolina kudzu, and add to data chaos for organizations that don't take quick, smart steps to guide intranet deployment. The state of intranets today is much like the state of client/server computing several years ago. It's a great time to get involved with a promising new technology, and an easy time to make mistakes.

The main intranet flavors

Right now, the most common intranet flavors are:

- ✔ Document publishing
- ✔ Database publishing
- ✔ Groupware and collaboration
- ✔ Extranets

The following sections include short descriptions of each type. The categories aren't hard and fast — some intranets have features from more than one category — but they're useful conceptually and, most of the time, practically.

Document publishing

The first kind of intranet is the *document publishing* intranet (ta-daa!), the kind that this book addresses. This sort of intranet is perhaps most closely matched with Internet technologies, in that publishing and reading documents is what the Internet has been all about ever since its inception.

As a result, document publishing is fairly easy to set up and doesn't require a lot of fancy, expensive software. Most organizations are getting their first taste of intranets by using them for document publishing.

For a more detailed definition of intranet publishing, see the early pages of Chapter 1.

Database publishing

Now that intranets are starting to mature, organizations are using them to provide easier access to data stored in depositories (databases). Most of the early intranet database publishing applications are *read-only,* meaning that the user can see the data, but not change or update it. Some organizations, however, are using intranets to update as well as read the data stored in mainframes and traditional network database servers.

The Internet hasn't been used as much for this sort of application, so that database publishing with intranets almost always involves some special-purpose software to link web servers to existing database machines. Compatibility issues crop up here, as companies use different systems to store their operating data, and web servers don't automatically know how to talk to those systems. Security can be a big concern, too.

Nevertheless, the potential an intranet brings for sharing databases more widely and easily is a powerful motivation, and most organizations will be using intranets as a way to access their database systems eventually, even if they don't do so right at first.

Groupware and collaboration tools

Intranets can host a variety of *groupware* and *collaboration* functions. Multi-user bulletin boards, electronic conferencing, chat facilities, group scheduling, collaborative product design, and even real-time interactive education (or *distance learning* as it is sometimes called) are all possible using the intranet substructure.

At this writing, the trade press is awash with articles debating whether the intranet is a better vehicle for such systems than special-purpose proprietary systems. As with intranet database publishing, special layered software is almost always required to implement these features.

Extranets (involving customers and vendors)

When you make your intranet available to those outside your own organization, such as customers, suppliers, or even the general public, it becomes an *extranet*. Extranets are more demanding (and complex) to build than intranets because of the increased importance of security, reliability, performance, and professional design. They may also have database publishing features and incorporate software to handle transactions such as order processing.

Although many intranet publishing techniques and tools work well for extranets, this book assumes that your first intranet publishing project is for internal use only — at least in its early evolution.

In any case, you're best off cutting your teeth on an internal project before embarking on an extranet that the outside world can see. Make your mistakes where they won't be quite as embarrassing — and where you feel more free to experiment a little.

Curing Mad Internet Disease

Since the mid-1990s, businesses have been wracking their brains trying to figure out how to make money on the Internet. I call this *Mad Internet Disease,* because it tends to become an obsessive and narrow focus. To cure yourself of this debilitating virus, forget about the Internet and intranets for a moment, and think about information distribution and your particular business.

What makes your business tick?

With rare exceptions, the most successful projects are those that start with a business need and then an attempt to find the right technology to meet that need, rather than the other way around. The first step in any successful intranet project, therefore, is to make a list of what makes your particular business tick.

Make a concise list of the five most important aspects of your business you could improve with an information publishing system. Make this list in pencil because, as you go through this book, you're likely to come up with more ideas. Don't worry about the details of what such a publishing system might look like — for now, think of it as a black box whose only characteristic is that it gets information into employees' hands.

If you're having a little trouble filling in the blanks, consider the flip side of the question: What business problems do you have that relate to information distribution? Can you think of examples where poor information flow caused your organization serious difficulty? Another suggestion is to think about how employees spend their time. What sort of information-gathering activities involve telephone tag and long wait times?

Later, after you build an extranet that has external links to customers, suppliers, regulators, and so on, you can go through the same exercise for that situation. Extranets, however, warrant a separate book!

Revenues and costs — asking the right questions

Now, back to the Internet. Take a moment to ponder whether the "How can we make money on the Internet?" question is really the only question you should be asking about the Internet, or even the best one.

Every business's bottom line is a combination of revenues and expenses. Maybe the better question to ask is, "How can we *improve our bottom line* with Internet *technology*?" This question broadens the focus to include cost savings, as well as revenue enhancement. It also broadens the focus to Internet technology, instead of limiting it to the Big I Internet. By asking this broader question, you may find that intranet publishing can be a big part of the answer, because intranet publishing can save your organization big bucks compared with the way you're currently distributing information.

My own preference is to ask an even bigger question: "How can we use Internet technology to make our organization more *productive*?" This question takes non-quantifiable factors into account, such as:

- **The quality of decision-making.** ("Who authorized developing a grape-flavored pasta? Doesn't anyone read our own focus group reports?")
- **How fast you can get things done.** ("How can we sell the 'Grape Noodle' to major accounts if it takes eight weeks for marketing to update the sales literature?")
- **How much time your employees waste in mindless busywork.** ("Bob's going around to everyone's looseleaf binder and replacing the product price sheets; he should be done in a couple of days.")

- **How much productivity your business loses because** *of Left hand–Right hand* **syndrome.** ("Why are we still ordering purple food coloring by the metric ton if marketing killed the Grape Noodle a month ago?")

- **How quickly people can become effective in a new job.** ("I'm the new marketing manager, and I have some ideas for new products. Where's the research on liver and cheese macaroni?")

These factors eventually filter down to the bottom line, but focusing entirely on dollars may blind you to some aspects of intranet publishing that can deliver longer-term benefits.

I now segue gracefully to Chapter 1, which explains those potential benefits in more detail, after defining exactly just what is meant by *intranet publishing*. Before you turn the page, however, please know that I'd like your comments on this book, and your ideas on how it can be improved in subsequent editions. I'm also glad to answer questions you may have about the book's contents. Please feel free to send me e-mail at my Independent Software Internet address, `gweadock@i-sw.com`. I can't always respond immediately (I travel a lot!), but I promise to answer every message.

Part I
Welcome to the Revolution!

In this part . . .

In the next two chapters, I introduce you to intranet publishing concepts and big picture issues. What is (and isn't) intranet publishing? Why are these "private Internets" driving a revolution in computer networking? What organization-wide effects is this revolution likely to incite? And how the heck do you pronounce "intranet"?

The answers to these questions await you in the following pages, along with some news about the costs you can expect to incur and the risks you need to watch for as you become an intranet publisher.

Chapter 1
What's Intranet Publishing?

In This Chapter
- Defining the elements of publishing on intranets
- Discovering the benefits that intranet publishing can bring to your organization
- Understanding HyperText Markup Language (HTML)
- Knowing when *not* to use intranet publishing
- Anticipating intranet technology's effect on your entire business

This chapter defines intranet publishing and looks at its many benefits. If you're just now planning an intranet publishing project, this chapter gives you a lot of ammo for your proposal. If you've already started such a project, this chapter provides a basis for promoting the project to users and managers.

If you feel you have a good handle on the meaning and benefits of intranet publishing, skip to Chapter 2 to make sure that you also understand the costs and risks involved!

Zeroing in on a Concise Definition

What do the following situations all have in common?

- ✔ Investment bankers at First Union Bank in North Carolina who need to find colleagues for a particular project can use a web browser to look up names in the company personnel directory. The intranet provides a database with details on employee experiences and roles in the organization.
- ✔ Xerox Corporation field sales representatives can use their notebook and laptop PCs to access customer history and product data from the corporate intranet while they're on the road.

- NetworkMCI employees looking for a change of scenery, pace, or salary can read job postings on the 14,000-user intranet.
- Employees of computer manufacturer Silicon Graphics can fill out purchase requisitions over the *Silicon Junction* intranet.

You've got it — they're all excellent examples of intranet publishing at work. In the Introduction to this book, I describe what an intranet is, and specifically how it differs from the public Internet. Now, to nail down what I mean by intranet publishing in a one-sentence definition:

Intranet publishing is the process of formatting and installing reusable documents, and their supporting programs, onto an intranet server where users can see and use them with their web browsers. I use the word *documents*, instead of the more general term *data*, because usually, when people think of intranet publishing, they think about newsletters, procedure manuals, and so on. The documents you publish can be more computer-oriented, for example, PowerPoint presentations, PageMaker layouts, or AutoCAD drawings. They can even be *interactive* documents that a user can modify, such as forms for creating expense accounts or product requisitions.

Data can also (logically enough!) mean information in a *database* such as SQL Server or Oracle. Most companies maintain financial and operational information in a database, including customer lists, product specifications, sales, expenses, and so on. While much of the material in this book is relevant for such intranet database publishing, this book doesn't get too bogged down in the specifics of database-to-intranet integration, which can get very involved.

Organizations with large document archives may use databases to store or catalog those archives. In this situation, intranet document publishing and intranet database publishing commingle, and you can't separate one from the other.

The term *publishing* implies a unidirectional act — someone publishes a document and that's that. However, remember that one of the coolest things about your intranet is that it can be a two-way street. For example, you can publish a form that an employee can then use by filling in the blanks and sending it back to you — that's intranet publishing, too, though it's a bit more complex than the one-way distribution of information you probably want to start with for your first project.

Intranet publishing doesn't encompass everything you can do on your intranet, by any means. Collaboration software, chat, groupware, and e-mail can all be bona fide intranet applications. However, these applications deal with the continuous exchange of constantly changing information in multiple directions. Intranet publishing, even interactive intranet publishing, essentially deals with reusable documents whose content or structure may change from time to time, but not with each communication.

Benefits of Publishing on an Intranet

Most of us hate paper, and already you're probably thinking that your intranet can cut down on paper use. *Paperwork* almost always has a negative ring to it, and the drive to eliminate paper sometimes drives people to irrational extremes. For example, I once consulted for an insurance company that wouldn't even let its Help Desk analysts have technical manuals in their offices — regardless of whether PWPM (Poorly Written Paper Manuals) was the only format in which certain information was available!

In many ways, paper gets a bad rap. Consider its virtues:

- It's portable.
- It requires no playback equipment to view its contents.
- It's readily editable, using common hardware (pens, pencils, and highlighters).
- It's highly standardized (it works essentially the same way in Paris, France or Paris, Texas).
- It doesn't crash, although it may burn.
- It's immune to viruses, but maybe not the family dog.
- The user interface is simple and intuitive.

If paper were a computer technology, people would consider it darn near perfect. If paper has so many great characteristics, why, then, would anybody want to publish documents on an intranet?

Accessibility

One of the biggest reasons is *accessibility*. With an intranet, everybody who can get to the intranet web server has access to your documents, whether the user is in the same building or half a world away. Because intranets use the TCP/IP (Transmission Control Protocol/Internet Protocol) networking language, which works well over Wide Area Networks (WANs), global publishing and document access is easy.

Accessibility also means that the documents on your intranet are available around the clock, every day (assuming that your server is reasonably reliable!). This 24/7 feature is great news for big organizations with a user base that spans time zones. The feature is also great for workaholics like ...*For Dummies* authors, who sometimes work at 2:00 a.m., and find that they need quick information.

Manageability

Intranets tend to use the so-called *fat server-thin client* model of computing, meaning that the user workstation doesn't have much responsibility for data or processing, and so can be relatively cheap and no-frills. Most of the intranet action (processing) is on the server, and this is especially true of intranets where a good deal of document publishing takes place.

The fact that you have a hundred, or a thousand, times fewer servers than you do workstations means that managing an intranet is a whole lot easier than managing other kinds of client/server environments that put more software and emphasis on the workstation. (You have the option of designing your intranet so that workstations shoulder more of the processing load, depending on the typical workstation hardware in your organization.)

Unlike the Internet, your organization is completely in charge of managing network performance. For example, if your network begins to run like molasses in January, you can upgrade by moving from regular Ethernet to Fast Ethernet, installing switching hubs, faster routers, and so on.

Also unlike the Internet, your business can manage intranet content. You control what information is available to your intranet users, assuming you put policies in place to govern the intranet publishing process.

Intranetting can bring unexpected management benefits, too. For example, users often need to print the documents they retrieve from the intranet, and printer management is a big time drain in most organizations. You can now buy printers that link to the intranet and permit administrators to manage the printer (set it up, check its status, and so on) with a remote web browser. You can expect to see similar capabilities in other network devices, such as hubs and routers, in the near future.

Development speed

Organizations can develop intranets rapidly because in most cases, the essential pieces are already in place. Those pieces include:

- A Network that speaks the Internet/intranet protocol: TCP/IP. (Remember that a *protocol* is a fancy name for a language that computers use to talk to each other)
- Network services to maintain computer network addresses
- Network servers that come with a web server program (as does Windows NT), or that can easily add one
- Workstations that already have a network connection, color monitor, mouse, and enough processing power to run a web browser

When you don't have to install a whole new network structure, and when just about every workstation in the organization already has the necessary software, the popular acronym *Rapid Application Development* (RAD) becomes more than a buzzword — it becomes a real possibility.

Distribution speed

Assuming that the workstations on your intranet are properly equipped for intranet access, intranet publishing is much faster than traditional paper or CD-ROM methods — as soon as you copy the data and supporting programs to an intranet server, the documents are available for viewing and use. Near-instantaneous distribution is a huge advantage when you compare intranet publishing to more traditional methods. If you publish a paper document, for example, you have to duplicate and distribute it, and users have to shuffle it from "in" boxes to loose-leaf binders or file folders. You also have to duplicate and distribute the material if you publish a document, or document collection on a CD-ROM, although users get fewer paper cuts this way.

Navigability

When I published my first book, in a fit of promotional zeal, I went to a local library to make sure they planned to order it. The first question the librarian asked me was, "Does it have an index? All *real* business books have an index." True enough. Without an index, a book is harder to navigate — getting to the information you need at any particular moment becomes a chore. Novels are generally excluded from this rule, although with Faulkner and Tolstoy, indexes may be a good idea (would have made college easier, anyway). Incidentally, *Exploding the Computer Myth* does have an index, but I don't think the librarian believed me. Maybe my beard put her off (it was in the Yasser Arafat stage).

Intranets go one step better than a book index — they use *hypertext* to provide easy and convenient document navigation. This book uses the Navigate icon to clue you in to when you may want to read another part of the book, but you still have to flip the pages. Hypertext, on the other hand, is like a book index that's spread carefully and intelligently throughout the text. You just click on a hypertext link, which is usually <u>underlined</u> and a different color from the surrounding text, and your computer jumps instantly to the screen or page containing the related information.

The ease of intranet navigation gives the user more freedom to determine which information is worth reading, and which isn't. It enables intranet document designers to create a single system that serves many levels of users. Intranet navigation also makes document access easier and faster.

HyperText Markup Language (HTML)

HyperText Markup Language, or HTML, is a text-based programming language for laying out web pages. Text-based means that you can write HTML code using even the simplest text editors, like Windows Notepad, or even DOS Edit. HTML uses codes in angle brackets, called *tags*, to specify text *markup* attributes, such as size, positioning, and italics. (If you've ever used WordPerfect for DOS, HTML tags are a lot like the special commands you see with that program's Reveal Codes feature.) For example, to make the word *Happy* appear in italics on a web page, the HTML code is:

```
<I>Happy</I>
```

The `<I>` turns the italics on, `Happy` is the text you want to display, and `</I>` turns the italics off.

HTML offers other tags to include graphic images on a page, tags to let you put mini-programs (called *applets*) on a page, as well as the hypertext links, so that users can jump to another document with the click of a mouse.

Figure 1-1 shows an Internet web page, and Figure 1-2 shows some of the HTML code that defines the same page.

Compared to other forms of programming, HTML is a walk in the park (and I don't mean Central Park). I don't intend to teach you how to become an HTML programmer in this book for two reasons: First, to do it right, you really need an entire book on the subject — *HTML For Dummies* by Tittel and James, or *Creating Cool Web Pages with HTML* by Taylor, are good ones (both from IDG Books Worldwide, Inc.). And second, these days, not everyone in an intranet publishing project needs to learn HTML, although you probably do need at least one HTML expert on board. Several excellent web publishing tools (Adobe PageMill, Microsoft FrontPage, Macromedia Backstage, and so on — see Appendix B) enable you to lay out a web page the way you want on screen, much as you would with a desktop publishing program. The tools then generate the HTML code automatically for you. These tools even come with *templates*, or page designs, already laid out.

HTML differs from a desktop publishing environment in one big way: It separates form from content. Using HTML, you can tell a browser what text and graphics you want on your page, and how to format the page in a general sense, but the way the page actually looks depends on how the user has set up the web browser. Fonts, text sizes, text colors, margins, and so forth can vary from computer to computer and from user to user. HTML's philosophy can be frustrating if you're a control freak, or liberating if you believe in giving power to the people.

HTML, as used today, includes several special formatting features for forms, tables, and frames. I cover these topics in sidebars in Chapters 5, 6, and 11 where they're more relevant. Also, check out Chapter 19 for a discussion of the HTML standard's past, present, and future.

You can see the underlying HTML commands behind any web page by choosing View⇨Source in Microsoft Internet Explorer, or View⇨Document Source in Netscape Navigator. See Figures 1-1 and 1-2.

Chapter 1: What's Intranet Publishing? 27

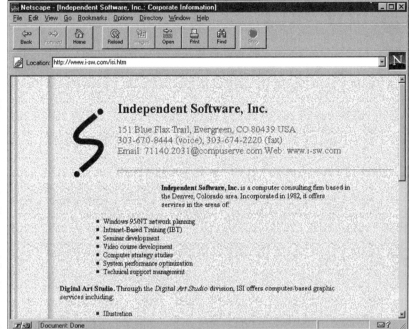

Figure 1-1: Here's a web page viewed in Netscape Navigator 3.01, that was created with HTML (courtesy of Independent Software, Inc.).

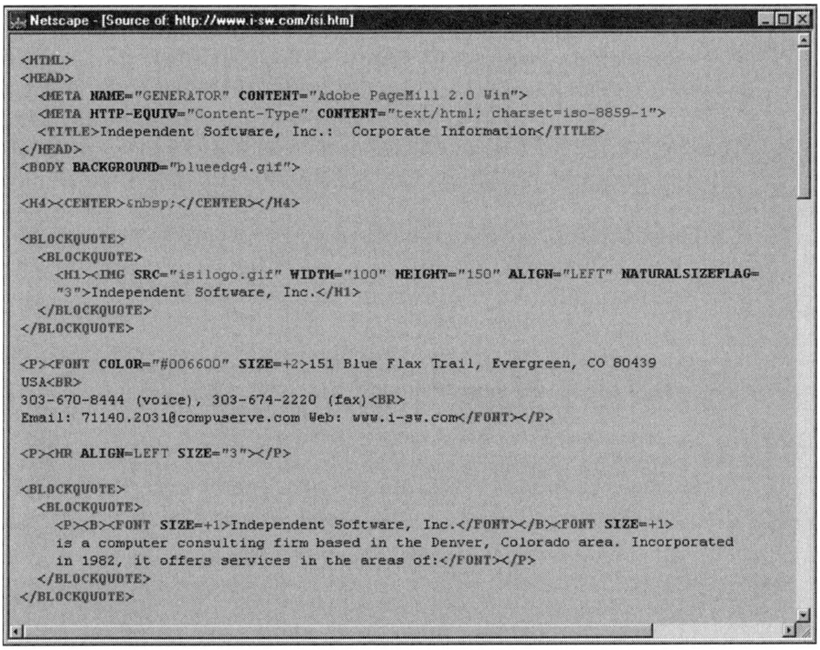

Figure 1-2: This is part of the HTML code that defines the page in Figure 1-1.

Integration

Most organizations that have been around a while have more than one kind of computer system. Bringing those different systems (mainframes, mini-computers, Local Area Networks) together at the user's workstation has been a gigantic undertaking for computer industry vendors and customers alike. Even after years of effort, though, many users still have to jump from program to program — even from system to system — to perform tasks such as word processing, e-mail, scheduling, graphics work, and so on. Windows-based environments make such bouncing around a little easier, but the seams still show with all those windows cluttering up your screen.

An intranet publishing environment can't provide total seamless integration overnight, but it can be a wonderful glue to hold different programs and documents together, and present them through the same window — the web browser. The magic that makes this possible, as I explain in the Introduction, is HyperText Transfer Protocol, or HTTP.

On a single intranet web page, you can create links to several different programs — heck, they can even be running on several different computers. Ditto for documents: They can be spread out all across the network, on different computers in different buildings, cities, or countries, and the user never needs to know, because the links all appear on the same web page, in the same screen window.

Intranets promise even greater integration for Windows users. Windows 98 uses the web browser as the user interface to the local workstation desktop, as well as to an intranet and the Internet. Running the web browser as a separate program to tap into an intranet isn't necessary in such a scheme — the user works from a web browser all the time, and just points it to the local workstation or the remote web server as needed.

Actually, you can use the web browser today with Windows 95 to point to the user's own computer, instead of to an Internet or intranet site. Figure 1-3 shows Internet Explorer browsing the user's own C: drive.

Familiar, standardized user interface

The intranet user interface is familiar for two reasons: Its controls look like those on consumer devices that people already understand, and many people have already spent time using a web browser to surf the public Internet.

Web browsers have buttons similar to the familiar ones on a VCR front panel, with a few extras thrown in, as shown in Figures 1-4 and 1-5.

Chapter 1: What's Intranet Publishing? 29

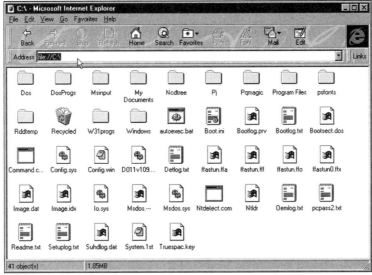

Figure 1-3: A web browser can also be a local computer browser. This figure shows Internet Explorer pointing to the user's own C: drive.

Figure 1-4: The Microsoft Internet Explorer toolbar.

Figure 1-5: The Netscape Navigator toolbar.

Most people with a home computer these days have figured out how to hook a modem up to it and connect to the Internet. The tool they use to browse the World Wide Web (WWW) for key lime pie recipes, potential romantic partners, or the text of the Gettysburg Address is the same tool you offer at work to connect to your intranet. Netscape estimated in 1996 that over 40 million people were using its browser — talk about familiarity! Many of your users are training themselves at home on their own time!

The user interface (web browser) is relatively standardized, for two reasons: Two popular browsers, Netscape Navigator and Microsoft Internet Explorer, dominate the market, and work almost the same way.

At first, Netscape Navigator was just about the only game in town. Now, ever since Microsoft decided (a little belatedly, but with astonishing energy) that they want to "do" Internet technology, Microsoft Internet Explorer has grown steadily in popularity. These two products cover over 90 percent of the browser market.

These days, the Netscape and Microsoft browsers look more like each other with every new release. Early on, Navigator had some nifty features for page formatting, known as *HTML extensions,* that Internet Explorer didn't, but current versions of the two browsers have borrowed features from each other to the point that both do most of what an intranet needs.

What's the big deal about a standard, familiar user interface? The answer is that training costs go down, support costs go down, and user productivity goes up. Despite the fact that so many companies spend so many zillion dollars each year on computer stuff, the biggest part of any computer system's life cycle cost is the people-related cost. Because intranets are easy to use, your company doesn't need to pay as many trainers, or hire as many tech support analysts. Even better, users can spend less time learning how to use the system and more time actually using it to do their jobs.

Compatibility with client workstations

One reason software is such a difficult business is that vendors have to practically recreate their product for every different type of computer in the target market. *Porting* (as it's called) a PC program to a Sun or Apple computer so that the Sun or Apple user can run the PC program is no trivial job. Naturally, software vendors try to figure out which platform can make them the most money, and then start there.

What happens is that not everyone in the organization can run the same version of every program, or heck, even the same program. Organizations that have PCs, Macs, and UNIX workstations waste huge amounts of time, energy, and money just dealing with the fact that the software isn't the same on any of those systems. Training and support costs far too much, and users can't communicate and collaborate as easily as they should.

Intranet publishing systems, however, suffer far less from such incompatibilities. First of all, just about every computer platform has web browser software available for it, which is often all the user needs to access your intranet. Second, as long as an intranet provides standard, least-common-denominator HTML, the screens look basically the same, whether viewed on a PC, Mac, SPARCstation, or Univac. And third — the best part — the intranetter doesn't have to design anything twice: A single system works for everybody.

(Relative) Ease of development

Compared to other kinds of computer information systems, basic intranet publishing systems are easy to build. If all you need is a system to present simple text documents to users over an existing TCP/IP network, an experienced intranetter can probably whip out a system in a couple of weeks or less. In most cases, even an inexperienced intranetter, who at least doesn't fear the technology, doesn't need more than four weeks. HTML is easy, and many of today's office applications have built-in abilities to convert documents to HTML.

Sandia Labs, a defense contractor that works mostly with high-energy physics, reports that its intranet projects take one-fourth the amount of time to develop than other kinds of computer projects. This is not to say that *all* intranet publishing systems are easy to build, and you can expect that Sandia Labs has some fairly network-savvy employees. Intranets with large, dynamic document databases can involve fairly serious programming. Obviously, as your intranet publishing goes beyond plain text and gets more high-tech, your projects begin to require more planning, take a bit longer, and require more specialized help.

And if you want to write your own Java code for web applets (mini-programs that run on a Java-enabled web browser, such as Netscape Navigator 3.01 or Internet Explorer 3.01+), I can report that Java is easier than C++ — today's most popular programming language. However, to me at least, that's a little like saying a 50-mile ultramarathon is easier than a 100-mile ultramarathon. I respect the people who do such things, but if an easier way exists to get from point A to point B (for example, a car), I usually go with that option.

Fortunately, for people like me, and maybe you, almost every week the industry pops out a new tool to help you automate parts of the process for even complex projects almost every week. Page creation programs, document conversion utilities, and intranet site design tools are becoming more sophisticated and reliable. Specialized document publishing applications provide canned templates and forms for very particular jobs, such as human resource policy documents. Intranet server management utilities are also getting easier to use. I cover all this stuff in later chapters.

(Also relative) Ease of upsizing

Need to expand your intranet? Doing so is easy (at least, up to a point). You can buy a bigger web server — the most powerful ones cost up to a million dollars, so the ceiling is high. Or you can add servers, and then divide out the programs and data files between them. Newer versions of web server software enable you to group several servers together and give them all the same electronic address so that they appear to the user as one big server.

You do have to be a little careful about design issues when you super-size your intranet — it's not quite as easy as it is at a fast-food burger joint. Chapters 2 and 14 go into this in more detail, but I can tell you here that an intranet architecture that works fine with 50 users can bog down with 5,000 users, even if you do put more servers on the job.

Outgrowing the architecture is more of an issue if you link your intranet web servers with separate, dedicated database servers for a database document publishing system. The early methods for a web server to fetch data from such a database server are inefficient, because the web server has to establish a communications channel, open a database file, read (or change) the information, close the file, and close the channel every time the user needs to read or change data. Newer methods permit the web server to maintain a continuous connection to a database server to reduce overhead and improve speed.

Here's the bottom line: As long as you make good design decisions about how your intranet runs programs and connects to databases — and not all intranets do these things — upsizing your intranet is relatively easy and simple.

Ability to publish many types of documents

You can use an intranet to publish a wider variety of document types than you can with traditional paper publishing. For example, intranets can handle the following:

- ✔ Text (such as a policy/procedure manual)
- ✔ Graphics, including color (such as product photographs)
- ✔ Binary data files (such as program updates)
- ✔ Programs (such as web browsers)
- ✔ Links to Internet locations (for example, your chief competitor's home page)
- ✔ Digital audio (such as the CEO's recent speech on strategic direction)
- ✔ Digital video (for example, how to assemble a subassembly from parts)

Certain types of documents require a little help on the receiving end, in the form of *plug-ins* or *helper programs* that allow the user's web browser to view data it normally couldn't. An example is *streaming audio,* a format for audio files that allows the user to start listening to an audio file over a network, as though it were coming from a radio — you don't need to wait to download the entire file before it starts playing.

Cheaper than paper publishing

This one's a biggie! Cogitate on these facts and figures:

- Management consultants at Deloitte and Touche estimate that most corporations spend 12 to 15 percent of revenue on internal and external paper publishing activities.

- Research firm International Data Corp. surveyed seven companies and found that the average return on investment from intranet publishing projects is 1,000 percent, due to paper and labor savings, and that organizations recover their intranet development costs in about 6 to 12 weeks.

- Dataware Technologies, a Cambridge research group, calculates that in 1997, delivering a megabyte of information on paper costs $3.50, while delivering the same amount on CD-ROM costs $0.0024 (granting that the average CD-ROM holds much more than one megabyte, and these figures are averages). Considering that intranet publishing is even cheaper than CD-ROM publishing, the difference is enormous.

- Silicon Graphics reports that it saves about $2.5 million a year in paper publishing and distribution costs from its intranet publishing projects.

- Sun Microsystems reports that it saves about $1.5 million every quarter by distributing software via its intranet, instead of through its old methods (again, paper publishing and distribution).

The reason intranet publishing is so much less expensive is simple: Organizations don't have to incur the substantial materials and labor costs of paper, printing, binding, order processing, and shipping.

In addition to being generally cheaper than paper publishing, intranet publishing enjoys a special cost advantage over non-intranet technologies: Much of the technology you need to do the actual publishing is free! You can download full-featured web server and client software from the Internet at no charge. Although most companies end up buying commercial intranet software, the fact that free alternatives exist goes a long way toward keeping prices down.

Intranet publishing may be much cheaper than paper publishing, but just so you know, it can carry higher front-end costs than paper publishing does. Your organization must pay out of pocket for a complete intranet information system — web servers and all — before you realize a dime of savings. In paper publishing, you pay as you go, and the front-end investment may be considerably lower. Cash-poor organizations may continue to use paper, until they can pony up for the costs of deploying an intranet system.

When to Publish with an Intranet — Not!

Despite its many benefits, intranet publishing doesn't make all other forms of document publishing obsolete. Here, for example, are a few situations in which you do *not* want to use an intranet for a publishing project:

- **Your target users don't have assured access to your web server(s).** For example, a sales rep in the field at a customer site may not have Internet/intranet access, and may need a printed, or CD-ROM-based, catalog or spec sheet to show a client.

- **The application calls for rich multimedia content.** If you need to deliver high-quality video or sound, most intranet *plumbing* (slang for the wires and hardware that connect your computers) doesn't cut the mustard — at least not yet. A multimedia CD-ROM may be a better publishing medium for very intense graphics, and other multimedia.

- **The document is going to external users.** If your document is intended for external users (for example, customers) as well as, or instead of, internal users (employees), you may find that a brochure or other paper document is a better way to go. If your intranet isn't accessible to external users on the Internet, your customers may have no way to retrieve the information except by paper.

- **Your publishing project has very demanding *uptime* and response time requirements typical of so-called *mission-critical* systems.** Most organizations should wait a year or two before putting their do-or-die applications that the business relies on for day-to-day transactions on an intranet.

- **You work for a paper company.** <grin>

You may be thinking that your users haven't been asking for an intranet system, so why supply one? Just remember that no one asked for a WalkMan either, until Sony created it. Users can't ask for something that they don't even know exists. And then once they have it, they wonder how they ever got along without it. Intranet-published documents are in many cases so much more convenient than traditional methods that your users will thank you and send you a fruitcake in December.

Intranet Publishing and the Enterprise

Attention Big Picture types who want to project what intranet publishing is likely to mean for business over the next decade or two: This section is for you. Those of you who are itching to get to the nuts and bolts stuff, please skip this section, with my blessing.

What happens if intranet publishing takes off?

First off, I'm here to tell you that it *will* take off.

In any enterprise, information flow is a key to survival and success. You want people who need specific information to be able to get it conveniently and quickly. You want to shield employees from information that they don't need in order to help prevent overload. You want the quality and accuracy of the information in your organization to be high. You also want to keep information of interest to your competitors out of their reach.

Over time, intranet publishing can have a big positive impact on your entire organization because it can help you meet every one of these goals. I'd go so far as to say that intranet publishing promises to be a bigger boon to most businesses than any use of the public Internet.

A successful pilot project is almost sure to inspire follow-up efforts. In a couple of years, your organization may have a dozen or more intranet publishing projects. Also, your business will very likely apply intranetting technologies and techniques to other kinds of activities, such as improving access to mainframe databases, and forging closer links to both customers and suppliers with *extranets*. (See sidebar.)

Sidebar: Extranets

Extranets are web-based systems available to individuals and companies outside your own organization for the purpose of streamlining business processes. For example, a supplier could check your sales system periodically, via an extranet, to see whether to stock more of a particular product in anticipation of new orders from you. Your intranet can be a stepping-stone to developing an extranet.

Extranets do *not* necessarily imply a public Internet presence. You can restrict extranet access to bona fide suppliers and customers. (You don't want competitors to know what your sales are!) Further, a public promotional Internet site isn't the same as an extranet; a promotional site may not offer any access to your internal operations, but may simply inform potential customers about your products or services.

In my own humble effort to bring some order to intranet and extranet terminology, I call a web-based system for both internal and external users a *multinet,* whether it includes public Internet access in either direction or not. If the term catches on, you heard it here first.

My point is that because the technology is likely to spread rapidly, be around for a long time, and perhaps become a springboard for other networking initiatives such as extranets and multinets, doing intranet publishing right from the outset is extremely important so that you don't end up building, trashing, and rebuilding these networks more often than necessary. And so, in Chapters 3 through 8 of this book, I help you identify the best candidates for your intranet publishing projects, and Chapters 9 through 16 devote a lot of time to implementing and maintaining your intranet publishing projects.

Intranetting is an evolving art (yes, I said "art") — intranets haven't been around long, after all, and no one person or book can give you a definitive handbook based on decades of experience. Nevertheless, you are best off getting hip to the current best practices so you can at least avoid some of the pitfalls that many companies have already encountered, and position your intranet for the rapid growth it's likely to experience.

What happens to all our existing systems?

Some people may believe that as intranets evolve, Local Area Networks (LANs) as we now know them will vanish into computer history. Any organization diving into intranet publishing needs to consider what impact it will have on their existing investment in information systems.

If your organization has many different computing architectures at work — microcomputers, network servers, midrange systems (like the IBM AS/400), maybe even big mainframes — you may ask how intranet publishing affects your ability to keep putting all those systems to work. So far, most intranets use microcomputers and network servers, but the folks who build minicomputers and mainframes aren't blind to the intranet phenomenon. Expect to see software that turns those bigger systems into monster intranet web servers.

The corporate intranet can provide a user-friendly front end to the programs and data on those big systems sitting in the air-conditioned glass houses. Software vendors everywhere are rushing to make their proprietary databases, mini computers, and mainframes accessible to browser users (witness Lotus' push to bring Notes to intranet users via Domino).

Intranetting doesn't invalidate any organization's investment in particular kinds of computers or systems. In fact, in many ways, that is the beauty of intranets and their success: The core TCP/IP network is available to just about every system out there. It does, however, put pressure on businesses that still rely exclusively on older *dumb terminals* to upgrade those user systems to bona fide microcomputers.

Remember that a *dumb terminal* is really just a monitor and a keyboard connected to a mainframe computer — you can't run a web browser on such a character-based terminal, and so you can't use it to connect to an intranet.

Intranets and Network PCs

The Network PC (or Net PC, for short) is a new concept that has become almost as high profile as intranetting. IBM, Microsoft, Netscape, Oracle, Sun, and many other vendors are hyping the Network PC concept feverishly. In a nutshell, the Network PC is just a PC with no disk storage. Anything the computer needs, from programs to data files, it gets from the network (see Figure 1-6).

Variations on the Network PC theme exist. Sun, for example, is building the *JavaStation,* a microcomputer that runs the Java programming language from an internal chip.

Network PC pros and cons

Why strip out the disk drives, especially these days, when their cost is so low? The big reason is *maintenance*. Consider these advantages:

- **Network PCs are easier to update with the latest software.** When user workstations run programs from their own disk drives, updating those programs is a Class A migraine, even with today's clever network management utilities.

- **Keeping Network PCs in sync is easier.** When users store data files on local disk drives, those data files can get out of sync with copies other users are working on. If everyone works on the same data file, presuming the supporting network software only lets one user change the data at a time, the latest version is always available.

- **Network PCs are less prone to user error.** When users add their own programs or modify configuration information on their own computers, not only can they make mistakes that hurt the computers' ability to run reliably (if at all), but they can also create a computing environment with very little consistency.

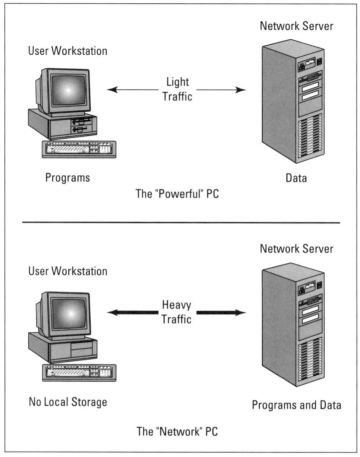

Figure 1-6: The Network PC has no hard drive or CD-ROM drive, and must retrieve programs and data from a network server, in contrast to the more typical *Powerful PC*.

Organizations are struggling to balance the power of full-fledged user workstation computers against the cost of maintaining and managing those distributed systems. Democracy is great, but it's expensive (check your latest tax return). Moving to an enlightened autocracy of NetPCs, where users have powerful workstations, but must run *approved* programs and get *approved* data from a central source, has great appeal. However, the NetPC autocracy has a few catches:

 ✓ **The increased traffic on the network is a major drawback.** Today's programs are bodacious — the industry term is *fatware* — because their creators assume that workstations have plenty of local disk space to hold them.

 ✓ **Users may resist losing control, choice, and flexibility over which programs they run.** They may perceive the Network PC as a thinly veiled return to dictatorial mainframe days.

- ✔ **Your in-house developers have to work harder.** In-house application developers may find their plates fuller than ever, as users who formerly wrote their own programs (spreadsheet templates, customized report formats, and even small database applications) must now abdicate that task to the Information Services group.
- ✔ **Users are helpless during system crises.** Overall, system fault tolerance can suffer: A Network PC can't do a darned thing if a needed server is down.

How intranets fit in

How does intranetting fit into this picture? Actually, intranet publishing can be a great enabler of the Network PC concept because it can reduce the number of programs a user needs to fetch from the network.

The primary program in an intranet publishing system is the web browser. The typical user can download the browser program from the network in the morning, and leave it running in workstation memory all day long. Sure, the user needs other programs too, but for many data access and entry chores, the browser is all that's required. Browsers aren't especially large programs, so they don't take long to fetch. And I expect that if Network PCs take off, they may soon come with a browser-on-a-chip that doesn't have to come over the network at all. If browsers rely on several *helper programs* to allow them to view the data coming down the network pike, however, network traffic increases. (Helper programs are add-in program components that allow a browser to display certain types of data, for example, streaming audio.)

The bottom line is that your intranet publishing systems will still work if your organization moves to the Network PC concept. However:

- ✔ **You need to work harder to limit network traffic.** The network will struggle just to send all the programs users need down to their workstations.
- ✔ **You must spend more time on performance optimization.** Network PCs don't have the local hard disk to use as a short-term memory for remembering pages and graphics the user viewed recently. (If you do plan to move to Network PCs, please read Chapter 14 especially carefully!)
- ✔ **You need to look at user programs that are smaller and more efficient than the ones most users work with today.** Little Java programs (see Chapter 12 for more on Java) that do 90 percent of what users need may be much more appropriate than fatware programs, having 9,000 features that most people never use.

✔ **You need to provide enough variety and capability in the programs that users can get from the network.** You don't want your users to scream bloody murder that you've taken away the very reason they like using small computers in the first place. The current PC provides a productive degree of independence from central authorities, who don't do things fast enough or flexibly enough for individual users.

Intranets as competitive weapons

The first intranet publishing projects your organization deploys are likely to focus on more effective ways to distribute information and reduce costs. As intranetting becomes an accepted computing method in your organization, however, you're sure to discover uses that go beyond cost reduction, and actually start to *contribute* to business success.

For example, intranet publishing can help your company adapt to industry changes by helping to change the way employees do their existing jobs, and by enabling new business functions. Often, such changes depend on sophisticated intranets that publish data in *real time* (that's computerese for *as things actually happen* instead of *a few hours, days, or weeks later*).

In other cases, the intranet can make huge volumes of data in existing databases more easily available for analysis and decision-making. This kind of intranet is also a more advanced type that can integrate closely with the database systems your organization already uses.

Finally, although companies rarely use intranets today for *transaction processing applications,* where performance is critical (for example, airline reservation systems), many computer companies are working on technologies that may make transaction processing feasible on intranets in the future. Chapter 3 discusses intranets and reengineering in more detail, but for now, know that intranet publishing can become a competitive weapon for your enterprise, in addition to a potent cost-cutting technology.

This chapter has clarified the benefits of intranet publishing and how it may fit into your organization's future computing architecture. You also need to know the costs and risks associated with intranet publishing before you take the plunge and start rolling out projects. By a remarkable coincidence, that's the subject of Chapter 2!

Chapter 2
Assessing Costs and Risks: Diving In with Your Eyes Open

In This Chapter
▶ Discovering the value of estimating and tracking project costs
▶ Getting ready for specific front end and life cycle costs your project may incur
▶ Finding out the risks of intranet publishing, to minimize them from the start

Before you jump into Part II, where I discuss all the cool things you can do with intranet publishing, this chapter offers a bit of a reality check, pointing out the costs and risks. Intranet publishing systems are business systems, and any good manager needs to understand the downside, as well as the upside, of a new venture. I've read dozens of intranetting books, and none of them addresses these issues adequately — but as a veteran of dozens of information system projects, trust me, they're vital to your success.

Intranet Publishing Costs

Intranet publishing is inexpensive as computer projects go, but it ain't free, and the cost factors aren't all equally obvious.

Some managers say that intranet publishing is so obviously cost-effective that a lot of front end analysis really isn't necessary. I agree with this to an extent. You can certainly get hung up analyzing costs down to the dime. You can't possibly measure benefits as accurately as you can measure costs, and the key criterion is the cost/benefit *ratio,* not costs alone.

Having said that, if you aren't aware, at least generally, of how deep a swimming pool is before you dive in, you may hit the bottom at high speed. Having to ask for a big budget increase because you didn't anticipate all the possible costs is a good way to torpedo a great project. By keeping tabs on intranet publishing costs, you can more persuasively make the case to deploy more intranet projects in the future.

Intranet development isn't as predictable as other types of information systems. Budgeting for time and money is, therefore, much tougher. When considering costs, err on the high side, commit your organization to tracking actual costs, and build up an experience base you can use for budgeting the next intranet project.

Who tracks intranet publishing costs in your organization? Is anyone doing it, at least informally? Can you reasonably expect project champions to assume this responsibility, with all that they invest in a project's apparent success? If financial managers track costs, are they aware of the indirect costs any information system imposes?

Software

As Athena sprang from the forehead of Zeus (*that* must've been painful), intranets emerged almost fully grown out of the public Internet. The good news for intranetters is that Uncle Sam did much of the technology development with tax dollars, and the software you need for basic intranetting is either free or cheap — please note that I said *basic* intranetting!

Everyone in the technology business, however, knows that even free software isn't *really* free. For example, a freely downloadable web server program may require a significant time investment to customize it for a particular site. Also, a company may not be able to receive vendor support for freeware, even if the company's willing to pay for it — which means the company must develop or hire sufficient expertise to support the software internally.

The freebies also generally just cover the basics of getting an intranet up and running. To do useful things with your intranet, you need special-purpose tools that you generally have to buy. This section takes a brief look at basic intranetting software, site development tools, and publishing applications.

Get the best intranet tools your budget allows. These tools tend to automate tasks that your system designers and administrators have to otherwise perform manually. You almost always come out ahead when you buy software that relieves the load on human beings — especially expensive human beings! Talk to colleagues, connect to resources on the Web for advice, and read the trade journals — the "best" intranet tool isn't always the most expensive one.

Don't hesitate to take a look at *Building an Intranet For Dummies* by John Fronckowiak (IDG Books Worldwide, Inc.) for some helpful advice on the nitty-gritty details of actually creating your intranet system. After all, you can't publish anything without an intranet in place.

Chapter 2: Assessing Costs and Risks: Diving In with Your Eyes Open

Basic software

If you do decide you want to be able to call a vendor for tech support, it's good to know that commercial software for the basics (web servers and workstation browsers) has to compete with the free stuff so it tends to be fairly inexpensive. Netscape FastTrack Server is only about $300, and its big brother, Netscape Enterprise Server, is around $1,300. Novell web server is $1,000, and Microsoft Internet Information Server comes bundled with NT Server. Workstation costs can be significant, however, if you have many workstations, and if you use a browser, such as Navigator, that costs something, even if it's only $50 a copy. (Microsoft Internet Explorer is free, by contrast.)

Site development tools

Commercial software for site development ranges all over the cost map, but you can get quite a bit of power for only a few hundred dollars. The $400 HoTMetaL Intranet Publisher from SoftQuad, the $300 Backstage Internet Studio (Desktop Edition) from Macromedia, the bargain $150 FrontPage kit from Microsoft, and the $500 Fusion product from NetObjects are all examples of inexpensive, soup-to-nuts packages that include workable web site development and management utilities.

Of course, you can spend more — up to $100,000 for a high-end site development package, that a major TV network may use, for example — if you need more features, or if you have a large intranet. Nevertheless, getting started with a medium to small project is perfectly feasible with a site development software budget of around $1,000.

If you need to secure your intranet against crackers, hackers, and other undesirables, create a budget for firewall software if you don't already have one. (*Firewalls* protect a trusted network, such as your intranet, from a public one, such as the Internet.) Plan on $1,000 to $3,000 to buy top-of-the-line protection for a small network, $20,000 or more for a large one.

Please see Chapter 15 for more on firewalls and other security measures.

Creating the content you want to publish over your intranet may not break the bank if all you need to do is convert existing documents to HTML format; most popular office-automation software suites have this capability built in. However, content development can get pricey if you have multimedia aspirations. A complete set of state-of-the-art graphics tools can set you back a few grand — more if you want to do high-end digital video work, or 3-D animation (even if it isn't *Jurassic Park*). Tools such as Adobe Photoshop, Adobe Premiere, Equilibrium DeBabelizer, Kinetix 3DMax, Macromedia Director, Sonic Foundry Sound Forge, and so on typically cost hundreds of dollars each, though less expensive alternatives do exist.

Converting data usually requires some software, too, whether it takes the form of Optical Character Recognition (OCR) scanning software to convert images to editable text (see Chapter 10) or utilities to translate WordPerfect files to HTML. Fortunately, you can get great conversion utilities for under $1,000.

Finally, your intranet project may involve custom programming if you plan to make your intranet heavily interactive with user input forms, database access, and so on. You're lucky here, too: Good program development tools, such as Aimtech Jamba, or Symantec Visual Café for writing Java code, tip the scales at $500 or less. Easily 90 percent of your programming costs go toward people who know the programming language you require.

Publishing applications

The more specialized any software is, the further you get from the basic intranet/Internet freebies, and the more the software is likely to cost. The area of publishing applications is, therefore, where you're likely to devote most of your intranet software dollars, and where you need to shop most carefully. The following list shows three examples of the jump-in price that occurs when software moves from the general to the specific:

- An industrial-strength, web-enabled document publishing system, such as Builder and SiteDirector from Folio, runs $10,000 or so; other products such as Information Dimensions Basis V8 cost $25,000 and up.
- A highly customizable, database-driven, document publishing system with groupware features for collaborative editing, such as NovaSoft NovaManage, costs $45,000.
- A tool for building intranet-based training can run from $2,000 for Asymetrix Toolbook II Instructor to $15,000 or more for Stanford Testing Systems IBTauthor (I discuss these products in Chapter 8).

I can see your jaw dropping to the floor about now. Relax! These tools are fast, industrial-strength products with the ability to handle thousands of intranet users; you may not need any such specialized tools for a small, basic intranet publishing project. Adobe Acrobat for $300 may well be all the publishing horsepower you require. Sometimes, vendors offer smaller-scale versions of their flagship products that can do the job just fine for a smaller project. For example, Asymetrix Toolbook II Assistant is half the cost of its more powerful sibling Toolbook II Instructor but provides most of the features you need.

Be aware that the cost of intranet publishing applications is usually proportional to the features you need to provide, the number (and size) of the documents, and the number of intranet users you anticipate. Large document repositories require a separate database, rather than a few web page directories, and after you start linking your web server to a secure back-end database that runs on its own dedicated server, complexity and cost start rising fast. The more users you have, the harder your publishing software has to work — and software to handle tougher jobs efficiently and quickly, of course, is more expensive.

Hardware

Hardware costs range incredibly wide. Your intranet hardware costs depend almost entirely on how many people you intend to serve and how much stress your applications place on server systems. A departmental intranet that publishes text documents for a couple dozen employees can run happily on a $3,000 PC; an enterprise-wide intranet server dishing up video training clips for several thousand employees can run you a quarter of a million smackers. A spectrum of options exists between the two extremes.

Definitely budget for at least one dedicated machine to run as your intranet server, even if your project is relatively small. Expecting the same machine to provide file and print services for standard LAN (Local Area Network) stuff, as well as web services for your intranet, is almost sure to make everyone unhappy with the performance of both systems.

If you're planning an intranet that needs to be running all the time (*high uptime,* as it's called), you probably want server *redundancy,* meaning that at least one extra computer can replace the main intranet server in a crisis.

If your intranet uses a database for storing and retrieving documents, you may need a separate machine to host that database.

If you have a *multinet,* where your intranet connects to the public Internet, you may need one or more dedicated machines to support security services (such as firewall software and proxy servers; see Chapter 15 if these terms are new to you).

If you currently rely on a paper-based document system, you may want to eventually convert your paper stuff to intranet documents. You can do so easily with a scanner and OCR (Optical Character Recognition) software. A simple flatbed scanner, suitable for digitizing a few dozen pages a day, runs $600 to $2,000. Higher-volume scanners with automatic paper feed that can easily handle hundreds of pages per day start around $7,000 and go up from there. Scanning services are an alternative if your document volume is too low to justify the hardware.

As with software, multimedia hardware gets pricey. An entry level digital video rig to capture, edit, and compress video clips can easily cost $6,000, and a fancy setup can run into hundreds of thousands of dollars.

The good news in this section is that you probably don't need any new hardware on the workstation side of things. If most of your users have a system with a color monitor, mouse, and enough memory to run the operating system, browser, and a couple of office applications without straining (usually 16 to 32 megabytes), you will be in fairly good shape.

Infrastructure

In Chapter 1, I mention that one of the great advantages of intranetting is that in most organizations, the basic network infrastructure already exists. However, intranets don't always just ride on top of an existing network without some enhancements (no more than you can hang a multi-ton snowplow blade onto your VW beetle without beefing up the springs a bit).

Intranets put more traffic on the network. You may need to upgrade your network performance to handle this traffic. The extent of your upgrades depends on whether you publish text-only documents or bigger stuff like graphics or digitized videos. The ease of dropping images into web pages tempts many intranetters into designing flashy sites that bog down networks. Doing so requires potentially expensive hardware enhancements, like different types of network hubs and increasing network transmission speeds (for example, from 10 megabits per second to 100 with Fast Ethernet).

Chapter 14 deals with intranet performance issues, including network traffic.

If you're making your intranet available to home users or other remote employees, you may need to add equipment for dial-up communications, if you don't have it already. A small dial-up server with half a dozen modems costs around $3,000. Faster remote access setups may require special phone company services, such as ISDN (Integrated Services Digital Network) lines, which can cost $50 to $100 per month for each line. Point-to-point leased lines supporting higher speeds than ISDN cost substantially more.

If you're putting a brand-new network into position, then you have to assume a whole gang of associated system costs, including cable, hubs, routers, servers, wide-area links (if any), and so on.

People costs

In a typical intranet publishing project, the people costs far outweigh the technology costs — as it should be. The temptation to concentrate on hardware and software costs, and forget about your *wetware* costs, is great.

Chapter 2: Assessing Costs and Risks: Diving In with Your Eyes Open

Wetware is nerdspeak for the human brain, which (as you know if you've ever had a head injury or watched a hockey game) is positively awash in blood. Computers are rarely wet, unless they're supercomputers cooled with liquid nitrogen to make them go faster. Don't go putting ice packs on your web servers, though: You have to hit 30 degrees below zero just to improve performance by 50 percent.

Warm bodies (wetware)

Most of the companies I've consulted with in the past few years overwork their technical staffs. The people who buy, build, program, manage, and support your information systems are generally already fairly busy, so you can't just assign them a big new project ("Hey, Alice, are you busy for the next couple of years? Wanna be a webmaster?") without providing any additional help.

Additional help may take the form of new employees, or you can *outsource* it (contract the work to other companies). Either way, costs are involved:

- **Employees carry direct salary costs plus fringe benefits (which can amount to 30 percent or more of direct salary):** Full-time webmasters aren't cheap — figure $75,000 and up for a good one. You may also need one or more web programmers, site designers, project managers, and network administrators.

- **Contractors don't get fringe benefits, but outsourcing has its own costs beyond direct contractor payments:** You have to figure in the time to evaluate and select contractors, the legal costs of contract review and administration, and the in-house personnel time required to get contractors savvy with what you need and to manage ongoing contractor performance.

Training

You need training for the people who design and support your intranet project, as well as for the people who use it. As far as the people who design and support your intranet, the number of people to train is small, but the depth of knowledge they require is great. The opposite situation applies for end-user training — not so much depth, but a whole bunch of people. Technical education can be expensive:

- Good outside instructors get $800 per day.
- Commercial, public seminars on intranet technologies range from $300 to $500 per day.
- Temporary help may need to take over for employees when they are in a training course.

    ✔ Off-site courses may have added travel costs.

    ✔ Computer books often cost $50 a pop. (My own intranet technology bookshelf easily represents a thousand-dollar investment. I keep telling my wife that one of these days I'll sell more books than I buy.)

Your training needs depend on how much intranetting expertise is already on the payroll. In any case, training for your intranet designers isn't an area where you should pinch the penny till Lincoln hollers.

Training costs are recurrent, not one-time as you may suspect. Whenever your company hires new employees, transfers existing ones, adds new features to your intranet, adopts new programs or modifies old ones, you have to turn around and get your users up to speed with the new stuff. These costs increase exponentially in a computing environment where you have many different kinds of software and hardware.

System management

Because intranets permit more frequent document updates, users tend to expect more frequent document updates. A big part of managing an intranet project, as I explain in Chapter 13, is keeping the content current. This can be a big job, especially if someone has to check new content for accuracy, completeness, organization, visual layout, and so on.

Somebody needs to answer user questions about the new publishing system. Initially, you need more help at your Help Desk to handle the load.

If you already have a network, someone is probably already monitoring that network for *uptime* (what percentage of the day, week, and year the network is running successfully) and performance. Adding an application, such as an intranet publishing system, adds to that workload.

Other indirect costs

Any information system also has various miscellaneous hidden or indirect costs. These include additional business insurance against theft, fire, and damage to hardware, software, and/or data; any additional physical facilities, such as space for servers and the associated rent; and so on.

Intranet Publishing Risks

So much for intranet publishing costs. What about the risks? This section identifies the top five: doing stuff twice, inconsistent user interface, bad design, poor print support, and inaccurate data.

Department of Redundancy Department

Every organization with more than one employee suffers to some extent from Left Hand–Right Hand syndrome: If one person or group doesn't know what others are doing, the risk of duplicated (and wasted) effort can be a real problem. Intranetting is a grass roots phenomenon that can spread like a disease because it's so easy. Don't be surprised if people catch the disease, and you find other workgroups and departments undertaking their own intranet.

I go nuts when I read articles in the trade press that urge workgroups and departments to go off and create their own *secret intranet projects*. That's fine for a small pilot project, but over the long term, coordinating and publicizing intranet publishing projects is the only way to avoid wastefully duplicating someone else's effort.

With some coordination and an open attitude toward your publishing project, you can avoid the problem of redundant effort. Publicize your intranet publishing project and then bring interested parties on board with their suggestions. The result is that you avoid duplicated effort, and you create an intranet that addresses everyone's needs. Then nobody feels like they need to start a secret intranet project.

Maybe the biggest potential benefit of intranetting is its ability to interconnect and integrate different systems. Specific groups can include links on their intranets to leverage the work that other groups perform. For example, if tech support needs to offer an employee directory, then with a little coordination, they can simply cross-reference the employee directory on the human resources intranet.

Inconsistent user interfaces

Huh? What about the key intranet benefit of using a single, consistent user interface — the web browser — across all projects? This is a valid benefit, but remember that the web browser is just a navigational tool, a window into a particular web site soul. Page layout, form design, navigational buttons and icons, backgrounds, headers, footers, and so on, can all vary widely within the browser window. To prove my point, take a gander at the web sites in Figures 2-1 and 2-2 — they reflect radically different approaches to web site design.

Chapters 9, 11, and 12 can help your organization standardize key aspects of your web sites, so that each publishing system doesn't have its own learning curve. You may want to enlist some help in creating your user interface guidelines from people who've worked with UI (User Interface) design before. Psychology, aesthetics, and technology all come into play in this area.

Figure 2-1: This web page uses an image map (the graphic at center has links embedded in it) for navigational purposes. The page is a single unit; the design is modern and clean.

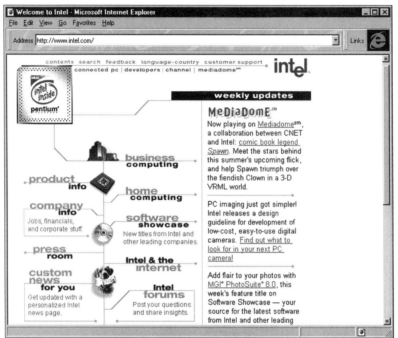

Figure 2-2: This web page is divided into multiple frames. Clicking an option in the left frame displays different information in the upper-right one, and frames on the bottom display various messages.

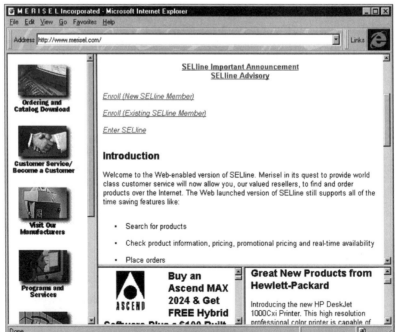

Overcentralizing development

Some organizations, in their zeal to standardize intranet development, overcentralize the process. While the spontaneous and uncoordinated development of intranet projects carries risks, such as inconsistent web site design, you can't be successful treating intranets like mainframes, either.

One of intranetting's key advantages is that projects can be small in scale and developed by individual departments or teams. You can avoid overcentralizing development, ensure consistency, and sidestep the Left Hand–Right Hand syndrome by publishing design guidelines, encouraging communication between intranetters in different groups, and centrally reviewing intranet projects. Chaos is bad, but so are dictatorships — try to find a happy democracy of contributors.

Dangerous dilettantes

A possible drawback of how easy it is to develop an intranet is that a given intranet publishing project may not receive the careful attention it would get if it required a heftier investment of new technology. The very ease of intranetting opens it up to dilettantes who know just enough to be dangerous, and who may find themselves in over their heads in short order (the theme for this chapter is *swimming pool analogies*).

For example, novice intranet designers may make design decisions that limit the project's ability to *scale up* (grow with your organization) over time. Using a connect-each-time tool (such as Microsoft Internet Database Connector, bundled with FrontPage) to access a document database may work fine for a few dozen users, but the tool may turn to sludge with a thousand users. Intranet projects are inherently scaleable, but the choice of software toolkits may well work against you, if you don't plan ahead.

Another mistake intranet newbies make frequently is to do things from scratch, when commercial software vendors have already done the work and can provide a better way. Those intranetters with limited experience aren't likely to know about the wide range of tools and utilities that can simplify their lives.

Another problem here is that intranet programming toolkits aren't as mature as most other programming environments (such as C++ or COBOL), meaning that some responsibility shifts to the system developer, who may have to be a bit more disciplined because the tools don't impose as much structure. The developer may also need to budget more time for debugging, to compensate for the lack of sophisticated debugging features in today's intranet programming software.

Put people in charge of your intranet publishing projects who at least have some experience with Internet technologies, make up for any gaps in experience with solid education and training, and hire expert help if you need it. And by all means, start simple. As I explain in Chapter 3 in more detail, don't tackle a complex, interactive, highly programmed intranet project until you cut your teeth on less ambitious systems.

Printing pitfalls

Computer applications have finally come fairly close to the goal of What You See Is What You Get (WYSIWYG, pronounced "wizzy-wig" — didn't Dr. Seuss write a book on the wizzy-wig?). That is, when you print a document, it looks more or less the same as it does on screen.

Alas, intranet publishing takes a step or two backward in the WYSIWYG department. The framers of HTML never intended it to function as a print processing language: HTML is designed strictly for screen viewing. As a result, printing an HTML document from a web browser often produces output that looks different (and, usually, worse) than screen output. Here are some examples:

- Many web pages include miniature programs called *applets,* written in the Java or ActiveX programming languages. Java applets can do many different things, and web designers often use them to provide cool-looking interactive buttons that appear to push down when you click them. However, if you try to print a document with a Java applet button on it, the button probably doesn't appear at all. In fact, depending on where the applet or applets are placed on the page, you may not get *any* text on the printout!

- Long HTML pages don't have any way to tell a printer when it's time to start a new physical page. (Think of the HTML screen orientation: The browser scroll bar enables a web page to be as long as the designer wants.) As a result, a web page printout may break the page at an awkward point and may even horizontally bisect a line of text.

Partial solutions do exist today. The Portable Document Format, which I discuss in Chapter 10, along with its enabling Adobe Acrobat products, does a much better job at achieving WYSIWYG printing than HTML does. The computer industry is taking steps to fix the HTML printing problem. For example, Adobe Systems is revamping its PostScript printer language to better accommodate HTML print jobs (for more on this, see Chapter 19). Intranet printing is still a problem area, though, and is likely to remain so for a couple of years.

Electronic lies

Mark Twain once said that there are three kinds of lies: plain old white lies, malicious damned lies, and statistics. Statistics can be the worst because although they are often inaccurate or incomplete, they assume the appearance of truth — just like information that a computer system spits out.

Inaccurate information is bad, but inaccurate information delivered by a computer is far worse. The orderly tables of figures and neatly laid-out documents on a user's screen tend to inspire a false confidence. Remember when you were a kid and you believed everything you read? Even grown-ups, who don't honestly think that three-eyed aliens are cloning Elvis just because a tabloid prints the story, tend to believe what they see on a computer screen.

Sure, data inaccuracy is a problem with any kind of computer system. But it's a bigger problem with intranet publishing, for several reasons:

- You're distributing information to a wider audience, so any inaccuracies become more widespread and potentially more harmful.
- You're moving information formerly on paper into a computer system, but without many built-in ways to check the accuracy of those paper documents. An OCR scanning program (see Chapter 10) can check for spelling mistakes in a text document, but it can't flag mistakes of fact.
- If your intranet is successful, it becomes the sole source for certain kinds of information.
- More people may be involved in publishing information on an intranet, so more opportunities exist for inaccuracies to creep in than if fewer people are creating the content.

Resistance to change

For any new information project to succeed, it has to overcome both the habits of the organization and the attitudes of users within that organization. Users' resistance to change — if severe — can badly undermine the success of your intranet project. Businesses vary widely in how heavily they drag their feet, but you can bet some users just won't want to use the new system, for any of several reasons:

- They love the old systems (hey, it's possible).
- They're burned out learning new computer systems.
- They're too busy to learn new computer systems.

- They hate the Internet, and, by association, your intranet.
- They don't see the immediate benefits.
- They *really* don't see the long-term benefits.
- They want to coast into retirement without learning anything new.

You may encounter some resistance to change on the part of information systems employees, too. These folks may have invested a lot of time and effort just getting the current systems to work, and now you come along ready to replace them with your newfangled intranet. Be sensitive to their concerns — everyone has to eat. Think of ways to enlist their help, rather than make them dig in their heels.

Ways exist to overcome organizational inertia, and Chapters 9 and 16 can help here. Starting with a pilot or prototype is one good approach; persuasively demonstrating intranet benefits with a mock-up intranet is another. In any case, unless your employees consist exclusively of fresh-faced kids right out of school, bringing change into an organization requires some effort.

I present more potential costs and risks here than you may have known about, but none of them means that you shouldn't embark on intranet publishing projects. The benefits are almost sure to make the overall cost/benefit ratio look mighty appealing.

Chapters 3 and 9 demonstrate that some advance planning can reduce the costs and risks in a big way.

Here's the final aquatic analogy: Now that you know a little more about how deep the pool is, it's time to dive in!

Part II
Intranet Publishing Applications

The 5th Wave   By Rich Tennant

"Well, the intranet isn't perfect. Some departments still seem to get more information than others."

In this part . . .

Part I gives the big picture view; and now in Part II, I zoom in and focus on the creative, effective ways you can meet business goals by publishing certain types of information on your intranet. This part also explores what that information may be — policy-and-procedure manuals, product specifications, and on-line training for critical business tasks such as refilling the coffee machine in the break room.

I open with a very important chapter on project selection, then examine applications in five categories: company information, routine business procedures, sales support, technical support, and Intranet-Based Training (IBT). These aren't the only possible applications, but they're ones that have strong potential to save you money and improve productivity.

Chapter 3
Choosing Your Project (Choose with Care!)

In This Chapter
▶ Understanding the differences between simple and complex intranet systems
▶ Evaluating the needs of users and managers
▶ Conditioning expectations for a more successful project reception
▶ Matching project demands with technology capabilities
▶ Evaluating key features of popular web servers and browsers
▶ Measuring success with your first intranet
▶ Clearing up intellectual property issues

Many more ways exist to put intranet publishing to work than I can cover here. Choosing your project isn't easy with so many applications that make good business sense. This chapter gives you a few issues to think about as you decide which application makes the most sense for your intranet's maiden voyage.

Chapters 4 through 8 look at specific intranet publishing applications from A to Z (well, maybe B to Y), but please read this chapter first if you see this message.

Start Simple

If I were creating stone tablets of intranet publishing commandments, the first one I'd chisel would read as follows: "Novice intranet publishers should start with the simplest system they can imagine that meets a demonstrable business need." If you take nothing else away from this book but this one precept, I'm gratified, because it's perhaps the most important advice I can give you.

"Okay, Glenn," you say, "define 'simple.'" My pleasure! Intranet publishing simplicity means simple *data,* simple *data flows* (how you get to the data), and simple *technology* (minimal bells and whistles).

Simple data

Another way to categorize intranet publishing systems is by the data types they publish. For example, here are different types of systems, in ascending order of complexity:

- **Plain text publishing system:** Deals with plain old words, and nothing else. No formatting — no **boldface**, *italics,* ^{superscripts} or $_{subscripts}$ — just plain old words!

- **Rich text publishing system:** Deals with words, but dresses them up with formatting attributes. These systems may need to inject technology beyond the standard web page language of HTML, to achieve faithful text formatting.

- **Basic text and graphics publishing system:** Serves up documents with rich text and also simple graphics, such as web-standard GIF and JPEG files. (If you aren't sure what these acronyms mean, I explain them in Chapter 12; for now, just know that they're the usual kinds of images every web browser can display.)

- **Advanced text and graphics publishing system:** Incorporates complex graphics, such as animations (which incorporate motion) and vector images (such as engineering drawings).

- **Multimedia publishing system:** Does everything an advanced text and graphics system can do, and adds the elements of sound or video.

Chapter 10 deals with formatting data, simple and complex, for intranet compatibility.

Simple data flows

One way to categorize intranet publishing systems is by how the information in them flows. Here are examples:

- **One-way, one-to-many system:** Publishes documents for users to retrieve and read, but doesn't let users send any data back to servers, as illustrated in Figure 3-1. Systems like this may publish static documents, which rarely change (such as lunchroom rules), or dynamic documents that change often (for example, horoscope readings).

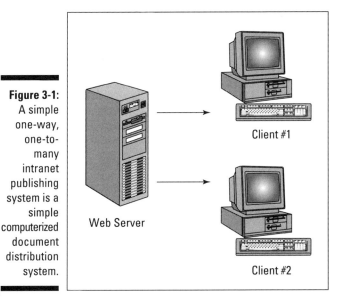

Figure 3-1: A simple one-way, one-to-many intranet publishing system is a simple computerized document distribution system.

✓ **Two-way, one-to-many system:** Publishes documents, but also lets users send data back to servers, as shown in Figure 3-2. The simplest example of this type of system is a user filling out an electronic form, such as an expense report. Information still flows in a channel between web servers and clients, but some sort of program must process the data returned by the user and (usually) respond in a way the user's browser can understand.

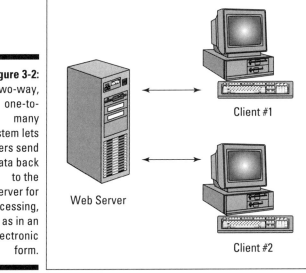

Figure 3-2: A two-way, one-to-many system lets users send data back to the server for processing, as in an electronic form.

Part II: Intranet Publishing Applications

- **Multi-way, many-to-many system:** Involves document publishing, editing, and collaboration, such as a newspaper performs when preparing stories. Information not only flows back and forth between a server and a client, but it also flows back and forth between the server and other clients working on the same document, as illustrated in Figure 3-3. Systems like this, which often go by the moniker *groupware,* usually require a back-end database running on a dedicated server to keep track of the documents and changes.

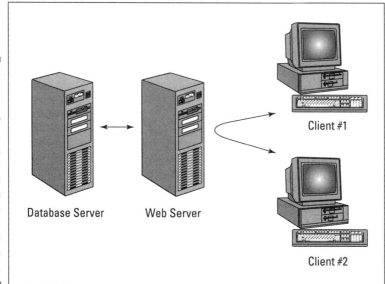

Figure 3-3: A multi-way, many-to-many system lets users exchange data with other users and often includes a back-end database system.

Simple technology

Finally, intranets can be divided according to the technology necessary to bring them into the world.

- **Basic technology intranets:** Require only a simple web server, a network, and a client-side browser. An example is an intranet used to publish Human Resources documents.
- **Medium technology intranets:** Add programming to the mix, but usually with application-specific toolkits that insulate the designer from low level details. An example is an intranet used for training new employees — the *courseware development tool* (the software used to create the training programs) makes designing interactive self tests relatively easy, and the designer doesn't need to be a hypernerd to get the job done.

✓ **Advanced technology intranets:** Require more heavy-duty programming, such as server-side or client-side scripts that perform customized processing functions. Most intranet database publishing systems fall into this category. Advanced technology intranets also usually involve more than one server.

My recipe for a successful first intranet publishing project is to start with the first choice from each of the preceding three lists: a one-way, one-to-many, plain text, basic-technology system. After you build this sort of system right (and that ain't terribly difficult if you read this book and heed my wisdom), you can confidently move on to the fancier stuff with a notch already in your belt. Start with the fancy stuff, however, and your first intranet project can end in disaster. Everything in computing is more complex than it first appears — even simple intranet publishing systems have their "gotchas" — and you really want to come in on time and under budget your first trip to the plate.

I talk about some medium to advanced intranet applications in Chapters 4 through 8, not in great detail, but mainly to familiarize you with the issues and technologies and to show you what's possible down the road. Just remember that one reason the Internet — every intranet's parent — has enjoyed such success is that it's essentially a *simple* computing environment. That, as they say, ain't no coincidence.

User Needs

"What do users really want?" can be almost as much of an enigma to those designing a new information system as "What do managers really want?". The intranetter had better spend serious time figuring out answers to both questions.

The user survey

Users know their jobs better than anyone, and they're likely to have great ideas for improving and streamlining those jobs. After you read over Chapters 4 through 8, and you have a good idea about what you want your first intranet publishing project to do, design a survey to get user feedback on the project. It can be paper-, e-mail-, or telephone-based, but keep it short enough so that busy users don't regard the survey as an unreasonable imposition on their time.

Many users don't have the faintest idea what the heck an intranet is. A good survey needs to include a brief description of what an intranet is, so that users know what you're talking about. Feel free to crib bits and pieces of this book's Introduction and Chapter 1 to get you started.

The manager survey

Sometimes users' desire for an information system doesn't tell the intranetter everything he or she needs to know. For example, users want to do their jobs better, but they don't care so much about how much the system that lets them do that is going to cost. ("The company can afford it. Sheesh, have you seen the new Range Rover the CEO's driving?") They also may not worry much about the turf battles that can ensue when a company starts shifting around responsibility for maintaining and distributing corporate information.

So, it makes sense for intranetters to spend time chatting with any company managers their intranet project is likely to affect. Your goal as an intranetter is to identify managerial concerns and address as many of them as you can. As a simple example, if a human resources manager wants to know how many people are using the new online benefits system, you can plan to install a *hit counter* program, or other similar software utility, to track usage.

Conditioning expectations

After matching the project to user and manager needs, the savvy intranetter pitches the project to the user community to garner their support and enlist their help as the project moves forward (see Chapter 9 for further discussion). Part of your pitch, however, should be to condition user expectations to a realistic level. Here are some questions that you may want to answer in your proposal:

- What can the project do for users?
- What can it *not* do?
- How soon can users expect to see short-term and long-term benefits?
- What are the project benefits that users may not see, but that are nevertheless real and valuable?

One of the pervasive computer myths is that automating a system instantly improves organizational productivity. Ba-low-ney. Automating a system initially *reduces* productivity as users devote time to learn the new system. Don't promise instant benefits.

Watch the temptation to oversell your project's virtues, too. You may believe it will be great, but the smart approach is to pitch it as being *good* and then let users discover that it's *great* on their own. If, for reasons beyond your control, the project turns out to merely be good, then it's not a letdown!

Chapter 3: Choosing Your Project (Choose with Care!)

Users with experience on the public Internet tend to have high expectations for any intranet publishing system's currency. Such users know that many companies update their Internet sites on a daily or weekly basis, and they may expect the same of your intranet system. Personally, I'm in favor of meeting this expectation rather than conditioning against it. However, if you can't perform frequent document updates, explain why in your promotional activities, before and during the project rollout.

Technology Fit

You don't want too much technology or too little. Use a chainsaw to cut butter, and the effect tends to take away your appetite. Tow your Winnebago with a Yugo, on the other hand, and your car is toast. (See how I tied in *butter* with *toast?* That's why I'm a professional author.)

But seriously, folks, as you go through the process of figuring out your first publishing project, ask yourself a few questions:

- If your organization already has web servers, how much work can they handle? What sort of work can they do?
- If your organization doesn't have a web server, how powerful a server should you get? Can you afford it?
- How fast is the typical user workstation in your organization?
- What jobs are you planning to ask of that workstation?
- Is your network plumbing in shape, or are the pipes already rattling under its present workload?

The following sections take a closer look at each of these key areas. Once you arm yourself with the basics, don't hesitate to hire an intranet consultant to help you evaluate whether your computing environment is a good technology fit with your planned intranet publishing project.

What can your servers handle?

Matching project demands to your technology boils down mainly to the intranet server platform. Client capabilities are important, but secondary — most user workstations can run the required web browser with no problem. The basic choice you need to make is between more industrial-strength servers that can handle hundreds of users, and casual servers more appropriate for small-scale projects, pilots, or prototypes.

Industrial servers

Apache, Microsoft, and Netscape own the lion's share of the intranet server market. Other good servers exist, and I don't mean to ignore companies like Silicon Graphics, but my editor made me keep this book under 400 pages.

Apache

Probably the most popular industrial-strength web server is Apache, from the Apache Group. Apache is a UNIX-based system and it enjoys the same benefits and headaches that attend all UNIX products. UNIX programmers can tweak and twiddle the product to their heart's content, but intranetters light on UNIX skills may find the product more work to get going compared to servers from Microsoft and Netscape. Apache also runs on a wide range of UNIX systems, in contrast to Microsoft Internet Information Server, which only runs on Microsoft NT Server. Best of all, Apache is free, free, *free!* — and is developed and maintained by a group of Internet professionals who contribute their time and energy for the greater good.

Check out www.apache.org for a ton of information on the Apache server and a download site.

Microsoft Internet Information Server (IIS)

The big boy server from Microsoft is called Internet Information Server (IIS), which debuted in early 1996 and which Microsoft has been upgrading like mad ever since. Version 2.0 is included with NT Server 4.0, which is the operating system IIS requires. You can get the newer, improved version 3.0 (code name: Denali) in the NT Service Pack 2 or Service Pack 3. You can always download the very latest version of IIS from www.microsoft.com/iis. IIS doesn't run on Windows 95, but if you need a Windows 95 server, see the following section on casual web servers.

In addition to its built-in support for web, FTP (File Transfer Protocol), and gopher intranet services, IIS comes with a bunch of bundled goodies:

- **Seagate Crystal Reports:** For custom server log file reporting and database reporting
- **FrontPage:** For web page design and site management
- **Index Server:** For search capability
- **NetShow:** For multimedia publishing

You can run the IIS management tool, Internet Service Manager, from the NT Server console, from any Windows workstation on the network, or from any network HTML browser — that is, from anywhere you want.

For programming, IIS 3.0 offers Active Server Pages (ASP), enabling intranet publishers to write server-side program scripts and access standard databases via HTML pages, without using the Common Gateway Interface (CGI) (for more on CGI, see Chapter 5). Nine out of ten programmers agree that database access with ASP is easier and faster than with an earlier Microsoft effort, the Internet Database Connector (IDC). IIS also supports Java, PERL, JavaScript, and VBScript.

In terms of speed, IIS 3.0 is a fast product that can compete head-to-head with most other popular web servers. For security, IIS leverages NT Server security. NT Server also handles the details of IP addressing (see Chapter 13 for more on that important subject). If you're standardizing on Windows NT Server, IIS is the compelling and even overwhelming choice, and keepers of the corporate coffers are sure to love the price tag of $0.00.

Netscape Enterprise Server

Netscape offers the Netscape Enterprise Server as its industrial strength variety. Enterprise Server, which gets high marks for its reporting and administration capabilities, as well as its generally zippy performance, costs $1,295 with the LiveWire software bundle, and runs on several UNIX flavors, as well as on Windows NT. Netscape sells its web server separately, or bundled with SuiteSpot, a software array of nine (count 'em, nine) server products which include e-mail, groupware, and search utilities. SuiteSpot costs $4,995 for an unlimited-server license at the time I'm writing this.

In terms of programmability, LiveWire Application Manager is loosely analogous to Microsoft Active Server Pages, offering a variety of program development tools. Enterprise Server supports JavaScript, NSAPI (Netscape Server Application Program Interface), and CGI programs. For management, LiveWire Site Manager can track broken links, and you can manage Enterprise Server remotely from any browser that supports frames (see Chapter 11 for more on frames).

For database integration, Enterprise Server has an edge over IIS, if you're running Oracle or Informix database managers. Another neat feature Enterprise Server has that Microsoft IIS lacks is the ability to map to file directories on other servers. For an intranet that you expect will grow, this capability makes adding servers, and splitting file directories across the servers, easy. (IIS Version 4.0 will probably add this feature, but this is just a guess.)

In terms of security, Enterprise Server has the handy capability of restricting access by web host or domain name. And if you run Enterprise Server on an NT machine, you don't have to create a separate security database for intranet access. Finally, Enterprise Server is known for being a product you can tweak and tune to your heart's content. The techies love it.

Other servers

Other excellent full-featured web servers exist besides those from Apache, Netscape, and Microsoft. Here are two of the more popular ones:

- **Novell NetWare Web Server:** Comes with NetWare 4.1+ (it doesn't run on NetWare 3.x) and has many powerful features that organizations already using NetWare are sure to appreciate, such as the ability to integrate with NetWare Directory Services (so that users can navigate the whole network from within the browser), and the ability to run on computers with multiple processors.

- **O'Reilly and Associates WebSite Professional:** ($499) For Windows 95 and NT, this is another good choice, offering excellent documentation, a CD-ROM with lots of programming goodies, the Allaire Cold Fusion database toolkit, and fine activity logging features. It doesn't offer remote browser administration, however, and doesn't automatically recognize NT Server users and groups.

Casual servers

The casual web servers this section discusses can all run on workstation-class machines, and they don't need to take over the computer like the industrial web servers do. However, you need to run a fairly beefy client machine if you want it to do double-duty as a light web server — consider at least 32MB RAM and extra hard drive space for the server software, activity logs, documents, custom programs, databases, and so on.

Netscape FastTrack Server

Netscape offers the FastTrack Server for Windows 95 as the downsized alternative to Enterprise Server. FastTrack costs $295 at the time I'm writing this. FastTrack server comes with *Wizards* — automated question-and-answer dialogs — to speed setup tasks. It also comes with the Communicator bundle, which includes the Composer page creation tool. Here are other features of FastTrack Server:

- HTTP but no File Transfer Protocol services (the lack of FTP isn't as big a deal because Netscape supports file transfer in both directions using HTTP)
- Excellent administration tools
- Extensive HTTP event logging (so you can see what's happening in terms of usage)
- Flexible configuration for multiple servers and addresses
- Support of Java and JavaScript programs

Microsoft Personal Web Server (PWS)

The Microsoft Personal Web Server (PWS) for Windows 95 is a scaled-down version of the Internet Information Server (IIS). PWS is free for the downloading from www.microsoft.com/ie/download/ieadd.htm. You already have it if you're running Windows 95 OEM Service Release 2, which comes preinstalled on today's PCs. Here are some features of this little server:

- Both HTTP and FTP services (no gopher, but that's usually okay)
- Low disk space requirements (about 1MB, which is refreshing)
- Remote administration from a web browser
- HTTP event logging
- Programming support for ISAPI (Internet Server Application Program Interface) and CGI, but not Java (see Chapter 5 or the glossary if this is Greek to you)

Microsoft also offers a variant of the Personal Web Server for Windows NT Workstation.

O'Reilly and Associates WebSite 1.1

The O'Reilly and Associates WebSite 1.1 light-duty server is the baby version of the full-featured WebSite Professional product. It lacks the high-end database and security features of the full version, but remains a serviceable light-duty web host for Windows 95 and NT.

What can your clients handle?

Although server capabilities take first priority, intranet publishing project selection depends on what sort of user workstations exist in the organization, too. Here's why:

- **Workstations run the web browser that links users to the intranet publishing system.** Browsers do differ in what they can handle, especially when it comes to non-standard or semi-standard HTML *extensions* (non-standard formatting in the HTML documents that only certain browsers understand).
- **Workstations need to run any *helper programs* that the browser may call on to view or use a particular type of data, such as a multimedia presentation or a word processing file.**
- **Workstations have to physically handle the incoming network traffic.** Fast servers and fast network plumbing don't matter if the workstation is a bottleneck.

- **Workstations have to cooperate with servers regarding security.** Chapter 15 explores intranet security in more detail, but I can say here that workstations with built-in security capabilities have an edge if you're thinking about choosing a publishing project that may require security for confidentiality.

Netscape and Microsoft clients

Netscape and Microsoft cover something like 90 percent of the web browser market between the two of them. Netscape has the lead at this writing, and is trying to maintain it by including more features in its browser package. Microsoft is gaining market share, largely because it gives away its browser for free. Both companies have aggressively upgraded these products, giving birth to major new releases every nine months or so (coincidence?).

If you have the luxury of being able to standardize on either Netscape or Microsoft browsers, the choice can be difficult, but you really can't go wrong in either case. Organizations with a wider variety of workstations may favor Netscape because of its better cross-platform compatibility; organizations running Windows almost exclusively may favor Microsoft because of its support for Windows software via *ActiveX controls* (Microsoft's proprietary applets). If your budget is tight, the Netscape solution does cost something ($59 a head, at this writing), although the Communicator bundle undeniably offers a lot of bang for the buck with its integrated e-mail, conferencing, scheduling, and other features.

Lots of companies currently support both intranet browsers; however, the cost to these businesses of doing so is rising, and will continue to rise. You may want to pick one of these horses to ride exclusively, if you want to keep intranet support costs as low as possible. Just ask your technical support manager how much more work is involved supporting two different word processing programs instead of one, for example. Two products, even with similar capabilities and uses, can require almost twice the support resources as a single, company-standard product.

Netscape Navigator

Netscape Navigator may be the world's most popular workstation program. The first version shipped in late 1994, followed by Version 2.0 about a year later, Version 3.0 in May 1996, and 4.0 in February 1997. Navigator runs on Windows, Macintosh, UNIX, OS/2, and OpenVMS computer systems — darn near all of 'em.

Navigator 4.0 comes with the Communicator package, which also includes the following tightly integrated elements:

- **Composer:** A relatively simple and limited HTML creation and editing tool similar to that provided with Navigator Gold (the high-end version of Navigator 3)

- **Messenger:** An e-mail module that adds security features and better window management, and can handle just about any intranet or Internet e-mail situation you want to throw at it
- **Collabra:** A newsgroup reader that can function as a discussion group client when used with Collabra Server
- **Conference:** A real-time video conferencing application including web-based voice transmission, whiteboard, and file transfer
- **Calendar:** (Professional Edition only), a small personal information manager that works with Calendar Server to create and publish personal schedules
- **AutoAdmin:** (Professional Edition only), with centralized management capabilities

Microsoft Internet Explorer

Microsoft Internet Explorer is the upstart in the browser wars, and is a solid product that offers goodies for organizations that have mostly Windows workstations. Internet Explorer offers less compatibility with different computers than Navigator provides — if you need to bring UNIX systems into the fold, you're out of luck at this writing, although Microsoft promises UNIX support eventually. Here are some salient features of Internet Explorer 3.x:

- **Provides ActiveX technology:** Enables Windows shops to leverage their investment in Visual BASIC and other Microsoft programming environments
- **Runs on Windows 95, NT, Windows 3.x, and Macintosh platforms:** Solaris support promised soon
- **Free, free, free!**
- **Runs Java programs and supports nearly all Netscape HTML extensions**
- **Is expected to be the new user interface for Windows 98**

With almost every major upgrade, both Netscape and Microsoft have followed the initial release with a maintenance release to fix bugs and security holes. The browser wars are forcing products out the door a little sooner than is prudent. You don't want to run Navigator 2.0, 3.0, or 4.0 any more than you want to run Internet Explorer 2.0 or 3.0. Use the .01 or .02 versions so that users have fewer technical problems.

Client performance bottlenecks

Regardless of whether your company uses Internet Explorer, Navigator, or a mix of both, workstation hardware pretty much determines the browser software's speed. Take a look at the data pipe that runs into the typical client workstation: the Network Interface Card (NIC). If your intranet project depends on downloading Java programs, large documents, or documents containing graphics or multimedia, the NIC must be able to suck that information quickly into the workstation. Without getting horribly technical, here are a few points to keep in mind:

- ✔ **So-called 16-bit NICs are much faster than older, 8-bit cards.** 32-bit cards are faster yet, but probably aren't necessary for most intranet tasks.
- ✔ **A NIC that sits in a high-performance slot on the workstation's main circuit board can move data faster.** For example, most PCs today come with two kinds of slots: Industry Standard Architecture, or ISA, and Peripheral Component Interconnect, or PCI. You want a NIC that can plug into a PCI slot for the fastest data throughput.
- ✔ **A 32-bit workstation operating system, such as Windows 95 or Windows NT Workstation, vastly improves the client's ability to receive information quickly.** A Windows 3.*x* machine handles network tasks roughly half as fast.

What can your infrastructure handle?

You can have wonderfully powerful servers and highly competent workstations, but if the hardware and software that *links them together* isn't up to snuff, all that hardware doesn't do you a lick of good. For example, an NT Server running IIS 3.0 and Windows 95 clients with high-speed network cards are still likely to struggle with graphics and Java programs if your intranet sits on a network running regular old 10-megabit-per-second Ethernet.

In Chapter 14, I talk about network infrastructure performance and ways to beef it up, so no point rehashing that here. For now, be aware that network *plumbing* (cables and other hardware) is an important factor affecting the kind of content you can publish with your intranet. Plan to spend some time with your network administrators discussing whether your publishing project is likely to put a severe traffic burden on your data highways. You may have to make do with a text-only pilot project using the existing network to prove the boon that an intranet provides, and then seek a budget for a network upgrade to handle graphics and other large document elements.

Can You Measure Success?

I always like picking a pilot project that can show a clear, unambiguous benefit if it succeeds. Often, your first intranet publishing project determines whether, and how vigorously, your organization will pursue new intranet projects. If you can demonstrate a quantifiable cost reduction with the first project, those follow-ups become much easier to sell.

Usually, measuring cost savings is easier when you're replacing an existing printed publication than when you're delivering new information that doesn't directly correspond to a print document. Although you may be tempted to create a new publishing system with unique content, consider saving that project for your second system. Have the first one assume a more mundane, but more measurable job — such as cutting in half the number of employee directories the company prints each quarter.

Do You Own the Data?

Whether you're setting up your intranet that is simple or complex, with powerful servers or casual ones, or that incorporates reengineering steps or not, one fact is constant: You're going into the publishing business. Like any publisher, you should know a bit about *intellectual property* law: copyrights, trademarks, and trade secrets. This field is becoming more and more important because information is replacing money as the global currency of value.

Copyrights

Copyrights protect the expression of an idea or ideas. (If you want to protect an idea itself, then you want a *patent*.) People, other than the content creator, can't reproduce copyrighted material without permission, unless it's a fairly small chunk of material, as defined by the *Fair Use Doctrine* — usually a few lines or so. If you want to quote a few lines from this book on one of your intranet pages, you probably don't need a letter from my publisher. If you want to quote an entire chapter — which I can understand, as each one is a rich store of knowledge, delivering both fact and insight with a lighthearted, dry wit — you need a letter.

In the U.S., copyrights usually last for the life of the creator plus fifty years, and a creator doesn't even have to formally register a copyright to enjoy some degree of protection. Copyrights aren't just for books and magazines: Creators can copyright blueprints, catalogs, directories, newsletters, software, price lists, tech notes, and so on.

Trademarks

Trademarks are a little different from copyrights in that trademarks protect titles, names, associated graphics, and brief phrases, rather than entire documents. You can generally use trademarks (for products) and *service marks* (for services) on your intranet, as long as you include the appropriate symbol, and acknowledge the trademark owner. *TM* is a pending trademark, *SM* denotes a pending service mark, and ® signifies a registered mark of either flavor. If you download a trademark graphic from its owner's Web site, you may need to receive a permission letter to use the graphic.

Copyright and trademark law has been slow to adapt to the new realities of electronic information publishing. As a result, businesses are wise to err on the side of caution when evaluating whether they own, or even have permission to use, the content they publish on an intranet. If you have any doubt, check with a lawyer experienced in these matters.

For example, a resort company may license pictures of attractive vacationers sipping silly-colored drinks under tropical sunsets from a professional photographer to use in print ads. Including these photos on the resort company's intranet sales-support page could be risky — doing so assumes that the license extends to electronic distribution as well, and not all licenses do. The company wouldn't want to shut down its publishing system for a few days to remove those images everywhere they appear, nor would it want to pay a hefty fine ($10,000 per violation isn't uncommon) for violating the license agreement. U.S. courts are tough on copyright violators.

What about material that displays neither a copyright nor a trademark? You can't necessarily always use such material safely, without written permission. Before publishing any content that your organization did not create internally, check with the creator and, to be on the safe side, obtain a brief letter granting you the permission you want. This suggestion even applies to graphics images someone in your organization may have borrowed off of a public Internet page. New digital *watermarking* technologies permit the owners of such images to positively identify a copy, even if the so-called borrower modified the image (for example, by changing the color palette).

Letters of permission often expire after a specified time period. Someone in your organization needs to track these dates, and ensure that you apply for permission extensions several weeks in advance.

Trade secrets

Also, take care before putting anything on your intranet that might constitute a *trade secret* — knowledge, techniques, and procedures your organization develops internally to give it a competitive edge. Get some legal advice as to whether the act of intranet publishing could jeopardize the legal requirement that your organization treat its trade secrets as secrets, and keep them confidential. Also know that you may have a legal obligation to protect the trade secrets of your customers, suppliers, and contractors.

The whole issue of copyright, trademark, and trade secret protection becomes much more complex when you link your intranet to the outside world to create a *multinet* (see Chapter 1). Not only do you have to be more careful with the content that you publish, you also have to consider the effect of putting corporate content in a public forum — content that you may want to copyright yourself. The global nature of the Internet means that you may need to copyright material internationally to fully protect it. You also have to ensure that even your multinet's domain name (www.domainname.com) doesn't infringe on someone else's trademark.

Chapter 4
Company Information

In This Chapter

▶ Using HTML tables to present structured information
▶ Publishing an employee directory and organizational charts on your intranet
▶ Distributing policy/procedure manuals and employee benefits information
▶ Publishing career management data
▶ Creating intranet-based newsletters
▶ Putting company schedule information on the network
▶ Publishing emergency and disaster plans
▶ Building a page of useful Internet links

*P*ossibly the simplest intranet publishing applications are those that post company information on the network to create a cyberspace bulletin board. You don't need fancy extra software for many of these applications — in most cases, a good web page editor does fine. The applications in this chapter are great for new intranet publishing projects.

HTML Tables

Although some of the applications in this chapter work fine using simple lists or text paragraphs, many of them call for a row and column format, and look much cleaner when you use HyperText Markup Language (HTML) *tables*. HTML tables deserve a few words of introduction here.

Tabular data and HTML

You see tabular data in books, magazines, and computer spreadsheets just about every day. HTML tables, pioneered by Netscape, and now also supported by the Microsoft Internet Explorer, provide the same row-and-column organization that these everyday tables provide. In fact, when you create an HTML version of a Microsoft Excel spreadsheet with the Excel Internet Assistant (built into Excel 97 or an add-on to Excel 95), the resulting page uses HTML tables. Creating tables with Word 97 or FrontPage 97 is just as easy.

HTML tables are very flexible. Here are some of the variables you can control when you create an HTML table:

- **Border width:** How many pixels, or dots, make up the horizontal and vertical gridlines
- **Overall table width:** Either in pixels, or as a percentage of the displayed web page width
- **Column width:** In pixels, or as a percentage of the total table width
- **Cell spacing:** The space between adjacent cells, where a *cell* is the container for a particular row and column
- **Cell padding:** No, not the insane asylum kind, rather the distance between a cell's contents and the cell border
- **How the table aligns horizontally within the browser window:** Against the left or right margins or centered, as well as how cell contents align horizontally and vertically within the cell
- **Row and column headings:** One thing to remember is that although HTML provides tags for table headings, regular text may be more flexible, depending on your page design tool
- **Table caption:** Can appear at the table's top or bottom
- **Table background and individual cell backgrounds:** Color or image

Figure 4-1 shows some of these formatting options.

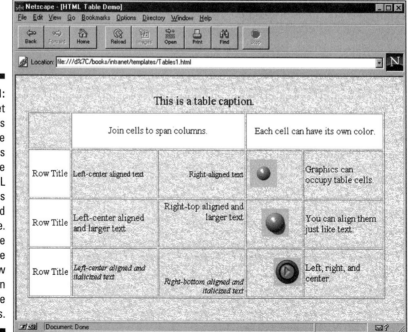

Figure 4-1: This intranet page shows a table that uses many of the HTML extensions developed by Netscape. Notice the cells at the top row that span multiple columns.

Chapter 4: Company Information

Use percentages for your table widths, rather than absolute pixel values. This way, your table contents resize themselves so they still look reasonably good when users shrink the browser window.

The versatility of HTML tables makes them a royal pain to code by hand if they're even moderately complex. Fortunately, modern web page design tools, such as Adobe PageMill, have excellent table creation features that hide the underlying HTML commands from the designer, and that show you how the table would look in a web browser as you edit and refine it.

Grid and bear it

Savvy intranet publishers apply tables for other reasons than just to display rows and columns of data. A one-cell table, for example, is a simple way to highlight a text element. The one-cell table frames the text element with a nice-looking raised border. The most powerful use of HTML tables, however, is as a positioning tool.

Before tables came along, HTML didn't provide convenient mechanisms for placing information exactly where you want it on a page. Tables, however, effectively allow the page designer to place a *grid* over the page for positioning text and graphics — much like the light blue gridlines on graph paper, or the grid in a graphics program such as Micrografx Designer, AutoDesk AutoCAD, or Microsoft PowerPoint. By specifying a border width of zero, the HTML table becomes an invisible grid that doesn't clutter up the page. Very slick! Bravo, Netscape!

Using tables as a positioning tool works really well because you can put anything in a table cell: text, graphics, form elements such as check boxes (see Chapter 5), even another table. The technique works so well, in fact, that some of the specialized intranet publishing applications that I cover in later chapters use tables as a layout mechanism on every single page (Asymetrix Toolbook II Instructor is an example — see Chapter 8).

Now it's time to table this discussion (sorry) and look at some company data publishing applications.

Sample Applications

Almost every company in the world has to use reams and reams of paper to publish company data, directories, manuals, and so on. Here I am again to say, "Intranets to the rescue!" This section outlines a number of good possibilities for publishing company data and documents on your intranet.

Employee directory

If your organization is small enough for each employee to have his or her own speed dial button for every employee on your phone system, you can skip this section. You may want to glance at the sidebar on bookmarks.

Anyone working in a large organization who has ever used one of those voice-mail employee directory systems ("Spell the letters of the employee's last name, using the pound key for *Q*, and then press the star key and spell the letters of the employee's first name, and hope against hope that there aren't two employees named *Mary Smith*") knows that there must be a better way.

As Figure 4-2 shows, you can build a simple employee directory out of regular HTML pages that employ simple lists and the navigational aid called the *bookmark* (see the sidebar for more information).

An intranet employee directory is perfect for publishing the following information:

- Name
- Photograph
- Division
- Department
- Building
- Employee number (if preassigned)
- Phone number and extension
- Sign of the Zodiac
- Emergency contact information
- E-mail address

Some products, such as Microsoft Word 97 and FrontPage 97, include wizards that let you easily create employee directories. More sophisticated employee directory software, such as programs from Oracle Corp. and SAP America, Inc., permit project leaders to search the employee résumé database for relevant skills and experience when looking for team members. Most project leaders would never rely on a database alone to assemble a team, but the intranet system surely speeds the process of creating a short list of interview candidates.

If you publish employee résumés, make sure that you implement security measures to protect the confidentiality of the data. See Chapter 15 for more on intranet security.

Figure 4-2: A user can click on the *W* at the top of the page to jump immediately to the *W* section in the directory. The *back to top* link at the end of each letter section lets users easily look up multiple names.

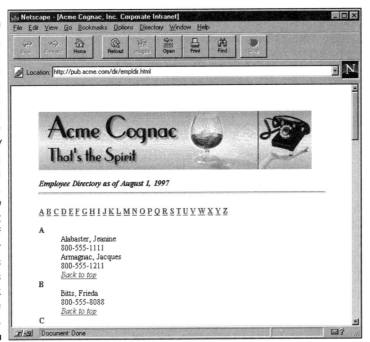

Organizational charts

Some organizations now use a *matrix organizational structure,* which does away with traditional organizational charts, and makes sure that no one knows exactly who does what, or who reports to whom (which, incidentally, can work fine in an organization of responsible, flexible, and highly motivated employees). Other businesses still find the top-down, tree-structured charts useful for describing reporting hierarchies, however. Publishing organizational charts (*org charts,* for short) helps employees find the people they need within the organization, and also helps orient new hires.

Your intranet is a great avenue for distributing org charts, but standard HTML needs a little help because it doesn't have built-in charting capability. You can get around HTML charting two ways:

- **Use an industrial strength flowcharting tool, such as Visio** (www.visio.com) **to build your org chart, and convert it to HTML with Visio Internet Assistant.** You can get fancy and include summary and detail views.

- **Use the Microsoft Organizational Chart applet included with Microsoft Office.** You have to run this applet from another program, such as PowerPoint 97:

    1. Click <u>I</u>nsert⇨<u>O</u>bject⇨MS Organization Chart.

    2. Create the chart (see Figure 4-3).

> ## Bookmarks
>
> A *bookmark* is simply an HTML tag at a certain place on a long page. Navigational buttons, such as the row of letters at the top of Figure 4-2, are actually *hyperlinks* to the bookmarks located at the beginning of each new letter section. Effectively, a web page bookmark consists of two parts: the bookmark itself, and a link to the bookmark location (usually near the top of the page).
>
> Netscape uses the term *bookmark* to mean stored shortcuts to intranet or Internet pages of interest (Microsoft calls these *favorites*). This usage is confusing, but I use bookmark here to mean a link to a different place on the same page, rather than the Netscape meaning. (You may also see the term *anchor*, which used to be more common but has now given way to *bookmark* in most page design programs.)
>
> For better speed, leave out the page's full Uniform Resource Locator (URL) when creating a link to a bookmark. If you just specify the bookmark name, which incidentally must be unique within a given HTML document, the browser assumes you want to stay on the same page. Specify the full URL, and the browser reloads the whole page. Make sure that you use the full URL if you're linking to a bookmark on a different page.

  3. Select File➪Exit and Return.
  4. From the PowerPoint menu, choose File➪Save As and save the slide as a GIF graphic.

You can now place the GIF file onto an intranet page using your favorite web page editor.

If you want, you can create a Microsoft PowerPoint slide show consisting of several organizational charts, and make an introductory slide with navigation buttons to take the user to the specific chart of interest. You can save the slide show as an HTML presentation using File➪Save as HTML and then link to the slide show's primary page from your intranet page.

You can also include links to photographs of individuals represented on the org charts, so that employees can recognize the people they should kiss up to.

Policies and procedures

Ah, the good old policies and procedures manual, perhaps the single largest PWPM (Poorly Written Paper Manual) your business uses. Putting this Human Resources manual on the intranet can be a dramatic cost saver. Even better, by relying on an intranet-based system, you can almost eliminate the problem of outdated manuals floating around (and employees making decisions based on that outdated information).

Policies and procedures manuals can include information on employment, employee records, payroll, working conditions and hours, drug and alcohol

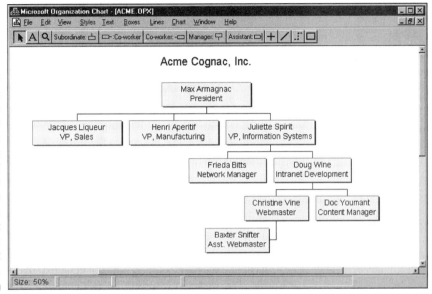

Figure 4-3: An inexpensive way for Microsoft customers to create org charts is to use the Organization Chart applet included with Microsoft Office.

use, business travel, leaves of absence, employee conduct, and disciplinary actions. Specialized software, such as Policies Now! from KnowledgePoint, can help you build an online manual. Figure 4-4 shows the Policies Now! selection screen from which you can choose specific modules to include in your manual. When finished, you select File⇨Export⇨Export as HTML and voila! A web page spews forth. Remember to have your legal counsel review the results to ensure compliance with laws in your state.

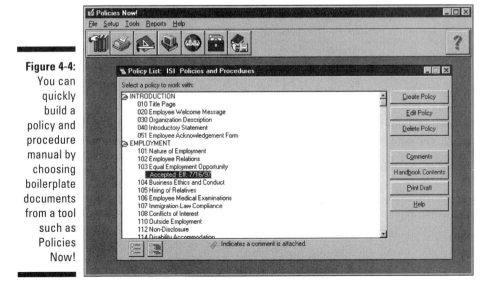

Figure 4-4: You can quickly build a policy and procedure manual by choosing boilerplate documents from a tool such as Policies Now!

Any time you make a major policy or procedure change, addition, or deletion, don't just post the updated content on your intranet. Send out an e-mail, or include a notice on your internal newsletter advising employees to check out the changes.

Include an e-mail link on your policy/procedure intranet home page so that employees can easily submit questions to Human Resources. An example might be, "Can I ask out an employee I manage without making the company vulnerable to a sexual harassment lawsuit?" to which the reply would be, "Certainly, Acme Cognac policies would never stand in the way of any employee discovering personal happiness. All you have to do is resign first."

Benefits

Benefits information can be part of the overall policies and procedures intranet the previous section discussed, or it can be a standalone intranet application. You can use your intranet to post information about employee benefits, such as the following:

- Vacation time, as a function of years worked
- Policy on sick days and other leaves of absence
- Child day care
- Credit union membership
- Health or workout facilities
- Employee discounts on products or services
- Insurance policies
- Retirement plans
- Stock purchase plans

The next few sections focus on the last three items as examples.

Insurance plan data

The billion-dollar Marshall Industries Inc., an electronics component distributor, publishes employee insurance policy details on its intranet — a smart idea, partly because just about everyone needs this information, and partly because it tends to change often.

If an employee isn't sure about coverage details, researching them becomes a simple matter on an intranet, especially one equipped with a keyword search engine. For example, the hapless toothache suffler can search on the phrase *root canal* to see whether the company picks up the tab, or the eyeglass wearer can search on *vision* to see whether the plan covers prescription Vuarnet sunglasses for looking cool on the beach.

If your medical insurance plan uses preferred providers or Health Maintenance Organizations (HMOs), your intranet can provide details so that employees can easily obtain medical care through approved channels.

Employees can use intranet-based insurance plan systems for one-way and two-way communication, for example, to perform the following tasks:

- ✔ Identifying dependents
- ✔ Identifying beneficiaries
- ✔ Choosing from multiple available insurance plans
- ✔ Submitting claims

To learn more about creating two-way intranet forms, check out Chapter 5.

Retirement plan data

The intranet can distribute information about your company's retirement plan, such as how long it takes to become partially or fully vested in the plan, details of pension payments, how to designate beneficiaries, and so on.

The value of a retirement data publishing intranet can grow if it links to outside financial services companies managing retirement funds. For example, the PeopleSoft 7 intranet suite from PeopleSoft (in development at the time I'm writing this) permits employees to link to Charles Schwab & Co. to get 401(k) information. This is a good example of how big client/server software vendors are webifying their applications for corporate intranets.

Stock purchase plan data

If your company offers employees special terms or options for purchasing stock, your intranet is a good place to publish details on what those options are, and how employees can take advantage of them. The page can even include links to brokerage houses on the Internet. Current stock prices can be updated daily and posted on your company data intranet's home page, along with a rolling one-year stock price average, which may be used as the basis for calculating employee discounts.

Career management

Career management applications can be as simple as a job description page, or as complex as a full-featured (and expensive) suite of tools, such as the Oracle Corp. Career Management product. This section takes a closer look at two career management applications: a *jobs available* bulletin board and an employee education intranet. Other possible career development subjects include:

- ✔ **Career track descriptions:** so-called *job ladders*
- ✔ **Job performance assessment forms:** for managers
- ✔ **Compensation plans:** including bonuses

Job board

An intranet job board can contain listings and descriptions of available positions throughout the company. You may even want to post detailed job descriptions (codes, classifications, duties, and so on) for every position on a separate intranet subsystem, and cross-reference these in the *employee wanted* section, using hyperlinks. Doing so enables an employee to survey brief descriptions of job openings, and click a hyperlink for more details on positions of interest.

Not everyone in your organization may have intranet access. The intranet job board, therefore, may have to be a supplement to other systems that reach everyone in the organization.

To minimize content management headaches, offer instruction (and network privileges) to department administrators so that they can make their own postings on your intranet job board.

Two-way communications using HTML forms also enables employees to apply for available positions via the intranet.

Educational opportunities

You can use your intranet to facilitate employee education by publishing information about training opportunities. You can also deliver courses over your intranet, which is the subject of Chapter 8. This sort of system isn't complex, but if you're a large organization, you may want to look at software specifically designed for publishing course information, such as the PeopleSoft 7 application suite from PeopleSoft.

The sort of material this system may publish includes:

- Schedules for in-house courses
- Schedules for public seminars from approved vendors
- Registration details (a two-way intranet can use HTML forms for this)
- Course approval procedures
- Commercial book titles to supplement classroom training
- Details on any cost-sharing or tuition reimbursement plans you offer for formal continuing education

Newsletters and periodicals

Newsletters are common communications vehicles in medium to large organizations where several layers of management, and the sheer number of employees, make it impossible for everyone to know everything through the grapevine. Technology-oriented businesses have been distributing newsletters by e-mail for some time, but this technique has the disadvantages that employees rarely keep back issues, and attractive page formatting (including color) isn't necessarily easy. Enter the intranet!

Chapter 4: Company Information

Some of the material companies provide via newsletters includes:

- **Long-term strategic directions:** "We are changing our focus from providing the best cognac money can buy to providing the cheapest cognac money can buy."
- **Public press releases:** About company products, services, reorganizations, takeovers, and so on
- **"Personal" messages from senior managers:** "You've all heard rumors that we've been targeted for a takeover by ABC Liqueurs, and, as CEO, I want to assure you that this *absolutely will not* happen, unless ABC offers me a suitable golden parachute."
- **Clippings from industry journals:** About the company (with appropriate legal permissions, these can be read into the intranet using Optical Character Recognition software and scanners — see Chapter 10)
- **Promotions and reassignment announcements**
- **Personal employee information:** Marriages, births, and other happy events making better copy than divorces and untimely demises
- **Company success stories:** Such as your new intranet publishing system!

Figure 4-5 provides a sample newsletter layout excerpt.

Figure 4-5: You can't see the table borders because their width is set to zero, but HTML uses the invisible grid to position the data on the screen and create the two-column format.

Smart newsletter editors let employees do some of the work by contributing articles. Placing a *mailto* link on the newsletter web page provides a convenient vehicle for employees to submit material to the editor via e-mail.

Larger organizations may publish several print periodicals to which employees can subscribe. Your intranet can become the vehicle you use to enable employees to choose which of those periodicals they'd like to receive during the transition period when you still make those periodicals available on paper. Microsoft Publisher 97 allows users to automatically convert their paper newsletters to online versions within the program. Microsoft Word 97 also provides a newsletter wizard and can convert the resulting document to HTML.

Government regulations

If your business has the mixed blessing of being a state or federal government contractor, you have to keep up with the various regulations governing products and procurement. Regardless of whether you're a government contractor, you probably have to keep up with certain other regulations: the Occupational Safety and Health Act, the Equal Opportunity Employment Act, and so on. Government agencies are voracious tree-killers, and all that paper documentation presents a prime opportunity for intranet publishers.

If you connect your intranet to the public Internet, employees can connect directly to the latest version of these regulations and view them online instead of on paper. The U.S. Federal government is helping you in this endeavor by providing many on-line documents in the Adobe *Portable Document Format* (PDF, discussed more in Chapter 10). Equip your browsers with the PDF plug-in (included on this book's CD-ROM) and create a page of links to the relevant government agency Web and *File Transfer Protocol* (FTP) sites.

Schedules

Effective employees have to understand company timetables. Organization-wide scheduling information includes:

- **Paid holidays:** Independence Day, Arbor Day (if you're a bank), and so on
- **Key financial dates:** Due dates for budgets and sales projections
- **Key operational dates:** Plant inventory, trade shows
- **Intranet publishing dates:** Newsletter content submission deadlines
- **Corporate events:** Shareholder meetings, company barbecues, Initial Public Offering When We All Get Rich

The intranet can host more than simple organization-wide schedule information, however. Check out these other possibilities for department-level intranet schedules:

- **Schedules for shared facilities:** Such as conference rooms (and information on those facilities — for example, Sandia National Laboratory posts photographs and descriptions of conference rooms so that employees can reserve appropriate facilities for their meetings)
  - **Computer user group meetings:** "Java programmers," "Desktop publishers," and so on (often called SIGs for Special Interest Groups)
  - **Departmental functions:** Planning meetings, budget discussions, and so on

If you run Microsoft FrontPage, you can create web-based calendars using the Calendar Wizard in the FrontPage Development Kit (similar features exist in Word 97 and other office automation suites). Alternatively, you may be able to use web browsers to interact with calendar functions in your existing groupware products, such as Lotus Domino or Novell GroupWise.

Emergency and disaster plans

Emergency and disaster planning is like flossing your teeth: Everyone agrees it's a good idea, but many don't do it. Three major impediments to a disaster recovery plan are:

1. **Getting procedures into the hands of those who are likely to need them.**

   "Quick! Where's our copy of the disaster plan?"

   "Oh, Bob has it; he's revising it."

   "Where's *Bob?*"

   "I think he's on vacation in the Caymans."

2. **Creating a document that employees can use quickly.** "For bomb threat procedures, please see Section I on emergency procedures, Subsection II on threats, paragraph 4 on explosive and incendiary devices."

3. **Keeping procedures updated as the organization changes.** If a cloud of dust arises from your desk as you plunk down the plan document, it isn't likely to help.

The intranet can be a good tool for distributing emergency preparedness and disaster recovery information that employees can read ahead of time to get familiar with the procedures. The procedures are available to anyone on the network, and intranet documents are easier to update than paper documents. Advance education isn't the only way you can use an intranet for emergencies.

Although intranets aren't generally considered *real-time* computer systems, using an intranet may be faster than looking up a procedure in a printed manual. In many emergency situations, the computer network remains up and running (joined, sometimes, by employees).

For example, if someone discovers a potential computer virus, the employee can check your intranet for a list of things to do and people to call. (The mere act of accessing read-only intranet web pages isn't likely to spread a virus, by the way.) In a manufacturing environment, the intranet may be no replacement for the large emergency procedure posters on the shop floor, but it can be a useful supplement to them in computer-equipped plants. A PC workstation may be much closer and easier to access than the first aid handbook.

If you design your intranet system to publish information employees might use in a time-critical situation, tailor your intranet pages so that vital information appears on the main emergency page. Enable users to easily click links for specifics on a particular subject (tornado, flood, CPR, severe paper cuts, and so on). Don't use any graphics on an emergency intranet system unless they're essential to conveying a procedure, and if you need a graphical image, keep it black and white so that the time to load the page is as short as possible. Finally, keep the emergency web pages on your web server, not on another server that the web server has to go out on the network to find. You want those emergency pages to appear *very quickly*.

Pages of useful links

If your intranet is a *multinet* — that is, it also connects to the public Internet — consider publishing a page, or set of pages, consisting of useful Internet links. These may link the employee to external Internet sites such as:

- **Government agencies that the company deals with**
- **Contractors, suppliers, and customers**
- **Competitors** (gotta keep an eye on 'em)
- **Market research databases and reports**
- **Academic institutions performing relevant research** (these are also a potential source of new hires)
- **Technology forums and vendor sites** (such as the links in this book's Appendix B)

The previous examples should be enough to get your brain cells firing. I haven't even mentioned daily company news bulletins, annual reports, meeting minutes, campus and facilities maps, employee home pages, and an employee classified-ad page — well, *now* I have.

Just about all of the applications in this chapter address the simpler kind of one-way, one-to-many publishing that Chapter 3 explains as a great candidate for your first intranet publishing project. In several places, though, I suggest how a two-way intranet can make these company applications more useful. Chapter 5 addresses how to implement more complex applications that require feedback from intranet users, and how to use two-way intranet communications to streamline everyday business tasks.

Chapter 5
Procedural Support: Streamlining the Routine

- -

In This Chapter
▶ Using intranets for one-way and two-way communication
▶ Learning about the gizmos that standard HTML provides for your intranet forms
▶ Jazzing up HTML forms with extra software, plug-ins, and helper programs
▶ Doing something useful with your intranet form data
▶ Combining your intranet project with a reengineering effort
▶ Streamlining office routines with cool intranet applications

- -

This chapter concentrates on using the intranet to publish forms and tables that help ease the day-to-day tasks of the typical business office, regardless of industry, division, or department.

Many applications discussed in this chapter require two-way communications, unlike most of the applications in Chapter 4, which involve the simple distribution of data to users and don't require a response (one-way communication). Using the intranet to streamline routine office procedures normally requires users to contribute some content of their own, for example, by filling out a supply purchase requisition or other form.

Two-way intranet communication uses more complex technology, just like building a spacecraft is tougher if you want it to return to Earth. Two-way communication, therefore, demands more expertise from intranet designers. You may want to gain some experience with one-way intranet publishing before you design a two-way system. However, you can design an effective two-way intranet publishing system, without a lot of rocket science, when two conditions hold true:

- **The user doesn't require instantaneous confirmation or results.** This is usually the case for many office procedures that employees expect to take hours or days, such as submitting an expense report.
- **The user-to-server communication lends itself to structured formatting,** such as selecting options from a multiple choice list or providing short answers to questions.

This chapter starts with a section on the built-in form capabilities that are part of standard HyperText Markup Language (HTML), then discusses ways to design fancier forms with a bit of extra software. Next, it presents the basics of intranet programming (you have to *do* something with that submitted form data, after all), and finally, a few practical ways to streamline office procedures with the help of intranet-based forms.

Formfitting HTML

HTML forms are special pages or page fragments that provide places for the web page user to enter information right in the browser window. HTML doesn't enable you to specify precisely what to do with that information — an external program does that. HTML can collect the information, pass it along to the external program, and then display any information the external program sends back.

Standard HTML forms

Regular, unadorned HTML supports several little predesigned form gizmos. Here's a list:

- **Plain text:** Allows you to specify a maximum length for the text a user can enter.
- **Text area:** For multi-line text, such as comments or questions. Alas, no way exists to limit how much text the user can enter. You can specify the text area width and height, but the user can still use the scrollbars to enter the entire contents of *War and Peace*.
- **Password text:** Actually has nothing to do with network passwords; Password text displays asterisks when the user types information, but doesn't actually encrypt the information or do anything special once the user sends the data over the network.
- **Check boxes:** Can have *values* (a bit of text associated with the check boxes), and can preset as checked or unchecked when they first appear; the user can check as many check boxes in a group as desired.

Chapter 5: Procedural Support: Streamlining the Routine

- ✔ **Radio buttons:** You define these in a group. Only one radio button in a group can be selected at a time, kind of like the pushbutton car radio buttons of yore, which were great because they didn't need reprogramming when you replaced the car battery.
- ✔ **Drop-down selection lists:** You can preset these to a default choice, and design as scrollable or non-scrollable.
- ✔ **Special Reset form and Submit form buttons:** Clear the form's contents to its original state, and then send the data off for processing, respectively (you can change the button names to read anything you want).

Be glad that I don't have the room to go into the boring details of how you create these elements on a web page form. Remember: this isn't an HTML manual. You can add these form elements the hard way, by manually editing a web page's HTML code, or (far easier and more preferable) by using a good HTML page design tool, such as Adobe PageMill or Microsoft FrontPage 97. Each page design tool has its own easy commands for creating the standard form elements, called *fields,* as shown in Figure 5-1.

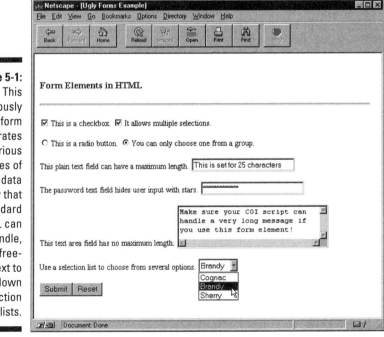

Figure 5-1: This hideously ugly form illustrates the various types of user data entry that standard HTML can handle, from free-form text to drop-down selection lists.

Whatever method you use to build your forms, here are a few design tips to make you look like a pro:

- Don't use a form at all if the only thing you're putting on it is a text area field. An e-mail link works better and is simpler for this sort of communication.
- HTML enables you to put multiple forms on the same page, but make sure that you have a good reason for doing this, because doing so can make the page confusing to the user. Remember, also, that each form on the page has to have its own reset and submit buttons.
- Use a standard text field rather than a text area field if you know the data fits within a certain maximum length.
- Take advantage of the HTML ability to assign default values that reflect the most common or likely choice. Doing so means less work for the user.
- Include sample text or instructions in text area fields.
- Include *none* as an option in a radio button group or a drop-down selection list, if it's a valid answer.
- Use drop-down lists instead of radio buttons wherever you can — they take up less screen real estate.
- Use the HTML ability to set a maximum response length whenever possible. Not only does this help you sort through responses, but for entries such as a phone number, it can help the user avoid making a mistake.
- Use HTML tables to format your radio buttons and check boxes, so that they stay neatly organized when a user resizes the browser window. For more on tables, refer to Chapter 4.

Fancy forms

Simple, standard HTML forms are fine for many uses. If you want to put some hot mustard on your egg roll, however, extra software is available to do nifty chores, such as:

- Precisely position form elements on the web page. (HTML doesn't do exact field placement.)
- Scan a paper form and building an intranet form that looks just like it.
- Perform mathematical calculations, such as row and column totals.
- Permit a user to submit only a single field of data, as opposed to transmitting an entire form.
- Check an entry's accuracy or validity before submitting it, and defining different rules for each form element.

Chapter 5: Procedural Support: Streamlining the Routine

Caere OmniForm Internet Publisher and Adobe Acrobat are examples of products that extend HTML to provide some of these desirable form capabilities. See Appendix B for contact information. Incidentally, Caere is pronounced "care," as I found out when I tried to be smart and said "kay-AIR-ee" to a manager there. I still maintain that's the *right* way to say it, but it's thaere company.

Extending the capabilities of standard HTML forms is a great idea, but as always when extending your intranet standard, you run the risk of tying your publishing system to a particular vendor. You also have to include a "helper" program or plug-in that enables standard web browsers to deal with the special form formats. For example, Caere's OmniForm Markup Language (OFML) format isn't one that a browser understands how to use without the helper program, which Caere supplies at no extra cost.

Data Processing, Intranet Style

After you know how to put together an HTML form for two-way communication with intranet users, you're rounding second base and looking good. However, you're not home free until you deal with one big question: Once the user submits the form, what do you do with the data it contains? Here's where the intranet designer has to go a little bit beyond the usual web technology, because remember: The World Wide Web started life mainly as a one-way information distribution vehicle.

I know, you may be in a position to leave the details to programmers, but you're better off if you at least understand the big picture of intranet data processing. Here are the broad brush strokes, and I leave the details to authors of other books (such as the popular titles *CGI is from UNIX, NSAPI is from Netscape* and *Why Bad Code Happens to Good Programmers*).

Common Gateway Interface (CGI)

Several years ago, CERN (pronounced *sern*), the European nuclear research center, came up with the Common Gateway Interface (CGI) idea. CGI provides web developers the ability to add features (via programs) to their servers without the server software itself having to incorporate the excess code. CGI has gained widespread acceptance, and all web servers nowadays support it, so it has all the appeal of a standard. CGI is best for occasional, light-duty data processing, and that's all many organizations require.

Right off the bat, I should tell you that CGI is not a programming language. It's an *interface* (the *I* in *CGI*), meaning that it defines how a server moves data between an HTML form and some other program.

What happens in a typical CGI system is:

1. **The user fills out an HTML form and clicks on the Submit button.**
2. **The browser tells the web server where to find the *external program* (so-called because it isn't part of the web server software itself).**

   The external program, called a *script,* normally resides in a directory called CGI-BIN. The name and location of the script are specified in the HTML form when you design it. You need to have a separate script for each different form.
3. **The browser sends the form data to the script located on the web server (or, possibly, on another web server).**

   The form data that the browser sends can be in the form of a Uniform Resource Locator (URL) with a special format (the URL is the address of the particular web page). You've probably seen some of these sneaky, complex URLs in your browser's location window when surfing the Internet — this is the *Get* method, for you aspiring HTML programmers. Or, the browser can send the data separately from the URL — this is the *Post* method, which designers prefer for complex forms, because it isn't subject to any maximum length limitation.
4. **The script — which can be written in a variety of programming languages, including C++, PERL, JavaScript, Pascal, and so on — handles the form data passed along by the browser (which can contain weird characters that need stripping out or translation), and does whatever it needs to do with that data.**

   For example, the program may update a database running on another computer, send a confirmation e-mail to the user, or even display a whole 'nother web page.
5. **If the script sends information back to the user, the web server presents it to the user's browser in HTML format.**

Very slick! Figure 5-2 illustrates the data flow.

CGI programming does have a few *gotchas,* and you need to know them:

- **Somebody's got to write the scripts.** The degree of difficulty for this dive varies depending on the programming language used — PERL is a double flip, C++ is a triple gainer with a twist. In any case, if you don't have a professional programming staff in house, you may need to hire or contract some help. You can get publicly available CGI scripts from the Internet, but they require testing and may not work in all environments (such as NT Server).
- **The web server has no control over what that script does, so no safety net exists to ensure that the external program doesn't accidentally do harm.** For security reasons, slap some access restrictions on the CGI-BIN directory.

- **CGI programs run on an *open-and-close* model, so each program starts from scratch.** For example, if a particular CGI program has to access a back-end database server, then every time the CGI program runs, it has to reconnect to that server — causing slow performance.
- **CGI programs run in a separate memory space from the web server software.** Again, this means that CGI programs can run slowly, imposing more load on the server. Heavy CGI activity can bring a server to its little semiconductor knees.

Quite a few *gotchas,* I know. You can, however, work around most of them fairly easily, except the performance problem. If you anticipate lots of users submitting forms and needing to run special server programs to handle that data, take a look at a different approach — for example, writing programs that the web server itself can run, as I explain in the next section.

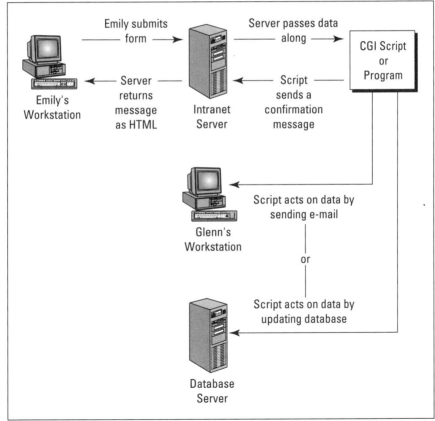

Figure 5-2: Intranet programming, CGI style. The CGI script may run on the same physical machine as the web server, but it's a separate piece of software.

Web server Application Program Interfaces (APIs)

In the arcane lingo of the computer industry, an Application Program Interface (API) is nothing more than a set of commands that a program can use to get things done. If a Windows program wants to draw a little message box on the screen that says "You need more memory on this PC, you cheapskate," the program uses standard Windows API commands, called *calls,* so the program doesn't have to draw every little dot on the screen.

Today's industrial strength web servers come with a built-in set of commands that programmers can use to perform many of the actions you might otherwise use a CGI program to perform. The big advantage here is that the built-in commands run in the same memory space as the web server itself, so they don't impose the large overhead of a CGI program, which must take time to set up its own little private memory space before it can get to work. On the other hand, the drawback of shared memory space is that a program using a web server API can possibly crash the web server itself, something that isn't as much of a concern with CGI. Also, programs that use web server API calls are *compiled* (made ready to run in advance) rather than *interpreted* (processed a line at a time when they run). Compiled programs run faster than interpreted ones.

If you didn't quite follow all that, it doesn't matter! Just remember that programs using the web server API can typically do things much faster than a CGI script can.

Some of the popular web server APIs are:

- Internet Server API (ISAPI), provided with Microsoft Internet Information Server
- Netscape Server API (NSAPI), provided with Netscape Enterprise Server
- Web Site API (WSAPI), provided with O'Reilly Web Site Server

By now, you can probably guess that web server APIs aren't as portable as CGI. For example, a program that uses ISAPI doesn't work on a Netscape server, so if you decide to switch server platforms, you got some reprogrammin' to do.

That's why I say at the start of this section that you will probably want to use CGI for occasional, light-duty data processing — it's a portable standard and the performance is fine in this situation. For frequent and heavier-duty data processing, for example, with a large user population, the web server API approach may perform so much faster than CGI that you don't mind locking yourself into a single vendor's server software.

Another type of program exists that runs within a web server's memory space, and it's called a *Server-Side Include* (SSI). SSI is barely supported by some web servers, is a potential security hole, and is normally only used to do minor tasks, such as tossing the current date and time onto a web page. I only mention it here because someone is sure to send me an indignant e-mail if I omit it entirely.

Java, east of Krakatoa

Several years back, a disaster movie appeared titled *Krakatoa, East of Java*. The movie producers never bothered to look at the map — Krakatoa is actually *west* of Java. Of course, Java, at least in this book, is a programming language — and one that can do even cooler things with your web page forms than CGI or server API programs can. Not many Java forms tools exist right now — hardly any, as I write this — but it's only a matter of time, so Java forms are worth a brief discussion.

HTML forms have a few important drawbacks. For one thing, they're *static*. The information a user plugs into one data entry field doesn't modify the appearance of the next data entry field. For example, if you're filling out an equipment requisition form, it would be nice if after you filled in your name, your phone number and department appeared automatically (from the company directory database) so you wouldn't have to retype it. Plain old HTML can't do that — Java can.

Another drawback has to do with data *validation,* that is, making sure that the data a user types into a form is reasonable and accurate. For example, typing **90r10** as a zip code, instead of **90210**, is an error you'd like to catch before the computer stores the form in a database. You can perform data validation with CGI, but only after the user fills in the whole form and submits it, creating traffic on the network, and work for the server. The better way to do this is to perform these sorts of accuracy checks at the workstation, before the user ever submits the form. Plain old HTML can't do that — Java can (and so can JavaScript and VBScript, discussed in Chapter 12).

Finally, if your forms link up to an external database, a Java program running on the workstation machine (which is where Java programs run, incidentally) can talk to that database directly, without even involving the web server as an intermediary. This trick is nice from a performance standpoint, because user workstations usually have far more processor speed to burn than stressed-out web servers.

As far as databases and Java go, Java programs communicate with databases via the Java Data Base Connectivity API, or JDBC, which permits Java programs to interact with databases that adhere to the popular Open Data Base Connectivity (ODBC) standard. Just so you know.

The bottom line is that if you use forms in two-way intranet communications, as some of the sample applications this chapter discusses do, keep your eye on Java form development tools. They're likely to overcome the key drawbacks of HTML forms, and some industry gurus believe they are already sounding the death knell for CGI scripts. That may be premature — I'm more comfortable that Java is sounding the *dangerously ill* knell for CGI — but I suppose that's quibbling. For more information on Java, as well as other intranet programming tools, check out Chapter 12.

Sample Applications

In this section, I discuss ways that you can put your intranet to work on routine office tasks. The advantages include reducing paper flow, saving employee time and effort, reducing the lag time for printing paper forms, reducing the need to keep paper form archives, allowing employees to submit forms from remote locations, allowing administrators to change form designs without trashing thousands of preprinted and obsolete copies, and in some cases, tying in with other intranet publishing systems for convenience and synergy — not to mention saving trees.

That's quite a list! Considering that over half of all business documents are forms, using your intranet instead of paper has the potential to save your organization megabucks. BellSouth, for example, estimates it saves $17.5 million each year using the intranet versus paper-based forms.

Purchase requisitions

Silicon Graphics, maker of high-performance workstations and servers, uses its Silicon Junction intranet to reduce internal purchasing process time by over 80 percent. Every corporation has a procedure for employees to order office supplies, computers, software, file cabinets, reclining massage chairs, and so on.

What sort of things can *your* intranet purchase requisition publishing system accomplish? It can:

- Provide forms-based data entry for the initial requisition, thus eliminating a paper form.
- Publish a page detailing your company's standard purchasing procedures and policies, such as when a request has to go through a multiple-bid process, along with typical time frames.
- Publish a page listing approved vendors.
- Explain how to use a vendor who isn't on the approved list.

✔ Trigger an e-mail to the applicant, once the requisition request is approved or denied ("A $2,000 reclining massager chair? Thought you could slip that one by, did you, Reinhold?")

✔ Allow the applicant to submit an e-mail when his or her Binford Executive Power Stapler 9000 hasn't shown up for two months.

Expense reports

Most companies offer expense report forms so that the company can reimburse employees for out-of-pocket cash outlays. In my corporate employee days, I always preferred company credit cards, but sadly not all companies trust their employees to that extent. Heck, some even guard the petty cash box like it contains Michael Jackson's other glove.

You don't necessarily have to go on a trip to incur reimbursable expenses, but this is the most common example. Figure 5-3 shows a sample trip expense report form that I created with Caere OmniForm Internet Publisher, one of the fancier form programs.

One nice aspect of intranet-based expense reports is that you can submit the form from your notebook PC, using a dial-up connection. For example, on the last day of your trip, when you know you've incurred all the expenses you're going to incur, you can dial in and submit your expense report. In theory at

Figure 5-3: An Acme Cognac employee could use a form like this to submit a trip expense report. Note the extra toolbar beneath the browser's regular controls, and the similarity to a paper form.

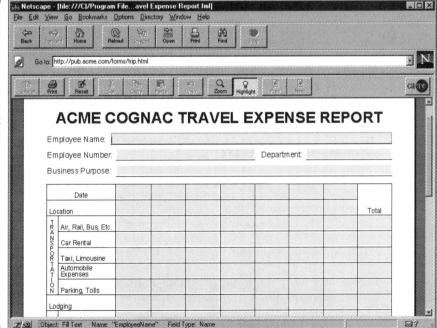

least, the sooner you get that form in, the sooner you get reimbursed. Okay, you still have to turn in your receipts. Even so, many organizations today streamline expense report processing by processing your check as soon as they get the form, and then docking you or firing you later if the receipts don't match up. In any case, you've got one less piece of paper to turn in.

Include a free-form text area field on your expense report form, where an employee can explain why it was necessary to tip a taxi driver $35 so that he would drive 80 mph on the shoulder of Chicago's Kennedy Expressway to make the last flight out after a sales meeting ran long. You know the friendly bookkeepers are going to ask for an explanation, so putting this text area field on the form can save a phone call.

Budgeting

The budgeting process in most companies involves departments and workgroups submitting projections for the coming year in spreadsheet form. You may be able to use HTML forms for budget submissions, but it isn't easy because standard HTML forms don't have the ability to calculate totals or do the other calculations a typical budget spreadsheet does. A budget form is a good application for one of those programs that I mention earlier in the "Fancy forms" section of this chapter.

When the budgeting process for the upcoming year is finished, and the numbers are cast in stone, you don't care that HTML can't do calculations, and it's a piece of cake to publish the figures for one-way distribution on your intranet. For example, if you use Microsoft Excel 97 as your budget spreadsheet program, just choose File⇨Save as HTML and follow the Internet Assistant dialog boxes. (You can add in the Internet Assistant feature to Excel 95 if you don't have Excel 97 — the software is on this book's CD-ROM.) Excel automatically creates an HTML table with all the budget numbers in it, ready for incorporation onto your intranet web page, as shown in Figure 5-4.

Document editing

One of the more complex intranet publishing applications is *collaborative document management,* a type of *workflow* or *groupware* application in which multiple individuals work on the same documents at different stages in the life cycle. That life cycle includes creation, editing, proofing, approval, and production. Each stage may have its own deadlines and timetables. Simple HTML forms don't cut the mustard at this level!

Before intranets got hot, the pre-eminent groupware solution was Lotus Notes. Notes remains very popular, and Lotus is tying Notes in with intranets via its Domino and Domino.doc products. Even so, some companies prefer solutions that work with open-format (that is, non-proprietary)

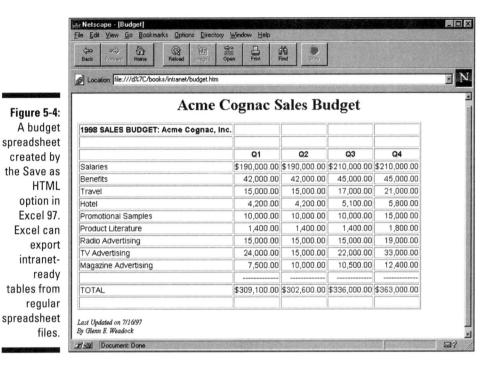

Figure 5-4: A budget spreadsheet created by the Save as HTML option in Excel 97. Excel can export intranet-ready tables from regular spreadsheet files.

document databases. Others believe Notes is still too expensive, although web-based groupware is sure to put continuing price pressure on Notes and Domino as time goes by. Domino.doc is also less expensive than many other document groupware tools.

Lotus Notes is more of a general purpose solution (although certainly less so with Domino.doc), but expensive, specialized document management software has also been around for years. Many vendors of such software, such as NovaSoft and Documentum, are adding intranet capabilities to their existing products. Some, such as Open Text, have designed ground-up intranet systems, such as LiveLink Intranet.

These products typically use a database approach to track documents, and they provide features such as security, shared libraries, change audit logs, automatic notification of slipped schedules, document searching, and document routing. They can do lots of things Notes can't easily do, such as create new documents from existing ones, treat a group of files as a single document, and generate online and print documents from a single source.

If your organization already has a ritzy document editing workflow product, intranet-enabled versions and add-ons may disappoint you at first blush. Web browsers don't generally offer tight, precise layout, and they can't easily do slick operations, such as pan and zoom. However, it's probably just a matter of time before intranets gear up to the task of sophisticated editing and publishing — likely with the help of Java, or perhaps SGML (see sidebar).

Travel information

Your organization may be large enough to have its own in-house travel bureau, and if so, you can design an intranet form that enables employees to send in ticket requests over your intranet. Employees could specify travel start and end points, dates, best times, preferred airline (gotta rack up those frequent flyer miles), whether the boss is springing for Business Class or not, and if you have enough miles to put in for an upgrade. You could design a fairly simple CGI script to send this information via e-mail to the travel office.

Even if your organization uses an outside travel agency, you can set up a travel request form as described in the previous paragraph, assuming both you and your agency have Internet e-mail capability.

The travel office can also use your intranet to provide details on employee travel schedules, so that, for example, dashing bachelor sales rep Don can try to get on the same flight to the big trade show as cute bachelorette sales rep Felicia, or so that Don's manager can check the schedule online and know when to expect Don back in the office. This application will probably require that your intranet connect to a database of ticket information at the travel office and allow users to submit queries via an HTML form. Simply slapping all the data onto a long web page wouldn't be practical, either to create or to use. To learn how to set up this sort of intranet system, check out Chapter 10.

Design and manufacturing

Intranet publishing can streamline routine product design and manufacturing tasks in many ways, such as by allowing designers and production managers to exchange blueprints, product specifications, bill-of-materials lists, parts supplier information, quality control test specifications, International Standards Organization (ISO) certification documents, equipment repair manuals, and so on.

You can post some types of design and manufacturing documents on an intranet for immediate viewing with a web browser. For example, many computerized technical drawings use the Autodesk AutoCAD file format (DWG). DWG files can be very large, but Autodesk offers an Internet Utilities package that converts DWG files into much smaller, single-layer snapshots called DWF (Drawing Web Format).

You can't edit a DWF file, but this file is fine for viewing purposes. Autodesk also offers plug-in software called Whip, for Internet Explorer and Navigator browsers, that enables intranet users to view DWF drawings from within the browser. For more information on Autodesk Internet Utilities and Whip, point your browser to www.autodesk.com.

What about two-way communication? A design or manufacturing intranet may use HTML forms to allow users to request specific documents or files.

A CGI script can then process the form data and automatically e-mail the desired file to the user.

Forms are convenient for distributing documents when a company has a lot of them, because users don't have to wade through long file download lists. They just specify what they want on the form. If you have only a few dozen files, and they don't lend themselves to automatic viewing within a web browser, consider an intranet-based file download site. Chapter 7 discusses how to build a download page.

Another possibility is to link the manufacturing intranet with the purchase requisition intranet I discuss earlier, to facilitate ordering parts and supplies.

Standard Generalized Markup Language (SGML)

The Standard Generalized Markup Language (SGML) is darned interesting for several reasons. SGML is the parent of HTML, which you know and love as the language of the Web. SGML also offers some powerful features for document publishing, and an entirely different philosophy than HTML's focus on screen viewing. Finally, SGML underlies some of the nifty features of intranet publishing applications, like SoftQuad HoTMetaL Intranet Publisher.

A key to understanding SGML is its almost fanatical dedication to separating form and content. While Netscape and Microsoft are extending HTML so that web designers gain more control over page appearance, and Java is doing the same, SGML advocates take the position that by specifying how a page looks, you sacrifice flexibility in using the core document to generate versions for different applications. SGML is a *create once, publish many ways* technology that doesn't depend on what Microsoft or Netscape are doing with HTML extensions. Anybody who spends much time printing HTML documents can appreciate the value of the SGML approach. SGML allows document publishers to create other HTML-like languages suited for tasks other than merely displaying a document on the screen.

Besides using SGML to generate different versions of a document for different situations (such as printing versus viewing, or an expert reader versus a novice reader), you can use it to provide *dynamic table of contents* generation. With this feature, the user can see, and navigate to, any part of a page: lists, headings, graphics, chapter titles, and even special tags your company creates to make document navigation easier. If you change the document's content, the table of contents updates itself automatically, without requiring you to change links anywhere. Wouldn't *that* be nice!

Another cool capability is more refined searching. Intranet search engines (see Chapter 11 for more on search engines) can help users find specific documents, but SGML makes it possible for a system to take users right to the specific *place* in the document where the search term appears. SGML also makes it easier for users to add document *annotations* (notes and comments) that don't actually modify the document, but travel along with it.

What does all this mean to you? If any of the above features appeal to you, look for intranet publishing systems such as SoftQuad's that offer SGML capabilities in addition to HTML. The two aren't mutually exclusive, but SGML features do require a browser helper program or plug-in because the browser can't understand them otherwise.

Although most design engineers have a computer workstation (usually a fancy one at that), many employees on the shop floor may not. Industrial workstations that can handle dust, metal shavings, varying temperatures, and paint particles in the air can be almost as expensive as *mil-spec* workstations (that's *mi*litary *spec*ification for us civilians). An intranet system for manufacturing support may, therefore, act primarily as a supplement to existing systems. For example, legally, you still have to post those safety notices on physical bulletin boards where everyone can see them (such as in the break room, next to those vending machines that dispense sandwiches made during the Eisenhower administration).

One area of special interest to designers and manufacturers is *project management*. Although project management software has been around for a long time, it hasn't always been easy for all participants to see an updated version of a schedule. That's no longer a problem with intranet-enabled project management tools, such as Primavera Project Planner 2.0, or P3 2.0 for short, from Primavera Systems. P3 2.0 includes a web publishing feature that places project data on an intranet page, and allows users to take a *zoom out* view for the big picture or a *zoom in* view for details on specific tasks and task groups. Now you can see how far behind schedule you are, right from your own workstation.

Incidentally, Microsoft Project can export HTML data with the HTML Converter add-on utility (free from Microsoft), but Project's web publishing abilities aren't as well integrated or as convenient as Primavera's.

User surveys

Intranet forms are great for user surveys. You don't really even need fancy form features here, because the types of data a user enters into a survey match just fine with standard HTML form capabilities.

Keep in mind that it's possible to survey employees to death. I recently conducted a survey of corporate employees and found out that they spend almost as much time completing interoffice surveys as they do handling their regular e-mail. ("Please fill out this survey about the visibility of the new paint markings on the company parking lot. This should take only 45 minutes to complete.")

The intranet is a nice way to ease the survey burden, because users can fill in an online survey when they want to. Of course, this increases the chances for bias, because a user is more likely to submit a survey after something great or awful has happened. As they say on Broadway, you're only as good as your last performance. But you can adjust for that skewing when you analyze the results. If you need to get a round of survey results within a particular time period, you can always e-mail the target group and say, "Please fill out the survey located on the human resources intranet."

Many organizations use e-mail forms for user surveys, but I like putting surveys on an intranet because it's an easy way to get new users familiar with the system and working with forms. Besides, during the early stages of your intranet, user feedback is very valuable, so you're smart to make it as easy as possible for someone who's actually using the new system to offer comments and suggestions. Figure 5-5 offers an example.

- Place a link to the appropriate user survey screen on the home page of each intranet publishing system.

- Periodically publish survey results on your intranet. Doing so is a way to show the user community that you actually read the surveys and care about them. You *do* care about them! I know you do!

New hire information

Ah, here's where you can really enjoy intranet publishing synergy. Remember the employee directory from Chapter 4? (Okay, so you haven't read Chapter 4 yet — in it, I discuss an employee directory that users can use through a corporate intranet.) Where does the data come from to feed such a directory? One possibility is an intranet form that can update the same database that the employee directory page uses.

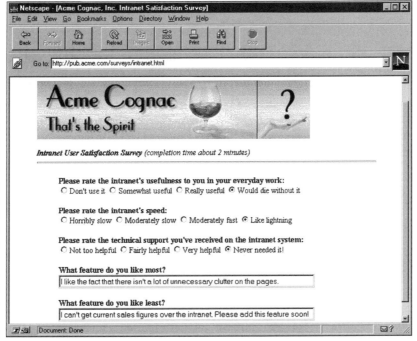

Figure 5-5:
Here's a user survey form for reporting satisfaction (or gripes) with the Acme Cognac intranet. This form uses plain old HTML.

Obtaining technical support

For computer users, getting good technical support quickly when users have a question or a problem is critical to the productivity of your intranet. This application for intranet publishing is so important that I've given it its own chapter — Chapter 8.

This chapter barely scratches the surface of the possible procedural support applications. Based on the examples in this chapter, try to think of two or three additional routine procedures in your office setting that you can automate with an intranet publishing system. What forms do your employees submit on a regular basis? What procedures do you already have set up on a vendor-specific computer network that may benefit from migrating to the open, standardized, and flexible intranet world?

Reengineering Opportunities

Another issue to ponder as you plan to apply your intranet to streamlining business processes is whether your intranet publishing project may dovetail nicely with a *reengineering* effort — that is, whether you can (or even should) change a business process at the same time that you automate it.

Big question, huh? Answering it means thinking a minute about what *reengineering* is. Whether you are a manager or a technical type who works directly with the network, you need to think about why business processes work or don't work, and how your intranet can make them better.

Basics of business process reengineering

Business Process Reengineering (BPR) is one of the few business buzzwords that actually means something — BPR means modifying the flow of work and information to realize gains in speed, service, cost, quality, and productivity. BPR looks at existing business processes with the understanding that many of them were never really *engineered* in the first place, but sprang up as a quick solution to a problem, and became Standard Operating Procedure by default rather than by design. When you reengineer, you ask whether the company can change those processes for the better — or, more radically, discard and replace them entirely. BPR usually involves combining several jobs into one, letting workers make more decisions, and performing work where it makes the most sense.

For example, a lot of companies have separate departments for credit and order processing. Combining the two functions into a single process saves time and reduces overhead. "Ms. Jones, the order you've placed for 90 cases of Acme Cognac would exceed your credit limit with us, but I see you have an excellent payment history. I'm going to raise that limit today so we can accept your order. Would you like a few thousand cigars with that?"

Michael Hammer and James Champy wrote *Reengineering the Corporation* in 1993, based on an article that appeared in the esteemed *Harvard Business Review*. BPR has come to mean many things since 1993, and some view it as a catch phrase companies hide behind while laying off hordes of employees. "We're sorry we had to let you go, but we're *reengineering,* you see." Small wonder something like 70 percent of all reengineering projects fail. BPR doesn't necessarily mean downsizing, though, and a high failure rate doesn't mean the concept has no merit.

Sometimes reengineering fails from weak leadership, as Hammer claims, but other reasons may be more to blame. For example, the business culture may not permit reengineering efforts to succeed. Many managers I've worked with would rather have a root canal *sans* novocaine than rock the corporate boat. Other managers fear the loss of control that decentralized decision-making can bring. Employees often resist any kind of top-down project purely on principle, especially if its success may lead them to the unemployment line.

Sometimes BPR fails because it requires something extremely difficult: better communication across departmental boundaries (between groups using different computer systems bought at different times for different purposes). Cross-departmental communication also requires major employee cross-training.

Are you beginning to see the role of your intranet emerging here? (The correct response is "Yes, Glenn, I am! Tell me more!") I'd be delighted, since you ask.

Can your intranet project implement a process change?

Information systems can either make business process reengineering easier, or absolutely impossible. Customized, nonstandard, and rigid information systems often get in the way; standardized, flexible systems (such as intranets — hurrah!) make reengineering easier.

One way your intranet system can make a reengineering project easier is by saving some steps in a process. A simple example is publishing a policy manual via your intranet, which saves the steps of printing and distribution. By saving steps, you reduce costs and speed up the process.

Intranets support BPR efforts in other, more important ways, too. Intranets help you link together different sorts of computer systems and provide a common cockpit (the web browser) from which users can get anywhere they need to go, and exchange information with anyone in the company. Intranet systems can, therefore, help overcome those interdepartmental computer incompatibilities that so often stymie efficient work habits. For example, an intranet tip-sharing system for customer service agents enabled AT&T to consolidate support numbers for its toll-free number service customers from 23 to 1.

Intranet publishing can also make the cross-training that BPR often requires a practical possibility: If the intranet is in place, users are already familiar with the one piece of necessary software (the web browser) to do the additional tasks that reengineering may require.

Finally, intranets tend to enjoy wide grass-roots support because they give employees an opportunity to steer their own future in a reengineering effort — just the kind of support that those top-down, unilateral "You *Will* Reengineer and You Will *Like* It" projects tend to lack.

You may worry that measuring your intranet's impact becomes more difficult when it accompanies a process change. You can't say that "60 percent of the cost savings is due to the intranet and 40 percent to the process change," any more than you can calculate whether a car's engine or suspension is more responsible for getting you to work in the morning. What you *can* do is measure the combined impact of a process change and your new intranet system. That's what everybody cares about, anyway.

The bottom line question is: Can your intranet project proceed hand-in-glove with a BPR project? Better than that, intranetting may be the key that unlocks BPR's true potential. Often, the very best time to think about BPR is when you are planning a new computer system. If your organization is experimenting with BPR, make sure your intranetters are in on the conversation, and also think about a little BPR education for your intranetters. The synergies may surprise you.

The ideas in this chapter may get you fired up about the intranet's potential for streamlining office procedures. I have a very specific office procedure for finishing a book chapter: I take a nap. See you on the next page.

Chapter 6
Sales Support: Getting and Keeping Customers

In This Chapter
- Publishing on your intranet, for the benefit of sales reps and customers
- Using your intranet to help clinch sales
- Distributing sales and marketing bulletins
- Improving salesperson access to customer information
- Eight miscellaneous sales support ideas

*I*ntranet publishing can do more than simply reduce paper-related costs and streamline routine procedures. This chapter shows how your intranet can provide key sales support data through a common interface and navigational structure.

Today, salespeople don't have things easy. Increased global competition and faster changing markets lead businesses to vary their products and services more often than in the past. Customers expect higher levels of service and responsiveness than they used to. As your sales force is trying to keep up with product changes and pamper existing customers, they're probably being asked to also beat the bushes and drum up new business. These folks can use some help, and as an intranet publisher, you can provide it.

Next to a generous expense account, your intranet can become your sales force's favorite asset. Intranets permit quick, global changes to sales-related documents, and relieve staff from having to keep track of quite so many pieces of paper. They also provide an efficient way to reach geographically dispersed sales reps, and act as a glue to bind different information systems together into a common window (the web browser).

In this chapter, I take a look at how intranet publishing can help your salespeople concentrate more on customer care and new business development, and less on paperwork — just as companies like Eli Lilly, HBO, and Xerox are discovering in their own sales organizations. Figure 6-1 shows a possible intranet sales support home page, with links to the various features I discuss.

Figure 6-1: The Acme Cognac sales support intranet home page is just a page of links to the various subsystems that sales reps can use from their web browser.

Use e-mail hand in hand with your intranet: Announce new intranet pages and significant revisions to sales documents by e-mail, and refer sales staff to the relevant intranet site.

Product Information

Good, effective salespeople know their product well. Your corporate intranet can help keep this knowledge timely by putting spec sheets, feature lists, diagrams, price lists, testimonials, references, competitive analyses, and sales bulletins online for easy sales staff access.

Spec sheets and configuration data

Salespeople often refer to specification sheets or features lists to understand product capabilities, and to help customers make the appropriate choice. A problem for sales staff in the past has been that this information changes frequently. The problem is bigger in some industries than others — semiconductor spec sheets change more rapidly than chainsaw spec sheets. However, even if the product doesn't change much over time, model designations and product families may.

HTML tables are a good way to present specification charts in row and column format on intranet pages. See Chapter 4 for details on creating web page tables.

If your products or services carry any industry certifications or endorsements, you can publish this information in a specifications page as well.

Complex products may require detailed *configuration data* prior to the sale, in which case the salesperson must select components and create a final bill of materials. However, some components may be incompatible with other ones, and some product options may be limited to particular models.

You can handle configurations and options in different ways with your intranet. If the possible combinations aren't too numerous, you can publish the configuration guidelines in text form, and perhaps even present tables laying out all the possible configurations.

For more complex products, you may prefer to give your salespeople a configuration tool, or *Wizard* — a program that steps the sales rep through a series of questions and answers to build the custom product, disallowing any impossible combinations (like an oil-and-water cleaning solution). You may already be familiar with a Wizard program from installing software — the steps and questions you go through to install many software packages are often called an *Installation Wizard.* A decent web programmer can write such a program in Java, ActiveX, JavaScript, or VBScript (see Chapter 12). Or, you may be able to use a *dynamic form* product such as JetForm 5.0, which changes the form's design, based on data the user enters along the way. A third approach is to use plain HTML forms and server-side Common Gateway Interface (CGI) scripts (see Chapter 5 for more info).

The bottom line is that you have many options for using your intranet to help sales reps both find out about the products they sell, and configure those products for specific applications.

Diagrams and illustrations

Visual aids, such as product diagrams and computer-based demos, are more likely to be useful for salespeople than for customers, unless the customers visit the salesperson's office. The reasons for this are that network speeds are much faster than modem speeds, and not every intranet allows remote dial-up connections. By all means, do some testing — if you can serve up attractive product illustrations reasonably quickly over a dial-up link, the salesperson equipped with notebook computer and cellular phone can be a one-person, custom-product literature rack.

One way to keep modem traffic to a minimum is to provide a links page for product pictures. Instead of placing the image file *inline* on the page, that is, so that the image automatically downloads as part of the web page, you can place a *link* to the picture on the page, along with descriptive text. This way, the graphics don't cross the modem connection until the salesperson or user clicks an image link, at which point, the browser downloads and displays the image. The browser doesn't download images the salesperson doesn't need, so that traffic goes down and speed goes up.

As long as your product pictures are in a *bitmap* format (that is, rows of dots), you can probably convert them to the intranet-friendly GIF and JPEG file formats using a page design tool such as FrontPage 97 or a graphics program such as JASC PaintShop Pro (included on this book's CD-ROM) or Adobe Photoshop (a tryout version of which is included on the CD-ROM also). (See Chapter 12 for more on GIF and JPEG.) However, if your product illustrations use a *vector* format (lines and curves), like most computer-based technical drawings use, you need to use a different approach: Either convert the images to bitmaps with a utility such as DeBabelizer, or equip the sales staff with *viewers* that enable the web browser to display the vector illustrations over.

Your intranet isn't likely to eliminate the need for glossy product brochures. By helping the customer zero in on particular products, however, you can give away only the brochures that cover products in which the customer has demonstrated an interest.

Price lists

Prices change often enough to be an excellent candidate for intranet publishing. The great advantage of intranet-based price lists is that as long as administrators keep the system current, salespeople don't need to worry that the prices they quote may be out of date.

You may be able to avoid redundant effort by linking your intranet to an existing database that contains current price information, if you have such a database available. You can retrieve data from standard databases and present it over your intranet in HyperText Markup Language (HTML) format using a variety of techniques, including CGI scripts and Java *applets* or mini-programs (see Chapters 5 and 12 for more info).

Your intranet can provide not only tabular price data, but also related information, such as the amounts and breakpoints of volume discounts and typical terms and conditions for payment, shipping, and product returns. If you include such information, place links to it onto all pages that present numeric price data. The fact that such links may cross departmental boundaries (for example, the legal staff may be responsible for the terms and conditions language) illustrates the power of intranetting.

Computer-based presentations

In recent years, computer-based sales presentations have become practical enough to challenge the older style 35mm slide and overhead transparency presentations. Computer-based presentations, using programs such as Microsoft PowerPoint 97, have several advantages over the other methods:

- They can be easily shared (for example, on an intranet download page).
- They can incorporate animation effects, sound, and even video clips.
- They're easy to change (for example, you can customize a presentation by replacing the customer name on a title slide in about ten seconds).
- A salesperson can easily copy a computer-based presentation and leave it with the customer for later viewing or reference — try that with a tray of 40 slides.

You normally don't want to play back computer slide shows live from an intranet, due to performance limitations (especially over a modem link). The nifty slide-to-slide transitions available in presentation software (wipes, fades, dissolves, and so on) are slick when fast, but clunky when slow. You can definitely use your intranet as a software distribution vehicle for computer-based presentations, however. Create a download site as I describe in Chapter 7, where sales staff can download a variety of canned presentations that they can then mix, match, and customize as desired to make a customer presentation.

Another way you can make the lives of sales staff easier is by posting multiple versions of computer-based presentations on your intranet download page. For example, many staff may still be using PowerPoint 95 rather than PowerPoint 97.

If a big part of your job involves creating or using computer-based presentations, you may find *Creating Cool PowerPoint 97 Presentations* by Glenn E. Weadock (me) and Emily Sherrill Weadock (my wife) helpful (IDG Books Worldwide, Inc., 1997). If you're just discovering computer-based presentations, check out *PowerPoint 97 For Dummies* by Doug Lowe (IDG Books Worldwide, Inc., 1996).

Testimonials and references

Smart customers and prospective ones want to chat with other firms that have experience with the products or services you sell, before making a commitment. You can use your intranet to store a history of customer testimonials and references ("I can serve Acme Cognac and impress dinner guests, without spending more than I would on jug wine."). You may want to organize these quotations by product on a primary links page.

For documents like testimonials and references, which sales staff may want to print and leave with customers, double-check how the HTML pages print. Make sure that the page breaks are clean and the output is legible. Watch out for Java applets that may render the page unprintable in whole or in part.

Competitive analyses

When I receive press kits from computer product manufacturers, the kits usually include a market comparison matrix that shows beyond a shadow of a doubt why Brand X is better than Brand Y. Sometimes this document takes the form of a simple chart with a list of features down the left edge, and separate columns for Brand X and Brand Y populated by little check marks. In other cases, the competitive analysis takes the thinly veiled form of a customer checklist, which just happens to include many of the features Brand X has that Brand Y doesn't. For example, a question may be, "Question 1: When buying cognac, does the brand name suggest a peak or pinnacle of performance and excellence?"

Use HTML tables to present such competitive analyses on your intranet. Make sure that you bear in mind whether the document is for sales use only, or for both customer and sales use, because the audience affects the tone of the document. If you mean for sales reps to print the checklist for the customer, you probably don't want to be as blatant as you may be in a document for internal consumption only. For example, you may say, "Check to see whether the bouquet is aromatic and alluring" for a document with external consumers, as opposed to, "Brand Y's cognac smells like a cow pie" for an internal document. Business can be war, but people respect companies that adopt at least the *appearance* of civility.

If your intranet links to the public Internet, you may want to include links to competitor home pages on the competitive analysis home page for the benefit of the sales staff.

 This sort of material may be sensitive, and although businesses routinely obtain copies of each others' competitive analyses, this doesn't mean that you want to make it easy for them. Slap restrictions on these intranet pages to limit access (see Chapter 15 for advice on the details).

 Do check into whether you need permission to use competitive analyses published by third parties, such as industry rating groups, consumer reporting organizations, and so on.

Sales and marketing bulletins

These sorts of sales and marketing bulletins go out to the sales staff all the time:

- ✔ "A newly-discovered defect in the Model 1100 chainsaw can result in severed limbs and expensive lawsuits; discontinue sales of this model immediately."
- ✔ "Our consulting group is now offering intranet design services, as well as traditional client/server network services."
- ✔ "The California warehouse is overstocked on this year's cognac, so we will be diluting it with water and repackaging it as sherry at a special price."

Such bulletins used to take the form of paper memoranda. More recently, they're e-mail messages. The trouble with e-mail is that many users delete a message once they read it. Your intranet provides a convenient way to publish sales and marketing bulletins in reverse chronological order. If a salesperson wants to review the bulletins, it's simply a matter of pulling up an intranet page with one-line summaries and clicking for complete details on items of interest.

Consider setting up a separate page for product-related press releases that sales reps can print and leave with customers.

Customer Information

Product information is great, but your intranet can also provide sales and marketing staff with a full range of customer information:

- ✔ **Sales contacts, key managers, decision makers.** You may include personal information (birthdays, for example) here, in addition to the usual addresses, phone numbers, and e-mail addresses.
- ✔ **Size, profitability (if a public company), recent growth, and other company traits.** If your intranet connects to the public Internet, you can include links to public information sources, such as 10-K forms providing financial information required by the government and maintained by the Securities and Exchange Commission (www.sec.gov) in their EDGAR database (Electronic Data Gathering And Retrieval). (EDGAR is a fun name. Who says civil servants can't be hip?)
- ✔ **Recent sales activity, especially to follow up on lapses in orders.** For example, Xerox provides customer history information on an intranet that field sales reps dial into, using their notebook PCs. The reps no longer have to place phone calls to sales support staff to retrieve data on past customer orders.

✔ **Credit information.** This can come from your own business records, or from sources such as Dun & Bradstreet (www.dnb.com).

Many companies use a database management system to keep track of customers. These programs fall into two categories: *desktop databases,* such as Microsoft Access, which can run on a small computer along with other programs, and *server databases,* such as Microsoft SQL Server or Oracle, which need a more powerful dedicated computer.

Many tools exist to help an intranet publisher tie into such database programs in order to put database information onto web pages, and, in the reverse direction, modify database records from a browser. Some of these tools come as part of web server programs such as Netscape Enterprise Server or Microsoft Internet Information Server. Some tools are bundled with intranet publishing kits like Macromedia Backstage Internet Studio. Finally, some are separate products, such as WEBase from ExperTelligence.

A complete discussion of database-to-intranet integration deserves a book of its own, but I can at least give you the following two tips here:

✔ Integration is much easier if your database program supports two standards called ODBC (for Open Data Base Connectivity) and SQL (for Structured Query Language). Both standards make it easier for a web server to read from and write to a wide variety of databases.

✔ If you want to put the workload onto user computers rather than intranet servers, JDBC (Java Data Base Connectivity) is a standard to watch closely, as it enables Java programs to connect to ODBC databases directly, without involving the web server.

Beyond publishing customer-related data, another special use of your intranet is to publish *sales leads.* You can even get fancy here and automatically distribute sales leads to individual reps. Say you do a direct-mail, radio, or TV promotion, and you plan to allocate the resulting sales leads to reps according to geographical region. You can create a little database application with a data entry field for sales leads and then create a table in the database that relates zip codes to individual sales reps.

Now, when a rep logs into your intranet and clicks over to the Sales Leads page, a CGI or Java program can be triggered to look up all the sales leads in the database with zip codes assigned to that rep, and then present them in a new web page. This near-real-time system can provide sales reps with up-to-date lead information whenever they want it.

You can take the concept a step further and allow the sales rep to click over to a separate page to report the status of each lead: *promising, doubtful,* or *told me what I could do with my chainsaw.* Another CGI script can then update the status code in the primary database, so that the next time the rep visits the sales leads page, the status code appears, and the rep doesn't accidentally call the same prospective customer twice.

General Sales Support

You can use your intranet in other ways than to provide product and customer information. Here are a few examples:

- **Post a Frequently Asked Questions (FAQ) document for rookie sales reps.** The FAQ can provide details on everyday procedures, from how to book an order to how to requisition literature.

- **With a public Internet link, you can create a special online newsletter for key suppliers and contractors.** For example, you can use such a newsletter to communicate changes to terms and conditions.

- **Publish sample conversation scripts for telemarketers to use.** For example, "Hello, I'm calling today to inform you of a special promotion for Binford chainsaws. You say you live in an apartment? Well, have you considered remodeling?"

- **Design a web application for on-the-spot quote generation.** For example, you can use web page forms and some Java or other programming to retrieve the price data and even check inventory levels.

- **Design a web application for querying an order-processing program to discover a particular order's status.** Customers generally call their sales rep when an order is late.

- **Publish sample documents or document excerpts for sales staff to include in proposals, quotations, and estimates.** Always have your legal eagles review such standardized text before putting it out on your intranet, though.

- **Post sales quotas, targets, and forecasts.** You can publish these figures by region, office, product, or all three.

- **Provide sales staff with access to the employee directory discussed in Chapter 4, so that sales reps can easily find the right person to help out with unusual questions.** For example, "Is this Carina Robin, design engineer for the Model 1100 chainsaw? Ms. Robin, I have a customer who does construction in Venice, Italy, and wants to know if that model works underwater."

Profits begin with sales. By focusing on intranet publishing only as a way to reduce paper-related costs, you may miss out on opportunities to make your sales team more effective in the field. Giving salespeople more (and more productive) *face time* with customers may just generate enough revenue to pay for that $50,000 high speed web server you have your eye on — or at least to bump up those expense accounts a bit for your hard-charging road warriors.

Chapter 7
Technical Support: Making Your Technology Work Better

In This Chapter
▶ Discovering what an effective Help Desk can do for your organization
▶ Learning five intranet applications for the Help Desk
▶ Six intranet applications for technical support users
▶ Using the intranet to support the intranet

A *Help Desk* is a group of analysts (also called technicians) usually within a business's Information Services (IS) department, that fields questions and problems from computer users throughout the organization.

For as long as I've been teaching Help Desk management seminars — since (gasp!) 1988 — companies have given short shrift to technical support organizations, expecting them to do their very challenging jobs with far too few people and minuscule budgets. The reasons for this are many: Managers believe that users read manuals, they don't know how trouble-prone or difficult their information systems are to use (partly because they may not use them personally), and they don't have a convenient way to measure productivity loss due to user downtime.

That's a cryin' shame, because the Help Desk can make the difference between productive, efficient technology that people actually enjoy using, and annoying, error-prone technology that users hate and only use because their jobs demand it. True, the Help Desk doesn't actually *design* information systems, but it collects information about how those systems work. Help Desk data is incredibly valuable if you're interested in making systems better through design, configuration, documentation, and training. In fact, the data that Help Desks collect is (or should be) far more valuable than the day-to-day user support responsibilities that they provide, important though the routine responsibilities are.

As organizations from Federal Express to the Federal Trade Commission have discovered, intranet publishing can help the Help Desk analysts do their jobs better within the tight budgets most companies impose.

No amount of cool technology can make a Help Desk successful if its responses to users, who need personal attention, aren't timely and accurate.

In this chapter, I discuss two kinds of intranet Help Desk applications: those for internal use within the tech support group, and those for use by Help Desk *customers* — your organization's computer users.

Systems for Internal Help Desk Use

If your first intranet publishing system addresses technical support, you may want to cast it as a Help Desk-only system, that is, one users can't access. Here's why:

- A Help Desk-only intranet solution is smaller in scale than one intended for general user access, so it's easier to manage, and a friendlier place to make mistakes as you get happy with the technology.
- The support analysts who use the system are technically savvy, and can concisely describe or document system problems (or maybe help you fix them).
- Providing information first to those whose jobs require them to be experts with that information just makes sense.
- If Help Desk analysts currently use slow and tedious systems (such as PWPMs — Poorly Written Paper Manuals) for information retrieval, a Help Desk intranet can increase productivity.

Internet access

The current trend is for Help Desks to have Internet access even if no one else in the organization does, for the excellent reason that a lot of vendor technical support information is available quickly, or even exclusively, on the Internet. Flat out, the Information Systems industry *expects* IS professionals to have Internet access. For example, Netscape offers extensive technical information, including a keyword search engine on its Web site (see Figure 7-1).

If your tech support group has Internet access, remember to register unique domain names and IP addresses for your intranet servers to avoid messy conflicts. In Chapter 9, I offer some details, if you need them. Also, look through Chapter 15 and consider whether you need additional security to protect your intranet from evil outside influences. Finally, check out *Building an Intranet For Dummies*, by John Fronckowiak (1997 IDG Books Worldwide, Inc.) for coverage of some of the basic security and intranet networking issues.

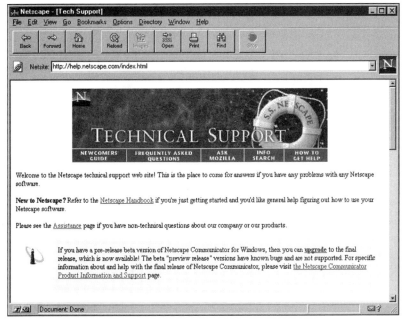

Figure 7-1: Your company's tech support staff needs access to Internet resources, such as this extensive technical information site from Netscape.

Inventory and configuration data

Here's an excerpt from a tech support conversation that happens 2,120 times every day:

> User: "I'm having trouble accessing the Human Resources intranet system."
>
> Support Analyst: "Okay, let's start with some information. What kind of computer are you using?"
>
> User: "Beige. Really more of an off-white."
>
> Support Analyst: "No, I mean is it a PC or a UNIX box?"

I'm exaggerating for effect — the point is that users may not know much about the computers on their desks. And yet, a support analyst may need quite a few details about the computer to troubleshoot a problem. A Help Desk can overcome the problem of a user's lack of familiarity with his or her computer equipment by maintaining a record of *inventory* and *configuration data* for each user. Inventory refers to the particular hardware and software products the user has, and configuration refers to how those products are set up. Such records may exist in a database that the support analyst can consult via the Help Desk intranet, or simply a few HTML pages that contain the data the analyst is most likely to need for quick access.

Any network larger than a few dozen users can benefit from inventory programs that speed the process of assembling inventory and configuration data by automatically collecting it. One good example is NetCensus from Tally Systems, which creates a dBase-compatible database. (dBase is a popular database program from Borland.) To make the database available on the intranet, you need to use a product such as Borland Visual dBase Professional. Other products, such as Microsoft Systems Management Server, can help you build an inventory and configuration database, too.

User information

Before the Help Desk analyst can start to solve the caller's problem, the analyst needs various pieces of contact information from the caller:

- Name
- Phone number
- Fax number
- E-mail address
- Snail mail address (in larger organizations)
- Department
- Job title

Asking users on the phone for all of these dirty details about themselves is a major time drain, and it tends to frustrate the user who has a pressing problem. Putting a user directory on a Help Desk intranet makes life (and creating problem reports) much simpler. For example, the analyst only has to ask the user's name, and can then look it up on the user directory. If the name appears there, and is unique, then the analyst doesn't have to enter all the other user contact information into the problem management system (which stores and tracks problem reports). If the analyst has to call, e-mail, or fax the user, all the information is in the directory. Furthermore, if you have an inventory and configuration database set up, as I describe in the previous section, the Help Desk is already halfway to solving the problem just by getting the troubled user's name!

Here's a good example of how multiple intranet publishing projects can work together for the greater good: If a user directory already exists, for example, as part of a Human Resources intranet, the Help Desk web designer can simply place a hyperlink (web page links to other web pages) to that directory on the Help Desk's intranet home page.

Network maps

Often, a big part of helping users with network problems is simply figuring out where the heck they are on the network. Putting *network maps* on the Help Desk intranet can be a big help for analysts who are trying to troubleshoot communications and connectivity problems. Network maps can include the following components:

- **Servers:** computers that share data, programs, printers, and so on with network users
- **Hubs and switches:** centrally located network devices that link computers to each other in a star wiring configuration
- **Routers:** devices that not only pass network traffic from one computer to another, but route it the fastest way when more than one path exists
- **Gateways:** devices that connect different types of networks (such as a Novell network and the public Internet)
- **User workstation computers:** (if there aren't too many of them!)

One of the more popular tools for network diagramming is Visio Professional, from Visio Corporation. Version 4.5 of this product includes an *Internet Assistant* that enables you to save network drawings in HTML format for inclusion on an intranet web page — perfect for your intranet map. You can also create hyperlinks associated with specific shapes on the map, so, for example, you can start with a high-level map and drill down to a more detailed map of a particular subnetwork. If you have an earlier version of Visio Professional, you can retrofit the Internet Assistant add-on by downloading it free from `www.visio.com`.

Knowledge bases

For years, Help Desks have used *knowledge bases* to provide better technical support. A knowledge base is simply a collection of troubleshooting information that analysts can use to zero in on solutions faster. Simple knowledge bases consist of technical notes that an analyst can search by keyword, with a query such as `Navigator AND HTML AND tables`. More advanced knowledge bases may take a question-and-answer approach, in which the system narrows down the probable solution by asking the analyst successive questions about the problem's symptoms.

Knowledge bases come in two flavors:

- **Canned knowledge base:** One you buy from a vendor who has already assembled information about troubleshooting a popular application (such as WordPerfect). ServiceWare, for example, offers several canned knowledge bases.

Part II: Intranet Publishing Applications

- **Custom knowledge base:** One you create, or that a problem management system creates for you, based on the particular problems and solutions that occur in your own organization.

The type of knowledge base your company's Help Desk needs depends on how much of the user software is popular commercial applications, and how much is custom in-house software.

If you go the custom route, most Help Desk managers prefer knowledge bases that they don't have to manually maintain. Several problem management programs create and update the knowledge base automatically as analysts enter new problems and solutions into the tracking system.

The trick to adding a knowledge base to your intranet quickly and easily is to use knowledge-base software that speaks HTML (HyperText Markup Language — the language of your intranet). For example, Taco Bell uses Web Advisor and Knowledge Builder from ServiceSoft to publish knowledge bases on their intranet. Knowledge Builder is able to work with the problem management tool Taco Bell already had in place (SupportMagic from Magic Solutions) to create an intranettable knowledge base. As a result, employees didn't have to create a new knowledge base from scratch.

Other problem management systems now supporting knowledge-base publishing via HTML include:

- Astea PowerHelp
- Frontier Technologies Intranet Genie
- Magic Solutions WebMagic
- Molloy Group Top of Mind and Internet Knowledge Kiosk
- Quintus ImpaQ
- Remedy Action Request System
- ScopusWebTEAM
- Software Artistry SA-Expert Web
- Vantive VanWeb and Vantive Enterprise

Additionally, companies who have built their own custom Help Desk systems using Lotus Notes can make those systems available on an intranet using InterNotes Publisher.

Check out the list of problem management software at www.servicenews.com/reviews/prrvtoc.htm

Intranet Publishing for Call Support

Phone calls to the Help Desk are expensive. One respected consulting firm estimates that computer phone support costs an average of *$2743 per user per year!* That figure doesn't even include the value of employee time for users waiting around on hold to speak to an analyst, or the toll that the John Tesh hold music takes on users' mental health.

What about using the intranet to provide technical help to users in the field? As new as the idea is, 25 percent of all corporate Help Desks are already taking advantage of web technologies to provide support directly to the users.

Initially, people who are already familiar with computers are generally the only ones who try, and use, self-serve intranet help. Novice computer users who are having a tough time getting the hang of the mouse aren't likely to muster up the courage or energy to try to find the tech support intranet. My point is that such a system doesn't instantly remove the need for phone lines.

Of course, intranet-based technical support doesn't need to replace the phones to have merit. Intranet-based tech support can, in fact, *supplement* phone support nicely. If the intranet can replace even 10 percent of the tech support phone call volume (remember, those calls cost almost $3000 per user per year), it can pay for itself in a matter of weeks. And as users become more comfortable over time with Internet browsing, for example, from their experience with home computers, they become more comfortable with intranet-based help.

For a tech support intranet to catch on, and attract newbies as well as seasoned veterans, it has to be super-easy to use and super-fast. Ease of use is important because beginning users tend to have many technical questions, and make many unintentional mistakes. Speed is critical when you consider the context: People use the tech support system when they've hit a snag on their computers and they're *dead in the water*. Often, a deadline's looming and they're already in a big hurry to get the problem fixed.

See Chapters 11 and 12 for ease-of-use design issues, and Chapter 14 for speed discussions.

Software distribution

If you're a computer user and you've ever called a tech support line, either within your own company or outside of it, chances are that you've heard these words: "We've fixed that problem with the latest software update."

Here's soapbox speech #94: Application software has become so complex and so feature-laden (or feature-troubled, depending on your perspective) that no software vendor can possibly test it completely before it ships out the door. As a result, the buying public is a software vendor's beta test site. Vendors *patch,* and fix, and tweak their software many times after a supposedly reliable, commercial version ships. *Bugs*, and the updates to fix them, have become a fact of life in modern computing, and there's no sign that things will change anytime soon — despite vendors' laudable *zero administration* initiatives, which lure you into the false sense that the software can basically run itself.

A *patch* is a file that modifies a program to correct a bug, just like a rubber bicycle tire patch fixes a tire bug (blowout). Patches may actually change a program file that already exists on the user's computer, or just replace one of the component files that contains the buggy (faulty) code.

Your Help Desk may already be in charge of distributing application software updates, or another group may handle it. Regardless, the intranet is a great vehicle to publish software updates that users must install on their own workstations (or, even better, that install by themselves quickly and automatically when the user accesses them). Just be sure you adhere to any distribution or licensing restrictions the vendor imposes.

You can reduce network traffic and transmission time by compressing the patch files you need to send. For example, PKZIP is a popular file compression program for PC users. The trouble is that you're never completely sure whether the file recipient has the necessary decompression software, and even if he or she does have it, an extra step is involved to actually use the software. You may want to use compression programs that can create *self-extracting archives* that automatically decompress when the user double-clicks them. For example, the shareware WinZip compression utility (included on this book's CD-ROM) enables you to choose Actions⇨Make.EXE File to create a self-extracting archive.

The two methods of distributing software over an intranet are *pull* and *push*.

Pull systems

In a *pull* software distribution setup, the user has to initiate the request, for example, by clicking on a link that points to the specific file the user needs. Pull systems are a little bit like those postcards you get in magazines — you have to choose to mail them in to receive the information.

Pull systems are super-easy to create with intranet tools. The most common way to set up a download site with an intranet is to use the File Transfer Protocol (FTP) service (see sidebar, "What is FTP?"). If you want to get fancier, you can use specialized software tools to handle more complex

> ## What is FTP?
>
> FTP (File Transfer Protocol) has been on the scene for quite a while—thirty years and counting so far — way before the Internet began hosting e-mail services. FTP is a TCP/IP (Transmission Control Protocol/Internet Protocol) application, just like the HyperText Transfer Protocol (HTTP) that dishes up web pages. Originally a Unix text-based program, FTP enables network users to both download files (to the user from the server) and upload them (from the user to the server), even between different kinds of computers and over dial-up connections. The files can be anything — text, programs, graphics, video clips, and so on.
>
> Web designers still use FTP to copy files from a remote location onto an intranet server. If you're using an Internet Service Provider (ISP) to host your intranet or your public Internet site, you normally use FTP to load your web site files onto the ISP's server.
>
> In the early days of Internet technology, you had to have a special FTP program to upload or download files. Today, nearly all web servers and web browsers include built-in support for FTP, so that you don't have to run a separate program.

situations, such as automatically performing special setup steps on the user's workstation, if such steps are required to use the software files you're making available. An example is Net-Install from 20/20 Software (see Appendix B for contact information).

The details vary according to which web server software you use, but here are the basic steps to create an FTP software download site on your Help Desk intranet:

1. **Make sure that your web server and browsers provide the FTP service — most of them do.**
2. **Create an FTP directory on your web server.**

   Your web server software may have already done this for you when you installed it.
3. **Set the FTP service to list files using the Unix directory format.**

   This step ensures maximum browser compatibility. Some browsers don't work with the MS-DOS directory format, which is just a different way to display directory structures.
4. **Decide what security model you want to use.**

   If you run your intranet on a LAN, such as Microsoft Windows NT Server or Novell IntraNetware, you can use existing user IDs and passwords to control access. However, you may find it easier to set up

Part II: Intranet Publishing Applications

your FTP directory for *anonymous login*. Anonymous login enables anyone to get to it. However, you can still control what users can do at the FTP site by setting security options for the single anonymous account. For more on anonymous login and LAN-based security, see Chapter 15.

5. **Set permissions for the FTP directory.**

    You normally want users to have *read-only* access to this directory, meaning that they can look at and open, but not change or save, the files. With read-only access, users can still open a file and save it as a different file on their own machine if they want to. If you want users to be able to copy files to the server, set up a separate upload directory for this purpose.

6. **Copy the software that you want published into the FTP directory.**

    If you're lazy, all you need to do at this point is put a single link on the intranet web page that points to the FTP directory. Users can then see the files much as they'd see a directory on their local computer (see Figure 7-2). I suggest that you *not* be lazy in this case (although I'm not against laziness in general), and continue with Steps 7 and 8, so you can give users more information about the files.

7. **Create a separate intranet web page for downloading, and place links onto the page that point to the files in the FTP directory.**

    If you format the link using the `ftp://` prefix instead of the `http://` prefix, for example, `ftp://acme.pub.com/userfiles/file1.exe`, you're telling the user's browser to get the file using FTP when the user clicks the link. It's automatic! Neato!

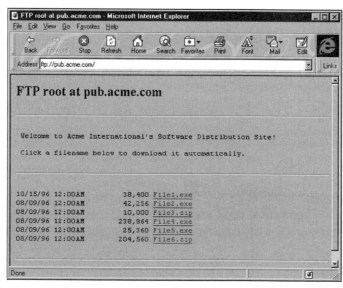

Figure 7-2: You can point users to an FTP site with a single link from an intranet web page. However, while this approach is simple to administer, it doesn't let you provide file details.

Chapter 7: Technical Support: Making Your Technology Work Better

8. **Include any necessary instructions or descriptive information about the files on the download page.**

   I like to include detailed file descriptions, sizes, and types there, plus any decompression instructions that users may need. You may also want to include an FTP hyperlink to the necessary decompression software. The goal is to include enough information to make sure that users get the file they need, and can use it once they've got it. You do have to keep the links maintained manually when you add or delete files. For an example, see Figure 7-3.

Security consultants may advise against using FTP on servers that connect to the Internet, partly because (unlike standard HTTP) FTP supports file transfer both *from* and *to* a server. The fear is that mischievous individuals may upload nasty files to your FTP site. Most FTP server software lets you designate whether to permit uploading, as well as downloading, in any particular directory (see Step 5 in the preceding list). If you *do* wish to create an FTP upload directory, separate it from other, read-only directories so that you know to check the upload directory for dangerous files before you use them.

You're best off separating files that you intend users to download, instead of creating one large archive (for example, with WinZip). The reason is that FTP has no way to pick up where it left off if a communication error occurs.

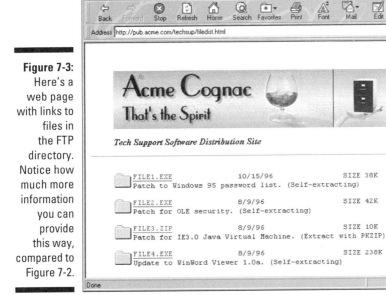

Figure 7-3: Here's a web page with links to files in the FTP directory. Notice how much more information you can provide this way, compared to Figure 7-2.

A user who hits a glitch 90 percent of the way into a large file download has to start all over again. Admittedly, communication errors are rarer on intranets than on dial-up Internet links, but they can still happen.

Push systems

Push software distribution systems enable the Help Desk analyst to send a software update or patch over the network to the user who needs it. All the user has to do is log on to the network, or check e-mail, and the patch or software is automatically sent out to the user. Push systems work like junk mail that you get because someone thinks you should have it (only in this case, the information isn't junk).

The simplest example of a push system is the e-mail *attachment*. By attaching a patch or update to an e-mail message, the Help Desk analyst sends it over the network along with a text message (which may say nothing more than Here's your patch!). If your intranet has e-mail capabilities, attaching files is usually no big deal. However, you should test the system to make sure that it works.

Different e-mail systems treat attachments differently. Ideally, you want an easy, automatic procedure in which a user can just open the message and the e-mail software saves the attachment to the user's hard disk. Slightly less convenient e-mail systems have a Save Attachment command that the user can choose when viewing the message.

Another example of a push system is the user's network logon script. The logon script is just a little program that specifies what happens when a user logs on to the network. Administrators can add lines to the logon script to perform a file download. Using this method depends on your already having a network that users log on to to access your intranet.

When you use any sort of push system for software distribution, you run the risk of forcing the user to receive a file at a time that may not be convenient. Very large files, for example, a major program update, can take a while to transmit, even over a fast network. A user who's checking e-mail for an urgent message from the boss may not appreciate having to wait for five minutes while a large attachment moseys down the wire. As a result, many businesses only use push systems for smaller files, and distribute larger files using pull systems.

Even if you think you may implement a *push* system for software distribution, setting up an FTP service is so easy that it makes sense to start with a *pull* system so that your software is available to users right away. Meanwhile, you can evaluate and test the different push systems on the market.

A classic example of how *not* to use a push system is the way America Online (and, sometimes, Microsoft Network and CompuServe) uses push technology to distribute software updates to its customers. A recent upgrade to the AOL Internet browser took about an hour, and was forced upon customers when they logged off the service. As with many push systems, the user couldn't cancel the file transfer. You don't want to pull boneheaded stunts like this if you want your users to love your intranet.

Publishing the troubleshooting hit parade

You can categorize the calls most Help Desks receive into *questions*, for example, "How do I do such-and-such?", and *problems*, for example, "Such-and-such isn't working." Some overlap exists, but separating your inquiries in this way can be useful. You can use your lists of questions and problems to prepare a *hit parade* list of *FAQs* (Frequently Asked Questions) and *FEPs* (Frequently Encountered Problems) to publish on your Help Desk intranet.

Frequently Asked Questions

Frequently Asked Question (FAQ) documents are all over the Internet, and for good reason. A well-designed FAQ is a quick way to find answers to common questions. On a web page, a FAQ is nothing more than a series of questions and answers in text format. Usually, the questions are in boldface, and each question-and-answer group is set apart slightly from the next, as shown in Figure 7-4.

You may want to separate FAQ documents by product or system, for example, "10 FAQs about Netscape Navigator" or "15 FAQs about the Help Desk Intranet." If you separate your FAQs like this, you may want to create a FAQ home page. Doing so enables users to have a consistent starting place for their computer woes, and link to the appropriate FAQ from there.

Your intranet-based FAQ can serve up detailed descriptions of the same kinds of solutions that your phone analysts provide in a concise form. For example, "Here's how to do it, and if you need more information, check out the Problem 34 page" — with a convenient link to that web page.

You can see a good public example of a Web-based FAQ by visiting Florida's Barry University at www.barry.edu/acchome/howdoi.html

Frequently Encountered Problems, or FEPs, put a slight spin on the FAQ concept by focusing on cases where something doesn't work. You can make the format for your FEP identical to your FAQ format, for consistency, and you can break FEPs out by product or system just like FAQs.

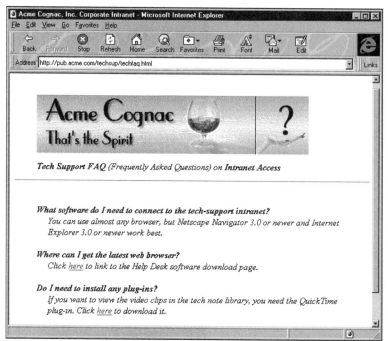

Figure 7-4: A typical FAQ page uses bold or italics for the questions, and normal text for the answers. Keep your questions and answers fairly brief so that users can quickly find the information they need.

The whole goal of publishing FAQs and FEPs over the intranet is to reduce the frequency of routine, repetitive calls to analysts who've answered the same question thirty times before. Users should only have to make a phone call to the Help Desk when a problem is so unusual that the intranet doesn't address it. The greater the uniqueness and complexity of the typical Help Desk phone call, the better the job the Help Desk intranet is doing. (I sometimes have a hard time explaining that to Help Desk people, who would just as soon have the calls get easier instead of harder. . . .)

Your Help Desk intranet is sure to be much more successful if user questions and problems that aren't yet in the FAQ or FEP pages find their way in. Get scientific with it: Use the reporting features in your Help Desk problem management system to report common questions and problems sorted by frequency of occurrence, automatically create FAQ- and FEP-list web pages from the reports, and then revise these intranet pages every month.

Searchable documentation

A lot of computer users out there refer to a PWPM (Poorly Written Paper Manual) only as a last resort. I know that when I install new software, I like to figure out as much of it as possible just by working with it, and checking the online help occasionally. I have to shake my head a little bit at IS departments that issue gigantic loose-leaf binders to every user of the organization's information systems and say, "Read this."

Rule number one of information system support: *Users don't read.*

Not that they don't *want* to; it's more that they don't have time to read a huge manual. They're not being paid to read computer documentation, and if they do read it, their bosses are likely to come down on them for sticking their noses into books instead of "doing their jobs." I've written a lot of system documentation in my salad days as a programmer and technical trainer, and although I'm darn sure that I don't intend to refund the dollars I earned doing so, I don't think the clients got a very good return on their investment. Consider putting documentation on the Help Desk intranet and making it *search-able* by key word. That way, your users can enter a confusing term, or the name of a device that's misbehaving, and retrieve a set of links to intranet web pages with possible help. You can make your intranet web searchable by installing one of the several web search engines available. You may not need a separate search engine if your document publishing software provides its own, as, for example, Folio Views does. Searchability makes it much easier for your users to find the specific info they need.

Examples of the type of documentation you may want to publish on your intranet include:

- New software version release notes
- Product hardware requirements
- A glossary of technical terms. (You may want to use the same web page design techniques I cover with regard to an employee directory in Chapter 4.)
- Three good reasons not to throw your computer out the window even though it constantly locks up: 1) Your paycheck will be docked for the damage; 2) The replacement computer will be just as bad; and 3) Pedestrians
- Complete product documentation for commercial software and hardware
- Complete product documentation for custom software

The following two sections take a closer look at the last two items. Up to now, creating online product documentation in traditional client/server networks has not necessarily been an easy task. The intranet changes all that with its built-in hyperlinks, universal browsers, and specialized Help file utilities. In your Help files, you can embed links that point to your FAQs and FEPs, individual tech notes stored elsewhere on your intranet, or your intranet-based Help Desk problem report form.

Take advantage of your intranet's hyperlink capability everywhere you can! Hyperlinks make your technical support systems much more helpful to your users.

Publishing documentation for hardware and commercial software

For hardware and commercial software, you already have some sort of documentation that the vendor provides along with the product. If the documentation is printed, you can either scan it into a computer using Optical Character Recognition (OCR) software, or petition the vendor for an electronic file and the right to publish it on your intranet. Which method you choose depends on how sticky the vendor is about giving you limited internal publishing rights.

More and more, product documentation comes in the form of Help files instead of more expensive printed manuals. In the PC world, the standard is Microsoft's WinHelp format, which converts Rich Text Format (RTF) word processing documents into a Help file. However, two new standards are emerging that are of particular interest for intranet publishers: Microsoft's *HTML Help* and Netscape's *NetHelp*.

Both HTML Help and NetHelp offer the big advantage of potential cross-platform compatibility, as compared to WinHelp, which is a Windows-only tool. Both systems also take advantage of features that WinHelp doesn't have, such as true-color graphics and frames for navigation. Both HTML Help and NetHelp also enable you to place links on help screens — for example, to FAQ and FEP pages.

HTML Help uses HTML together with special *ActiveX controls* (Microsoft's mini programs, or *applets,* which run on your browser) to provide HTML compatibility while maintaining most of the features of the current WinHelp engine (contents, index, full-text search, and so on). HTML Help supports pop-up windows, and is a compressed format (making it quick to download from your intranet). At the time I write this, HTML Help is available for Windows 95 and Windows NT platforms only.

NetHelp is tailored specifically for users running one of the Netscape Navigator browsers and focuses on cross-platform compatibility. NetHelp doesn't yet support pop-up windows and is an uncompressed format. However, it does support a wide variety of workstation platforms, including OS/2, Unix, and Apple Macintosh. In addition, a variety of third-party plug-ins for NetHelp add capabilities to the basic product.

If the commercial software you use today doesn't offer an HTML-based help file, you may be able to convert the help file it does offer into an HTML format. Help-2-HTML from Blue Sky Software automates the process if you're starting with a WinHelp format file, even if you don't have the original RTF (Rich Text Format) documents. The product enables you to choose between the Microsoft and Netscape formats, or plain old HTML.

To get the Microsoft HTML Help beta, go to `www.microsoft.com/workshop/author/htmlhelp/htmlhelp.exe`

The Netscape NetHelp site is at `//home.netscape.com/eng/help`

Figures 7-5 and 7-6 show some of the differences between a standard WinHelp file and an HTML Help file. Notice in Figure 7-6 that the Contents and Index tabs are to the left. A special ActiveX control permits pop-up windows (lower right), which HTML doesn't support on its own.

Publishing documentation for custom software

Your organization owns the documentation for any software you create in-house, and that documentation is probably already in electronic form. You've passed two hurdles already! The only challenge to putting it on your intranet is converting it to a web-friendly format. Chapter 10 deals with document conversion in depth, but for now, take my word for it — you can turn almost any electronic document into an HTML document with very little trouble.

As your company develops new custom software for in-house use, you may want to follow the Netscape and Microsoft approach, and create help files in HTML from the very beginning. Whether you use HTML Help, NetHelp, or plain vanilla HTML depends on whether you run mainly Windows workstations or a wider variety, and on how many special help system features you need.

Figure 7-5: A typical WinHelp file running on Windows 95. Notice that you can't see the topic tree and a specific help screen at the same time.

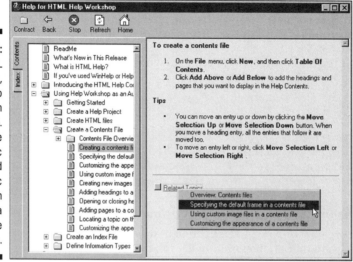

Figure 7-6:
An HTML Help file, also running on Windows 95. You can see the topic tree and a specific help screen within a single window.

You can't use a regular HTML editor, such as PageMill or FrontPage, to create files in the specific HTML Help or NetHelp formats. Instead, use a tool such as Microsoft HTML Help Workshop or Blue Sky Software RoboHelp 4.

User knowledge bases

Earlier in this chapter, I discuss *knowledge bases*, sort of like indexes of a department's expertise, that contain troubleshooting information for use by Help Desk analysts. If the user interface is friendly enough — that is, *really, really friendly* — the Help Desk can publish knowledge base information outside the Help Desk. Doing so enables the fairly advanced users in your organization to do their own troubleshooting, if they want (or need) to. Whether you call user knowledge bases *call support* or *call avoidance* applications, they can help reduce call volume and ease the lives of users whose technical problems don't necessarily coincide with the Help Desk's 9-to-5 schedule. (I always seem to run into software snags after the vendor's working hours. On the plus side, I now know lots of friendly security guards on a first-name basis.)

Problem reports and HTML forms

After you get employees used to tapping into the tech support intranet for FAQs and quick help notes, you can consider broadening the intranet system to enable users to submit problem reports as well as read information. Many companies (including CNN Interactive in Atlanta) use intranets to provide an avenue for users to report problems. This approach tends to work better in organizations with reasonably computer literate users, who can provide enough detail in the initial problem report for the analyst to begin solving the problem without calling back for more information.

The typical way to ask for problem reports is with an *HTML form* on your FAQ and FEP pages. An HTML form is simply an area on a web page with edit boxes where your users can enter text, and a Submit button to send the report to the appropriate people (in this case, the Help Desk). Chapter 5 discusses HTML forms in more detail.

If you already use a problem management tool, ask the vendor whether it offers (or is developing) HTML form templates and supporting programs to integrate intranet-based problem reporting with the existing tracking system. If you don't use a problem management program, you can either buy one that runs on your intranet, or roll your own from scratch.

Typical fields that you may want to set up on an HTML problem report form include:

- Date and time of report
- Date and time of problem occurrence
- User name, phone, and e-mail
- Perceived urgency
- Program involved (including version number)
- Hardware involved (Pentium PC, UNIX workstation, Power Macintosh)
- What, if anything, the user changed before the problem cropped up ("Who, me? I didn't change anything! Unless you mean that memory upgrade I performed last night with a crowbar and hammer." I must admit that I've been guilty of this sort of thing myself.)
- Description of the problem

Technical videos

Now things get a bit fancier! I throw this topic in to get you thinking about future applications, even if video publishing isn't the first application you choose for your intranet (it probably shouldn't be).

Certain technical support topics lend themselves nicely to visual demonstrations. If you want to show computer users how to install an internal modem, change a laser printer toner cartridge, or refill the break room coffee machine, you can do so with an intranet — if your network is fast enough to play the videos back smoothly. The best way to find out is by experimenting. Every network has different performance characteristics, and the amount of network speed you need depends on the quality of the video you want to achieve (desired video window size, frames per second, number of colors, and so on).

The general procedure for creating and publishing technical videos on the intranet is as follows:

1. *Capture* **(as it's called in computer video parlance) the videotape to a digital format using a computer equipped with a video capture board.** Another possibility is to record live video directly into a computer using one of the new digital video cameras.

2. **Edit the video clip with a tool such as Adobe Premiere,** which enables you to do everything from simple cutting and pasting, to resizing the playback window, adding titles and special effects, and inserting subliminal messages such as "Use the intranet . . . Uuuuuse the intranet."

3. **Compress the video clip so that it's smaller and downloads more easily across the network.**

   Again, a tool such as Premiere can perform several different kinds of compression.

4. **Save the edited and compressed video in a format that's compatible with the computer video player you plan to use on the intranet.**

   Common formats are AVI, QuickTime, and MPEG. AVI is convenient if most users run Microsoft Windows; QuickTime may work better if you have some Macs in the mix; and you may favor MPEG if your users' computers feature MPEG acceleration hardware (many newer ones do).

5. **Copy the digital video to your web server and include the necessary links on the web page for users to connect to view the video.**

6. **Install any required helper program or plug-ins on the client workstations.**

   Most browsers don't support digital video as a standard file type, and require a plug-in.

Although this six-point list may make the process sound simple, you probably want to get some expert assistance from someone who's done digital video work before. The software and hardware tools are complex, and have a fairly steep learning curve, and digital video is still a young (and buggy) technology. If you are really turned on by this stuff and want to learn it yourself, *Multimedia & CD-ROMs For Dummies*, 3rd Edition by Andy Rathbone (1995 IDG Books Worldwide, Inc.) is a good place to start. The end result can be a technical support tool matched in its effectiveness only by personal, one-on-one demonstrations.

Check out intranet video products from Progressive Networks and VXtreme (see Appendix B for contact information). The VXtreme Web Theater has some especially cool features, such as enabling users to jump directly to specific parts of a digitized video via a table of contents.

The Tool that Explains Its Own Use

Ever hear of *Cobbler's Children syndrome*? The term refers to an old tale about a village cobbler who was so busy making shoes for all the villagers that his own children wandered around barefoot. My wife Emily is familiar with the concept — the new PC in her office *still* isn't connected to our company LAN. My point is that intranetters deploying Help Desk applications should include a facility for explaining how to use the intranet itself.

At first, you may think, "Wait a minute, if a user can get to the intranet-based help system, he or she already *knows* how to use the intranet." I thought the same thing until I really examined the issue. A user that can connect to your intranet home page may still need to know about the following procedures:

- How to configure the browser for encrypted connections using *Secure Sockets Layer* (a communications security protocol — see Chapter 15)
- How the navigation buttons on the page itself differ from those on the browser toolbar (see Chapter 11)
- How to save bookmarks to frequently accessed intranet pages
- How to configure the browser to either run, or not run, Java and ActiveX programs
- How to change the automatic home page that opens when you start the browser
- How to change the browser font size settings for easier reading
- How to download and install *helper programs,* and plug-ins
- How to access the Dilbert Internet site — useful if your organization uses a *multinet* with both internal and external (Internet) connectivity
- How to improve workstation performance, for example, with *caching* (see Chapter 14)
- How to use an HTML form (see Chapter 5)
- How to set up a dial-up link to the intranet from a notebook computer
- How to apply for a network account (if the user presently connects to the intranet with an *anonymous login*; see Chapter 15)
- How to apply for different security privileges

Okay, the browser's own online help may address some of the obvious issues. However, some browsers, such as Netscape Navigator, rely heavily on help documents stored on the Internet. If your intranet doesn't connect to the Internet, providing help via your intranet makes sense. You can also tailor your intranet-based help system to only include information about your users' particular common questions and problems, so the online help is more relevant to your organization.

Further, intranet users who have an interest in creating their own publishing system may be curious to know how you created yours: what software and hardware you use, how long it took to set up, what the ongoing maintenance requirements are, and so on. Users may want Help files on how to help build the intranet!

For more info on Help Desks, check out the Help Desk Institute Web site at www.helpdeskinst.com

Chapter 8
Intranet-Based Training (IBT)

In This Chapter
- Comparing Intranet-Based Training (IBT) with other methods of training
- Deciding what kinds of courses to publish on your intranet
- Training that IBT is *not* well suited to deliver
- Delivering training with IBT
- Designing your IBT program
- Succeeding with IBT

*I*ntranet-Based Training, or IBT, is a great intranet publishing application that few intranetters have explored yet. This chapter presents some ideas for course content, how to deliver that content over your intranet, and a few guidelines for effective IBT design.

Quick — what's your company's most important asset? (Pick one.)

- ✔ Knowledgeable, competent employees
- ✔ Savvy, far-sighted management
- ✔ Loyal, prompt-paying customers
- ✔ Cash in the bank
- ✔ A secret product formula (Coke, WD-40, that miracle sticky-note adhesive)
- ✔ The ability of employees to learn new things

Many folks don't immediately pick the last option — wouldn't you rather have employees who *already* know a lot about their jobs, versus employees who know how to learn? — but the last answer is precisely the one some of today's top management thinkers would give. And they have a strong case:

- ✔ In a dynamic, global marketplace, no matter what a company's employees know today, they have to know something different tomorrow in order to help the company stay competitive.

- ✓ Every organization has turnover. Helping new or reassigned employees learn what they need to know in their new positions makes them productive sooner.

- ✓ Many organizations have fewer employees today than they did ten years ago, and the ones who remain may have to master several skills and play multiple roles.

You can help employees learn faster, better, and at less cost by publishing educational courses on your intranet.

Training Topics

Some subjects are great for IBT, some are better left to other methods. The success of your IBT project is directly related to how well you match the subject matter to the delivery vehicle. Teaching someone skeet-shooting is much more successful when you deliver hands-on instruction as opposed to merely giving the student a book and a shotgun (it's also less dangerous). By the same token, it makes sense to choose subjects that people can really pick up effectively over the intranet.

Good prospects

A sage once remarked that the best tools are those that teach their own use, and the intranet can be very useful for teaching people how to use information systems — especially because the topics change so rapidly.

The demand for computer education is growing as a result of the following factors:

- ✓ Computer products continue to get more complex and require more knowledge from the user and, thus, continued training.

- ✓ New technologies (intranets, multimedia, and so on) continue to pop up in the marketplace and, therefore, in the workplace. Each new technology that a company begins to use requires additional training.

- ✓ The *rate* of introduction of new computer products and upgrades to existing products is increasing, and your training methods need to be flexible and able to respond to the constant flow of new tools.

Two distinct markets for Information Technology (IT) education exist: *professionals* and *users*. Probably no field exists in which continuing education is more essential to the professional's career than in IT, where the emphasis is on supporting and troubleshooting IT products, as well as training the users. More and more, though, the burden of learning how to use computer products, especially operating systems and application programs, falls on the end user, where the emphasis is on learning features and functionality.

So, some of the computer-related courseware possibilities that may be appropriate for IBT include:

- **End-user training on operating systems.** For example, many organizations are migrating from Windows 3.x to Windows 95, and the users need to learn the new operating system quickly so they can get back to work fast.
- **End-user training on specific applications.** For example, you may want to offer training in the creation of PowerPoint presentations
- **End-user training on how to use the intranet.** Well, you *had* to figure that would be in here!
- **Technical computer training for support staff.** For example, new Information Systems (IS) staff may need training on how to install the Windows NT Workstation software from a LAN server.

Although in many ways it's a natural fit, Intranet-Based Training isn't just a way to deliver computer training. Other, non-computer education applications could include:

- **Product training for salespersons.** For example, you may need to educate your sales staff how the Binford 1000 radial saw differs from the Binford 2000 (and they are radically different, which is why you need to buy one right now for only $19.95!).
- **Procedural training for common office tasks.** For example, you may have new temporary help to process payroll, and you need a way to train them quickly without taking up the time of the other staff.
- **Shop-floor training in a manufacturing environment.** For example, some employees on the shop floor need to know how to reset a PC workstation controller in an automated plant.

Not-so-good prospects

What sorts of educational material are *not* appropriate for IBT? The following categories are usually better suited for other delivery methods:

- **Education that benefits heavily from videotaped scenarios or interactive role-playing.** For example, customer service telephone skills often require intensive role-playing practice.
- **Highly specialized education that only a few people in your organization need.** Examples include the skills required to configure a computer network management system or mailroom duties.

✓ **Education where trainees need hands-on experience.** For example, PC hardware technicians need to get in front of a "dumb box" and open it up, see what's inside, and know where all the little doo-dads are. An IBT document, even done in the best 3-D technology, still can't adequately show you how to find doo-dad number X-345-N-7 easily.

Using the above points as a thought-starter, see if you can think of four specific IBT applications that can help your organization meet some immediate training needs. You're allowed to scribble them in the margin (your grade school teacher will never know).

Delivery Techniques

You can deliver training over an intranet in several ways. You can publish (in ascending order of both complexity and usefulness) simple text, files designed for CD-ROM training, and files designed for intranet training.

Making text-based training materials available on your intranet

Making existing, text-based training materials available for downloading is easy and fast, but it doesn't create very compelling courseware — even if you take the time to convert the text into a web-viewable format, such as HyperText Markup Language (HTML) or Portable Document Format (PDF). Getting training materials up onto your intranet quickly won't do you much good if nobody uses them, and nobody will if they look like Figure 8-1.

Publishing computer-based training materials on your intranet

Your intranet can publish Computer-Based Training (CBT) products your organization may already have purchased, new CBT products you can buy from any of the dozens of vendors in the marketplace, or CBT that your organization has already developed in-house, for example, with tools such as the following:

✓ **Aimtech IconAuthor 7.0** ($1,295) is a venerable CBT development product. Its test creation features are useful for creating IBT but somewhat harder to use than similar features in ToolBook II Instructor. IconAuthor dominates the IBM OS/2 operating system courseware market.

✔ **Macromedia Authorware** ($5,000) is a good authoring tool for projects with heavy multimedia content, largely because of the bundling of Director, Sound Forge, and xRes with Authorware. Authorware uses a flowcharting metaphor to help you create your training materials. Authorware is not very well-suited to creating self-tests (such as multiple-choice questions that the student can answer on-line and that the program can "grade" automatically).

✔ **mFactory mTropolis** ($1,195) has a powerful language that allows you to create all kinds of cool stuff and is targeted at creating CD-ROM presentations. Think of it as Microsoft PowerPoint on steroids. It supports cross-platform authoring (for both Windows and Mac), and so is great for companies with art departments where Macs still reign supreme.

Take a look at Figure 8-2, a screen shot from a fairly typical CBT product, and note the heavy use of large, bandwidth-gobbling graphics.

The trouble with most CBT courseware designed for CD-ROM or hard drive playback is that it assumes a very high *bandwidth*, or data transfer rate. A PC can read files from a CD-ROM or hard drive much faster than it can pull files across a Local Area Network (LAN) from an intranet server. Therefore, most CBT courseware you can buy today isn't well suited to being run from an intranet — that's a nice way of saying it runs like a slug.

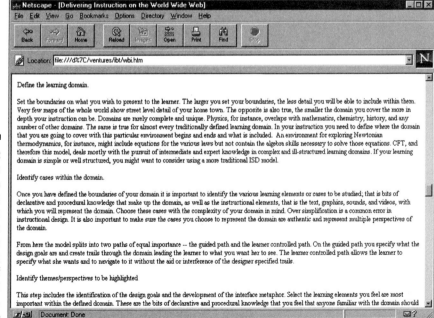

Figure 8-1: This figure illustrates how not to publish training on an intranet: long streams of uninterrupted text.

Part II: Intranet Publishing Applications

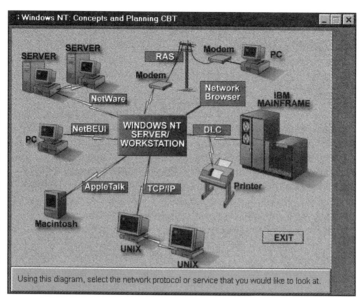

Figure 8-2: This CBT product's graphics load quickly from a hard drive or CD-ROM, but slowly over a network connection.

One way around the bandwidth problem is to have users download CBT files to their local hard drives before running them. However, these files can be quite large (many megabytes) and they can clog up user disks in a hurry. With this method, you also give up platform independence because your CBT programs have to be different for PCs, Macs, UNIX systems, and so on — undermining one of intranetting's key advantages, as discussed in Chapter 1.

 If you decide to go with the download-and-run approach, select courseware that's self-contained in a freestanding EXE (executable) file. Such courseware requires minimal or no configuration at the client side. Your users just need to grab the necessary file, and then run it on the host computer — the rest happens like magic.

If the CBT vendor provides a *browser plug-in*, or *helper program*, you can set up the user to "view" the courseware without having to download it in its entirety right up front. The plug-in is a program that works with a web browser to allow certain types of non-Internet standard files to be transmitted via your intranet and viewed with the web browser. The student must either already have the plug-in on the client computer (unlikely) or must download it over your intranet.

The advantage is that once the student has installed the plug-in, he or she can view a CBT program originally designed for CD-ROM or hard disk over the intranet, without having to download the whole doggone course. The flipside to this advantage is that such plug-ins may have very large installers (the Neuron plug-in installer from Asymetrix is over 3 megabytes).

You may find a few additional difficulties with the plug-in approach:

- CBT materials usually aren't written with the intranet in mind, so they may still rely heavily on graphics, animation, sound, and video — all of which run slowly, even with the plug-in.
- Adding plug-ins to client Web browsers complicates client system configuration and causes your information systems department to loathe and detest you for giving them extra work.
- You need a different plug-in for every different CBT vendor.
- Most CBT plug-ins don't work perfectly with all CBT products. You may encounter features such as pop-up windows, for example, that don't work properly.

Publishing courseware designed for the intranet

The best approach by far is to buy (or build) IBT that is designed from the start to use intranet standard files (HTML, GIF, JPEG, and Java), and to run across a LAN rather than from a CD-ROM drive. Intranets are still new, IBT's even newer, and you don't find a lot of courseware available for purchase yet, though this situation is changing. Fortunately, you can get some pretty cool authoring tools that you can use to "roll your own" IBT. Here are two:

- **Asymetrix Toolbook II Instructor 5.0** ($2,000) is the latest in a long line of well-regarded courseware products from Asymetrix, founded by Paul Allen (Microsoft's cofounder). Toolbook Instructor is the high end of the Asymetrix product line and includes many tools for courseware design, including powerful self-test capabilities and wizards for developing glossaries and tests. It uses a metaphor of a book with chapters and pages to help you lay out your IBT — a system that is intuitive for both users and developers alike. You can distribute your Toolbox II documents in both EXE (executable) and HTML (web page) format. Asymetrix has made most of Toolbook's features exportable to Web formats via HTML and Java, although the Web format does not support the OpenScript language.
- **IBT Author from Stanford Testing Systems** ($3,995 for Starter Edition, $9,995 for Professional Edition) is a high-end tool specifically designed for IBT authoring on Windows 95 and Windows NT platforms. The product supports multimedia, test question templates, scoring, and several administrative and reporting features (setting up course permissions, student groups, and so on).

If you're on a very tight budget, you may want to consider using good old Microsoft PowerPoint for some low-end IBT authoring. PowerPoint permits hyperlinks for both text and graphics, although you have to design your interactive tests from scratch. PowerPoint 95 (that is, version 7.0) can be retrofitted with an Internet Animation Publisher feature, available at www.microsoft.com/mspowerpoint. The Animation Publisher allows you to create a web-compatible version of a PowerPoint presentation that includes animated slide transitions, clickable screen buttons, and all! The Internet Animation Publisher is already included with PowerPoint 97 (that is, version 8.0), and gets activated when you select File⇨Save As HTML.

In either case, you need to be sure that the client browsers have the PowerPoint Animation Player plug-in installed (it comes with AXPUB.EXE). Figure 8-3 shows a PowerPoint slide show being viewed from within Microsoft Internet Explorer to give you some idea of the possibilities of IBT on a shoestring.

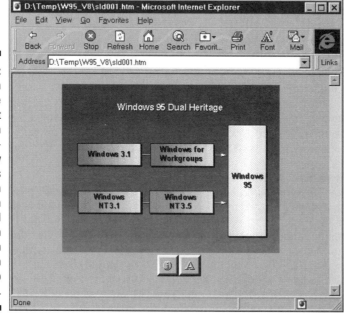

Figure 8-3: Users with the PowerPoint Animation Player plug-in can view slideshows with animation and transition effects from within their Web browser.

IBT Design Guidelines

If I am as persuasive as I'd like to be, you agree that IBT can be a great supplement to other training methods. Already I can see it: You're thinking about courseware subject matter and you can appreciate that designing IBT specifically for the intranet is the way to go. Man, that is exciting! Before you jump in and create the IBT equivalent of the labyrinth, you may want to consider a few examples of IBT design techniques: navigation, interactivity, modularity, and multimedia.

Navigation

Figure 8-4 shows a sample screen from an IBT application created with Asymetrix Toolbook II Instructor and running in the Microsoft Internet Explorer browser. Note the use of small, graphical navigation buttons at the lower right, for jumping back to the menu, going back a screen, and going forward a screen. Note also the hyperlink for Java.

If the user clicks on the hyperlink, the IBT system displays a new screen showing a definition of the term (see Figure 8-5). This technique helps more advanced students avoid slogging through material they already know, and keeps screen clutter down.

In "straight" HTML, overlapping objects (such as the help tips you see in Internet Explorer by pressing the F1 key) aren't allowed, so the definition must appear in a separate page. If you use definition screens in your own IBT projects, it helps to keep the definition pages small so they'll appear more quickly. (Note that you may be able to add pop-up window capability with certain browsers and servers, but ToolBook doesn't support it, so you have to graft it on after the HTML export from ToolBook — for example, with an ActiveX control or JavaScript program.)

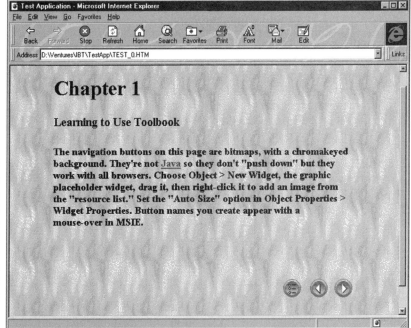

Figure 8-4: The navigation buttons are transparent GIF files with associated hyperlink behavior.

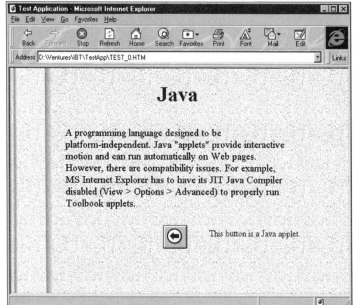

Figure 8-5:
Definition screens are accessible by hyperlinks.

The backgrounds in both Figures 8-4 and 8-5 are *tiled GIF* images (see Chapter 12 for more info), so they don't take long to download. Figure 8-5 uses a special type of tiled GIF called a *combo GIF*, to create the border on the left, which is a lovely blue color in real life (see the enclosed CD-ROM).

Use the same background, title style, and layout for all hyperlinked definition screens. This consistency makes the IBT materials you create easier to use (the student always knows when he or she is at a definition screen as opposed to a lesson screen).

Navigation with buttons and hyperlinks is great, but what about those situations where a student wants to look up a topic by a keyword, without having to wade through pages looking for hyperlinks? A *search engine* can help — some IBT authoring tools have their own glossary function; another option is to *layer* a search engine on top of your IBT course. For example, you can use the popular Excite or Alta Vista search engines to beef up your site. (For more on search engines, see Chapter 11.)

Interactivity

IBT becomes much more effective if it includes interactive elements. HTML doesn't help much in this department, so we turn to Java. Chapters 5 and 12 provide more info on the Java programming language if you want it. For now, just know that Java programs run on the user's machine, within the web browser window.

Chapter 8: Intranet-Based Training (IBT) 149

The quiz question in Figure 8-6 uses a predefined ToolBook Java *applet* (a small program) featuring random sequencing of the answer buttons, and a feedback field to help the student understand why a given answer is true or false. The example in Figure 8-6 actually uses *two* Java applets that work together: the set of buttons on the right, and the feedback field toward the bottom of the screen. When you work in Toolbook II Instructor, you can right-click on the button set and choose the applet's properties: button names, feedback responses, whether you want the buttons to appear in random order, and so on. Figure 8-7 shows the button set's property sheet when in you are in the Toolbook Authoring mode (as opposed to Reader mode).

When you use specialized Java applets, or *widgets*, such as the one in Figure 8-6, you need to make sure that the web server stores the Java code where the browser can find it — an example would be a folder named "Java" in the same parent directory that contains the IBT's HTML and GIF file folders — and you should also make sure that the client contains a special file, required by the Java language, listing the specialized applets. For ToolBook users, the file is TBJAVA.ZIP and should appear in the CLASSPATH environment variable in a PC's AUTOEXEC.BAT file.

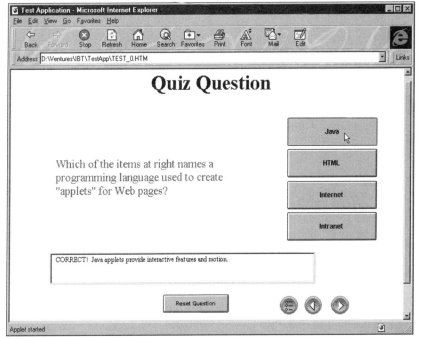

Figure 8-6: The feedback field toward the bottom helps the student figure out why a certain answer is true or false.

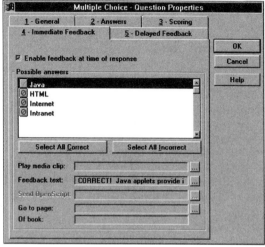

Figure 8-7:
You can specify feedback text and timing in the Java widget's property sheet in Toolbook.

A handy aspect of better IBT authoring tools is the ability to score test results cumulatively for a session, and perhaps store them in a database for system administrators to review. Whether scoring is a big deal for your company depends on how formal you want to be about on-line training. You may decide that unscored test questions are fine if you're putting the courseware out there on a voluntary, here-it-is-if-you-want-it basis. On the other hand, if you plan to make IBT courses a prerequisite for employees to advance or qualify for certain company positions, more formal scoring features become important.

Some vendors of IBT authoring software make a test-score database an extra cost option, and the extra cost can be significant — $10,000 or more. If recording test scores matters to you, be sure to ask the vendor whether the capability is included in the bundle you plan to buy.

Modularity

Another key element of designing good IBT is *modular organization*. A modular course makes it easy for students to select the lesson they want when they want, and modularity is important if students are expected to use the course on an occasional basis for Just-In-Time Training (JITT) — or if they can only spare five or ten minutes at a time to take the training in the first place. Figure 8-8 shows a sample table of contents screen that makes navigating the course fast and easy.

One mistake even professional courseware authors make is to include introductory pages that the user must wade through before getting to the table of contents. Such material may be useful and appropriate the first time a student takes an intranet course, but in subsequent sessions, these pages

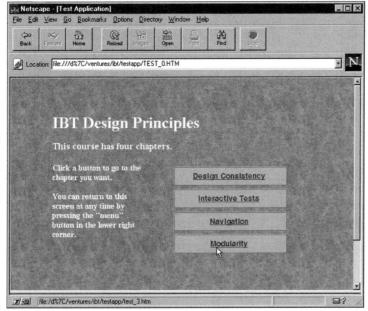

Figure 8-8:
A modular IBT course uses menus to lead the student quickly to short, topical lessons.

just get in the way — much like those voice mail systems that state the obvious each time you call. Be considerate and include a hyperlink on the course's first page to take the student directly to the table of contents.

Multimedia

What about adding sound and video to IBT to give it more punch? Tread carefully here, maestro.

First, ask yourself if the typical client workstation has the capability to play sound. Most office PCs don't have sound cards, and although many newer ones come with sound integrated onto the computer's main circuit board, that doesn't mean the computer has speakers.

Second, ask whether sound or video will really enhance your course in a way that text and graphics won't. If a sound or video clip doesn't contribute to the learning experience, don't bother with it. An IBT training course on payroll deductions and employee tax rates is hardly enhanced by some winky MIDI file playing the Brandenburg Concerto #1.

Third, if you do use sound and video, try to use a *streaming* format such as RealAudio if the network is fast enough to support it. Download-and-play sound is too much trouble for users trying to concentrate on the training material.

And fourth, test your multimedia-enabled course to ensure that the files download fast enough to sound or look good. No multimedia is better than clunky multimedia.

Keys to Successful IBT Publishing

In a nutshell, here are the most important tips for designing successful Intranet-Based Training:

- Use an IBT development tool to speed up the authoring process. I've seen companies try to roll out IBT using nothing more than a generic web page editor, and it doesn't work.
- Go for a clean, uncluttered design.
- Design for speed: Use large graphics, animated GIFs, and video clips sparingly (if at all).
- Make your IBT course very easy to navigate with consistent, simple buttons.
- Take advantage of hyperlinks to let users click on difficult or important terms.
- Make all screens of the same type (such as definitions) consistent in appearance.
- Take advantage of Java applets that add interactivity, for example, in self-tests (important for training validation). For more about Java, please check out Chapter 12.
- Use good organization: Don't force users to go through some of the same material over and over; keep lessons about the same size.
- Modularize the lessons so your IBT is more useful for JITT.
- Include some form of text search capability so users can find JITT information and quickly return to topics they want to look at again.
- Don't build your IBT around sound annotations unless you know that every potential student has the hardware to hear them.

The intranet is a great new tool for educating employees. Although most of the intranets that organizations have built so far haven't focused on education, IBT is one of the biggest-payback intranet applications, especially for companies in fast moving fields. Publishing training on the intranet is a great way to help build a *learning organization* — one that is more productive, competitive, and able to adapt to its changing needs over time than merely smart organizations.

Part III
Strategies, Techniques, and Tools

The 5th Wave — By Rich Tennant

"No, they're not really a gang, just a particularly agressive intranet."

In this part . . .

If Part II covers the *what* of intranet publishing, Part III deals with the *how* — *implementation* issues. Here you can find chapters on project planning, formatting and converting documents for intranet compatibility, structuring your intranet for ease of navigation and management, and designing a web site that's interesting, functional, interactive, and good-looking.

I mention a lot of products that can help you perform all these tasks faster and easier, on the assumption that you're as inherently lazy as I am. I can only present a sampling of what's out there, and the intranet tools marketplace is constantly changing these days. However, even if the specific products I mention here mutate or die by the time you read this section, you can still have a good background to go shopping on your own.

Chapter 9
Plan Your Work and Work Your Plan

In This Chapter
▶ Identifying and involving key groups
▶ Deciding the prototype versus pilot question
▶ Tracking the project
▶ Outsourcing, partnering, and consulting
▶ Deciding who may publish
▶ Preparing for growth and extranetting
▶ Measuring success

Before you dive into the technological nuts and bolts of actually getting documents onto your intranet, do a little planning. By thinking ahead and addressing the issues I raise in this chapter, you vastly improve your odds of intranet publishing success.

If you're already neck deep in an intranet publishing project and you think it's too late to plan anything — STAY RIGHT HERE and read this chapter! (Fooled you!) You are never too late to build consensus, think about dividing the labor, and plan for your project's future.

Building Consensus

One magazine article I read a few months ago took the position that because intranets are relatively easy to set up, project teams and work groups should just get out there and create them, with or without the blessing of management or Information Services (IS).

This advice isn't necessarily completely wrong. The "full speed ahead, damn the torpedos" approach may be okay for a small intranet publishing system that won't be around for very long — for example, a little web server posting a few documents for the convenience of team members working on a four-month project. Setting up a guerrilla intranet is also a possible way to force others in your organization to appreciate what intranet publishing can do for them. ("Don't say it's impossible. We did it over here.")

A consensus-building approach is probably better, however, if your publishing project meets any of these criteria:

- You expect it to be around in a couple of years.
- You may need big bucks to expand it if the publishing project is a success.
- You need cooperation from those who control the information you want to publish, such as human resources managers or Help Desk managers.
- You want to attract and involve users who currently have other options for getting the information they need.

I know that many of you gung ho, grassroots intranetters out there are severely allergic to getting your managers involved in a skunkworks project that you now control only because it's below the corporate radar. You're results-oriented, hip to new technologies, and intolerant of office politics. Get management involved, you may think, and they'll just muck things up.

Fact of life: If you really want to make an impact and help your organization be more productive, at some point you have to go public with your intranet and get a bit political. If your project has true business merit, you're in much better shape than the mainframe programmers who are still trying to convince everyone that COBOL is great so they still have jobs tomorrow. Push intranet publishing into the mainstream, and you can work on many more cool projects.

Top-down, bottom-up, or all together?

Things happen different ways in different organizations. *Top-down* projects start with management. *Bottom-up* projects start with users or groups and later draw the attention of managers. Intranets are often bottom-up projects because they don't require massive centralized administration either to start or to maintain; they're inherently easier to use than many other kinds of information systems; and they appeal to employees who are more concerned with sharing information than controlling it.

Chapter 9: Plan Your Work and Work Your Plan **157**

Intranet publishing systems can succeed no matter where they start, and every business has its own culture. However, the most successful projects in most organizations, in my opinion, arise from a coordinated effort at all relevant levels. Even if you can't drum up the ideal all-together-now effort, you need to at least ensure that all the key groups know what's going on.

Who *are* the key groups? Any intranet publishing project has the following four constituencies, as illustrated in Figure 9-1:

- **The managers:** They approve, fund, support, and take credit for it (just kidding — sort of).
- **The project leaders:** They get their hands dirty, make it happen, and then get miffed when anyone tries to change it.
- **The content providers:** They give the project leaders something to publish and help keep the documents updated, after they understand that they won't lose their jobs in the process.
- **The users:** They benefit from the system and help continually improve it by complaining regularly.

Involving the project's constituencies does *not* mean creating a large project team. Intranet project teams should be fairly small and flexible, so that they can move quickly and adapt to new needs. The technology permits quick development, and over-staffing can stifle that advantage.

Find some champions for your project

Try to build a team of champions in each of these four key constituencies. The term *champion*, as used in modern business, means someone who sticks his or her neck out on behalf of an idea or project and takes a leadership role in making that project a reality.

You want your champions to be facilitators, advisers, boosters, red-tape cutters, and, if you're lucky, morning baked-goods bringers.

These champions mean more to the success of your project than a large budget or an expensive webmaster. Identify candidates (usually people who already have an interest in technology), explain your idea to them, discuss why you need their help, listen carefully to their advice, keep them informed as your project moves along, and thank them many times along the way.

Part III: Strategies, Techniques, and Tools

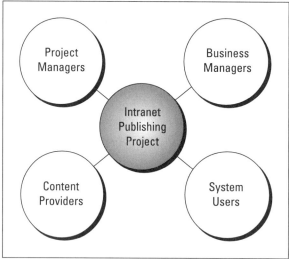

Figure 9-1: The key constituencies in an intranet project are, ideally, all involved in it from the design stage forward.

A message to business managers

If you're a midlevel or senior business manager, please know that your intranet publishing project managers must have your support to succeed. *Your support* means the following:

- **Get project managers the people and products they need in order to demonstrate the return on investment they promise.** If you don't give them the resources they need, they are sure to produce less than satisfactory results or even fail.

- **Help project managers stay on track with business priorities and publish documents that fulfill business goals.**

- **Work with other business managers and with content providers to iron out turf issues.**

- **Don't impose unrealistic expectations on your intranet publishers.** Intranets are new, most of the document publishing programs are new, and nobody has much experience with any of this stuff! Mistakes do occur. Just let your people know that you expect them to learn from their experience, and that you do look for a payoff at some point.

- **Don't demand heavily documented return on investment (ROI) analyses.** ROI for information systems is notoriously hard to quantify. Some of the benefits are intangible. Obviously, you need to ask for cost savings estimates, but if you get too bogged down in ROI, IRR (Internal Rate of Return), and all those other numbers you look at when you buy a new sheet metal press, you can miss the boat.

- **Don't micromanage!** Make your priorities clear and check in periodically, but let the people responsible for implementation do their jobs without a lot of back seat driving. Resist the temptation to rush into project meetings waving a recent magazine article and say, "Here's the product we need! This article says it's great! I think we should buy it right away! Maybe we should buy two!" Pass those tidbits along, but let your project team weigh the product's pros and cons.

How can you help your intranet publishing project team? Do they need a hardware or software tool that you can help them get? Can they use another warm body? Do they want to attend a public seminar on a certain aspect of the technology? Do they need someone to help evangelize intranetting to other managers? If you can't think of anything, as a last resort, ask them!

A message to project leaders

Make your case to management early in the intranet publishing project to build support in high places. You need this support for the following reasons:

- **Managers control ongoing project funding.** Intranets tend to grow quickly, and staff, servers, software, and network infrastructure improvements don't grow on trees (and they ain't always cheap either).

- **Managers provide ongoing reality checks to see that your publishing projects tie in closely with business goals.** These reality checks make sure that you don't go off on tangents and end up with an orphaned project. Intranet technology is cool, but it needs to have a business purpose.

- **Managers can help smooth over information ownership issues and arrange access to the content your users need.**

The most important bit of advice in this chapter for project leaders is right here: *Write an intranet publishing business plan*, whether your management say they need a written document or not. A good project plan document can persuade managers in ways that no verbal discussions can. It shows your managers that you take the project seriously. It also helps you organize your thoughts and raise issues that require discussion and negotiation with other team members. To beef up your pitch, crib some material from Chapter 1, which presents intranet publishing benefits.

A message to content providers

Content providers can be department heads, financial administrators, human resource executives, manufacturing engineers, technical writers, Help Desk managers, and so on. Whoever controls a bit of information to be published on the intranet is a *content provider*. If you fall into this category, you can make or break an intranet publishing project.

In an economy where information has become a business's most valuable asset, employees have become very protective about the information that they control. Many employees' main function is to collect, maintain, and distribute certain information. They worry that intranet publishing systems could render that function — and them — obsolete.

You can probably relax a little. If an intranet is likely to make your job obsolete, you need to plan for a change anyway, and getting actively involved in the intranet project can be a great place to start. Intranetting is a growth industry! Intranet publishing systems rarely do away with content providers' jobs. More commonly, intranets intensify these jobs, because documents, or data, that the providers used to update monthly can now be updated more often, and project leaders need help converting and formatting data for the intranet (see Chapter 10 for more on conversion and formatting).

A message to key users

If you're a key user of an upcoming intranet publishing project — that is, someone with input into the project's design, or maybe even a member of a committee that helps guide the project — here are a few suggestions:

- **Be a help, not a hindrance.** Most people resist change to some degree — that's natural. Ask the project leaders to clarify what benefits they see for the user community and then be open-minded about it, even if you like the way things are right now. A new system can be even better, and you won't know until you give it a try.

- **Help the intranet publishers understand your needs in the design stages.** Explain the problems and concerns you experience today relating to obtaining company information. What are your main beefs — speed, quality, amount, degree to which the information is up-to-date? Intranet publishers have to know this stuff if they're to succeed in making your life easier. When they come to you with questionnaires, forget the fact that you receive more surveys in a typical year than paychecks. Fill 'em out thoughtfully and be glad the project managers are even asking the questions. If they *don't* come to you with questionnaires, go knock on their cubicle partitions and say, "Hey, I hear you're building a document-publishing intranet. Have you got a few minutes? I've got a few ideas."

- **Let project managers know how they can improve their systems once they're in place.** Users unfortunately often assume that they have zero input into the information systems they use, and develop a jaded, world-weary fatalism about ever improving those systems. The technological and organizational barriers to changing information systems can be frustrating for everyone, but the only way system designers know which direction to push is if you help them understand what you need. Recognize that one of the great things about intranet systems is that designers can modify them more easily than most other kinds of information systems. Don't assume that just because the publishing system has been formally rolled out that its design is fixed. Heck, intranet systems are *never* finished.

The First Project

Okay, the plan takes all the relevant groups into account, and recognizes the importance of their contributions. What does the project itself look like?

Chapters 3 through 8 cover application selection issues — the type of material to publish, identifying your target audience, and so on. All those issues need to be in the project business plan.

Prototype or pilot?

One big early decision is whether to create a prototype or a pilot project. The tools you use, which I discuss in the next three chapters, depend on this decision.

A *prototype* is a model of a system that demonstrates the system's look and feel, and may even work with a limited set of documents (a *working prototype*). Intranetters have created intranet publishing system prototypes in a relatively simple presentation program, such as PowerPoint 97. A *pilot project*, on the other hand, is a fully functional system, but usually having a limited and clearly defined scope.

One big risk of a prototype system is that some technology projects don't *scale* well, meaning that they begin to fail in significant ways when they grow beyond a certain size. For example, a plain Ethernet Local Area Network (LAN) can provide adequate speed for a prototype intranet publishing system serving a few dozen documents to a few dozen users. Add ten times as many documents and ten times as many users, and the system may run like molasses in January.

Here's a classic case in point: Denver International Airport's automated baggage handling system worked great in the prototype stage, but ultimately ran millions over budget and delayed the airport's opening several months when technologists attempted to scale it up to full size. (By the way, it still isn't fully functional, and probably never will be.)

A pilot project approach has more appeal than a prototype for most businesses because you can develop a small, tightly focused intranet publishing system in a matter of weeks, and the end result is a functioning business system, not a mock-up. You can even think of a pilot project as the first component of the larger intranet you envision. Prototypes are valuable for larger projects, but if you go that route, see if the demo tool you're using can introduce specified time delays at points where the system is likely to be slow in the real world. You can't predict delays precisely (they shouldn't be as bad as those on the public Internet), but use your test network (which can be one server and one workstation) to get a feel for them. Raising unrealistic expectations is a fast way to torpedo a new technology. If you don't bother with time delays, do advise your audience that the demo runs faster than the production system will.

Track and learn

Whether your first intranet publishing project starts as a pilot, or as a prototype that (you hope!) evolves into a pilot, look on it as an experience that you can draw from in future intranet projects. The only way you can do this is if you track the first project's progress and make notes along the way — what took longer than expected, what went smoothly, and so on.

Use a project management program, both to manage the initial project and to analyze it later, when you move on to new projects. Figure 9-2 shows a screen snapshot from the most popular microcomputer project management program, Microsoft Project. Other products to consider are Scitor Project Scheduler, Primavera SureTrak, and Primavera Project Planner (see Appendix B, "References and Resources," for contact information).

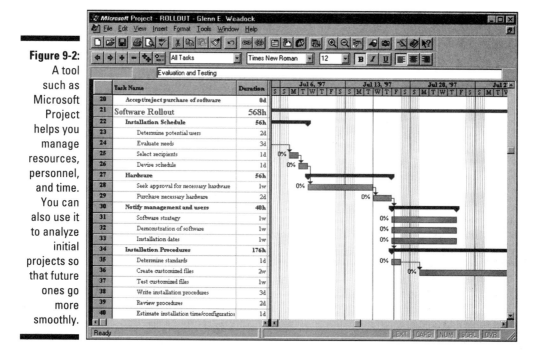

Figure 9-2: A tool such as Microsoft Project helps you manage resources, personnel, and time. You can also use it to analyze initial projects so that future ones go more smoothly.

Who Does the Design?

Now that you know what sort of project, pilot or prototype, you need to build, you have to figure out who is actually going to build it.

Home-grown intranets are appealing partly because many organizations already have the knowledge and staff necessary to implement them. If your organization already has an Internet presence and your own employees design and host the Web server(s), you're more than halfway there.

Even if you do have a gaggle of Web-savvy people at hand, getting some outside help for your first intranet publishing project may be smart. Intranets differ from the Internet in several key ways. For example, intranet sites tend to be more productivity-oriented and less glitzy, and you can sometimes make assumptions on an intranet that you can't necessarily make for a public site (such as which browser everyone's using). Intranets also usually carry more, and denser, information than public Internet sites.

Intranet publishing demands talents other than tech savvy, too. You need people who can write (English, that is — not code), and people who have a strong visual design sense. You may be able to find these people in-house.

Consider involving professionals who've done intranet work before, either through *outsourcing*, *partnering*, or occasional *consulting*. You may have to pay more up front, but usually the overall cost of the project decreases because the in-house project team avoids mistakes that can increase expenses later.

Outsourcing

Outsourcing is basically just a new word for contracting with other companies for a service. You may want to outsource some or all of your publishing project. Doing so can be expensive — plan on paying in the neighborhood of $70 per hour or more — but if you're in a big hurry, and you need your pilot project to look good from the get-go, outsourcing may be your best bet.

When considering the outsourcing option, ask yourself these questions:

- How fast do you need this project to be finished?
- How complicated is the project?
- What skills does the project require that I don't have in-house?
- How long would acquiring those skills, either through hiring or training interested employees, take?
- Can we conveniently outsource part of the project, rather than all of it?

TIP

The biggest drawback of outsourcing isn't that the contractor may not deliver — most experienced ones do — it's that you miss out on an opportunity to gain experience by doing. If you do outsource some or all of an intranet publishing project, ink a deal that entitles you to the contractor's work notes, project management schedules, internal memos, and so on. You can certainly benefit from these materials, but most outsourcing arrangements don't include them in the package. On a related note, make sure that formal system documentation is part of the arrangement, too. If you ever take over your project and run it entirely in-house, this documentation can be a big help.

Partnering

Partnering differs a bit from outsourcing, and has the following characteristics:

- The outside company shares work with your in-house staff and works at your location most of the time.
- The hired partner educates your employees as the project goes along, meaning that the transition to running your intranet in-house can be much smoother.
- The process usually takes somewhat longer than straight outsourcing because of the training time.
- The end result is not only a completed project but also the expertise your organization gains.

Partnering may be either more or less expensive than outsourcing, depending on how quickly your in-house staff pick up concepts and can start doing productive work on the project. You may find partnering to be a good middle-of-the-road option for organizations that want to get trained in intranet publishing, but need to get a specific project off the ground faster than would be possible by relying on in-house expertise.

Consulting

Professional information system *consultants* have the advantage of working with multiple companies and applications, so they bring a valuable perspective to your project. You can get helpful advice from intranet consultants on a less formal basis than outsourcing or partnering.

For example, you can hire a firm to take a gander at your publishing site and make some suggestions for user interface design improvement. Sometimes, consultants are also useful for pointing out new technology your in-house people (and, perhaps, contractors) don't know about. ("Yes, you can certainly *do* it this way, but have you heard about. . . ")

Chapter 9: Plan Your Work and Work Your Plan 165

Bringing in a consultant for any less than a day or two usually doesn't provide good value for your money. Any consultant worth a darn needs to spend a little time with your systems and people before dispensing advice.

Consultants who belong to professional associations are more likely to take their work seriously. If you don't already work with consultants who have intranet experience, you may be able to find some through the Independent Computer Consultants Association (www.icca.org). Vendors with certification programs can also help out. Novell and Microsoft, for example, can provide lists of consultants in your area who have passed exams on intranet-related products (NT Server, IntraNetware, and so on).

Thinking Ahead

The smartest thing to do is to plan on your intranet publishing project being a smashing success, for the following reasons:

- The cost and time savings are so significant that these projects very often do succeed.
- You're reading this book, which improves your odds even further!
- Nothing can kill a good project faster than too much success.

I should explain that last point: Back in 1981, when I was a design engineer for a solar energy product called a *heat exchanger* (basically two copper tubes mashed together), the company I worked for went to a big trade show in Chicago to announce the product. We put together the most gorgeous sales literature the heat exchanger community had ever seen, our manufacturing people assembled glittering prototypes, and I documented engineering test results that showed we knew how to mash two copper tubes together more effectively than anyone else. We handed out three hundred business cards and won many customers — and it was the worst thing that could have happened to us.

We got back to our offices to find more orders than we could possibly fill. Customers didn't get as much product as they wanted, and what they did get came late. Many wrote us off and didn't bother to come back when we built up our manufacturing capacity. The moral of the story is that if your intranet publishing system succeeds, and user demand grows so fast that you can't manage it, you end up concentrating on keeping up with administrative chores rather than publishing useful and timely content, and ultimately you turn off your users.

So what can you do to handle growth more gracefully? Two suggestions are setting guidelines as to who can publish content and automating the process of assigning new computer addresses so that you don't have to worry about it as the user population grows.

Who may and may not publish?

At my local grocery store, patrons can post *for sale* messages on a cork bulletin board by the exit. Local merchants are prohibited from posting, which leaves room for the patrons' notices. The notices can't be larger than an index card, and every so often a store employee takes down postings that have been up for a long time (or that advertise something the employee wants). The bulletin board works well because a few ground rules are in place. After an intranet publishing system starts to catch on, two things are likely to happen:

- Employees approach the project managers with data they feel should be published on the system.
- Other employees take things a step further and begin creating their own mini-intranets. (Remember, any computer on an intranet can potentially act as a server.)

Some organizations are very relaxed about who publishes data on an intranet and about who can set up an internal web server. Sun Microsystems, for example, has over a thousand internal web servers in its organization — then again, Sun has a bunch of very web-savvy employees who can probably handle a network of that complexity. Your company may be in a different situation.

If your organization isn't careful, the intranet phenomenon could easily get out of control before you know it. This matters if network traffic increases to the point that everyone's intranet now runs slowly, or if you want to present corporate documents and data to employees in an organized and consistent manner. Maybe you need some ground rules like the ones that exist for the cork bulletin board at my local store.

Organizations can never manage and control intranets the same way they controlled mainframe systems. Control probably isn't necessary, but guidance and direction certainly are. Set a few ground rules, preferably organization-wide (enlist your champions' help with guiding who can put what on the intranet). Here are some suggestions:

- Create a small group, or designate one individual, to review requests to publish documents on existing intranets, or to create new intranet systems. Review meetings should be held at least monthly.
- Draw up a list of minimum requirements that any new intranet publishing project must meet in order to merit consideration (for example, if the information isn't already available on any intranet).
- Publish formatting and content guidelines (for example, maximum suggested words per web page, maximum suggested links per page, required links to main organizational pages, what constitutes appropriate content, and so on).

Don't want to think about publishing policies now? Trust me — six months of use with no guidelines, and that grocery store bulletin board becomes a useless mess.

Domain name and IP address registration

Once your publishing project begins winning hearts and minds throughout the organization, people inevitably start murmuring in the hallways about what could be done with an extended intranet, or *extranet*, that permits customers or suppliers, or both, to connect to corporate web servers. Establishing that link to the outside world is challenging enough without your having to change all your host addresses (like `207.69.207.251`) and domain names (like `www.i-sw.com`), but that's exactly what you may have to do if you don't provide a globally unique address and domain name ahead of time.

Just because a network of intranet computers has unique IP addresses and domain names with respect to all other computers *inside* the organization doesn't mean that those addresses and names are unique in the world. Your best bet is to ensure that worldwide uniqueness ahead of time. I'm sure that sounds like a huge government red tape hassle — fortunately, it's fairly easy and all done through the InterNIC registration authority in Virginia.

Here are the steps to follow, in a nutshell:

1. **Pick one or more domain names you like for your servers.**

    I usually suggest choosing more than one, as the fee isn't large ($100 per name for two years, as I write this) and the good, short names are starting to disappear.

2. **See if the names are already taken.**

    An easy way to do this is to connect to `http://rs.internic.net/cgi-bin/whois` and specify the name you want. If someone else has it, that company's name and contact information appears on the screen.

3. **Follow the instructions at the InterNIC Web site (**`http://rs.internic.net/rs-internic.html`**) to register domain names and network numbers (see Figure 9-3).**

    The details are all there in the form of Frequently Asked Question (FAQ) documents and procedural flowcharts. You can fill out the templates online, and then send your check by mail.

A major part of thinking ahead is figuring out how you can maintain and manage your intranet project over time. Fast-forward to Chapter 13, skim it, read it, or paste it on the inside of your glasses, and make sure your publishing project business plan addresses the issues I raise in that chapter.

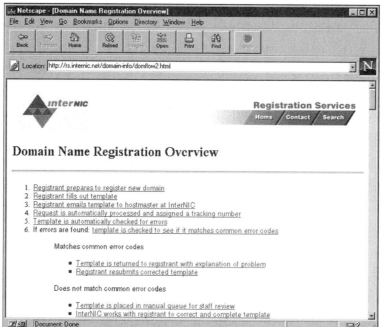

Figure 9-3: The InterNIC authority offers detailed registration instructions on its Web site. Procedures and costs are subject to change, so scan the site thoroughly before registering.

Measuring Success One User at a Time

Many technology project plans leave out the part about measuring success. Make sure that you don't make this mistake.

I attended a networking seminar where the instructor said that asking whether a computer network is cost-effective is like asking whether a phone system is cost-effective; some things you just don't question. Without phones, people can't do their jobs, and without great computer networks the same holds true.

I agree in spirit, but the fact is that most organizations do a heckuva lot of cost-benefit analysis before putting a fancy new phone system in place, and computer systems aren't any different. Further, we're not talking about a computer network versus no computer network — we're talking about a new *kind* of computer network, one that many organizations don't quite understand yet.

Why it's important

Measuring success is important for these reasons:

- To validate and reinforce the support everyone provides the project in the first place
- To gain support for expanding or enhancing the publishing project
- To gain support for new publishing projects
- To give you a leg to stand on when you ask for a raise, after sticking your neck out on this intranet thing
- To identify projects that aren't meeting their goals, so that you know they need fixing

How to do it

How can you measure the success of an intranet publishing project? Here are a few possibilities:

Number of users

Well, this is a starting point. A document system that only five people out of a thousand actually use can't be considered a success. On the other hand, a large active user population in itself doesn't indicate success.

For example, people may use the system because they can't get to the information any other way. I spent forty minutes navigating a PC manufacturer's labyrinthine Web site the other day to find out how to perform a specific hardware upgrade because nobody on the tech support hotline knew the answer.

Also, if you just look at the number of people who use the system in a given time period, say a month, you don't know whether they used it one time or a hundred times in that time period. They may have only checked out the home page, become hopelessly confused, and given up.

You can get information about the number of users who access your intranet application using web server logs. Several tools exist to help interpret web server logs and make them more understandable. Chapter 14 treats this issue in more detail.

Number of hits

A *hit* is a web page access, and you can also get this data from web server logs. Now we're getting a little closer to some meaningful data. Fifty users and five hundred hits in a month's time means that, on average, every user accessed the site ten times during the month.

You may see a large hit count in the first few weeks or months after you roll out your new publishing system. Don't assume this means that everyone loves the system and is putting it to productive use! Early on, users explore the new system just to see what's there. Similarly, don't worry if the hit count drops off after this early usage spike. A decline can just mean that users figured out what areas they needed on a routine basis and are now only visiting those pages.

Number of satisfied customers

The number of satisfied users is a fairly reliable measure of success. You can estimate satisfaction levels various ways, including phone and e-mail surveys, paper-based questionnaires, and so on. You can also create a form on the intranet itself and put a link to the form on the system's home page — a "tell us what you think" link.

Cost savings

Here's a language that managers can really understand: If your intranet publishing system replaces a paper-based system, measure what that old system used to cost the organization in terms of paper, processing (duplicating, binding, and so on), filing, distribution, and staffing. If the new system replaces a CD-ROM-based system, do a similar calculation. Estimate the intranet project's payback period and then document the ongoing cost savings over the next year, two years, and five years, considering that intranet content updates don't require redistributing CD-ROMs or paper materials on a regular basis.

Success stories

Sometimes measuring success in numbers isn't an accurate reflection of the truth. Intangible benefits may very well outweigh all the quantifiable cost savings data. Your human-resources intranet may allow employees to understand their benefits more easily, your sales-support intranet may enable reps to master new product specifications more quickly, and your tech-support intranet may enable computer users to get faster answers to technical questions. These benefits have value even if you can't easily express that value numerically. Chapter 16 discusses how you can use such success stories to promote the system.

Okay, you've done some planning. You have a concept of how to get this intranet system rolling, who its constituencies are, how to involve them, where the project needs to go, how you may measure performance, and how you can deal with what the future may bring. Now you're ready to think about the technological tools and techniques you need. The first step is to look at what you must do to take the documents you already have — or plan to create — and format them to be intranet-friendly, as Chapter 10 explores.

Chapter 10
Formatting Data for Your Intranet

In This Chapter
- Deciding whether your intranet is the only place you need to publish documents
- Choosing between stock HTML, custom HTML, and Java to deliver your documents
- Publishing from paper, word processing, desktop publishing, graphics, and database formats
- Using the popular Adobe Acrobat *Portable Document Format* (PDF)

*I*n this chapter, I describe how to put the information you want to publish on your intranet in a format that users can view. The documents you want to publish may be in any of hundreds of different formats and, unfortunately, intranets can only deal with a handful. Therefore, you have to create a plan: either for document *conversion*, in which you translate documents from their original formats to an intranet-friendly format, or for document *accommodation*, in which you equip client browsers with software capable of viewing documents in their original formats. Most intranetters end up doing a bit of both.

A *format* is just a way to store information on a computer system. You may know that a word processing program, such as Word for Windows, typically uses a format (normally with the file suffix DOC) that stores not only the text content of a document, but details about text and page appearance (formatting, margin settings, and so on) as well. On the other hand, a simple text-editing program such as Windows Notepad uses a format (normally with the file suffix TXT) that only stores the bare-bones text and doesn't support any fancy text characteristics. You can have the exact same words in both formats, but the editing and printing capabilities are different. Different kinds of programs — desktop publishing, spreadsheet, database, graphics — also have their own formats, each optimized for the particular program.

If you use Windows 95 or Windows NT, you can view the list of file formats your computer is equipped to handle by opening My Computer and choosing View⇨Options⇨File Types, as shown in Figure 10-1.

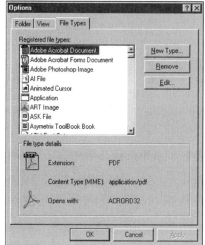

Figure 10-1: You can view data formats on a Windows 95 or Windows NT machine alphabetically in the File Types list.

In this chapter, I address how you can convert the format of a document that you already have or are now creating to a format for publishing on your intranet. I take a look at publishing strategies, delivery strategies, sample data types, and one especially popular program to give you an overview of the key points to consider. I also mention several specific products that may make life easier for you as you reformat your documents for intranet delivery.

Two Publishing Strategies

The first question you face when dealing with document format issues is whether your intranet is to be your sole publishing audience. The answer determines how you manage document conversions and content updates, as the following sections explain.

Intranet only

If your only intended use for a particular document is to publish it on your intranet, your life is reasonably simple — at least, at work it is. You have to figure out a way to convert that document into a format your intranet can handle, or provide a browser plug-in that enables users to view the document in its original form. You *don't* have to worry about whether the document needs to be used in a brochure, annual report, or other print format, however.

Your big decision is how to handle content changes. If you use a document accommodation approach (for example, if you provide users with the Shockwave browser plug-in so that they can view a Macromedia Freehand illustration in its original form), such changes are easy: Only one file exists, so it's the file you change!

If you use a conversion approach, however, set a policy for whether content providers need to make changes to the source document or to the converted intranet-format document. Technical considerations may force you to perform changes in the source document, in which case you have to run your conversion utility again — for example, if you have complex technical drawings that you want to convert to a *Graphics Interchange Format* (GIF) or *Joint Photographic Experts Group* (JPEG) graphic for easy intranet publication (GIF and JPEG are explained in more detail in Chapter 12).

Intranet plus

Repurposing is the dopey term people use to describe the process of taking information in one form and changing it to another. (First, *purpose* is a noun, not a verb. Second, do you *purpose* things once before you *repurpose* them? I must be in an Andy Rooney sort of mood today.) If you need the same document to serve multiple purposes, such as intranet document and printed document, life becomes a bit more complex compared to the *intranet only* situation I describe in the previous section. You have two basic options:

- **Maintain two completely separate sets of documents: one for print and one for intranet publishing.** This solution may be acceptable if the documents rarely change, or if you can change the print-destination document and then easily regenerate the intranet-destination document with a conversion utility.

- **Maintain a single source document from which you can easily generate print-destination and intranet-destination documents.** You make any necessary changes to the source document and then automatically generate the updated print-destination and intranet-destination documents.

For a long time, the second option has only been available to companies that can afford high-end document management systems, costing tens of thousands of dollars and more. New, less expensive tools are beginning to appear, however. For example, Design Intelligence offers *i publish*, a $149 program that enables you to create desktop publishing-type documents and easily reformat them for print or intranet destinations.

Part III: Strategies, Techniques, and Tools

The i publish product makes extensive use of predefined page element combinations and behaviors, so a page *knows* how to readjust itself to look good on a web site or on the printed page. This philosophy is quite different from the philosophy behind Adobe Acrobat, for example, which essentially takes a snapshot of a print-page layout and then reproduces that snapshot in a browser window. Building pages in i publish is easy with drag and drop for text and graphics elements, and the user interface is actually a customized version of Microsoft Internet Explorer (see Figure 10-2).

Along similar lines, Adobe PageMaker lets you automatically reposition a page's text and graphics when you change the page orientation from *portrait* (long side vertical) to *landscape* (long side horizontal). PageMaker also adjusts page elements when you change page size or apply a different page *master* (template).

For documents that must serve multiple uses, make any necessary changes to the source file, and then regenerate the intranet and print format files. Remember that any manual modifications you make to files (for example, HTML files) are lost when you make a change to the source document and regenerate that document for publication!

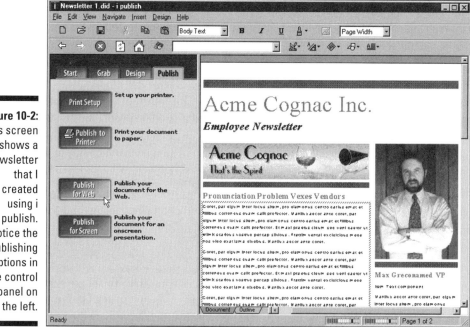

Figure 10-2: This screen shows a newsletter that I created using i publish. Notice the publishing options in the control panel on the left.

Three Delivery Strategies

After you decide on a publishing strategy that specifies how you manage original and converted documents (and how to manage document changes), you must decide on a publishing *delivery* strategy. Basically, your choices are to stick with plain HyperText Markup Language (HTML), use customized HTML, or use Java. In a continuing effort to lace this book with my world-famous Weadock analogies, I now compare choosing an intranet publishing technology strategy with choosing a new car.

Stock HTML

Say you see a great classic car that you want to buy — an Alfa Romeo spider, maybe. Sure, it's a little cramped and it doesn't have any cupholders. The model has been around a while; however, a lot of mechanics know how to work on it, and spare parts are readily available. I call this car *stock HTML*.

In intranet publishing, this car is analogous to a document system that uses only plain vanilla, market-standard HTML, straight text, and GIF or JPEG graphics. Every reasonably modern web browser can read such stock HTML documents without modification.

Converting existing documents into stock HTML may entail losing a certain amount of formatting information, but the ability to publish documents in a format that every computer user can read makes that an acceptable compromise. Some specialized conversion programs, such as the $495 HTML Transit from InfoAccess, make a laudable effort to provide some web-like interactivity to converted documents. HTML Transit can generate a table of contents from major headings, place navigation buttons at the top and bottom of HTML pages, and create web pages with frames, as shown in Figures 10-3 and 10-4.

Of course, you may not need a specialized conversion utility. Many programs today have a Save as HTML option. Conversion utilities can give you more control over the process, however, if you need it.

One problem with the stock HTML approach is that the source documents often contain design elements that don't automatically translate to the more limited HTML format. For example, if you design an intranet-based training course in Asymetrix ToolBook, you discover quickly that overlapping windows don't export to the HTML format.

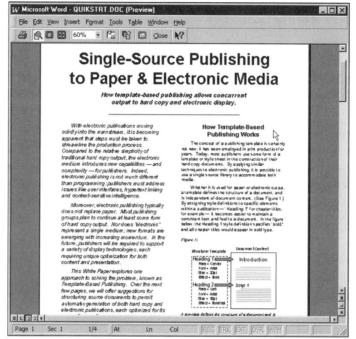

Figure 10-3: Here's what a word processing document looks like when previewed in Microsoft Word.

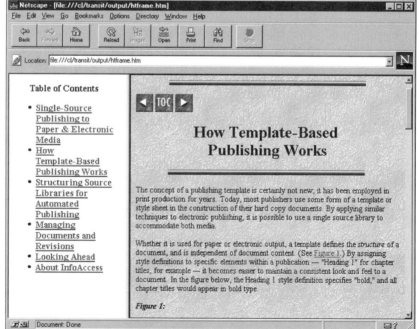

Figure 10-4: Here's the HTML version, after conversion by HTML Transit.

Unsupported design elements are one thing, but you also have to deal with *ambiguous* design elements when converting to stock HTML. That is, you have to tell whatever conversion utility you use how to treat document elements that can be interpreted two or more different ways. A program such as HTML Transit has literally dozens of settings you have to specify to create a conversion *template* that guides the process. If the source documents use inconsistent designs themselves, you may need to create special conversion templates for each different design.

If content providers can contribute documents with formatting that is consistent enough to make automatic template-based conversion tools reliable, you may want to look at utilities that automatically convert source documents placed into a designated web server directory. Transit Central from InfoAccess is an example. At $3,995, you pay for the convenience, but this sort of solution certainly eases the burden of handling document updates and changes.

Custom HTML

Back at the car lot, you start thinking about what you have to give up if you decide to go with stock HTML. You really want a nice CD player, better handling, or more horsepower. The salesperson agrees and shows you a car that just came in as a trade-in. The previous owner poured cash into it, adding all the cool features you wanted. Of course, this car — which I call *custom HTML* — may not be as easy to work on, what with all the customizations and modifications, and there may be only one place in town you could go to for repair work. It has an undeniable appeal compared to the stock model, however.

In intranet publishing, stock HTML's limitations as a general purpose document-formatting framework are well known: no precise positioning of page elements, limited fonts and font sizes, and practically no support for accurate printing. HTML's appeal as a universal format remains a strong motivation for keeping it, however, and if you can somehow extend it to address the major formatting problems, you're really in luck.

Custom HTML extensions do just that, by using independently developed, proprietary portable document formats. With such formats, you can publish documents with their original fonts, column layouts, and graphics placement. You can also have confidence that when users print the document, pages break where they're supposed to break.

Portable document format software typically includes one or more document conversion utilities and a browser *add-in*, or *helper* program, that permits the user to read, display, and print documents that have been converted to the portable format. Vendors often include indexing and search utilities as well, which is a good thing because general-purpose web site search engines may not be able to find text in a portable document format.

You may need a larger version of a portable document viewer if you want users to have search capability. For example, Common Ground provides a MiniViewer and a ProViewer (only the ProViewer supports searching).

The major players in this market are:

- **Adobe Systems Inc.,** whose $295 Acrobat software uses *Portable Document Format* (PDF). Viewers are available for Windows 95, Windows NT, Macintosh, and UNIX. This solution is the most popular on the public Internet — the common browsers support the PDF format and Acrobat handles multimedia well, although file sizes are large.

- **Hummingbird Communications Inc.,** whose $195 Common Ground Web Publishing System uses the *DigitalPaper* (DP) format. Viewers are available for Windows 95, Windows NT, Macintosh, and UNIX. Common Ground has better compression than Acrobat does, and the package includes utilities for publishing to CD-ROM media, as well as an intranet site.

- **Tumbleweed Software Inc.,** whose $249 Tumbleweed Publishing Essentials software uses the Envoy format licensed by both Novell and Corel. TPE is the best of this lot at file compression, so consider it if your network is on the slow side.

When you need to convert a single document, these three products provide a slick way to do it. You don't need to run a separate conversion utility. You simply *print* the document to a *virtual printer*. The virtual printer isn't a real printer (that's what *virtual* means in computer lingo), but it shows up in the print dialog box as though it were. When you print to it, you create a file in the appropriate format instead of a printed document.

When you need to reformat a bunch of documents, you don't want to load each document into a word processor and print to a virtual printer. Fortunately, the portable document format vendors provide batch-processing utilities that can handle multiple conversions with a single command. (The DigitalPaper Express batch processor for Common Ground runs only on Windows NT at the time I write this.)

The requirement for a browser add-in or helper program is the largest remaining drawback for portable document format software, as it complicates the client workstation setup. You can include a miniature viewer with your DigitalPaper or Envoy document if you want, so that all the user has to do is double-click the file to see it. This approach adds to the file size of every document, however. The other major drawback used to be that you had to download an entire document file, even if you only wanted a single page. These days, all three vendors provide *page-on-demand* capability (also called *byte serving*), so an HTML link can reference a specific page in a portable document, and the server downloads only that page.

Acrobat is such a popular tool that I devote a special section to it at the end of this chapter: "One Popular Standard: Acrobat."

Pure Java

A third technology strategy is to forget about the stock Alfa, forget about the customized Alfa, forget old cars entirely, and buy a brand new car built from the ground up — with almost all the features that you want. To be really clever, choose a *world car* (that is, one that consists of a single model that's legal everywhere in the world). I call this car *Pure Java*.

The market is just now beginning to offer web page design tools that dispense with HTML almost completely, and rely on the Sun Java programming language to present text, graphics, multimedia, and applets in a browser window. I say *almost completely* because you still need an HTML file to tell the browser the name and location of the Java page. For more about Java, take a look at Chapters 12 and 5.

The advantages of a pure Java approach are pixel-level control over object placement and platform independence (Java runs on most hardware and software). The disadvantages are that Java is still developing and that different, sometimes incompatible, versions exist of the *virtual machine* software that interprets Java programs to run on a specific workstation type (such as PC or Mac). In addition, the speed of viewing Java-enhanced documents is usually a bit slower than straight HTML, depending on the specific page.

Two products illustrate different uses of Java in intranet publishing: Coda and Net-It Now! The Coda program from Randomnoise, Inc., in addition to creating pure Java pages, was actually *written* in Java (I respect companies that practice what they preach). The software is oriented towards people who are building new web pages from scratch and want to drop their text and graphics clips onto the page by hand. Coda looks and feels like a page layout or image editing program. Version 1.0, shown in Figure 10-5, runs on Windows 95, Windows NT, and Macintosh platforms. The Coda development environment treats individual page elements as objects, each having its own set of properties. The Object Palette lists all the objects on a page, and the Properties window shows the properties of the currently selected object — in this case, the page's central pushbutton.

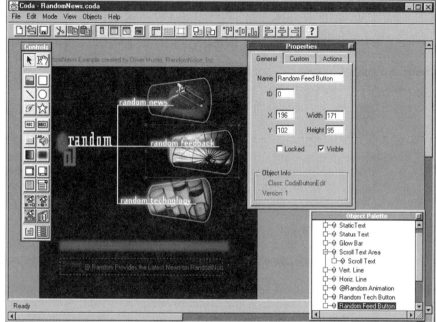

Figure 10-5: The Coda development environment treats individual page elements as objects, each having its own set of properties.

Net-It Now! from Net-It Software also creates Java pages with HTML wrappers, but Net-It Now! is oriented towards people who are creating web pages from existing Windows documents. You create a Java page much like you create a portable document format file using Common Ground, Acrobat, or Tumbleweed — that is, using a virtual printer driver. Net-It Now! version 1.5 runs on Windows 95 and Windows NT 4.0 and costs $295. After the conversion, you can add cool page elements, such as pop-up graphics, and page-to-page transition effects.

Figure 10-6 shows the same document as shown in Figure 10-3 converted using Net-It Now! Notice that Net-It Now! faithfully maintains the original document's layout and formatting. The window on the right shows how the page looks when viewed by Internet Explorer or Navigator. Java's precise positioning ability allows this page to look nearly the same on your intranet as it does on a printed page.

The company also offers an automatic tool called Net-It Central, with intranet drop boxes into which content providers can copy source files for automatic conversion and linking. Prices range from $1,995 to $6,995 per server.

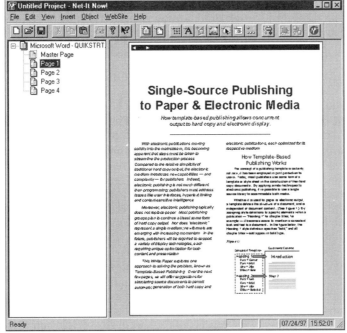

Figure 10-6: Here's the result of a *printout* from Word 97 to the Net-It Now! virtual printer.

Four Data Sources

Okay, so you've figured out how you plan to manage documents and changes, and you have chosen a technology delivery strategy from the three choices in the previous section. The last step in your data-formatting plan is to consider any special issues that have to do with specific source data types. Formatting data for your intranet involves different steps and technical issues, depending on where you're starting. In this section, I zero in on four possibilities: paper documents, word processing or desktop publishing documents, computer graphics, and databases.

Paper

You may assume that you have to contract with one of those keyboard sweatshops, with row upon row of bleary-eyed data entry clerks clicking away, to move the information from paper into a computer. Depending on the quality of the paper documents, you may be able to use *Optical Character Recognition* (OCR) scanning.

OCR works in conjunction with scanning hardware to *read* a paper document, recognize the letters and numbers on the page, and convert them to electronic text suitable for plunking down onto an intranet web page or editing with a word processing program.

OCR scanning sounds expensive, and you certainly can spend many thousands of dollars if you need a high-speed document feeding solution. However, for scanning the occasional paper document, a $600 flatbed scanner and a $500 program (such as OmniPage Pro for Windows 95, from Caere Corporation) may suit you right down to the ground. One of the slick things about OmniPage Pro is that after it scans your document, it can save it in HTML format, thus saving you a separate step.

How accurate is OCR scanning? OCR has gotten much better over the last few years, and 99 percent accuracy is achievable with clean originals. The error-detection capabilities are better, too. For example, good OCR software automatically identifies scanned words that don't exist in a dictionary, so you can fix an error manually, or accept the word and add it to the dictionary, if it's a proper name or unusual term. If your documents use unusual typefaces, you can train the OCR software to learn those typefaces.

In Figure 10-7, I use OmniPage Pro to scan one of Caere's own sales brochures. The scanned image is on the left, and the OCR results are on the right. The program did well, missing only the large *OmniForm* word at the top, and misspelling only one word.

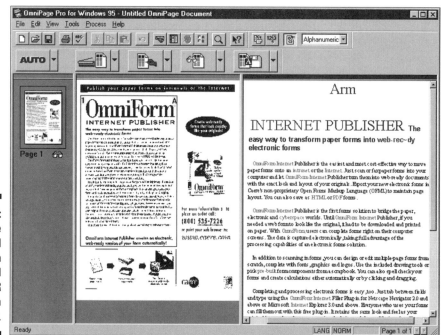

Figure 10-7: The scanned image is on the left, and the OCR results on the right.

Nagging accuracy problems still exist, however. Consider a hyphen at the end of a line. Most OCR programs remove the hyphen, which may be fine most of the time. What if the hyphen is part of a word that *requires* a hyphen, though, such as in the classic Homeric expression *rosy-fingered dawn*? The OCR software has no way to tell, and you get *rosyfingered dawn*.

How fast is OCR? With a reasonably modern workstation and scanner, figure on roughly 30 to 45 seconds for a full page of text from a clean original. Still, you usually need to spend longer than that to go back and fix errors by hand.

Word processing and desktop publishing programs

Several of today's word processing programs have added built-in web publishing capabilities. For example, Word 97 from Microsoft includes a File⇨Save as HTML command that converts a regular Word DOC file to stock HTML. The program generates HTML tables and converts graphics to GIF format, unless the graphic was originally in JPEG format — in which case Word 97 keeps it as JPEG during HTML export. Word saves drawing objects, WordArt effects, and text boxes as GIF images, too. Any hyperlinks in the document are saved as hyperlinks, and Word 97 does a good job of translating formats, such as bulleted and numbered lists into their HTML equivalent.

If you have an earlier version of Word, you can use the Internet Assistant add-on to achieve HTML export capability.

Word 97 includes a number of features that enable you to create new documents designed especially for HTML export. Choosing File⇨New⇨Web Pages⇨Web Page Wizard brings up a series of screens that guide you through creating a new document using one of Word 97 web page templates (see Figure 10-8). The web-page features Word 97 supports include background image, horizontal rules, tables, hyperlinks, and form elements.

Of course, you don't have to use your word processor's built-in HTML save feature. If you need more precise control over the finished product, you can use a separate conversion tool, such as HTML Transit, as I discuss earlier in this chapter.

Consider the more complex issue of desktop publishing software (usually abbreviated DTP). Almost by definition, DTP documents include graphics, and carefully positioned graphics at that. Can you convert DTP documents into HTML format?

Part III: Strategies, Techniques, and Tools

Figure 10-8: Microsoft Word 97 includes the Web Page Wizard that enables you to create a new document, specially formatted for export as a web page.

Yes, within certain limits. Recent versions of leading DTP programs either include an HTML export capability or can add this capability through a program plug-in. For example, Microsoft Publisher 97 supports HTML export through a menu command (File⇨Save as HTML). Here are some details on other popular DTP programs and, where applicable, companion products:

- **Adobe PageMaker 6.5:** Priced at $895, it can save a file as stock HTML. It doesn't save table of contents or index elements as hyperlinks, however, so you have to create these manually. PageMaker converts multicolumn documents to HTML using tables, and it honors existing hyperlinks.

- **QuarkXPress:** Another popular DTP program ($995), enables you to add the program CyberPress from Extensis (www.extensis.com) to enable XPress to save a DTP document in stock HTML format. BeyondPress, from Astrobyte (anyone remember the Jetsons?) is the $595 *big* version of CyberPress, with more nifty features.

- **Adobe FrameMaker 5.1:** Excels at creating and managing longer, more complex documents (such as entire books), and supports Unix, Macintosh, Windows 95, and Windows NT. The $895 FrameMaker is better for creating Acrobat PDF files than HTML, but it does come bundled with WebWorks Lite from Quadralay Corporation, which adds HTML export facilities. The full WebWorks Publisher, which also converts FrameMaker documents, is $895. Another option for FrameMaker is the HoTaMaLe plug-in, which is free from Adobe and is simpler to use than WebWorks Publisher.

As with word processing software, you can use a separate conversion tool with these programs. You can also convert DTP documents into one of the three portable document formats mentioned earlier (PDF, DigitalPaper, or Envoy), if you're using the Custom HTML technology delivery strategy.

Most word processing and DTP documents use a double-space after a period at the end of a sentence. You may wish to replace such double-spaces with single-spaces for better-looking intranet text. If you use an automatic conversion tool that provides this option, so much the better. Otherwise, you may find it easier to do a search-and-replace operation within the word processor or desktop publishing program prior to HTML conversion.

Graphics

Say you have some straight graphics files (no text) that you need to convert for your intranet. Convenient options exist to make your life easier here, too, but you have to know just a little bit about the type of source document, and intranet graphics file formats.

You can place two kinds of graphic files onto a standard intranet web page: *Graphics Interchange Format* (GIF) and *Joint Photographic Experts Group* (JPEG). In Chapter 12, I discuss these formats in more detail. For now, just know that both are *bitmap* formats that describe a picture as a collection of tiny dots (*pixels*).

The word *pixel* is a combination of the two words *picture* and *element*. IBM called pixels *pels* for a while, but that never caught on — probably because *pixel* is more fun to say.

If your source graphics documents are in one of these two web-friendly formats, you don't need to do any file-type conversion at all. You may, however, want to reduce the number of colors to make the file sizes smaller, and, therefore, faster to transmit. If your source graphics are in a different format but still a bitmap file type (such as TIFF or PCX), you need to convert them. Fortunately, the process can be as simple as opening the file in an image editor (such as Adobe Photoshop, JASC PaintShop Pro, or Corel Photopaint) and then saving it in the GIF or JPEG format.

In either case, you can use a tool, such as DeBabelizer from Equilibrium, to convert a whole bunch of files at once, instead of one at a time.

If, however, your source graphics are *not* GIF or JPEG and, furthermore, are not bitmap files at all but rather *vector* files (which describe a picture with lines and curves instead of pixels, like Autodesk AutoCAD or Macromedia FreeHand drawings do), you have an altogether different kettle of fish! This leaves you with a choice to make:

- **You can still convert vector graphics to GIF or JPEG, but you must decide upon the final size of the graphic in pixels.** Unlike vector graphics, bitmap formats don't resize well, and you also give up the ability to zoom (move in and out) and pan (move side to side).

- **You can convert the vector graphics to a format that an intranet user can view with a browser and a helper program.** Programs such as Autodesk Whip, Macromedia Flash, or Macromedia Shockwave fit into this category. Shockwave, for example, allows users to view vector graphics created (or converted) by the $399 Macromedia FreeHand illustration program, with full zoom and pan capability.

Many intranetters aren't aware of the second option, but it has a lot of appeal. Check out the discussion in Chapter 12 on Flash and Shockwave, if you need to publish vector graphics (such as technical drawings) over your intranet.

When you drop bitmap graphics onto a web page, specify an exact height and width, in pixels. Many page design tools, such as Adobe PageMill, offer this option in an object properties window; you don't have to be an HTML guru to use it. Browsers can create rectangular placeholders while downloading such graphics, and the browsers don't need to rearrange the page once the graphics finish downloading, making page viewing faster.

Databases

A fourth possibility for source documents is documents stored in a database. Your organization may have a large number of documents and may have decided years ago to keep them organized and accessible using database software. How can you get documents stored in a database onto your intranet?

The answer depends on the particular database you use. A lot of document management systems use their own special database formats for storing, indexing, and retrieving documents. If this is the case in your shop, your best bet is to see whether the vendor offers web publishing tools. Here are two examples:

- **askSam document database system:** The Windows-based askSam document database system from askSam Systems has become popular for document databases, largely because it's easy to use (sorry, I don't know who Sam is). It reads a variety of text and database file formats, and provides for form-based data entry. Once you have documents in an askSam database, though, how do you let intranet users get at those documents? The short answer (and maybe the *only* answer) is to buy the askSam Web Publisher for $1,495, which contains prebuilt program scripts that allow intranet users to find documents and pages using sophisticated keyword searches. You can even use the askSam Web Publisher to add information to an askSam database from an intranet browser.

- **Folio infobase system:** If your business is on the larger side and your documents are more numerous and voluminous, you may want to use the popular, industrial-strength Folio system to store documents in an indexed, compressed, searchable database that Folio calls an *infobase*. You may be familiar with the Folio viewer product, Folio VIEWS, if you've ever used the online help system in Novell NetWare. Figure 10-9 shows the user interface. Creating an infobase (for example, with the Folio Builder product, which is designed for document publishers rather than users) is not a task for the timid, and if you're in a hurry, askSam is a lot easier. However, Folio handles large document databases with aplomb. Keyword searches are very fast, and infobases can include graphics and video clips as well as text. This is fairly powerful software and the vendor assumes you can justify some time to spend learning it.

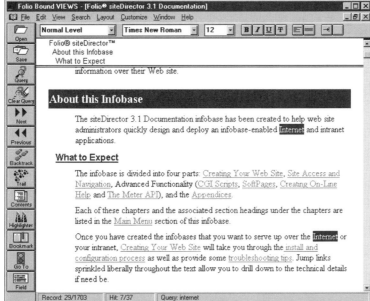

Figure 10-9: This screen capture shows the results of a Folio VIEWS search on the word *Internet*. A user can see each occurrence of the word using the navigation buttons on the left.

Say you have one or more Folio infobases set up, and now you want to let intranet users get to that information. As long as you have a spare $10,000, you're in luck: Folio siteDirector is a slick tool that works with popular web servers and dishes up infobase documents in HTML format on the fly. You can even add an extra layer of security, and you can create your own custom HTML template files to influence the look of the web pages users see. One caution: As I write this, siteDirector includes Folio 3.1 rather than the newer and zippier Version 4.0.

The bottom line is that document databases may use proprietary file formats, but the vendors are getting on the intranet bandwagon. If you have a vendor-specific document database that doesn't yet have intranet publishing capability, bug your vendor, by all means. Ten will get you twenty that they're already working on a solution for you.

One Popular Standard: Acrobat

Adobe Acrobat, for $295, with its *Portable Document Format* (PDF), enjoys widespread use on the public Internet and is therefore already familiar technology to many companies. I figure that Acrobat is popular enough to get its own discussion, but you need to remember Common Ground Publisher and Tumbleweed Publishing Essentials, both of which are competing formats with unique advantages of their own, as I discuss earlier in this chapter. In any case, Figure 10-10 shows Internet Explorer viewing an Acrobat document.

Acrobat, available since 1995 and now in Version 3.0, is really a collection of several programs:

- **PDFWriter:** is the *virtual printer* for creating PDF files from almost any application program (word processing, desktop publishing, and so on). You *print* to the PDFWriter device using the standard Print dialog box in whatever program you are using, and instead of getting an actual printout, the result is a PDF file.

- **Capture:** creates PDF files from paper by scanning them and performing Optical Character Recognition (OCR). A separate standalone Capture program has more features, such as batch processing, for an additional $895.

- **Distiller:** creates PDF files from PostScript files you may already have, and offers more control over image compression than PDFWriter. Distiller can also process multiple files at a time (batch process).

Chapter 10: Formatting Data for Your Intranet

- ✔ **Exchange:** enables you to view and edit PDF files. You can add forms, hyperlinks, image thumbnails, and even buttons that play sounds or videos when clicked. The hyperlinks, incidentally, even work across PDF files.
- ✔ **Reader:** includes the standalone PDF viewing program. Acrobat 3.0 files can be read from within Navigator or Internet Explorer on PC, Macintosh, and UNIX machines.
- ✔ **Catalog:** creates a full-text index for a PDF file, making searches of Acrobat documents run much faster.

Acrobat 2.1 files were not exactly optimized for intranet use: They were large, slow to search, and inefficient. Acrobat 3.0 has improved the situation by allowing you to optimize files so that repeated graphics are only stored once. Version 3.0 also only stores the font characters that a document actually uses, instead of an entire typeface definition.

The *page-on-demand* feature in Version 3.0 allows a user to select a single page instead of the entire document, and *progressive rendering* (also in 3.0) means that users see pages as they begin arriving at the browser. Page-on-demand requires web server support. Progressive rendering only works with files saved using the file optimization option. Even searching is faster and more flexible: You can search by exact word, synonym, phonetic similarity, and *proximity* (search for two words that are close to each other).

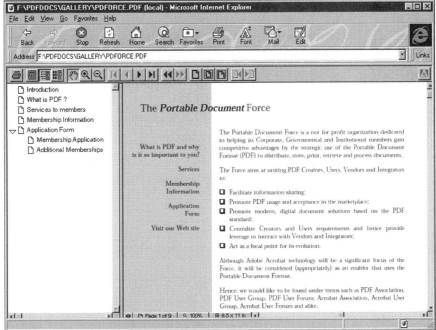

Figure 10-10: Acrobat adds a toolbar to Internet Explorer and displays a table of contents in the left pane and document pages in the right pane. The document prints just like it looks.

You can link to a PDF file within an HTML page, or you can embed the PDF file itself. Microsoft Internet Explorer users can navigate the PDF file using a window inside the browser window, but Netscape Navigator users must go to a full-screen view to navigate the document.

In terms of document accuracy, Acrobat gets high marks, although it doesn't embed fonts within PDF files. If a user doesn't have a font on his or her computer, Acrobat makes a substitution. Acrobat 3.0 provides better document printing control than Version 2.1 did, including half-toning and color options that make it quite a capable print engine.

Acrobat has never been exactly shy in terms of disk and memory requirements, and Version 3.0 is still gluttonous in these areas. Acrobat Exchange and its related files require 20MB of RAM, and 45MB of disk space to use all the bells and whistles; the Reader uses 2MB of RAM and about 8MB of disk space. The PDF format is now more portable than ever; however, the support for multiple computer platforms is excellent, the reader is free (as always), and the addition of interactive form elements, hyperlinks, and buttons makes PDF a jazzier way to deliver documents. At just under $300, Acrobat is worth your consideration for intranet document publishing.

Many different strategies, technologies, and products exist to help you get the data you want to publish onto your intranet so that users can download and view it. The bad news is that you have to learn enough about the options to make intelligent choices. The good news is that you're not limited by a single approach, technology, or product.

After you wrestle with the various formatting issues presented in this chapter and come up with good solutions for your situation, the next logical question is how to *structure* the content you publish on your intranet so that users can find what they need quickly and easily. Chapter 11 is waiting for you, and you'll be glad to know it's in standard book-page format, compatible with all readers.

Chapter 11
Adding Structure to Your Substance

In This Chapter
▶ Understanding the role of hyperlinks and Uniform Resource Locators (URLs)
▶ Using home pages, image maps, bookmarks, and frames for navigation
▶ Discovering product-specific navigation tools
▶ Evaluating intranet search engines
▶ Deploying push content

This chapter deals with structuring your intranet site so that users can navigate it easily, search for information, and even receive information automatically. After you go through the formatting process laid out in Chapter 10, you have data that's in a physical format suitable for intranet publishing. That doesn't mean, however, that the data is in an appropriate, *logical* format. You have the substance at this point, but without the easy access that good structure and organization brings.

Imagine trying to use the *Yellow Pages* without subject headings: Even the obscure headings the directory publishers use are more handy than none at all. Similarly, if you don't provide good structure and organization to your data, it is as good as unusable. For your intranet to be a productive tool, users must be able to quickly get the information they need, with no muss and no fuss. Maybe the best thing about an intranet is that it gives you several powerful ways to improve access to, and organization of, your content — regardless of the type of content you publish:

✔ Page and site organization that permits easy, intuitive *navigation*

✔ Site-wide *search* tools that bypass your intranet's navigational structure and provide a way to zero in on the information the user wants

✔ *Push publishing,* in which users specify the type of information they want and the network sends it to them automatically

By structuring your intranet pages, providing cross-structural search capabilities, and sending certain information to users automatically, you make it easy for users to access the content you publish.

Organizing Your Site for Easy Navigation

In this section, I chat about intranet navigational aids: hyperlinks, home pages, image maps, bookmarks, and frames. However, before any of that can make sense, you have to understand a fundamental characteristic of intranets that sets them apart from traditional computer networks: their *stateless* nature.

What Puerto Rico and intranets have in common

You don't have to read too many articles on intranet technology before you bump into the enigmatic statement that HTTP is *stateless*. (HTTP, remember, is the HyperText Transfer Protocol language that intranet browsers use to connect to web servers.) The statement "HTTP is stateless" simply means that your web server doesn't keep track of where a user has been.

Each time a user clicks a link on a web page, the server handles the link (usually by sending a new page to the browser) and then goes to sleep. Next time the user clicks a new link, the server regains consciousness and handles the new request, but the server has total amnesia: It doesn't know what the user did previously. It doesn't track the user's *state*.

"Hold the phone," I hear you say (I have good ears). "If what you say is true, how come I can hit the Back button on my browser and go back to the previous page?" Good question. The reason this works is that the *browser* keeps track of which pages you visited. The server couldn't care less.

HTTP by itself is not only stateless, but also *non-reentrant*. Being non-reentrant is a consequence of being stateless (this may be the most obscure sentence in the whole book, but bear with me here). For example, you may find that when you start filling out an HTML form, link to a different page to look something up, and then come back to the HTML form to pick up where you left off, all the blanks are empty. The server doesn't track the user's state, so it doesn't know or care that you filled in 19 of the 20 blanks before you went off to another hyperlink. The browser doesn't normally keep track of those form entries, either; all it can do is return you to previously visited pages, but each page request starts from scratch. You can't *re-enter* a page after an interruption, hence the term *non-reentrant*.

Ways around this HTTP limitation do exist, as some of you Internet surfers may know from experience. The point is that HTTP doesn't work this way by nature, and web sites that track state from page to page (such as Internet storefronts with shopping-cart features) must do so via custom programming.

Okay, so HTTP is stateless and non-reentrant. So what? These two facts actually explain a lot about how intranets work. Here are three examples:

- ✔ Web pages tend to be self-contained little packages of information — worlds unto themselves. A long HTML form requires a long page.
- ✔ Intranet designers tend to put a fair amount of information on each page, because moving to a new page requires a new wake-up call to the server and a new HTTP connection, which uses valuable processing power.
- ✔ Standard web pages don't support pop-up windows, like you may have seen if you've used the online help feature of a graphic-based program like Word for Windows. (Think about it — the server can't redraw the information underneath the pop-up window when you close it, because the server doesn't recall what's under there. Amnesia, remember?)

Certain browsers actually can support pop-up windows, but only with a little help from their *plug-in* friends. For example, the ActiveX control add-in for Internet Explorer can provide pop-ups that work with Microsoft HTML Help files.

Maybe most importantly, the statelessness of the web and the chronic amnesia of web servers means that the intranet designer can't easily build a sequence of pages that are guaranteed to automatically proceed in a specific order. HTTP pages generally load independently of whatever page the user was viewing the moment before requesting the current page. That would make intranet publishing systems pretty doggoned useless if it weren't for something called a *hyperlink*.

Hyperlinks to the rescue

Hyperlinks, as you may have discovered if you've read other chapters in this book, are little places on a web page where a user can click the mouse to go somewhere else. A hyperlink can be an underlined word or phrase, a graphical button, or a particular area inside a larger graphical image. The web designer determines where hyperlinks appear, what they look like, and where they go. The *where they go* part is defined by something called the *Uniform Resource Locator* (URL). See the "Uniform Resource Locators" sidebar for more information.

Hyperlinks allow intranet designers to turn HTTP's statelessness into an advantage. True, you can't force the user to navigate through a sequence of pages in a particular order. With hyperlinks, however, users can go where they want, when they want, without following a predetermined path. Users don't have to waste time looking at screens they don't need or want, and they can choose to find out more about a subject by clicking a link (intranet designers call this *progressive disclosure*). The hyperlink can be the best single technological weapon organizations can use against information overload.

Modularizing content and structuring it with hyperlinks is both necessary and good, but like all good things, you can overdo it: More than one hyperlink every couple of sentences gets distracting. Also, if your hyperlinks extend too many layers below the surface — that is, if users have to drill down through too many pages to get the specific document needed — users are likely to get lost, confused, and frustrated. Here's a general guideline: Users should spend 90 percent of their time on your intranet reading and 10 percent clicking hyperlinks.

You can gain an appreciation for how to use hyperlinks by visiting sites on the public World Wide Web and by experimenting with your own intranet. The other navigational tools I discuss in this chapter — image maps, bookmarks, and frames — all depend on hyperlinks. For now, I direct your attention to the first place all intranet users go before they start merrily hyperlinking hither and yon: the site's *home page*.

There's no place like home (page)

After clicking several hyperlinks, the intranet user may feel lost at sea. One great way to alleviate user confusion is to give users a lighthouse — a place they can always see that always corresponds to a fixed location.

In life, that fixed location is your house or apartment (or, if you live like the characters in *Cheers,* a bar). On an intranet, it's the *home page* (a.k.a. *start-up page*). You normally configure every user's browser to automatically go to your intranet's home page every time the user runs the browser. You can do this with the administrator kits that Microsoft and Netscape provide (the Internet Explorer Administration Kit and Navigator Administration Kit, respectively, both freely downloadable from the vendors' Internet sites). Users can manually change the home page location with menu commands, but it's nicer to use the administration kits so that the setting is the way you want it as soon as the user installs the browser.

The home page usually identifies the company and contains hyperlinks to the major subsystems the intranet dishes up, as in Figure 11-1. Each major subsystem can (and should) also have its own home page.

Uniform Resource Locators

The Uniform Resource Locator (URL) (usually pronounced *Earl*, as in *The Earl of Sandwich*) is the web address that points users to your publishing system. Every document, no matter what the data type (text, graphics, sound, video, program), has its own URL, and the URL is the key part of any hyperlink.

The format of a standard URL is as follows:

    service://host directory
        document.document type

When a URL refers to a Web page, the `service` is always `http`, for HyperText Transfer Protocol. If the URL refers to a file the user wants to download, the service may be `ftp`, for File Transfer Protocol.

The `host` is the particular computer where the web page or file is located. Usually, this is an English-type name, such as `yourco`. Understand that `yourco` is a convenient, mnemonic translation for the numeric Internet Protocol (IP) address. Your intranet should have a program running on a server somewhere that handles the translation automatically, so the computer knows that `yourco` refers to something like `207.68.137.40`. Typical translation programs are Domain Name Services (DNS) and Windows Internet Name Service (WINS).

The `directory` is usually just a file directory on the host server computer that specifies where the heck on that computer the desired document is. Directories may have subdirectories (like manila folders in a file cabinet), so more than one directory entry may appear in the URL. To extend the capabilities of the web server, the directory part of the URL can have a special format that tells the server to go run a program somewhere instead of looking in a literal file directory. This is typically how URLs allow users to click on a link and run a database query, for example.

The `document` is normally the actual file the user wants. It may, however, be part of the instructions for running a special program.

Finally, the `type` tells the web browser what sort of data to expect. A type of `htm` or `html` means that the data is a standard web page description. Other types may indicate that the file is a sound snippet, movie, graphic, and so on.

Now you understand URLs! Like most aspects of intranet computing, when you understand them, URLs are not as complex as they look.

 Always provide a link to the home page on every page of your intranet, always put that link in the same place, and always make it look the same. Often, intranet web designers include the link to the home page in the *signature,* or *footer* section, of every page. **Remember:** A lighthouse never moves, and it never changes shape!

 Some intranet designers advise against banner graphics, including the company name, on the premise that everyone using your intranet knows what company they work for. (In these days of mergers and mega-mergers, though, do they *really?*) My opinion is this: Your intranet's users are either already, or soon to be, Internet users, and an obvious visual cue that they're using your intranet and not visiting a public Internet site makes sense.

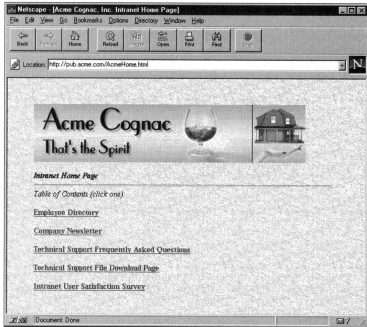

Figure 11-1: Employees can choose specific subsystems from Acme Cognac's automatically loaded home page.

Image maps

An *image map* is a graphical image that contains hyperlinks. Page design tools generally let you create image map *regions* that link to different locations. Image maps are nifty for presenting a visual map of an intranet site, with text legends corresponding to different hyperlinks. Refer to Figure 2-1 in Chapter 2 for an example. Site designers often implement an image map in the form of a horizontal menu bar that runs across the top of a home page. I always suggest using actual text in image maps rather than just icons so users can understand the navigational links more easily — icons by themselves can be obscure. The good news is that because you're creating a graphic, you can feel free to use whatever fonts and text styles your graphics editing program supports.

Two flavors of image maps exist: the old server-side kind, which requires the web server to process the mouse click, and the new client-side kind, which requires the browser to do so. Client-side image maps are faster and easier, so use them whenever you can (most newer page design tools offer the ability to create either kind).

Don't use hundreds of image maps in your intranet site, because they're difficult to maintain over time. For example, many site design tools don't let you use a single command to change an image map link in every map where the link appears, as you can usually do with text hyperlinks.

Users may not want to deal with the delays that graphic files introduce over slower links. For example, using a dial-up modem connection at a remote mountain location, the quality of the phone lines is crummy, and the best you can do sometimes is 9600 baud — even though you have the *latest high-speed modem* (sorry, I was ranting)! If the delays are really bad, just about all web browsers include a command to disable graphics. For example, in Navigator 3.0 and later, choose Options⇨Auto Load Images and disable the Auto Load Images option.

A problem arises when graphics are used as navigational elements. Novice intranet designers often forget to provide corresponding text hyperlinks. The solution, happily, is simple: Test the site by turning graphics off and see whether you can still navigate everywhere you need to go.

You can use image maps to create graphics-based *drill-down* documents, in which a user clicks on a web page to see more detail for the indicated topic. Rail transportation company CSX Corp. has an intranet called Transportation Work Station Net (TWSNet) that presents a map of the United States. Users can click on the geographical area they're interested in to see progressively more detailed maps — all the way down to rail hubs and even individual train cars. Users can then retrieve schedule and cargo data for the selected rail cars.

Bookmarks

Bookmarks, also called *anchors,* permit easier navigation of a long page. Typically, bookmarks are nothing more than text hyperlinks at the top of a page that point to specific locations further down the page. As a general rule, I suggest using bookmarks on pages longer than three screens. For an example of bookmarks in action, see Chapter 4 — specifically, Figure 4-2.

Frames

Frames, a browser extension popularized by Netscape, allow more than one HTML page to appear in the same browser window. Scroll bars let the user see frame contents that don't fit within an individual frame. Internet Explorer 3.0 and later supports frames, although several other browsers don't. Laying out frames used to be difficult, requiring manual HTML coding, but now several page layout tools (FrontPage, PageMill, and others) provide much more convenient frame commands. FrontPage uses the wizard approach to step the designer through frame design (see Figure 11-2).

198 Part III: Strategies, Techniques, and Tools

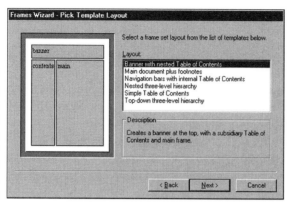

Figure 11-2: The Microsoft FrontPage Editor Frame Wizard.

Whether to use frames has become a matter of hot debate within the web page design community (which can feud more vigorously than the Hatfields and McCoys). Many designers advocate against frames, because they can be slow (the browser has to load a separate HTML page for each window) and confusing. Frames also chop up the screen, which usually isn't very large to begin with.

A good rule is not to use more than two frames if you can help it, and never use more than three. Whenever I'm tempted to use frames, I always try to ask myself whether I can accomplish the same effect more simply and efficiently with tables.

Probably the most common use of frames is to provide a table of contents window and a document window. Clicking a hyperlink in the table of contents displays a new document in the other window.

Most page designers locate the table of contents in the left window and the target document in the right one.

Printing documents from framesets isn't always intuitive. For example, a user can easily print the table of contents frame instead of the document frame. Some user training may be necessary if you anticipate users needing to print from windows with frames.

Product-specific navigation

In addition to HTML navigation features, such as image maps, bookmarks, and frames, you may have other product-specific ways to help users find their way around, depending on the software you use.

For example, HoTMetaL Intranet Publisher (H.i.P.) from SoftQuad includes a special viewer plug-in for Internet Explorer and Navigator that supports a table of contents view for an intranet project that you create with H.i.P. In the two-pane view in Figure 11-3, notice the specialized toolbar above the table of contents. The toolbar includes buttons for expanding and collapsing the table of contents, sorting the contents, searching the site for keywords, asking to be notified via e-mail if a specific page changes, annotating a page without actually modifying it, and so on.

For another example, Adobe Acrobat uses a portable document format called PDF (an unoriginal but descriptive name) for distributing documents across an intranet in a form that browsers can display and print accurately. PDF documents have their own internal bookmarks for navigation, which you can see in the left pane of the window in Figure 11-4. These PDF bookmarks aren't the same as HTML bookmarks, although their function is similar. Chapter 10 has a more detailed discussion of PDF acrobatics.

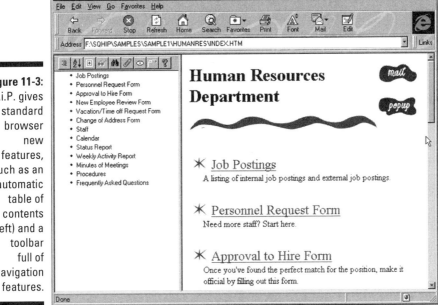

Figure 11-3: H.i.P. gives a standard browser new features, such as an automatic table of contents (left) and a toolbar full of navigation features.

Part III: Strategies, Techniques, and Tools

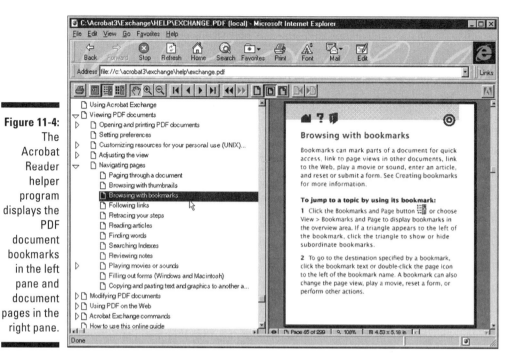

Figure 11-4: The Acrobat Reader helper program displays the PDF document bookmarks in the left pane and document pages in the right pane.

Search Engines

Search engines are server-based programs that create an index of an entire site, much like a book index, and permit users to locate indexed documents using criteria such as keywords, file dates, content authors, and so on. A user can specify a keyword or phrase, click a Submit Search button, and see a list of documents that contain that word or phrase. The search engine generally summarizes the documents in the list, or at least provides the first few lines of the document, so that the user doesn't go on quite so many wild goose chases.

An alternative to hyperlink navigation

Search engines are no substitute for a well-organized intranet web site, but they can come in handy and are now fairly easy to provide. They also introduce an element of serendipity to your intranet — a ten-dollar way of saying that they allow users to discover information and connections they didn't know about before.

When would an employee elect to use a search engine rather than navigate the site from general to specific, using the hyperlinks the intranet designers created? Here are a few occasions:

- When the employee wants to quickly see all the documents on your intranet that pertain to a reasonably specific word or phrase, such as *paid vacation* or *free food*
- When the employee wants to search an entire intranet server that may host multiple departmental intranets
- When the employee wants to search multiple intranet servers at once
- When multiple intranets have grown up randomly and chaotically and don't yet have a consistent navigational structure
- When your intranet has a navigational structure, but that structure is so messy that almost any alternative is preferable

Don't laugh *too* much at that last scenario — it's more common than you may yet realize.

If your workstation users store data files on their own machines as well as on the network, consider providing them a *personal* search engine that can index and scan files that reside on their local hard drives. Verity and AltaVista (see Appendix B) both offer such software, letting users search their own disks just as they would search the corporate intranet.

Evaluation criteria

Searching for a search engine? Here are some evaluation criteria to think about as you shop for a solution.

Indexable data types

You can almost assume support for plain text and HyperText Markup Language (HTML), but if you publish a lot of documents in Adobe Portable Document Format (PDF), be sure that your search engine can index them, too. What you really want in this case is a search engine that can not only find the relevant document, but also highlight the occurrences of the search term in the document. You may also want to know whether the engine can search Microsoft Office data files (Word, Access, PowerPoint, and so on), e-mail files in the format your business uses, and database file formats.

Search method flexibility

You want not only the ability to specify a keyword or phrase, but also the ability to make a more sophisticated search with *Boolean operators* (AND, OR, NOT), *proximity* statements that find words near each other, synonyms, and other file characteristics, such as the document author. Figure 11-5 shows examples of the kinds of searches you can make with Microsoft Index Server (the special punctuation marks are a bit of a pain, but they're not all that hard to learn). Some search engines offer *parametric* searching (using a data object's attributes or parameters — "Show me all the memos Cecily wrote in December").

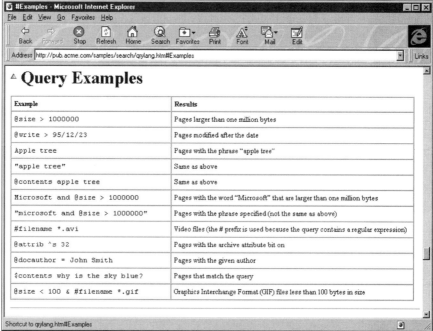

Figure 11-5:
This help screen for Microsoft Index Server shows several different search methods available to users.

Balance between thoroughness and selectivity

If you've ever performed searches on the World Wide Web, you've probably bumped into the frustrating situation in which your search returns 9,419 documents. The opposite problem ("Congratulations, your search returned **0** results") is equally frustrating. The better search engines try to be thorough but also selective. You can only really determine whether a particular engine strikes a good balance by testing the engine.

Ease of whittling

That is, if a search does return a large number of documents, does the program simply provide a long and unorganized list, or does it try to group the choices into categories somehow (*clustering* is the jargon term) for an easier time whittling down the possibilities?

Platform support

Some search engines only work with one or two web servers. This can be a problem if your organization has multiple intranets using different servers (Windows NT here, UNIX over there).

Ability to crawl

Crawling means that the search engine can visit multiple intranet servers and index them. You need a crawling search engine if you're trying to help employees find information on multiple *grass-roots* intranets that grew up chaotically because people in your company didn't buy this book soon enough.

Automatic indexing

Creating a full-text index is a heavy job — the search engine has to go through every doggoned document on your intranet and index every word. The ideal search engine updates its indexes automatically at a time you specify (such as 2:00 a.m., when no one is around). Just be careful not to set a time that your network also uses for creating data backups, another intensive activity.

Remote administration

Performing reindexing and configuration chores remotely (from a web browser anywhere on the network) can save some significant time compared to having to physically go to the server console.

Product choices

Here's a sampling of popular search engine vendors and products, which range all over the map in terms of costs and capabilities:

- **AltaVista:** Intranet Search Private Extensions is a search engine that works with Digital Equipment Corp. Alpha computers and runs on top of either Windows NT or UNIX. The cost is $16,000 and up, but you get some very fast technology. An Intel NT version is in process at the time I write this.

- **Excite for Web Servers:** From Excite, Inc., is free and runs with Windows NT and UNIX systems. Excite enables you to exclude files and directories easily but doesn't handle many data formats outside plain text and HTML.

- **Knowledge Network:** From Fulcrum Technologies, can index documents in Lotus Notes, Microsoft Exchange, Adobe PDF, and other formats. Figure 11-6 shows the versatile WebFIND! search utility from Fulcrum running within Internet Explorer 3.02. Knowledge Network runs on Windows NT Server and costs about $400 per seat.

- **Microsoft Index Server:** Works with Windows NT Server 4.0 and later and Internet Information Server 2.0 and later — and that's it. However, it's a reasonably complete solution and it's also free, if you already have Windows NT Server. Index Server is easy to install and can index Microsoft Office documents.

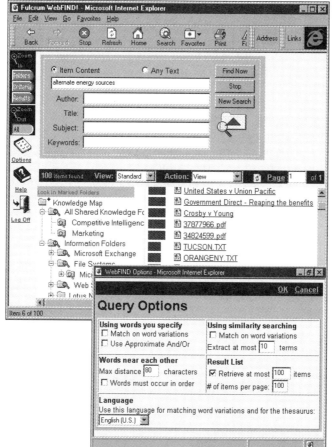

Figure 11-6: WebFIND! is the browser-compatible search component of Knowledge Network from Fulcrum.

- **Netscape Catalog Server:** $995 separately (it comes included in the $4,000 SuiteSpot software bundle) and handles a large variety of data types (Office, PDF, and others). It offers remote browser-based administration and compatibility with several web servers. Setup isn't as easy as with some other products, however.

- **Open Text:** If you have a *very* large document database, so large that the search engine's index is larger than 2 gigabytes (2,048 megabytes), you may need a 64-bit search engine, such as LiveLink Search 64 from Open Text. The cost is in the tens of thousands of dollars, but if your organization is big enough to need such a product, it's probably big enough to afford it.

- **Verity:** This company is a leader in search technology. Companies from Adobe to Lotus and Netscape license Verity products. Search '97 consists of a range of products and starts at $2,000 per server.

Getting Pushy

Site navigation structures and search capabilities are mandatory for a successful intranet. The third information access technique, *push publishing*, isn't. In fact, it may not do anything for you that your present e-mail system doesn't do. Push may have a place in your intranet publishing system, however, if employees have ongoing needs for very current information, if your networks can handle the extra traffic, and if you have a limited e-mail system that you can't easily change or upgrade.

Concepts

Intranet publishing has traditionally (if I can use that word for a technology that's younger than the car I drive) been *demand-driven* publishing. That is, if a user wants a web document, the user has to initiate the request — just as if you want to read a section of a newspaper, you have to go get the paper and turn to the section you want.

Push publishing (also known as *direct messaging, webcasting, content delivery*, or simply *push*), on the other hand, actively sends information to the user over an intranet, based on the user's own expressed preferences. Imagine having an assistant who already knows what sections of the newspaper you enjoy reading and who brings those sections to you without your asking for them. Now you're getting the push concept.

Push publishing can work well when users need a way to stay current on changes to important documents, company news, or specific project developments. You can also use push publishing to distribute software upgrades, such as for client-side antivirus utilities. Push is not usually appropriate for distributing historical or archival (noncurrent) information. Use a search engine for that stuff.

How does push publishing work in practice? Your intranet designers create different directories on a web server and create corresponding *channels* of content. Users link to the system with their browsers, augmented by extra, vendor-specific software, and choose the channels that interest them. Intranet managers or content providers add information to the channel directories, and the push software on user workstations periodically checks the server to see what's new. It then downloads and presents that content to users in a variety of formats, from screen savers to pop-up windows, Java applets, and marquee-style tickers.

So although everybody calls this technique *push* publishing, it's really more of an automatic, periodic *pull* of content. Use that more accurate terminology, though, and people look at you funny.

Look carefully at the volume and type of data you offer via push publishing. Perhaps no other technology has the capacity to overload a network faster than this one, which is why some network managers have banned it outright. Push client software also can drag down workstation performance, as can any software that runs in the background and watches the clock.

Before you start setting up push publishing systems, take a hard look at whether they can do anything for you that your present e-mail system can't. Also determine whether the site design tools you use can provide similar capabilities more simply. For example, HoTMetaL Intranet Publisher from SoftQuad can automatically e-mail users when pages that they select change.

Products

Here are some of the higher-profile push publishing software products:

- **BackWeb Technologies:** Provides both push technology and Internet-based push content — you choose whether you want one or both. BackWeb can do software distribution, too. Client software is free, and server software, which runs on Windows NT Server and Solaris, starts at about $10,000.

- **Castanet from Marimba:** Concentrates on software distribution for organizations that use Java programs. The product consists of the *Transmitter* server-side component and the *Tuner* client-side software. Both run on Windows NT Server, Windows 95, and Solaris machines. Pricing depends on usage and ranges from $1,000 to $25,000.

- **I-Server from PointCast:** Started the push publishing revolution on the public Internet. PointCast concentrates mainly on messages rather than software distribution, and like BackWeb, it provides technology and content. Companies with multinets that link to the World Wide Web can deliver PointCast messaging to intranet users, albeit with advertising. I-Server runs with Microsoft Internet Information Server.

- **Verity Intelliserv:** Part of the company's Search '97 offerings; works with Windows NT Server. Intelliserv can monitor web site files, databases that comply with Open DataBase Connectivity (ODBC), and some types of e-mail.

Chapter 12
Spinning Your Web

In This Chapter
- Creating an attractive, interesting web site
- Adding graphics, sound, animation, and video to your publishing project
- Adding interactivity to your intranet with Java, ActiveX, JavaScript, and VBScript
- Taking the drudgery out of intranet publishing with page and site design tools

*W*eb page and site design is another giant topic about which dozens of books have been written, and I only have one chapter for the subject in this book. Be sure to check out Appendix B for references, if you want more information on this subject. Don't forget to take a gander at the CD-ROM, which contains a grab bag of goodies to help you spin an intranet web that's both functional and beautiful.

Site Design Principles

Whatever applications you run on your intranet, and however you decide to format and structure the actual web site, a big part of your success is whether you can put everything into a gorgeous and friendly package.

Designing a computer information system with which users interact is a big challenge. Even big software companies have problems with the so-called *user interface.* That's not to say that you can't do a great job tying the various elements of your intranet together, but be sure to consider the nature of the medium, the capabilities of today's tools, and human psychology. This section gets you started along that path with a discussion of screen design guidelines and how to make your system *intrasting.*

A screen is not a page!

Similarities exist between a printed page and an intranet page. For example, short lines are easier to read than long lines, a little white space at the left margin can avoid a cluttered look, and dark text on a light background strains the eyeballs less than the opposite approach (regardless of artsy webmaster opinions to the contrary).

As you adjust your thinking from print design to computer design, bear in mind that intranet pages are smaller, resizable, more hidden, more independent, and more cosmopolitan than printed documents.

Smaller

The printed, typeset page has a typical resolution of 1,200 to 2,500 dots per inch, so many that you can't see them without a magnifying glass, and maybe not even then. The computer screen has a typical resolution of 72 to 96 dots per inch, or 12 to 24 times fewer than a printed page. The bottom line is that you just can't cram as much onto a computer screen as you can on a piece of paper.

The limited resolution of typical computer monitors is one reason so many web designers hate *frames,* which create multiple independent regions within the browser window (refer to Chapter 11 for more information on frames). These designers argue that the screen is so small to start with, why chop it up even further and incur more wasted space? They have a point, and if I do use frames in a project, I tend to keep the number down to two.

Resizable

You can't change the size of a printed page (at least, not without scissors), but you can resize the browser window. Remember that the browser is likely to be sharing the user's screen with other programs, so it may not occupy the entire screen. When evaluating intranet publishing tools and when designing your own custom intranet web pages, check whether the user can successfully resize the page —that is, whether the page gracefully adjusts to the new window boundaries.

More hidden

In a print document, every page is out in the open for all to see, much like a politician's romantic affairs. Not so with an intranet page. Pages longer than the browser window have a hidden section that the user must scroll down to see. If it just so happens that the viewable part of a page ends at a paragraph break, the user may assume that the page ends there.

Whatever you really, really want a user to see on a given intranet page should appear toward the top. Less important information should appear further down, so that if a user doesn't bother to scroll down that far, it's no big deal. Obviously, exceptions do exist. An employee directory needs to be in alphabetical order, even if Fred Zwxvy *is* the CEO.

More independent

A page in a book doesn't stand alone: It's surrounded by other pages and a front and back cover (at least, in my house, until one of my twins gets to the book). However, an intranet page may *need* to stand alone. For example, it may be the only page referenced in another document. As a result, your intranet pages all need to contain some basic information, which web designers typically include in *header* and *signature* sections at the top and bottom of each page.

The header can include a banner graphic, company name, intranet name (for example, if it's a separate departmental system), and page purpose. You may also want to consider including a link to a site map and a search engine as part of the header (refer to Chapter 11 for more on intranet navigation). In the fictitious Acme Cognac intranet screen shots that besprinkle these pages, the banner graphic is always the same, except for a rectangular piece at the far right that provides a graphical cue to the page's purpose.

The signature, or *footer* section, can include:

- The page owner (the individual primarily responsible for it)
- The page owner's e-mail address
- The date the page was created
- The date the page was last updated
- Copyright information (if relevant)
- Links to the top of the page
- Links to the system's home page

Some designers like to include the company name and intranet name in the signature, for example, "Acme Cognac, Inc. Technical Support System." You may also want to precede the signature section with a horizontal rule to set it off.

More cosmopolitan

Send a paper document to someone, and you know what country they live in. Publish a page on your intranet, and the employee viewing it (if you work for an international organization) may be in Boston or Beijing. Give a bit of thought to international formats for page elements, such as dates, postal codes, and so on. For example, spell out the month for all dates — the numeric month-date-year format you may be used to isn't universal.

How not to be boring

The often quoted cardinal rule of Internet web site design is "Never be boring!" This advice is good for intranet publishers, too. Even though dazzling intranet users, who view the system first and foremost as an everyday business tool, isn't as critical as wowing the general public with an Internet page, you still want users to come back and use your system repeatedly.

Slow is boring, too. Chapter 14 offers several tips on making your intranet run faster.

Text formatting

Traditionally, HyperText Markup Language (HTML) doesn't give the web designer any control over the typefaces used at the user machine, except for relative size, italics, and boldface. If the user sets up the browser to use the Times Roman font, then your pages appear in Times Roman, whether you think it's boring or not (it is). You can, however, always use different sizes and formatting options to make your intranet pages clearer and more interesting. For example, in a Frequently Asked Questions (FAQ) document, you can use bold (or large) text for the question, and regular (or small) text for the answer.

Don't go overboard — too many text variations make a page look cluttered and disorganized. Avoid all capital letters, unless you need to make a VERY STRONG POINT. Never use blinking text elements — fireflies of the computer screen that users want to swat away.

Plans are afoot to implement HTML extensions that support the two most popular font types: TrueType and PostScript (for more on this issue, check out Chapter 18). If you use Microsoft FrontPage or Internet Information Server, you can specify TrueType fonts for use in your intranet pages. Using unusual typefaces (sparingly!) is a good way to spice up your intranet pages.

You can't count on a fixed text color scheme, either, although your web page design tool gives you the impression that you control the color of visited and unvisited text hyperlinks, and any other text on the page. For example, in Navigator, a user can choose Options⇨General Preferences⇨Colors, and pick colors that always override the ones your page designers originally chose (see Figure 12-1).

Fortunately, you can override the override. In fact, you can lock down almost all aspects of Navigator using the Netscape Navigator Administration Kit. Microsoft provides a similar Internet Explorer Administrator Kit for its browser. See www.microsoft.com/ie for details. These tools let you preset just about every browser option a user can choose (everything from text colors to the default home page — even the funky little icon that appears in the upper-right corner), and lock out any user changes to these browser options.

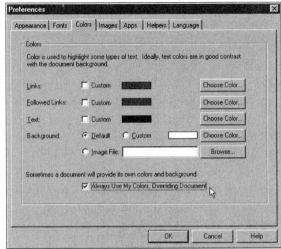

Figure 12-1: Users can choose their own text colors in Netscape Navigator, overriding colors chosen by intranet page designers.

Backgrounds

Backgrounds provide one way to make your intranet publishing system more interesting to see and more fun to use. The best and most common way to create a background is to use a small, rectangular image that the browser can automatically duplicate across and down the page (this duplication is called *tiling*). Because the tile is small, it downloads quickly over the network, and then the browser quickly duplicates it.

Most page design tools come with sample tiles. You can also buy them separately (for example, in the WebMorsels product from Image Club), retrieve some from the Internet (`the-tech.mit.edu/KPT/bgs.html` is a good place to start), or make your own — although creating a tile that duplicates without showing the seams between tiles requires a bit of experience with an image-editing program such as Photoshop. You can even use *combo tiles,* which run all the way across horizontally, but repeat vertically. (Refer to Figure 1-1 for an example of a combo tile background.)

You can use backgrounds to subtly underscore your intranet's organization, in addition to making pages look interesting. For example, you can use a different background (or background color scheme) for each of the different document systems on your intranet. You can also use one background for all your link pages and another one for all your content pages. Whatever strategy you adopt, applying it consistently is the key to making the strategy work.

Any experienced Web surfer has come across pages with backgrounds that make the text on top nearly illegible. Test your backgrounds with the smallest font size of text to make sure you don't give your users eyestrain. You can use grainy or complex backgrounds with large font sizes in bright colors and shadows, but doing so is risky because you never know when someone will put small text on that page.

A trick I found to make pre-built background tiles more text-friendly is to load them into a graphics editor, such as Adobe Photoshop, and reduce the contrast a few notches. You may have to convert the file to a full-color RGB (Red-Green-Blue) format for the contrast feature to work right. When you're done, convert it back to its original form (for example, to a 256-color GIF), and save it.

Not every page needs a background. Pages with small text or complex illustrations may look better with a plain gray or white background, so that the text or illustrations are more legible.

Funny bits

Throwing in a bit of humor can help make your publishing project more fun and interesting. If you feel your project is too serious for any kidding around, remember that there's a little cartoon in every issue of *The Wall Street Journal,* one of the more sober print publications around.

A quote or joke of the week on your main intranet page keeps things lively, but follow these suggestions:

- Don't leave the same joke on the site for more than a week (the expiration period for any joke).
- Don't make users pay for humor in terms of performance. Keep it text-only, or in a very small graphic, unless you have a really fast network.
- Keep your humor light and uncontroversial. I prefer politically incorrect humor myself, but the network probably isn't the place for it.
- Don't use any joke that begins, "A duck walks into a bar . . . ."
- If you borrow your humor from published sources, include the appropriate attribution to avoid falling afoul of copyright laws.

The Web and Multimedia

The definition of *multimedia* has degenerated to mean *something more than text,* which includes the whole gamut, from relatively simple 2-D graphics to complex digital video. Whatever you can create on a computer, a way probably exists to plunk it down onto your intranet page.

When incorporating multimedia onto your intranet, always ask yourself whether the multimedia really adds something valuable to the user's experience. Intranet multimedia takes time to run, and if all you are doing is adding a computer version of the *Flashdance* theme to the Human Resources manual, you are probably not really fulfilling any of the goals of your intranet.

Graphics

Graphic images for your intranet pages can come from several sources: photographs your company scans into digital format, computer illustrations your employees create, images that come bundled with graphics software, and pictures you buy from computer graphics companies. A few programs you may want to consider for creating intranet images include the following (see Appendix B for contact information):

- Adobe Illustrator
- Adobe Photoshop (a tryout version is included on this book's CD-ROM)
- Asymetrix Web3D
- Corel Photopaint
- Crystal Graphics Flying Fonts
- JASC PaintShop Pro (included on this book's CD-ROM)
- Macromedia Flash
- Macromedia FreeHand
- MetaCreations Painter (formerly Fractal Design Painter)
- Micrografx Designer
- Microsoft Image Composer (included with FrontPage 97)
- Ray Dream Designer

Most web browsers support two kinds of graphics files: *Graphics Interchange Format* (GIF), and *Joint Photographic Experts Group* (JPEG). The fact that browsers don't support the other nine zillion computer graphics formats is great news if you don't want to learn what the acronyms BMP, CGM, PCX, PCT, PNG, TGA, and TIF stand for.

On the other hand, you may have a library of images using one or more of these formats, in which case you're well advised to have an excellent conversion tool on hand (such as DeBabelizer from Equilibrium Technologies) to create intranet-friendly GIF and JPEG files.

Both GIF and JPEG are *bitmap* formats, meaning that they store information as a collection or series of arranged dots, or *pixels*. To display *vector* graphics, which store information as curves and formulas, and which most illustration and Computer Aided Design (CAD) programs use, you need a special browser plug-in (such as Autodesk Whip) that supports the particular vector format. Whip, for example, lets users zoom in and out of a CAD drawing without losing detail — something you couldn't do by merely converting a CAD drawing to GIF or JPEG.

GIF and JPEG formats allow you to create images that use different *palettes* (sets of colors). When using more than one graphic on the same intranet page, try to set them to the same palette (for example, with DeBabelizer). Otherwise, one or both of the images is likely to look crummy on a machine that can only display 256 simultaneous colors. Two GIF images can theoretically demand 512 different colors, in which case half the colors would be inaccurate. How gauche.

Graphics Interchange Format (GIF)

Graphics Interchange Format (GIF, pronounced *jiff*, not *giff*) files use a structure developed by the online information provider CompuServe. GIF files are space-efficient and can contain up to 256 colors from a palette of nearly 17 million colors. The GIF format doesn't have many sub-format variations, so you can generally assume that any popular web browser can understand and display almost any GIF file.

The latest GIF standard format (GIF89a, if you're interested) enables you to create a *floating* GIF that has a transparent background. Such an image looks nice on an intranet page, because the underlying page background can show through. For example, a floating GIF of a donut shows whatever background you have through the donut hole, instead of another color. The latest GIF format also enables you to create animated GIF files, which I discuss in the "Animation" section later in this chapter.

Another nice aspect of GIF files is that you can *interlace* them. Interlaced GIFs download alternate rows of pixels at one time, so that the image takes shape gradually, instead of all at once. If your intranet runs on a fast network, users don't see much difference. On slower networks, however, interlaced GIF graphics give the illusion that your network is faster than it really is and help prevent users from giving up on slow-loading images.

Good image editing tools, such as Adobe Photoshop 4.0, can easily create transparent and interlaced GIF files for your intranet. Good page design tools, such as Microsoft FrontPage and Adobe PageMill, enable you to make ordinary GIF files transparent and interlaced.

Joint Photographic Experts Group (JPEG)

Joint Photographic Experts Group (JPEG, pronounced *jay-peg*) is a popular image format because of its sophisticated compression abilities. Unlike GIF files, JPEG files can display millions of colors, so they're useful for photographic images, as long as your user workstations have true-color display capability.

Also unlike GIF files, compressing an image into the JPEG format may result in the loss of some image data — a *lossy* compression technique, as it's called. JPEG is smart about compressing photorealistic images: It knows how to squeeze an image into a small size by throwing away image information that the human eye isn't likely to notice. You can also control the compression percentage when creating a JPEG graphic from another format, so you can experiment to obtain the best compromise between file size and image fidelity.

When creating JPEGs from other formats, keep the original JPEG file on hand, to avoid the *fax of a fax of a fax* syndrome. You may want to make a new JPEG later at a different size or compression setting.

JPEG is *not* so smart about compressing non-photographic images, such as charts, or any images with sharply defined lines and curves, including text — JPEG tends to blur them. You're better off using GIF for such images, unless you really don't want users to know *exactly* how far sales have dropped since you started running the marketing department.

Sound

Over two dozen computer sound formats exist. Here's a completely detailed list of all of them! No, seriously; here are five common ones that intranet publishers are likely to encounter:

- **AIFF (Audio Interchange File Format):** This file format is common in the Macintosh world.

- **AU:** This is the most common type of sound file in the UNIX world (Sun SPARCstations and so on), and one of the older formats on the public Internet.

- **MIDI (Musical Instrument Digital Interface):** This file format makes for a small file and works well for synthesized digital music. MIDI files contain a sequence of codes, kind of like the holes in a player piano roll, that trigger a synthesizer on the user computer's sound card. The synthesizer then generates the actual sounds.

- **RA (RealAudio):** This is a proprietary *streaming* audio file format designed for intranets and the Internet. RA files start playing right away, unlike other sound files that must download completely before playing.

- **WAV (Waveform Audio):** This file format makes for a large file size and works well for voice recording and analog music sources. This is a common format in the Windows world and stores the wave describing the sound in full detail. About a dozen compression options exist to make WAV files smaller.

Sound isn't quite as easy to implement on your intranet as graphics are. First, unlike graphics, no sound file format is universally playable by all web browsers. Second, many user workstations don't have the necessary hardware to play sound files. Third, getting sounds into a computer isn't quite as simple as scanning a color photograph. And fourth, to have a sound file play as it downloads from server to client, the network has to guarantee a minimum *continuous* data transfer speed — a requirement that the TCP/IP (language of the Internet and your intranet) designers didn't worry about.

None of these problems is insurmountable, however. Internet Explorer handles AIFF and AU files via the ActiveMovie control, MIDI files through the Windows Media Player utility, and WAV files through the Windows Sound Recorder utility. Netscape Navigator plays AIFF, AU, WAV, and MIDI files through the standard Netscape audio plug-in (npaudio.dll). Both popular browsers can play RealAudio with a free helper program from Progressive Networks (www.realaudio.com).

Many computers come with built-in sound capability. Most Macintoshes can play back good quality stereo sound with the built-in speakers, but most PCs have built-in speakers that sound like they cost fifty cents (they do). Fortunately, adding sound cards and speakers to user PCs is simple and fairly inexpensive ($100 to $150 a pop).

You can record sounds with an inexpensive microphone that plugs into the sound card, and you can even connect a tape recorder or VCR directly to the sound card for digitizing prerecorded sounds. A good utility for editing and converting digital sound files is Sound Forge, from Sonic Foundry (see Figure 12-2). Sound Forge enables you to convert and manipulate sound files, for example, to clean up hisses and clicks, add special effects, or simply compress the file so it downloads more quickly over your intranet.

The problem of network transmission speed is thornier, but companies such as Progressive Networks (RealAudio) and Xing Technology Corporation (StreamWorks — see www.xingtech.com) have done impressive work delivering *streaming* audio, which starts playing back as soon as it begins downloading across the network. The only drawbacks to streaming audio are that you must add a helper program to enable browser playback, you usually need to designate a server to deliver the sound files, and streaming audio may play back with the occasional blip or skip due to limitations in TCP/IP.

So-called *network computers* typically have zero (count 'em, zero) expansion slots, so if you think you may use sound on your intranet in the future, look askance at non-expandable computers that don't have sound capability built-in and can't accept a sound card, either.

Animation

Animated graphics add the element of motion to a web page. Spinning wheels and moving arrows grab a user's attention even more effectively than multicolored graphics (and, incidentally, are *very* easy to overuse to the point of being annoying!). You can use computer animation on an intranet to

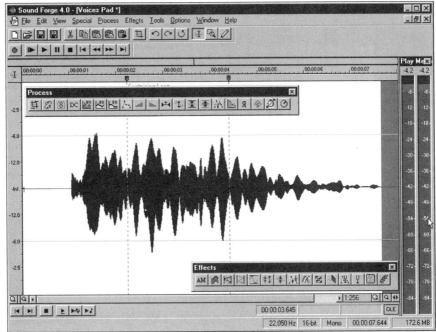

Figure 12-2: Sound Forge enables you to convert and manipulate sound files.

show a manufacturing worker how to combine component parts into a subassembly or to illustrate information flows relevant to a particular business process (such as designing a new product).

Animate your GIFs

The simplest form of web page animation is the *animated GIF* (see "Graphics Interchange Format (GIF)" earlier in this section, for a description of the GIF format). Remember in grade school when you made a series of drawings on book page corners, creating a mini-movie of a monster that enthusiastically devoured your teacher, one limb at a time, as you flipped the page corners? This *flipbook animation* is the time-honored principle behind the animated GIFs. Animating a GIF image amounts to nothing more than a series of two or more GIF images that display in succession to create the illusion of motion.

You can create animated GIFs with tools such as Asymetrix Web3D or Microsoft Image Composer (with the utility you can download free from `www.microsoft.com/imagecomposer`). Animated GIFs work well with small images, because larger ones take so long to download that the motion looks clunky.

Use repetitive animated GIF files very sparingly, if at all — they can be even more obnoxious than the dreaded blinking text.

A Flash in the pan

Next up the ladder from the animated GIF, in terms of both capabilities and price, is Flash 2 from Macromedia. This product started life as FutureSplash from FutureWave Software, which Macromedia acquired (if you've used the Microsoft Network online service, you've probably seen FutureSplash animations). The great thing about Flash 2 is that it uses *vector* images (lines, curves, and so on) rather than *bitmap* images that you use with animated GIFs.

If you don't care about computer graphics theory (and I wouldn't blame you), the bottom line is that Flash animations are packed into remarkably small files, and, therefore, can download quickly across the network. Flash can read most common vector image formats (such as Adobe Illustrator and Autodesk DXF files), which you can then program to spin and bounce and slide almost any way you want, for a variety of two-dimensional animation effects. You can add items using layers, and define how objects move using a timeline editor, as shown in Figure 12-3. The sample shown has five layers — you can create different motion effects for drawing objects in different layers, and Flash 2 combines all the effects for the final animation.

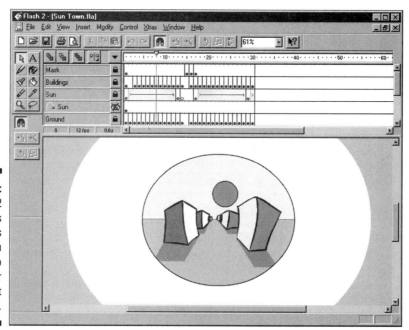

Figure 12-3: Flash 2 creates animations that you can drop into your intranet web page.

Chapter 12: Spinning Your Web 219

The basic animation procedure is to draw an object, position it, take a snapshot (called a *key frame*), move the object, take another snapshot, and so on. Flash fills in the intermediate frames to create a smooth animation. Flash can also handle sound files (AIFF and WAV formats — see preceding section). You do need a player program on the client side, but the Flash Player is freely available for both Internet Explorer and Navigator. A demo version of Flash 2 is included on this book's CD-ROM.

What I really want to do is direct

Going even fancier than Flash 2 means moving to Macromedia Director and the famous Shockwave plug-in (also included on the CD-ROM if you don't already have it). Director, which costs about $800 at the time I write this, can create flexible and complex animations. Each object in a Director movie is an *actor*, and the timeline is called the *score* (similar in concept and operation to the timeline in Flash 2).

After you create a movie with Director, you compress it with a tool called *Afterburner*. Shockwave-equipped browsers can then play your *shocked* animations, as they are called in the biz. (Macromedia has a lot of fun with its product names, unlike some companies I should not mention — IBM, IBM, IBM.) The penalties for Director's power are much larger file sizes and slower download times than what Flash 2 offers. Director also takes more time to master than Flash 2, just as a Ferrari takes more time to master than a Fiat. I suggest that you see whether Flash 2 can handle your animation needs before assuming you need to step up to Director.

Shockwave-equipped browsers can also play multimedia applications created with Macromedia AuthorWare and view illustrations created with Macromedia FreeHand.

Video

Computer video puts real-life movies (anything you can film with a video camera) onto an intranet page, as opposed to computer animation, which displays moving images that an artist creates on the computer. Publishing digital video clips over an intranet is the most technically challenging multimedia application. However, it can be a powerful tool, especially for employee training and technical support (refer to Chapter 7), guided facilities tours, filmed product demonstrations, and managerial briefings.

The process of creating a digital video clip is more or less the same, regardless of the hardware and software you choose. You connect the camera or VCR to a computer with a video capture card. The card translates the video signal to data and stores it as a file on the computer's hard drive. You can then edit, compress, and save the video to your web server, using a tool such as Adobe Premiere (a tryout version is on this book's CD-ROM). Create a link to the video file on the relevant page, install the client viewer program, and you're done. If you use a streaming video technique such as RealVideo, you must also set up a video server on your network.

Here are some popular file formats to consider for intranet video publishing:

- **AVI (Audio-Video Interleave, or Video for Windows):** The Microsoft standard supported by Windows 3.0 and later, Windows 95, and Windows NT. Many different compression options exist.
- **MPEG (Motion Picture Experts Group):** A compressed video format supported by Microsoft ActiveMovie. MPEG-1 is designed for single-speed CD-ROM drives and runs in a 352-x-240 playback window at 30 frames per second. MPEG-2, the newer version, is more ambitious and runs in a 720-x-480 at the same 30 frames per second.
- **QuickTime:** The Apple standard — the typical file suffix is MOV. Apple makes QuickTime players freely available for Internet Explorer and Navigator. As with AVI, you can choose from several compression options, to strike a balance between speed and quality.

RealVideo from Progressive Networks is a streaming video format that requires a special server and client-side plug-ins. VDOLive from VDONet Corporation, MediaServer from Vosaic Corp., and Web Theater from VXtreme are other streaming video formats that compete with RealVideo. Most of these products can encode digital video into their own proprietary data formats from AVI, MPEG, or QuickTime source material.

Interactivity

The traditional way of providing interactivity to a web site is to add a HyperText Markup Language (HTML) form and write a server-side Common Gateway Interface (CGI) script to handle the results (refer to Chapter 5 for more details). In contrast, Java and ActiveX programs run on the user's workstation, and thus provide interactivity without burdening the web server. Still other options are *JavaScript* or *VBScript* programs, which also run on the user's workstation and are easier to create than Java or ActiveX programs.

Java: a client programming language

Despite the fact that programmers usually refer to Java programs with the diminutive term *applets,* Java is a full-fledged programming language, similar in many ways to the popular C++ language. However, Java — developed by SunSoft, a unit of Sun Microsystems — has several unique features.

For one thing, it runs on a wide variety of computers, and Java programmers don't even have to create different versions of their programs for, say, PCs and UNIX systems. The programmer writes the code once, and the Java *virtual machine* software on each different computer interprets the code for that particular computer type. Write once, run everywhere — just like Salman Rushdie.

Platform independence is a compromise, though, because a programmer can't *optimize* a Java program for a particular computer type. And the virtual machine takes some time to interpret the Java program's commands, slowing things down a bit. The speed problem is lessened somewhat by the *just-in-time compilers* both Internet Explorer and Navigator include with their web browsers. Although these compilers don't work with all Java programs, they can run many of them faster by optimizing the program code for the particular kind of computer (PC, Mac, whatever) when the program is run.

Java applets can add nice interactive touches to web pages, such as a button that *pushes down* when the user clicks on it. Java can do much more than add window dressing, however — it can check user forms for correctness before submitting data to a server, create interactive question-and-answer dialogs for use in intranet-based training, and communicate directly with databases using Java DataBase Connectivity (JDBC) commands, to ease the web server's processing load. Java also permits intranet programmers to place graphics and text precisely on the page with pixel-level control, something standard HTML doesn't allow. (For more on Java page formatting, refer to Chapter 10.)

Java includes a bunch of security features that make it a bit safer than ActiveX. Java programs don't muck about with files on the user's computer, run programs other than themselves, or speak directly to the client operating system.

Does Java have any drawbacks? A few:

- ✔ Formal standardization by an independent body doesn't really exist yet. Time will probably take care of this issue.
- ✔ A Java program that runs fine on one kind of computer may crash on another. This issue may prove more difficult to solve: Java programs download from server to browser every time they're used. If a user visits a particular Java-enabled intranet page 30 times in a month, the Java applets make the trip across the network 30 times — adding to network traffic.
- ✔ Java programming isn't especially easy, and good programming toolkits for Java are just now starting to appear. Visual Café from Symantec, Visual J++ from Microsoft, and Jamba from Aimtech are examples.

ActiveX: making use of Microsoft programs

ActiveX, with a name that sounds as though it's straight out of a Marvel comic book ("Spiderman Meets ActiveX!"), may be the hottest Internet technology that nobody quite understands. ActiveX is an evolution of the Object Linking and Embedding (*OLE* — pronounce it like a bullfighter would) technology in Windows that, for example, enables a user to graft a chunk of spreadsheet into a word processor and create a *compound document*.

In similar fashion, ActiveX enables a web browser to fire up ActiveX-compatible applications, such as the programs in the Microsoft Office suite, *inside* the browser window. Also, programmers can use Visual BASIC 5.0 and later to create ActiveX *controls*, self-contained and reusable mini-programs that can do everything from displaying a movie to fetching records from a database. A particularly interesting ActiveX control, HTML Layout, enables you to create an HTML page that doesn't change appearance as the user resizes the browser window. Another cool control enables you to create pop-up windows, for example, for glossary definitions.

Unlike Java applets, ActiveX controls remain on the user's hard disk after their first use. Organizations that use Windows enjoy access to thousands of commercially available, ready-made ActiveX controls.

Here's an irrelevant but fun fact: The BASIC programming language doesn't mean *basic* in the dictionary sense. BASIC is an acronym for *Beginner's All-purpose Symbolic Instruction Code*.

Microsoft offers a free utility, the ActiveX Control Panel, for placing ActiveX controls onto an HTML page (you can download this utility from www.microsoft.com/workshop/author/cpad/default.htm). If you use FrontPage 97 as your web page editor, you can place ActiveX controls by choosing Insert➪Other Components➪ActiveX Control.

Critics of ActiveX point out that its complexity can lead to slow performance. Also, unlike Java, ActiveX is so closely tied to Windows that it doesn't do much for non-Windows platforms. For example, at the time I write this, you can't buy any Macintosh, OS/2, or UNIX ActiveX controls.

Internet Explorer 3.0 and later supports ActiveX, but Netscape Navigator 3.0 requires a plug-in, which you can download from www.ncompasslabs.com/products/scriptactive.htm

Scripting: JavaScript and VBScript

Java and ActiveX are full-featured programming environments, and they're not easy for non-professionals to master. Even Java and ActiveX programs sometimes need some programming glue to paste them appropriately into a web page. Enter *JavaScript* from Netscape (not Sun — Sun created *Java*) and *VBScript* from Microsoft, two web programming languages that mere mortals can get the hang of in a few hours.

Both JavaScript and VBScript (the *VB* is for *Visual BASIC,* on which VBScript is based) work by embedding program code into an HTML file, surrounded by the <SCRIPT> and </SCRIPT> tags. (The first tag also specifies which of the two programming languages the script uses, such as <SCRIPT language="JavaScript">.) JavaScript is *case-sensitive* (capitalization matters), while VBScript is not.

When the user's browser reads the HTML page and bumps into the <SCRIPT> tag, it knows to interpret what follows as a JavaScript or VBScript program. Unlike CGI programming (refer to Chapter 5 for more information on CGI), these programming languages typically don't involve the server. The browser does all the work — typically, but not necessarily.

You can use VBScript in server-side programming with Internet Information Server (IIS), and Netscape sells a server-side version of JavaScript under the name *LiveWire*.

Good programming practice dictates that you hide the JavaScript and VBScript program lines from old web browsers by enclosing them in HTML comment tags, so that the browser doesn't interpret script lines as text to display.

So what can you *do* with these languages? One important application is performing client-side form data validation. For example, if a user keys in **555-1q34** as a phone number instead of **555-1134**, a script can catch the error before the form data gets shipped off to a server. Other applications include:

- Changing a page's appearance on the fly, based on a user menu selection or form entry
- Designing forms that automatically remove or modify later choices, based on information the user supplied earlier in the form
- Designing intranet pages that use different layouts or features, depending on which browser the user is running (handy for businesses with a mix of Netscape and Microsoft clients)
- Displaying the current date and time
- Playing a sound file when a page loads or a user clicks a link
- Displaying a scrolling message on the browser status bar

How to choose between JavaScript and VBScript? If your programmers know Visual BASIC, VBScript is probably easier to learn. JavaScript, however, is better documented and enjoys more support in the Internet community. JavaScript is better at math, VBScript better at text handling. If you have a mixture of Microsoft and Netscape browsers, JavaScript is your ticket to ride (as I write this, VBScript works only with the Microsoft browser).

Page and Site Design Tools

A couple years ago, many web page editing tools worked as add-ons to an existing word processing program. Even today, you can use Microsoft Word 97, for example, as a HyperText Markup Language (HTML) editor. However, tools specially designed for web page editing are guaranteed to make you much happier, which is what this section addresses.

FrontPage

When Microsoft acquired Vermeer Technologies, it acquired FrontPage. FrontPage 97 makes significant strides over the earlier Version 1.1, and constitutes a good all-in-one solution for page and site creation. FrontPage 97 (the current version at this writing) consists of the following main elements:

- **FrontPage Editor:** Is the page creation and editing tool. It supports tables; frames; drag-and-drop; browser preview; direct HTML editing; TrueType fonts; image maps; programming in Java, ActiveX, JavaScript and VBScript; and a page-oriented *to-do* list. The Editor comes with several sample page templates. It can also spell-check pages.
- **FrontPage Explorer:** Provides web site management features, such as mapping (see Figure 12-4), link verification, site-wide search-and-replace, site checking (with the included Personal Web Server), and site publishing (copying files to the intranet server).
- **The Bonus Pack:** Adds the Personal Web Server, for testing and staging, and the Image Composer graphics utility, among other miscellany.

FrontPage provides tools called *WebBots* (or, to save a syllable, *bots*), which are simply pre-written Common Gateway Interface (CGI) scripts to do things like process user forms, connect to databases, create tables of contents and search pages, and so on. These depend on the web server having the FrontPage server extensions installed. Fortunately, the extensions are freely available for most popular intranet servers (see www.microsoft.com/frontpage/freestuff/fs_fp_extensions.htm).

Figure 12-4:
FrontPage Explorer lets you click a page in the left window and see all the links to and from that page in the right window.

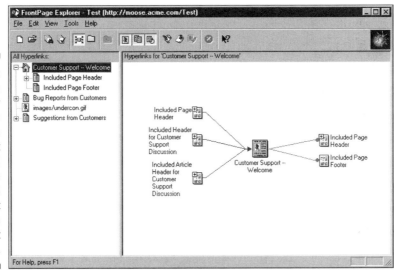

FrontPage supports good integration with Microsoft Office, supporting drag-and-drop with Office programs and a shared thesaurus, spell-checker, and clip art library. You can import existing web sites into FrontPage or build a new site with the various *Wizards* that step you through creating multiple web pages around a common theme. FrontPage reads many popular graphics file types and converts them to GIF or JPEG when you save a page.

FrontPage offers a lot of bang for the buck ($149). I personally could never get completely comfortable with Version 1.1's web page editor, but FrontPage 97 has corrected many of the earlier version's shortcomings. For site management, those with large intranets may want to look at the $1,500 Microsoft Site Server as an alternative and more powerful tool.

HoTMetaL Intranet Publisher (H.i.P.)

HoTMetaL Intranet Publisher is an interesting and even exciting tool, largely because SoftQuad includes several features of SGML (Standard Generalized Markup Language — refer to Chapter 5). These include the ability to generate a *dynamic table of contents* that changes automatically to reflect page additions or deletions, the ability to customize HTML, and the ability to allow users to see intranet data in different *views* (for example, simple versus detailed).

H.i.P. (pronounced *hip,* as in *Use our product and be hip*) is marketed as an all-in-one intranet solution, and is usable as such. The key elements are:

Part III: Strategies, Techniques, and Tools

- **H.i.P. Editor:** For creating and editing individual web pages; based on the popular HoTMetaL Pro product
- **H.i.P. Information Manager:** For site management (mapping, link maintenance, and so on — much like Microsoft FrontPage, but with document conversion utilities, too)
- **H.i.P. Viewer:** The client-side browser plug-in that lets users run H.i.P. pages (with their SGML features) from Internet Explorer or Netscape Navigator
- **H.i.P. Monitor:** A management utility that alerts administrators of unusual server events, tracks when pages go out of date, and automatically e-mails selected users of key page changes

I recommend the HoTMetaL web page editor for those already reasonably fluent with HTML. HoTMetaL brackets page elements with their associated HTML tags, which is great, but possibly a tad bit confusing at first (see Figure 12-5). This tool also includes a spell checker and thesaurus.

If your tastes incline to an all-in-one package, H.i.P. is worth a close look, mainly for the high-end SGML features it brings to standard web browsers. Even if you like other programs better for site management and monitoring, you can always get the HoTMetaL Pro editor separately, although the SGML capabilities go away if you don't use H.i.P. Viewer.

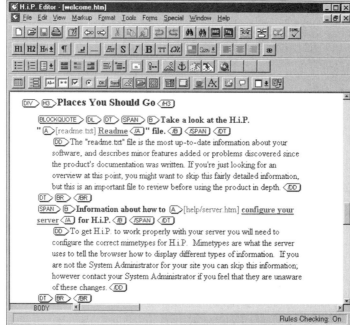

Figure 12-5: HoTMetaL lets you see the nuts and bolts of the HTML page you're working on and assumes that you understand HTML well enough to navigate a rather imposing set of taskbars.

Chapter 12: Spinning Your Web 227

For more info on H.i.P.'s navigation features, refer to Chapter 11.

PageMill

Long a favorite on the Macintosh, Adobe PageMill made the move to Windows in Version 2.0, giving Mac users one less reason to feel superior (bringing the total down to 2,159, by their count). As with most Adobe applications, PageMill hides much of its power behind a deceptively simple set of tools and commands. Creating forms, tables, and framesets with PageMill is a breeze, thanks to intuitive toolbars, drag-and-drop support, and a Help system that really does. PageMill can read Windows BMP and Macintosh PICT files and convert them to GIF or JPEG when you save a page.

PageMill is a graphical program that displays a fairly accurate version of your page while you edit it. If you want to see the underlying HTML code, type Ctrl+H and there it is, but you rarely need to.

PageMill uses an *object-oriented* approach to web page design, which means that the program considers HTML elements as *objects*, each with its own set of properties. After you get used to this way of thinking (and you are, if you use Windows 95 and have learned to right-click everything in sight), the PageMill *Inspector* becomes a handy way to change the appearance or behavior of most page items. Figure 12-6 shows a PageMill session where the user is setting table features with the Inspector property editor.

Unlike some of its competitors, PageMill comes very close to being a true WYSIWYG (What You See Is What You Get) editor. I say very close, because the PageMill Preview window doesn't always show precisely how the page looks in Internet Explorer or Navigator.

The aspect of PageMill I like best is that it makes tasks (such as designing frames) that are ridiculously complex, or even impossible, in other programs look simple and easy by comparison. It also generates good-looking HTML code.

Backstage Internet Studio

Backstage Internet Studio from Macromedia is another all-in-one product like HoTMetaL Intranet Publisher, but its strength is quick and easy database connections. The Desktop Edition ($300) works with desktop databases such as Access, dBase, FoxPro, and Paradox. The Enterprise Edition ($1,000) works with server databases such as Oracle, SQL Server, and Sybase.

Figure 12-6: The contents of the PageMill Inspector (the box on the right) change to reflect the page element you click. Here, the user changes table options easily in the Inspector window.

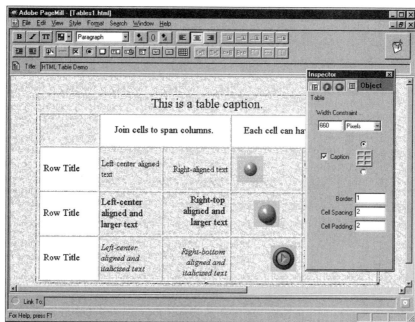

A nifty feature of Backstage Internet Studio is the ability to pass data from one page to another, something plain vanilla intranets can't do. Consider Backstage Internet Studio if you use a standard database to manage your intranet documents. It contains the following pieces:

- **Backstage Designer:** The package's HTML editor, and a popular product in its own right. It offers direct editing or WYSIWYG editing and supports Java, ActiveX, JavaScript, and VBScript. Designer handles tables but not frames.

- **Backstage Manager:** Includes features such as link verification, remote site management, discussion groups, and database access.

- **Backstage Server:** Runs in concert with your existing web server to manage Backstage Objects. These ready-made objects reduce the need for CGI programming and allow your site to generate web pages in response to user database inquiries. Other objects provide time and date stamps, the ability to select the next and previous database records, user authentication, and special form objects.

- **Various other bundled goodies:** Including O'Reilly Web Site, a Java creation tool (AppletAce), and an image editor (Macromedia xRes).

So now that you have a functional and attractive intranet publishing system in place, do yourself a favor and read Part IV on intranet care and feeding before you wing it to the Bahamas with sunscreen and Speedos. Nothing ruins a lazy day on a Caribbean beach like a call from your network manager saying, "Our intranet's fallen and it can't get up!"

Part IV
Intranet Care and Feeding

## The 5th Wave						By Rich Tennant

"...and, as we all know, departmental integration into the intranet project is still only 90% complete."

In this part . . .

Success in tennis or golf or baseball depends on your developing a swing with a smooth, complete follow-through *after* you hit the ball. Similarly, intranet publishing success depends on how (or if!) you manage the project after you roll it out.

Intranets depend on continuous refinement. They also tend to grow rapidly (especially if the application is truly useful and the execution is crisp). For these two reasons, proper intranet care and feeding is critical. In the chapters that follow, I deal with project maintenance, system performance, security concerns, and publicity and promotion — all of which should make your intranet follow-through more successful than my golf swing. (I have great form; I just keep missing the ball.)

Chapter 13

Webmasters and Beyond: Maintaining an Intranet

In This Chapter

▶ Discovering why intranets may need more ongoing maintenance than other information systems

▶ Setting up an intranet advisory board

▶ Hiring a webmaster

▶ Making sure your computer support staff can handle user questions and problems

▶ Designing maintainability into your intranet

▶ Keeping intranet publishing applications reliable and up to date

▶ Handling behind the scenes network, server, and client maintenance chores

These days, computer companies are talking a lot about Total Cost of Ownership, and not just because they want to create yet another TLA (Three Letter Acronym). Ongoing information system maintenance and support account for 85 to 90 percent of the system's total life cycle cost. This chapter can help you keep intranet maintenance costs down while keeping your intranet publishing system up.

All information systems need periodic review and enhancement, but intranet systems require more maintenance than most. Here's why:

✔ Starting an intranet publishing project is technically feasible, even with incomplete content and programming features (try *that* with a corporate general ledger system!). The result is that many intranets start active life in an embryonic state.

✔ Users tend to really like intranets, and, therefore, are more likely to push for intranet enhancement and expansion.

✔ In many companies, the network infrastructure is already in place, so intranet growth has fewer technical barriers than systems that require lots of new hardware.

Whether intranet publishing succeeds in your business depends on how effectively you maintain and nurture your intranet systems over time. Like a nuclear reaction, if you can control it enough to harness the power, intranet publishing is amazingly potent. If you can't, it tends to lay waste to the landscape in a hurry.

People Issues

Your intranet maintenance plan needs to start with people issues, such as who has high-level responsibility for system maintenance, who's in charge of maintaining the system on a day-to-day basis, what sort of reasonable publishing standards could make maintenance easier without cramping anyone's style too much, and how to maintain the client side of the people equation through ongoing user support.

Intranet advisory board

Depending on the size of your project, you may want to set up an *intranet advisory board* with at least one delegate each from management, Information Services (IS), content providers, and the user community. These are the four key intranet publishing system constituencies I discuss in Chapter 9 in the context of intranet design and implementation. Large organizations may even want to set up individual task forces under the auspices of the intranet advisory board. The advisory board can assume high-level responsibility for one or more of the following functions:

- Developing strategies to keep the corporate intranet in line with company growth
- Allocating resources (people, technology, education) for system maintenance
- Preventing the reinvention of the wheel (in the words of one MCI manager, "Collaborate, don't duplicate")
- Developing and enforcing publishing guidelines, including keeping things legal (more on that in Chapter 3)
- Providing for the delivery of effective intranet user support

Hiring and training webmasters

The *webmaster* is a job title that didn't exist five years ago but is in hot demand today. A webmaster is primarily responsible for the design and management of a web site. A good webmaster wears many hats: architect, planner, politician, visionary, artist, and technologist. Beyond all that, the webmaster also needs to help the organization understand what your intranet can and cannot do. A tall order, which is why salaries in the $75,000 to $100,000 range aren't uncommon for experienced webmasters these days.

In large organizations, webmaster functions may spread across several individuals, but normally the primary responsibility for each intranet publishing system sits with one person.

Finding and selecting a webmaster isn't easy. First off, there's no such thing as webmaster certification, and even if there were, it wouldn't mean much in an area that's evolving as fast as intranets are. When interviewing a potential webmaster, get online and look at what the candidate has done in the past. For example, consider the following:

- Is the site's functionality clear, or does it take a while to figure it out?
- Do the different pages show design consistency?
- Is it easy to tell where you are in the site?
- Do you need to click like crazy to get anywhere useful?
- Do the colors blend well?
- Does the site use any advanced features (forms, CGI scripts, transparent and animated graphics)?
- Do the pages load reasonably quickly?

Look for project management experience and a track record managing other people. Your webmaster may start out as a lone ranger, but if your intranet publishing system takes off, the webmaster won't be lone for long.

Programming in C++, Java, VBScript, JavaScript, Perl, and so on is all to the good, but intranet technology is starting to offer good higher-level tools that may reduce the need for a webmaster to be a good low-level programmer. Programming in HTML, however, is a must. A little hand-tuning of HTML code often comes in handy.

Don't be put off by a little eccentricity. Good webmasters have a strong creative streak, and that often surfaces as unusual dress, appearance, non-structural metallic body parts, and mannerisms. As long as the potential webmaster doesn't look or act so odd that he or she doesn't fit in the office environment at all, let it go. But it's okay to remind your webmaster of the old saying: The more eccentric your appearance, the better you have to be.

Ongoing webmaster education is important because intranet technology is in rapid flux. Here are some elements to consider:

- **Surf time:** Don't come down on your webmaster for spending a certain amount of time (say, 10 to 20 percent) online, checking out other sites. The Internet is a great source of ideas.
- **Magazine time:** The stigma of reading magazines in the office lifts for the webmaster. This person has to keep up with current intranet trends, and magazines are essential to doing so.
- **Tech seminars:** Send your webmaster off for public seminars on technical topics covering areas your intranet uses or may use: HTML, Java, ActiveX, scripting languages, and so on.
- **Aesthetics:** The occasional color theory or user interface design class or book is an essential supplement to the techie, nuts-and-bolts courses, books, and magazines. For example, I think every webmaster should read *The Design of Everyday Things* (Donald A. Norman, Doubleday) and *The Elements of Friendly Software Design* (Paul Heckel, Sybex).

Publishing policies

As intranet publishing systems grow and multiply, content ownership becomes even more important than at the project planning stage (see Chapter 3). In their zeal to deploy useful business solutions, intranetters can be a tad cavalier about who owns the data. For example, it's mighty tempting to surf the Web and snag copies of graphics and logos that look cool, even though such activity may be just as illegal as photocopying pages of a printed book for redistribution.

The intranet advisory board or, at least, the webmaster, needs to consult with your organization's legal counsel to produce content ownership guidelines and then publish them. Where? If you said "On our intranet," give yourself ten points and move on to the next paragraph.

Another publishing policy issue is *design consistency*. One technique is to create HTML templates for your web pages. For example, in Netscape Navigator, you can choose File⇨Save As⇨As Template to create a template. You can then store these templates on your intranet download site as an easy way for users to create intranet pages within an overall corporate design.

User support

A big part of maintaining your intranet system is providing technical support to those who use the system. If your internal Help Desk provides that support, do you need more staff to handle the intranet user workload? Do you need education on intranet technology for the Help Desk analysts? Do you maybe even need a special group of technicians who specialize in intranet support?

True, intranets are generally easy to use. But Help Desk support isn't just for usage issues — installation and configuration can befuddle even experienced mouse jockeys. If your users have to install their own browser software, they may need help. If they install browser plug-ins or helper programs to allow their browsers to view or play a wider variety of documents, they may need *more* help. On an ongoing basis, when a problem crops up with the network, a web server, a dedicated back-end database server, or a specific application, Help Desk technicians need to have the knowledge to find and fix the problem quickly.

Even if you move some support services to your intranet (see Chapter 7 for example applications), users are still likely to need phone support for several months, and perhaps indefinitely. Your organization must plan for chicken-and-egg situations: "Trouble accessing the intranet? Just follow the detailed troubleshooting flowchart we published on our intranet."

The bottom line is that intranets may, over time, reduce the need for personal user support. However, the mix of skills that your Help Desk analysts need certainly changes, and any staff reduction probably won't be feasible for the first few months of a new intranet project.

Designing for Maintenance

One of the biggest daily problems that system administrators may have to deal with is that the intranet designers don't think much about maintenance issues. If you haven't rolled out your intranet project yet, you're in luck! You have a great opportunity to build in maintainability from the start.

Hardware and software guidelines

Designing for maintenance means that you don't buy five different makes of web server for your intranet. It also means that you may want to consider standardizing on particular software environments, such as Linux (a popular freeware variant of UNIX) or Windows NT, for web servers.

User workstations are a more ticklish matter because most organizations already have a mixed bag of hardware and software. In the past, different departments, workgroups, and even individuals may have gone out and bought whatever they wanted. You may be able to publish guidelines that at least suggest to the user community the following:

- ✔ **How to configure their existing workstation hardware.** For example, through memory and processor upgrades.
- ✔ **Recommended minimum hardware requirements for using the intranet.**
- ✔ **Recommended hardware vendors.** For example, avoid no-name clone computers because of poor support or reliability.
- ✔ **Which web browser or browsers they should use.**

You probably want to publish these guidelines on your intranet, for sure; but also in company newsletters, new-hire orientation binders, online desktop help files, and any printed intranet documentation you distribute.

IP addressing control

This little section gets a wee bit technical. Okay, whole books have been written on what I'm about to cover in a dozen or so paragraphs. Less technically inclined readers may want to skip or skim this section.

The Internet Protocol (the *IP* part of *TCP/IP*) differs from other kinds of networks in the way it identifies who's on the network. Some networks use a unique number burned into a silicon chip on a computer's network card, and the network card manufacturers must take care never to use the same network number twice. (They're pretty good about this, incidentally — duplicate addresses do occur, but very rarely.) IP, however, uses a system that is both more flexible and (at least potentially) more of a "pain in the net." Any computer on the network can have one of a variety of *IP addresses*, each of which is a series of four numbers with periods between them, for example 207.68.137.40.

Making sure that no two computers on the same intranet have the same IP address is super important in order to avoid one computer accidentally getting another's "mail" (network data)!

As the intranet grows, the demand for IP addresses also grows. A few different methods exist for maintaining and managing IP addresses:

- ✔ **The central Information Services (IS) department can keep track of them and ensure uniqueness when issuing new addresses.** In this scenario, any new intranet user must request a fixed IP address from the IS department and then type that number in the appropriate place on the user's workstation. This approach can work well for small shops, but it becomes labor intensive for medium and large organizations.
- ✔ A method called *Bootstrap Protocol*, or *Bootp* (pronounced *boot-pee*), comes from the UNIX world and allows the system to make on-the-fly IP address assignments from a predefined pool of addresses,

Chapter 13: Webmasters and Beyond: Maintaining an Intranet

as users connect to the intranet. This method beats the heck out of trying to manage hundreds of addresses manually. Windows 95 workstations, however, don't support Bootp.

✓ **Dynamic Host Configuration Protocol, or DHCP, does pretty much the same thing as Bootp, but it's a little more automatic, and it does Windows, too.** When a user links to your intranet, a server running DHCP automatically *leases* the user an IP address for a specified period. When the user is done using your intranet, that particular IP address becomes available for another user.

You can build easier maintenance into your intranet by using Bootp or DHCP on the network. Which one you choose is largely a matter of whether you're primarily a UNIX shop or a Windows shop.

Besides making sure that users get unique IP addresses, maintaining a TCP/IP network also means making sure that those numeric addresses match up properly with user-friendly *domain names* such as acme.pub.com. A small shop can choose to manage its domain name match-ups manually, for example, by typing the associations into a workstation file named HOSTS anytime they change. Larger (or busier) businesses appreciate having the name associations handled more automatically and centrally, with the help of a *Domain Name Server* (often called, redundantly, a *DNS Server*). A DNS server simply maintains a list of IP addresses and the associated domain names, so that every time a user enters a domain name in an application, your intranet can find the IP address.

Finally, on Windows networks, computers can browse the network using special names called *NetBIOS* names (NetBIOS stands for Network Basic Input/Output System, and is just a way for applications to communicate with a local area network). A Windows network may include computers with the NetBIOS names Moose, Squirrel, Boris, and Natasha, for example. Those NetBIOS names need to match up with IP addresses, too. Just as with domain names, you can manage NetBIOS names manually with workstation text files (LMHOSTS) or automatically with a server (the usual choice for NetBIOS name management on NT Server networks is Windows Internet Naming Service, or WINS).

Figure 13-1 shows the many names a user workstation can have.

✓ You don't have to have separate machines running address management services like DHCP, DNS, and WINS. For example, on a Windows NT server, you can run all three on the same computer.

✓ If your network is *really* large, check out more industrial-strength IP address management products, such as DNS/DHCP Manager from Cisco Systems and NetID from Isotro (see Appendix B for more information).

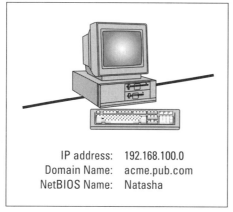

Figure 13-1: A user workstation on a Microsoft network has an IP address, an intranet domain name, and a NetBIOS network name.

The way IP addressing was originally conceived is for each computer to have one, and only one, address. However, as the world turns and the intranet grows, you may want the flexibility to have a single web server support multiple IP addresses, or, conversely, to have multiple web servers share the same IP address. Look for these capabilities when shopping for web servers to handle a potentially large intranet publishing system. If the server supports HTTP Version 1.1, it can probably handle these variations on the IP addressing theme.

Portability

Especially when it comes to web server programming, portability (being able to move programs around) should be a major concern. For example, webmasters can write programs using so-called Server Side Includes, or SSIs for short; but such programs, while fast, are limited to the type of server you set them up on. If you ever move your system to a different server type, for example, to upgrade performance as a new product becomes available, you can find yourself rewriting a lot of code. Common Gateway Interface (CGI) programs are more portable and, therefore, may be worth their generally slower performance (see Chapter 5).

One of the risks of using an all-in-one intranet publishing solution from one vendor is that the individual pieces may not be replaceable by other vendors' pieces. For example, when a different vendor offers a desirable feature you want to integrate into your existing system, you may simply be stuck. A portable system uses technology bits that you can swap around a little.

For example, say that you're using a database to manage a large library of documents. That database may be a special, proprietary design, such as Lotus Notes, which is fine as long as you use the same vendor's tools for HTML conversion, user queries, and so on. If you later decide that you want to use a different tool to convert the documents to HTML so that users can view them, or that you want to use someone else's search software for faster document location, you may be out of luck.

Highly integrated, non-portable software products are said to be *tightly coupled*. Look for dependencies between data formats, processing logic, and user presentation modules. Loosely coupled systems may not perform as well because they can't rely on shortcuts made possible by a tightly coupled product, but they are more portable and flexible.

A key to making your intranet portable is to use *relative links* rather than *absolute links* wherever you can. A relative link tells the web server to look in a directory at or below the current directory to find a new page or page element. An absolute link specifies the precise location, which can change if you decide later to push your web file structure down a notch or two in the directory tree. (You still have to use absolute links when pointing to resources on different servers.)

Case sensitivity

One speed bump most intranet publishers hit at some point is the issue of *case sensitivity*, meaning whether or not your server cares if text is uppercase or lowercase. Although Windows-based servers and clients are generally indifferent to capitalization, UNIX systems pay close attention to it, which can create problems. For example, a Windows-based program generates a file with all capital letters and a UNIX-based server looks for that file expecting lowercase. My recommendation for easier maintenance is that you require that *all* files use lowercase letters and make this requirement part of your intranet standards.

Documentation

Companies sometimes pressure their intranet publishing project managers to get systems online in a hurry. Usually, the first casualty of time pressure is proper documentation. Having no documentation can be a major problem over the long term, especially when personnel changes or when consultants come in to enhance or expand the site. ("Your first job is to get familiar with our intranet's design." "Great. Just point me to the documentation." "Uh . . . documentation? Just what do you mean by that?")

Comments, embedded into programs and HTML documents, are often the best way to document intranets because the comments appear together with the document HTML code itself. For example, you can easily add comments to HTML code with the tag pairs <!- and ->:

```
<!- This page requires a Microsoft or Netscape browser
        version 3.01 or above ->
```

Comments are especially valuable for fancy or tricky web pages that may not work with all browsers or that require particular helper or plug-in programs.

I also urge intranet designers to create and maintain a *design manual* that contains details about the intranet architecture, components, standards, and programming practices used in your organization. Such a document doesn't have to be massive, and ten pages are better than none. A design manual makes managing and maintaining an intranet much easier, especially in organizations with technical staff turnover or that outsource major pieces of the intranet project.

Maintaining Applications

Whether an intranet system is designed for easy long-term maintenance or not, certain application management chores appear on every intranet manager's recurring to-do list. The two examples this section explores are *link integrity* (making sure your hyperlinks point to something that's still there) and *document updating*.

Both these tasks become much easier if intranet managers have good tools to map a web site visually. Figure 13-2 shows a site map created automatically by the industrial strength management tool, Microsoft Site Server. (Other good site mapping utilities include Web Analyzer from InContext Systems and Astra SiteManager from Mercury Interactive Corp.) Note the tree view to the left and the graphical view to the right (called a *cyberbolic* view, because it uses hyperbolic curves rather than straight lines — looks weird at first but actually makes the map easier to read). Site Server enables you to view the map at greater or lesser levels of detail.

A good site mapper enables you to customize the display by choosing, for example, whether you want to include linked graphics or just the web pages themselves.

Chapter 13: Webmasters and Beyond: Maintaining an Intranet

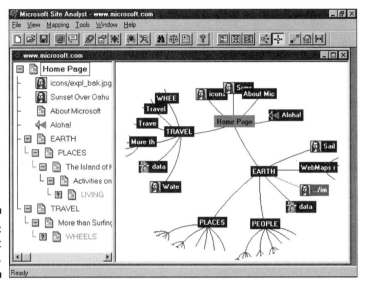

Figure 13-2: Microsoft Site Server.

You can certainly use flowcharting tools to create and manage your own intranet site map flowcharts manually, which is a great approach if you're managing an intranet and you want to ensure your job security through the year 2010. An automatic tool that builds the map for you can cut your intranet management time drastically, however, so that you can spend your time on more productive pursuits, such as enhancing your intranet or planning your football pool picks.

The case of the missing links

In any intranet, it's just a matter of time until someone deletes a page that's referenced by a link on another page. Such *broken* links are frustrating to users, who may see an `Error 404` when they try to connect to the links. Even with intranets, one can't completely escape coded error messages, although an English explanation usually accompanies the number. A misspelled link is another common type of broken link.

Happily, some intranet design and management tools provide a built-in capability to check for broken links. Microsoft FrontPage Explorer, for example, includes a Verify Links command that lists broken links and enables you to edit them so that they work again. Microsoft Site Server contains a module called Site Analyst, which not only presents a list of broken links, but even spins the graphical site map around to highlight that link — as shown in Figure 13-3.

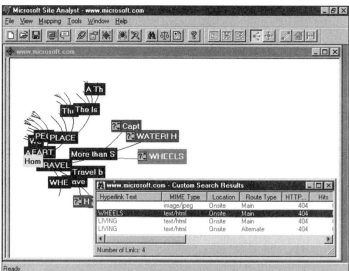

Figure 13-3: The Site Analyst component of Site Server presents a list of broken links in the Custom Search Results window.

A subtler variation on the missing link is what I call *dependent file syndrome*: An intranet page depends on a graphic that another department maintains and stores. For example, a product information intranet may use scanned product photographs that the marketing group keeps on its own network server. The intranet may depend on those graphics being a certain size, but the marketing folks decide one day that disk space is becoming a problem, so they shrink the files to half size — making your intranet pages look crummy.

You can deal with dependent file syndrome two ways: Appropriate the dependent files by copying them to your intranet server where you control them, or establish a communications channel for departmental content providers to alert you before changing files to which your intranet links.

When you change the Uniform Resource Locator (URL) for a frequently accessed intranet page or document to which users are likely to point directly, for example, via a *favorite places* list in the browser, consider notifying affected users with an e-mail message. Many e-mail systems today allow you to embed a new URL into an e-mail message so that the recipient can link directly to the web site by clicking the URL in the message.

Freshness dating

Here are other aspects of keeping intranet content current, besides the link management I cover in the previous section:

- **Assigning responsibility for particular content areas.** With some server management software, you can even assign an author to a particular web page and pull a report listing all pages assigned to that person.
- **Setting regular schedules for content updates.** These don't necessarily preclude ad hoc updates, which may be necessary at unscheduled times.
- **Monitoring which pages need updates.** If you have a site management tool, such as Site Server, that supports page expiration dates, use this feature so you can later pull reports listing pages due for updating.
- **Defining formatting guidelines for how content providers need to submit material.** Doing so relieves some of the burden on intranet managers, who can post content updates more rapidly if extensive reformatting and conversion isn't necessary.

If non-technical content providers update content periodically on your intranet, provide a user-friendly utility for this purpose — the Microsoft Web Publishing Wizard is one example. Expecting content providers to master the nuances of the File Transfer Protocol (FTP) command line to copy files up to web servers may be unrealistic.

If you publish software over your intranet, for example, with a download page (see Chapter 7), freshness-date it by both calendar day and version number, so that users can easily see whether they need a particular file or if it's no newer than the file they already have. Also, as I discuss in Chapter 12, you help users by putting the date of creation and last modification to every web page into a *signature block* at the bottom of every intranet web page.

Some intranet site management tools enable you to search for content by date. In this way, you can easily rank web pages by when they were last modified and pinpoint stale sites that are more likely to need an update — and to bankrupt users who just exercised their stock options based on a price that's two months old.

Maintaining the System

This section covers behind-the-scenes intranet maintenance: keeping the network, servers, and clients humming along smoothly and happily.

The network

How do you know when a server needs maintenance? By the time a user calls to report a problem, dozens or even hundreds of users could be running into the same problem. Fortunately, you have a better way.

Network Management Systems (NMSs) make proactive network monitoring possible for a wide range of devices. A simple way to think of an NMS is as a *red dot system*: A network administrator looks at a screen and sees a map of the network and its various key components (servers, hubs, power backup systems, and so on). The NMS monitors the state of those components and puts a red dot at the appropriate place on the screen anywhere a problem crops up (server down, hub down, link down, excess traffic on a Local Area Network segment, and so on).

The most popular NMS standard these days is the *Simple Network Management Protocol,* or SNMP. SNMP traces its roots to the UNIX world, so it would seem to be a natural fit for use with intranets, which also started on UNIX systems (even today, most public Internet servers run UNIX). The Internet Engineering Task Force, a standards-setting body, is, in fact, burning midnight oil to extend the SNMP standard so that it includes web and FTP (File Transfer Protocol) servers. Other groups are working to include network management capabilities for both HTTP (HyperText Transfer Protocol, the language of intranets) and Java. Meanwhile, a management system such as SNMP (or a similar vendor-specific product, such as DEC PolyCenter, Hewlett Packard OpenView, or IBM NetView) can still be a big help in identifying problems on the local area networks that host intranet services.

Modern network management systems go well beyond the red dot system. Some of the capabilities to look for when shopping for NMS software include

- **Software distribution:** The capability to send programs and program updates to users. Vendor-specific tools may offer more features than a more generic intranet-based distribution system.
- **Software license tracking and metering:** *Tracking* means keeping tabs on how many users are running a program concurrently; *metering* means limiting that number by locking out users above a fixed maximum. Sometimes necessary with proprietary intranet publishing systems.
- **Hardware inventory:** Processor, memory, disk space, installed options, and so on.
- **Capacity planning:** Features to help administrators project future usage patterns and demands.

Here are a few network management products worth checking out:

- Cabletron Spectrum
- Cisco Systems CiscoWorks
- Digital Equipment Corp. PolyCenter
- Hewlett-Packard OpenView
- IBM NetView

Chapter 13: Webmasters and Beyond: Maintaining an Intranet

- ✔ Intel LANDesk Manager
- ✔ Microsoft System Management Server
- ✔ Novell ManageWise
- ✔ Symantec Norton Administrator for Networks

You can now outsource certain intranet maintenance and management functions. NetSolve, for example, offers round-the-clock network monitoring services. Offloading some maintenance functions to contractors may free up in-house staff for new intranet projects. Be sure that the contractor is familiar with your system and is responsive to your particular needs and desires (for example, you may want a copy of the contractor's trouble logs).

The server

Generic Network Management Systems (NMSs) are useful for identifying server problems and alerting network administrators to those problems. Automated tools specially designed for intranet web sites can help alert intranet server administrators if something's wrong that a general-purpose NMS might miss. For example, the Red Alert program from Internet Resources Group periodically downloads web pages, just to make sure they're still downloadable, and can even page a technician if something's amiss.

The next question to ask is, "What do you do when an NMS or specialized web server monitor indicates a problem — especially when your network administrator or technician is at a remote location?" Being able to deal with server problems remotely is an important maintenance requirement. You don't want to make administrators physically go to the server location every time a problem crops up — especially if it's 2:00 a.m. and no one is at the office.

Technicians can use at least two tools for remote server troubleshooting: web server log files and LAN-based reporting tools.

Web server log files

Web servers have their own log files that track usage and traffic. Figure 13-4 shows the log file configuration screen for Microsoft Internet Information Server.

These log files provide details on intranet activity, such as:

- ✔ Every intranet access, including user address, requested document, and the associated traffic. If certain documents generate excessive traffic, you may consider paring back their graphics content, for example.

- ✓ All errors from the server and from programs run by the server (this is especially useful when you need to troubleshoot problems because you can see which scripts may contain bugs, for example).

- ✓ Which users connect to the intranet most frequently (you may need to upgrade network cards for frequent visitors to improve access speed).

- ✓ Which web documents and pages account for the most network activity (these become candidates for streamlining, for example, by reducing graphics file sizes).

- ✓ How many bytes of data traffic the web server handles at different times of the day, week, month, year, millenium, and so on.

- ✓ Peak web server data traffic for a given time period.

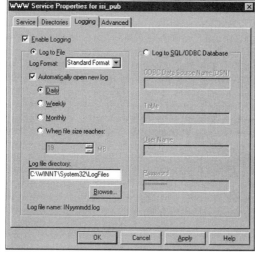

Figure 13-4: You can program Internet Information Server's Service Manager to log activity to a file or a database.

If your web server site management software permits remote access to these server logs, for example, via HTML pages, maintenance and troubleshooting becomes much easier. Graphical reporting capability is also a big plus, so that technicians don't have to interpret the log files by staring at hundreds of lines of text and numbers. Also, predefined reports help a lot by not making your administrators create their own.

Some server log file analysis tools can save log file data into a database format — for example, Microsoft Site Server supports Access and SQL Server formats. When shopping for a web site analysis tool, consider whether it supports the database you use in your organization. This way, you can easily create custom reports that include the information you're most interested in tracking.

Chapter 13: Webmasters and Beyond: Maintaining an Intranet 247

Although the trend is afoot to standardize web server log file formats, at last count about two dozen different formats exist. Make sure that the log file analysis utility you buy can read the formats your web servers create.

LAN-based reporting tools

Remote management tools for web servers aren't nearly as sophisticated as those for traditional Local Area Network (LAN) servers. Fortunately, if your intranet runs on top of a traditional LAN operating system, you may be able to solve many kinds of problems by using the remote access tools the LAN vendor provides. For example, if you run Microsoft Internet Information Server on a Windows NT Server, you can perform many server management tasks from a remote Windows 95 machine by using the Windows NT Server Tools, which include the Event Viewer (see Figure 13-5), Server Manager, and User Manager.

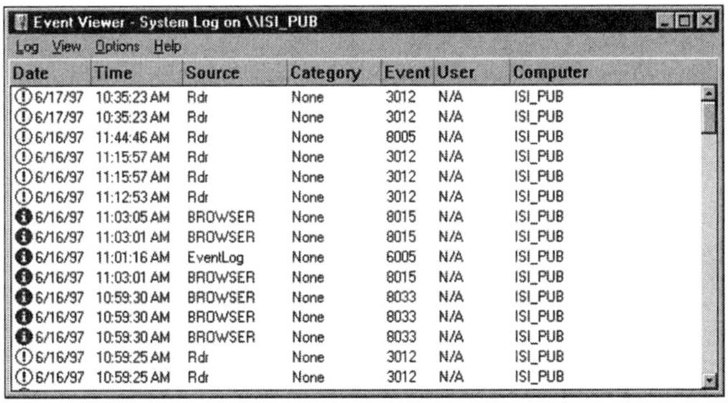

Figure 13-5: Here's a remote Windows 95 computer running the NT Server Event Viewer over a LAN connection.

The client (apologies to John Grisham)

Intranet maintenance usually focuses on servers and network infrastructures, but a big part of maintaining an intranet publishing system is to keep the client workstations in the best possible shape — that means hardware, but also workstation *operating systems* — the programs that control the machines' primary functions (Windows 95 and UNIX are examples).

An ounce of preventive maintenance is worth a pound of troubleshooting cure. Most network administrators can't possibly keep up with all the software patches and fixes that workstation users may need, however. A solution to this problem in most organizations is regular, two-way communication between intranet managers and the workstation support staff, as (in larger organizations) the group that manages the network is often different from the group that manages user workstations. Using two-way communication, at least the intranet administrators know when operating system patches are scheduled for application.

Sometimes, too, the intranet manager may run across a tidbit that he or she should pass along to the workstation tech staff. The following tip is just one example.

Windows 95 users can run out of memory prematurely if they perform many intranet links, due to a bug in the Windows 95 system software. A fix for this problem exists: The file is KRNLUPD.EXE at http://www.microsoft.com/windows/software/krnlupd.htm), and applying it to every Windows 95 PC that you expect to use your intranet is a great idea.

You can post operating system fixes and patches on an intranet download page (see Chapter 7 for how to set up such a page). Proactive organizations also e-mail users about fixes that could be important to their ability to use the system reliably and securely.

Plan for significant technical time on an ongoing basis to evaluate and test new versions of web browsers and plug-in programs. Merely posting the latest versions on a download page isn't enough, because sometimes a new version doesn't work properly with the HTML pages, documents, and publishing applications on your particular intranet.

Maintaining an intranet is a bit like keeping a racecar on the road by anticipating and fixing the problems that crop up. As with cars, if you start with a sound design, assemble a good team of mechanics for the pit crew, and equip yourself with good diagnostic equipment, maintenance isn't terribly difficult, and you can prepare to handle the unexpected. Chapter 14 goes a step further, and considers the situation where you not only want your *Formula I* intranet to keep running, but you want to keep it running *fast*.

Chapter 14
High-Octane Performance

In This Chapter
- Whipping your intranet servers into shape
- Beefing up network plumbing
- Tuning up user workstations
- Designing smart, speedy intranet publishing applications
- Monitoring performance, and spotting problems
- Planning for future capacity

This chapter provides guidelines and tips for tuning up your intranet so that document users don't grow old and gray waiting for pages to appear, forms to send, and files to download.

When you get to the bottom of this page, please count to 20 *slowly* before turning to the next page. Continue this procedure until you reach the end of this book.

Okay, that advice is silly, but I'm making a point here: If you don't expect someone reading a book, magazine, or corporate manual to endure long delays between pages, you don't want intranet document users to wait either. If users have to wait, then no matter what else you do to design a great intranet information system, they won't use it — at least not if they have other, faster ways to get the information they need.

Remember: In many situations, intranet publishing systems compete with paper, and paper documents don't need 20 seconds to *load*.

Some organizations take the view that the intranet user population is a captive audience, so performance is secondary compared with a public Web site, which has to perform well to keep visitors coming back. Even if a user truly can't obtain a particular document any other way than via your intranet, user productivity should remain a goal of your information system. Many scientific studies, such as those of IBM researcher Arvind Thadhani, show that computer-user attention wanders after as little as a two-second delay. Thadhani also discovered (way back in 1981) that user productivity increases significantly when computer response time improves even as little as from one second to half a second. If you have an intranet environment that's growing fast, such as the Lockheed-Martin system that tripled in one year to 140,000 users, performance can slip away faster than sand through chicken wire, and user productivity goes right along with it.

Other organizations may feel that because the "data pipe" is so much larger for an intranet than for a typical public Internet connection, performance issues don't matter. Here's my two cents' worth on this point: Optimizing your intranet for performance is certainly not as critical as optimizing a public Internet server for performance. Also true: If you have a brand spanking new network and only a dozen users, intranet speed isn't likely to be a big problem for you. However, if your network hardware is getting a little long in the tooth, if heavy traffic occasionally slows performance, if you have hundreds or thousands of intranet users, or if you expect your intranet to grow rapidly, performance is worth some attention. Performance concerns should never displace user-friendly design, relevant content, and system reliability in your priorities, but you shouldn't ignore it either.

Optimizing performance is a huge task, and the nitty-gritty details always depend heavily on the specific products you're using. My goal in this chapter is to mention some of the key aspects of whipping your hardware and software into intranet-ready shape.

One big-picture note before you dive in: High-octane performance can be labor intensive, and these days, in most organizations, labor is more expensive than computer hardware. One valid approach to performance management is to spend a chunk of money on some very high-speed servers, infrastructure, and clients. Sounds wasteful, I know, but it could be cheaper than throwing even more money at specialists who run around tweaking your network all the time.

Giving the Network a Tune-Up

In addition to purchasing newer, faster equipment, you can tune up your current equipment to get the best possible service. As shown in Figure 14-1, the main areas to target for a tune-up are *servers, infrastructure* (that is, all the wires and devices that connect computers to each other), and *clients* (see Figure 14-1).

Starting with servers and infrastructure is usually the best way to go, because you have the most control over these network pieces. Client tuning is important, too, but running around tuning up all those workstations takes more time and may not deliver the same bang for the buck (or hour's worth of effort).

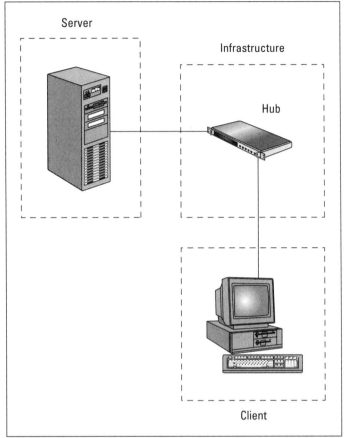

Figure 14-1: Intranet hot-rodding opportunities exist in three physical areas: the server, the network plumbing, and the client workstation.

Server tuning

In a typical intranet publishing system, the web server does most of the work. Some technologies are changing this situation: Java programs run at the user's workstation rather than at the web server. Nevertheless, the server still has to send all those Java programs out to the users over and over again (Java programs are downloaded each time they're used). Servers also have to handle any behind-the-scenes connections to document databases, requests to run programs on other servers, and user requests for files via FTP (File Transfer Protocol, often used to distribute software upgrades and updates). The servers also manage hyperlink activity in all web-based intranets.

Servers are busy little guys, and you want to get the most you can out of them. Rare is the server that's optimized for high performance right out of the box. Tuning up your server involves the processor, memory (RAM), disk, communications, and load balancing (dividing the workload between servers in a multiple-server network). I address these five areas in the following sections.

Other aspects of a server's design, such as the *data bus speed* (how fast information moves around internally in the server), can affect performance as well. You can't, however, do much to tune those features. You either have a fast data bus or you don't — so I omit a discussion of them here. However, if you are in the position to buy new hardware, you definitely don't want to omit them from your consideration.

Server tuning is great, but it only takes you so far. If you have an el cheapo computer running your web intranet, you can tune it till the cows come home and you still won't get fast performance (turbocharge a Yugo and it's still a Yugo). If your tech staff devotes time and energy to server tuning, and the system still performs like a slug, it may be time for a faster server, such as those from Silicon Graphics, Sun Microsystems, Digital Equipment Corporation (*Alpha* servers), Hewlett-Packard, and others.

A fun note for computer nerds: The Hewlett-Packard Exemplar X series servers can handle 64 processors and 64 gigabytes of RAM! Now that's *horsepower,* even if such servers do cost a cool million. Fortunately, in today's market, you can buy very respectable-performing web server boxes, software included, starting at $10,000.

Processor

Most designers agree that you want a lot of processing horsepower on your intranet servers. However, you're not necessarily stuck with the amount of CPU power your server comes with. For example, the Microsoft Windows NT Server operating System enables you to pack up to four microprocessors into one box to ramp up server brainpower.

Servers that support such a *Symmetric MultiProcessing* (SMP) scheme, as it's called, don't deliver precisely proportional speed gains. In other words, an NT server with two Pentiums isn't twice as fast as one with a single Pentium — it may be about 50 percent faster.

Sometimes you can do chip surgery and replace an older, slower microprocessor with a newer, faster one. In some cases, chip replacement is a good option, but tell whoever does it to be careful — you can easily fry those little chips with static electricity. Again, the performance boost you get is not directly relative to the CPU speeds ("your mileage may vary").

Memory

To nerdify an old cliché, you can never have too much money, be too good-looking, or have too much memory. Memory is key to server performance, and here's why: Servers *buffer* (temporarily store) files and directories in memory to increase speed, because getting information from RAM is *many* times faster than getting it from a disk drive. File buffering is a little like going to the grocery store: If you go on a bicycle, you need to take many more trips (and time) than if you go in a large truck — and some items are too big to transport at all.

Every server is a little different in terms of its memory requirements, but
don't even think of setting up a web server with less than 64 megabytes of
RAM. With RAM at all-time low prices — on the order of $100 for 16 mega-
bytes as I write this — memory is no place to scrimp and save.

Disk

Fast servers need fast disks, and tuning up a server often means replacing
hard drives with speedier ones. An ultrawide Small Computer System
Interface (SCSI, pronounced *scuzzy,* not *sexy*) disk drive runs rings around
garden-variety disks such as Enhanced Intelligent Drive Electronics (EIDE)
types.

Tuning the disks that you already have generally involves fixing file system
problems using the operating system's repair utility, and *defragmenting* disks
so that the server doesn't have to hunt all over the disk platter for files that
are stored in bits and pieces.

Sometimes the operating system comes with a *defragger* (slang for the program that defragments a disk), and sometimes, as with Windows NT Server,
you have to buy a separate utility. In either case, setting up a regular schedule
for tuning the disks is a great idea. Utilities even exist that defrag continuously
in the background whenever the server isn't too busy. Automatic defragging
is a far cry from the old days, when system managers would spend two to
four weekends every month laboriously performing this chore by doing a full
data backup and restore. The divorce rate for these technicians was high, at
least for the ones who found the time to get married in the first place.

Communications

Servers communicate with the rest of the network via Network Interface
Cards (NICs). NICs older than a couple of years are likely to be far slower
than newer models, which use a technique called *bus mastering* to pump
data in and out of the server faster.

Sometimes, simply updating the software that the server uses to talk to the
NIC — the NIC driver — can boost performance dramatically. NICs also have
zillions of configuration options that can impact speed.

In faster servers, the NIC can be a bottleneck. If you have a fairly large network, explore the possibility of tossing one or two additional NICs into the
server, and hooking them up to different pieces of the network — called
segmenting a network. You can only carry this trick so far — creating segments of fewer than six users probably doesn't make sense.

Load balancing: dividing the labor

Often, the best way to improve a server's performance is to give it a sibling:
Add another machine and divide the chores between the two, or three,
or four, and so on. Intranets let you easily balance network load this way

because the user's browser grabs data from wherever it needs it, and users don't need to know which server they're using at any given instant (Weadock's Rule #1 of successful networks: The less users have to remember, the better).

You can split server chores across multiple machines in several ways:

- **Split out files by type:** Put text documents on one machine and graphics on another.
- **Split out web server applications:** Put your HTTP (HyperText Transfer Protocol — your web pages) on one server, FTP (File Transfer Protocol, for file downloads) on another, DNS (Domain Name Server, for computer address management) on a third, and e-mail on a fourth.
- **Give traffic-intensive intranet functions their own server:** Doing so means that they won't bog everything else down. A good example of a traffic-intensive application is a groupware program like Lotus Notes.
- **Divide files up within a publishing application:** Put filenames beginning with *A* through *M* on one server, and *N* through *Z* on another. Remember, however, that if you do this, keeping the URLs straight can be a bit of a problem, because you have to remember which server hosts which files when creating a document link.
- **Divide files and applications by department:** Put the financial intranet on server A, the manufacturing intranet on server B, and so on.

Infrastructure tuning

Web-type intranet publishing systems make heavy use of the HTTP communication protocol (HyperText Transfer Protocol, the language of web servers and browsers — see the Introduction to this book). Much of HTTP's flexibility arises from the fact that it's a *connectionless* protocol, a $10 word that simply means each HTTP transaction is self-contained: Each time a user clicks a hyperlink, an HTTP connection opens, the web server ships the data to the browser, and the HTTP connection closes. This design means that a web server can handle many more users than is possible with traditional servers, but lots of users clicking on hyperlinks still means a lot of HTTP traffic over the network.

Web systems also permit publishing graphical data, which is *much* bigger than text data. A server can transmit thousands of words using the same amount of traffic as it needs to transmit a single graphical image (a picture really *is* worth a thousand words!). If you plan to publish sounds or videos over your intranet, the data files get huge in a hurry.

The bottom line here is that the network plumbing, or *infrastructure,* must be up to the task of moving that data around in a reasonably short amount of time if your intranet is to be a success.

How important is infrastructure tuning?

Wide Area Network (WAN) links are often a big intranet performance bottleneck. Specific tuning suggestions depend on the type of WAN, and are beyond — way beyond — the scope of this book. Your WAN gurus and access providers can suggest ways to speed up long-distance links.

If your network has a high-speed *backbone,* or *trunk* — that is, the part of a large network that manages most of the traffic and links Local Area Networks together — consider linking your intranet servers directly to it to bypass the bottleneck of a regular Local Area Network (LAN) workstation connection. Asynchronous Transfer Mode (ATM) is slowly growing in popularity for network backbones, and it has the appealing feature of being able to prioritize traffic (so that for a few seconds, for example, a video clip gets higher priority than e-mail traffic, so that the video can display more smoothly at the workstation). Gigabit Ethernet is on the horizon and coming up fast, too. If you're thinking about ATM, also think about gigabit Ethernet, which I discuss in Chapter 19 as a standard to watch.

If you're still using regular old Ethernet (speed limit: 10 megabits per second) for desktop communications, step into the light and move up to Fast Ethernet, which is up to ten times faster depending on how many users are on the network. You don't have to perform the transition all at once. You can start replacing workstation NICs (Network Interface Cards) with combo cards that can work at either the slow or the fast speed, and when you're ready, upgrade your network hubs.

Ethernet switching is popular because it sets up ad hoc, dedicated communications circuits between two computers. Switched Ethernet can help intranets that need to communicate high-traffic data types like video.

Figuring out your tune-up needs

Whether you need to worry a lot or a little about infrastructure tuning depends on your answers to these questions:

- Does your publishing system involve a lot of graphics?
- Are many of those graphics complex?
- Are you publishing pages with sounds?
- Do you plan to publish digitized speeches (video)?
- Are the documents you publish large (over 1,000 words)?
- Do they contain many hyperlinks (over 10 per page)?
- Are you using Java technology?
- Do users already complain about network speed?
- Are you using computers older than three or four years?

If you answer "Yes" to a few of these questions, you may want to consider some infrastructure tuning in addition to server tuning.

Part IV: Intranet Care and Feeding

When beefing up your network infrastructure, remember the age-old (well, it's at least a year old) adage: *Switch when you can, route when you must.*

Finally, look into products that enable you to prioritize intranet traffic, for example, by URL, user address, or traffic type (web server versus file server). Even if your organization isn't using ATM, products such as PacketShaper from Packeteer are worth exploring.

Client tuning

You can have a fast server and fast infrastructure, but the rubber meets the road at the user's workstation. Tuning a client (workstation) for performance involves some of the same steps as tuning a server, and a few different ones. Don't worry too much about processor performance or disk speed on workstations — these factors are much more important for servers.

Network software

See whether you're running the most efficient TCP/IP (Transmission Control Protocol/Internet Protocol) client software on user workstations. Such software links the user computer to the network. For example, Power Macintosh systems perform noticeably better with the newer Open Transport TCP/IP software than with the older, slower MacTCP.

Memory

The actual amount of RAM an intranet user needs varies by the type of computer and operating system (Sun SPARCstation, PC with Windows 95, PC with Windows NT, and so on), but a good rule of thumb is to have at least 16 megabytes of main memory for best browser performance. More RAM doesn't necessarily make the workstation run faster, but it does allow users to have more programs loaded at once while they're using your intranet, and it permits performance tricks, such as the following tip.

Here's a neat intranet performance trick that's especially useful on slower networks. Clicking a hyperlink to bring up a complex new page may freeze the browser and not allow the user to do much of anything until the next page appears. In Netscape Navigator 3.01, the user can right-click the hyperlink and choose Open in New Window. While waiting for the new page to load in a separate copy of Navigator, the user can continue reading and scrolling around in the current page and then mouse over to the new page after it's loaded.

Caching

Caching (pronounced *cashing*) is a general term that describes any short-term memory in a computer system. The whole idea behind caching is that users (and, therefore, their computers) tend to go back to the same place (or nearly so) for information over and over again.

That's certainly true of an intranet designed for document publishing. A web browser can cache, or store, pages and images that the user has visited earlier. The browser makes a copy on the user's local hard disk of the pages and graphics that the user accesses. The next time the user calls up those pages, the browser grabs them from the cache rather than from the network for much better speed. For example, Figure 14-2 shows the contents of a Netscape Navigator cache area.

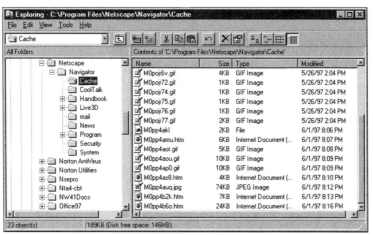

Figure 14-2: Navigator, like most browsers, caches remote pages and graphics to the user's hard disk for faster retrieval later.

Tuning the cache involves setting the maximum amount of disk space the browser may use. Increasing this value enables the browser to keep more pages and images in the short-term cache memory, but it also means that more hard disk space gets eaten up. To come up with the best compromise, make an educated guess as to how much free disk space the typical intranet user has, and don't exceed 20 percent of that amount. A 10- to 20-megabyte cache should improve performance for most users without gobbling too much of the hard drive.

Caching carries with it a risk that users may see the stale, cached version of a page that has since been updated. As you can see from Figure 14-3, you can set how often you want Netscape Navigator to verify documents to determine if they've changed. Once per session is a compromise that provides caching performance gains while minimizing the risk of seeing outdated pages.

To set up caching in either of the two most popular browsers, follow one of these steps:

  ✔ **In Navigator 3.01:** Choose Options⇨Network Preferences⇨Cache⇨Disk Cache to set the size (see Figure 14-3).

  ✔ **In Internet Explorer 3.x:** Choose View⇨Options⇨Advanced⇨Settings to set the size (expressed here as a percentage of total disk space).

You can also get specialized browser tools to perform *look-ahead caching,* for example, by downloading linked pages ahead of time so that when the user clicks the links, the new pages appear almost instantly.

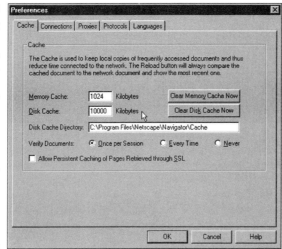

Figure 14-3: Setting Navigator's disk cache size to a higher value enables it to have more short-term memory and improve browsing speeds.

Communications

The workstation's physical link to the intranet can be a speed bump, and the comments I make earlier in this chapter about server Network Interface Cards (NICs) hold true for clients as well. Generally, you want a 16- or 32-bit NIC at the client, preferably one that can handle Fast Ethernet speeds of up to 100 megabits per second. If the client has some high-speed expansion slots where NICs can plug in, for example, PCI (Peripheral Component Interconnect) slots on an Intel machine, use NICs that can take advantage of those slots.

The good news here is that high performance workstation NICs are inexpensive. A hundred dollars a seat is usually all you have to spend to ensure the user-to-network link isn't a bottleneck.

Designing for the Best Performance

Back when I was a kid growing up in Dallas, and the LBJ Freeway (Loop 635) was first built, most residents thought it was monstrous overkill, and during the first several months, one rarely saw a car on it. Over the years, all manner of office buildings and retail malls sprang up along the LBJ corridor, and it's now one of the more congested roadways in Texas.

My point is that you can do a wonderful job tuning up your network as I describe in this chapter, but software applications and data files tend to grow and use up the available network capacity. If intranet publishers see that large graphics appear without delay over a fine-tuned network, they're bound to use more of them. To avoid the LBJ Freeway syndrome, your organization has to combine network tune-ups with design guidelines that help ensure good future performance.

Search engines

If you want to provide a search engine on your intranet, you may want to do some performance testing on a few different products before standardizing on one. Some publishing systems come with their own built-in search capabilities, which vary greatly in performance. General purpose search engines are available from a dozen vendors — Digital AltaVista is widely regarded as one of the quickest.

For more on search engines, hyperlink over to Chapter 11.

Link pages versus content pages

Link pages are navigational pages that consist mainly of links to other pages. An intranet table of contents is an example of a link page. *Content pages*, on the other hand, are those that actually present the information the user needs.

One great design tip is to make sure your link pages load quickly. Experienced intranet designers minimize graphics on link pages, because the user typically doesn't want to spend much time there anyway.

Long pages versus new pages

If you have to post ten book chapters on your intranet, a long web page with all ten chapters loads faster than a few separate web pages with portions of the total ten chapters. The reason for this is that every new page to which a user links requires a separate HTTP connection.

Of course, long pages can also be a regal pain for the user because of all the scrolling around that's necessary to find the important information. You can minimize the problem for the user by adding bookmarks at the top of the page. Doing so enables the user to click the bookmark and jump down to the part of the document he or she wants to read (refer to Chapter 11 for more on this subject). Breaking up long stretches of text into paragraphs or bullets also helps. In any case, don't design your intranet system with lots of little separate web pages, lest your users (and servers) go crazy.

Graphics optimization

One of the better ways to optimize graphics is to reduce the number of colors they contain. The GIF file format only permits 256 colors, but the JPEG file format permits millions of colors. The more colors, the bigger the file — and the longer it takes to download. If most of the users on your intranet are only running a 256-color display on their desktops, those extra colors won't make a prettier picture anyway.

The number of colors in a digital image (*color depth*) relates to how many bits define each *pixel* (dot on the screen). Here are the usual options:

- A 16-color file uses 4 bits.
- A 256-color file uses 8-bits.
- A file with thousands of colors (*high color*) uses 15 or 16 bits.
- A file with millions of colors (*true color*) uses 24 bits.

For digital photos of the company president or department head, use millions of colors so that he or she looks *mahvelous* on screen. For most everything else, 256 colors is best. If you use a slick tool, like Adobe Photoshop, color reduction can produce an 8-bit image that's almost as good-looking as a 24-bit image. (The enclosed CD-ROM provides examples.)

Here's how to reduce the color depth of an image in Photoshop:

1. **From the Photoshop menu, choose File⇨Open.**

    Open the image you want to color-reduce.

2. **From the Photoshop menu, choose Mode⇨Indexed Color.**
3. **Select the desired color depth.**

    You can tell Photoshop to optimize the palette so that it picks the best possible colors for that particular image, or you can use a specific palette (stay tuned for a minute to find out why you may want to do that).

4. **Choose File⇨Save to save your changes.**

If you have a large number of graphics files to convert, the one-at-a-time approach can be slow. You may want to look into a tool such as DeBabelizer from Equilibrium Technologies that can perform color-depth reduction for a whole group of files at a time. (Great name: The dozens of graphics formats really do constitute a Tower of Babel. I wish companies like IBM would come up with more creative names for their products. While I'm at it, I wish for a million dollars.)

You can take things a step further by making all your graphics conform to the *same* 256-color palette (yep, DeBabelizer can do that, too). The client doesn't have to spend time changing the palette from one page to another or trying to reconcile two images on the same page that have different palettes.

Background graphics are especially important to optimize, because the background must load before any other part of the page. Keep these files small (use tiling, as discussed in Chapter 12) and keep the color depth (number of colors) to no more than 256.

For large graphics, HTML provides a nifty way to handle the mix of fast (local network) and slow (dial-up modem) connections likely to be used by your intranet audience. You can store two versions of the graphic: one with full color and another with limited color. The limited-color file loads first, and the gorgeous but larger full-color file loads in the background after the rest of the page has finished. Here's a sample HTML command that instructs the browser to load the images in this manner and provides the file names:

```
<IMG SRC="HIGHRES.JPG" LOWSRC="LOWRES.JPG">
```

Remember the discussion earlier in this chapter about long pages versus new pages, and how each new page requires a new HTTP connection? Ditto that discussion for graphics. One medium-sized graphic usually loads faster than several small-sized graphics because the medium-sized graphic only requires one HTTP connection.

A specialized graphic type that you may be using for navigation (hyperlink) purposes is the *image map* (refer to Chapter 11 for more information on the image map).

Intranet advertisements

Most readers of this book have done a little surfing on the public Web — maybe even a lot of surfing. If you're in this category, you know that the graphical ads that seem to appear on darned near every Web page in cyberspace can really bog down performance. Animated advertisements, implemented usually as *animated GIF* files, take even longer to download.

Some intranet publishers apply similar techniques to their own internal web sites, for example, posting banner ads or animated GIFs on web pages, in e-mail messages, or in push publishing systems like PointCast to announce new system features or documents. By doing so, these publishers give up a key performance edge an intranet has over the Internet. By all means, make those announcements, but use text or text hyperlinks to do so. If you need to highlight the announcements, use a bright color for the text.

Back-end technologies

In Chapter 10, I spend a little time on how web servers connect to external programs for the purposes of accomplishing tasks that are too fancy for the web server by itself, retrieving documents stored in a database repository, or handling information provided by users in HTML forms. The mechanisms the intranet designer chooses to link to back-end services can have a big performance impact.

For example, using *Common Gateway Interface* (CGI) scripts is generally slower than using server Application Programming Interface (API) calls, and increases network traffic because of the repetitive Open and Close commands that flow to the back-end database. Even for non-database tasks, the scripted programs CGI usually calls tend to run slowly. A publishing application that offloads processor overhead to the client machines, for example, by using Java, puts less demand on the web server but may require faster workstations.

See Chapter 5 for a discussion of intranet programming and CGI.

Make sure that your intranet publishing system designers pay close attention to how the web server links to other services, programs, and databases. Where multiple options exist, try to test them out before choosing one for the production system. You may find that proprietary and nonportable solutions, such as using the programming features in specific servers to create standalone compiled programs, are faster than open and portable solutions that work with multiple web servers like CGI.

A classic tradeoff in computer technology is speed versus portability. My rule of thumb is that if the performance penalty isn't too great, or if you can budget a faster web server, go with the more open and portable solution.

File distribution

Intranets can be great for publishing software upgrades, as I point out in Chapter 7. However, downloading files may be the most performance-degrading activity an intranet user can perform. What are some techniques for alleviating the network load?

- **Limit** push downloads to those that are truly necessary and widely applicable in the user population. (See Chapter 11 for more on push publishing.)
- **Compress** files on the server so that they download faster. (Make sure decompression utilities are available for all users if you use this method.)
- **Separate** files that some users may not need into separate archives. For example, not everyone needs the technical documentation that accompanies a program update.
- **Label** file sizes on the web page.

Standard templates and central sites

One smart way to encourage intranet publishers to adopt some of the high-performance design techniques in this session is to simply post standard templates that use them and urge new intranetters to take advantage of the ready-made page layouts. The advantage for the webmasters is that they don't have to reinvent the wheel, and the big-picture advantage is that new projects use templates designed for low network impact from the start.

If you're part of a larger organization, you have another option: Suggest to departments and workgroups that they offload web site hosting to the Information Services group, where performance-minded professionals can apply performance enhancing methods and technology. To some, such centralization flies in the face of intranet traditions, but not every department wants or needs to maintain its intranet publishing system.

Performance Monitoring

Intranets are dynamic. You can tune a system and design it for performance, but the usage profile may change over time, changing performance along with it. The only way to keep a web publishing system in shape is to monitor performance on a regular basis, track the changes, identify the problems, and then deal with them. More scientific system managers use performance monitoring as a way of predicting future capacity requirements.

For some intranet maintenance functions, you can hire an outside contractor to do performance monitoring for you. CrossComm's ExpertWatch service is one example.

Network management systems

In Chapter 13, I mention the importance of a Network Management System (NMS) in maintaining a network. Turns out that a NMS can be useful for performance monitoring as well as just identifying downed links or crashed servers. Use the features of your NMS to set traffic threshold levels beyond which the NMS raises an alert. Just be aware that NMSs aren't yet very good at tracking performance problems that result from a combination of small delays at different steps of a computing transaction.

The Heisenberg Uncertainty Principle states that you can't observe something without changing it. For example, say you put a frozen pizza into a conventional oven. Every time you open the oven door to check whether it's ready, you let some heat out and inadvertently cool the pizza a little. (Here's a more abstract example for science fans: If you can see an electron, you must be bouncing light particles off it, which changes the electron's path, so you don't really know where it is anymore.) I once saw a bumper sticker, stuck on an apartment door, that read "Heisenberg slept here — maybe."

The Heisenberg Uncertainty Principle holds true for computer networking as well. Here's proof: SNMP (Simple Network Management Protocol, a popular NMS) traffic itself can contribute mightily to network congestion, as Stanford University found when it began monitoring web activity on campus. *Datamation* (November 1996) quoted Stanford network specialist Milt Mallory as saying, "We've found the enemy, and it is us." Easing up on some of the monitoring activities improved network speed.

If you have a large organization with many different kinds of networks, you may need an *umbrella NMS* to gather data from all the network-specific NMSs. Such software is affectionately called MOM — for Managers of Managers. Its duty is to package the other NMS data and present it to the network manager in one program.

Wide Area Network monitoring

If your intranet system extends beyond the LAN environment, and incorporates a Wide Area Network (WAN), performance monitoring gets trickier because wide area links usually involve public communications carriers whose systems you can't directly monitor.

One monitoring possibility is to use specialized programs that test end-to-end transmission performance across wide area links. Chariot from Ganymede Software Inc. is an example of such a product, which does stress tests using application simulations that mimic real-world use. Here's a hint: Run the stress tests at night or on weekends, to avoid having your car egged by irate users.

Other companies with WAN monitoring and testing software include Visual Networks, Inc. and Concord Communications, Inc. (See Appendix B for contact information.)

If you invest in WAN stress-testing or performance-monitoring tools, don't just use them to check the health of your intranet links. Use them to verify that you're getting the service levels you're paying for from your communications carriers.

Operating system tools

Most operating systems over which web server software runs have built-in or bundled performance monitoring utilities. For example, Windows NT Server comes with a Performance Monitor that enables you to track just about every performance-related quantity imaginable (see Figure 14-4). System-level tools like this don't separate performance by service or application, but they can give you an overall view of how the server's doing.

Web server tools

Tools for tracking intranet web server performance statistics are still maturing. Some software vendors of network and mainframe performance monitors (Computer Associates, Tivoli Systems, BMC Software, and others) are expanding their offerings to include web servers — a business strategy that falls into the "Well, duh!" category. If your organization already licenses such software, look into upgrades that have intranet monitoring features. If not, you may want to look into products that specialize in web server monitoring, such as Optimal Internet Monitor from Optimal Networks Inc., WebTrends from e.g. Software, WireTap from Platinum Technologies, or Access Manager from Sequel Net, to name just a few.

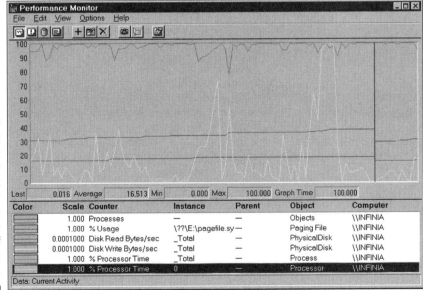

Figure 14-4: Windows NT Server Performance Monitor provides a real-time view of system statistics.

Look for the following features in performance reporting tools:

- **The ability to publish performance reports in graphical form.** I hate reading columns of figures, and so does everyone I know.
- **The ability to publish performance reports on a web server.** This ability enables an administrator to view reports with a web browser rather than a separate program, and more than one person can view them at a time.
- **Compatibility with more than one kind of web server.**

The next big issue in intranet care and feeding is maintaining adequate security. Chapter 15 discusses how to define "adequate" and what policies and technologies exist to implement it.

Chapter 15
Intranet Security

In This Chapter

▶ Deciding how much security your intranet project needs
▶ Using physical security as the first line of defense
▶ Configuring intranet servers to use LAN-based security
▶ Restricting remote access with firewalls and dial-up security
▶ Using Secure Sockets Layer (SSL) for encrypting communications
▶ Implementing measures to keep your intranet running at all times

Computer security means making systems available to those who need them, and unavailable to those who don't. Just about every intranet requires some level of security, to protect against both accidental and malicious threats. In this chapter, I look at the various kinds of security you may want to consider, whether you implement them all or not.

I admit right up front that this is not the easiest chapter in the book. Security can be a fairly abstract topic, and it's full of Unavoidable Alphabet Soup (UAS). Intranet security, however, is one of the more important subjects for intranet publishers. I do my level best to explain it well, but this is tough stuff — don't worry if it isn't all crystal clear on the first read-through.

Security? We Don't Need No Stinking Security

You may not need super-rigid security on your intranet publishing system, at least compared with other types of systems (the Information Services managers who are reading this book are now starting to get nervous). You do need *some* security, though, regardless of the sort of intranet publishing system you have. The trick is to provide the level of security that your organization and publishing system requires, while making that security as transparent as possible to the user, and reasonably inexpensive for your company.

Yes, we're Internetted

If your intranet links to the public Internet, you may need to put several security measures in place:

- **Limit user ability to connect to the Internet at all.** For example, maybe your support staff are the only people who should have Internet access.
- **Limit user ability to connect to certain sites.** For example, you may want to limit access to sites of a nature that is likely to corrupt the moral fiber of the employee, or simply waste a whole lot of time.
- **Restrict all Internet users outside your organization from linking to your intranet.**
- **Restrict all Internet users, except certain ones who meet some criteria you put in place.** For example, you may want to allow customers, suppliers, and so on, but exclude everyone else.

The ability to control employee access to the Internet may determine your ability to sell management on the intranet concept. Many managers hear *Internet* and mentally picture employees surfing instead of working. Managers who do a lot of unproductive surfing themselves on their home computers are especially prone to harbor this suspicion, especially if they have discovered any of the 9.5 million pornographic Internet locations, where you can spend hours downloading digital movies like *Behind the Green Web*.

Where you can distinguish between data for internal consumption from data that you want to make available to the outside world, reflect that distinction in your web site file directory structure. Separating internal-only files into their own directories makes securing them much easier.

No, we're not Internetted

If your intranet doesn't connect to other networks (such as — you guessed it — the Internet), you have 50 million fewer people to worry about and several major security concerns go away. Even though your intranet isn't linked to the *Big I*, you may still need to set up some security. For example:

- **If users can dial up your intranet from a remote modem-equipped computer, so, possibly, can industrial spies or mischievous 12 year-olds working out of a dimly lit bedroom in Albuquerque.**
- **Computer viruses can infect even seemingly isolated intranets.**
- **You don't want just anybody logging on to your intranet and posting files or changing pages around.**

Chapter 15: Intranet Security 269

> ✔ **You don't want the famous disgruntled employee to be able to *accidentally* spill coffee into your web server and trash it.** As recent lawsuits prove, coffee can be dangerously hot. The fact that it's *supposed* to be dangerously hot is irrelevant, immaterial, and inadmissible.

Physical Security

Physical security for intranets includes the following:

- ✔ Coded door locks to server rooms
- ✔ Detachable server keyboards that administrators can lock in a file cabinet
- ✔ Crushing old backup tapes with the heel of your shoe, before tossing them in the trash (cowboy boots work best)
- ✔ Placing user workstations where others can easily see them
- ✔ Security guards
- ✔ Alarm systems
- ✔ Electrified fences

You may need to consider physical security measures for servers, workstations, network hubs, and even printers, if the data they print may be confidential (paper shredders aren't just for people like Oliver North). Consider physical security for remote parts of your network, too, such as remote offices or users who link to the intranet through a dedicated line. From the intruder's standpoint, such remote sites are just as tempting as a workstation at your company's main office.

If you contract with an *Internet Service Provider* (ISP) to host your intranet servers, establishing strong physical security is all but impossible, because the ISP servers are outside your physical control. You *can* ask what measures your ISP takes to ensure physical security. Most have reasonable controls in place. After all, their business depends on good security, too.

LAN-Based Security

Many standalone web servers have their own security database of users, groups, and access privileges. If your intranet runs on a *Local Area Network* (LAN) that already provides security services, you may be able to use those services to control intranet access. This is a real boon for administrators, because you don't have to build two separate sets of user and group security databases. For example:

- **Novell's IntraNetware** can use the security features of the built-in NetWare Directory Services (NDS) to control which users can access specific intranet pages. NDS enables an administrator to assign restrictions to server files and directories by the user's IP (Internet Protocol) address (location on the network), or by user or group account.

- **Microsoft Internet Information Server (IIS)** works with the users and groups you create for Windows NT Server. User and group access privileges you define with the Windows NT User Manager also apply to intranet users. You can assign restrictions to server directories, or URLs by user or group account.

Certain web servers that use LAN-based security for authentication let users log in to the server without encrypting their user name and password, making both available to electronic eavesdroppers. For example, in Microsoft Internet Information Server (IIS), this is called the *basic login*. You may be able to improve security by using a more sophisticated *encrypted login*, which puts the transmission of the password and user name in a code that only the server can understand.

A big part of maintaining effective LAN-based security is keeping your network operating system updated with vendor patches and maintenance releases, which often boost security or even fix security holes. Another tip is to use the auditing and logging features built into your network software to help you identify break-in attempts.

Figure 15-1 shows the Account Policy dialog box of Windows NT Server 4.0 Manager for Domains.

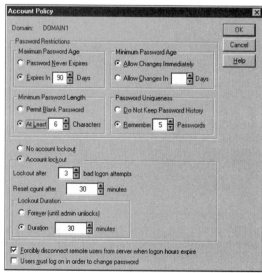

Figure 15-1: Windows NT Server 4.0 User Manager for Domains enables LAN administrators to slap all kinds of security requirements on users.

Special LAN-based security measures include *watchdog programs* that automatically log users off the network after a specified number of minutes of inactivity. These programs can help avoid the *he went to lunch and forgot to log out* syndrome. An unattended but logged-in workstation is a major security hole.

You can also get programs to test your LAN-based security, and they're a good idea. The UNIX world offers the Security Administrator Tool for Analyzing Networks (could it be . . . SATAN?). Windows NT Server and NetWare shops can look at the Kane Security Analyst (see Appendix B).

You don't have to use LAN-based security if you don't want to. For example, you can configure your intranet server to allow *anonymous logins*, as the next section discusses, if you don't need to set up varying security restrictions for different users. However, LAN-based security is convenient for many intranetters, because it provides an easy way to offer different levels of access to different users.

Application-Level Security

Application-level security is whatever security the programs (applications) running on top of, or alongside your LAN, provide. These applications include web server-specific programs, publishing programs, and Java or ActiveX applets.

Web server-specific programs

One set of applications just about all intranets run is web services. Some web server programs have their own security databases of users and passwords — Netscape Enterprise Server is an example. Others have extra security layers that work on top of the underlying LAN security features.

Microsoft Internet Information Server (IIS), for example, uses the NT Server security database of users and groups, but adds the ability to deny user access based on the user's IP (Internet Protocol) address. IIS can also assign *read* and *execute* permissions that layer on top of NT Server's built-in permissions (see Figure 15-2). Give *read* permission to content areas so users can look at the web pages, and *execute* permission to directories containing programs, such as Common Gateway Interface (CGI) scripts.

Finally, IIS creates a special account for *anonymous logins.* You can assign group-level security to the anonymous intranet account in Windows NT Server's User Manager utility, just as you would with any NT Server user account (see sidebar and Figure 15-3).

> ## The password is...
>
> LAN-based (Local Area Network-based) security typically relies quite heavily on passwords (these comments apply equally to web servers, which often have their own password security). Most network passwords, however, are about as effective as a chain lock on a New York apartment door.
>
> Users share passwords with each other. They pick passwords that are easy to remember and, therefore, easy to guess, and they write their passwords down. Contractors and consultants get passwords that administrators don't cancel when the jobs are finished. Users who leave the organization may enjoy password access for months — or even years — later.
>
> LAN administrators can program their networks to enhance password security by, for example:
>
> - Making users change their passwords periodically
> - Forcing a minimum password length
> - Requiring unique passwords that no one else on the network is already using
> - Removing the default passwords that come with preconfigured LAN user accounts such as Guest or Supervisor
>
> For example, figure 15-1 shows the password restrictions that Windows NT Server 4.0 can impose.
>
> A little user education on password selection can help, too. For example, users should choose passwords that:
>
> - Aren't in the dictionary
> - Have numbers and punctuation marks, as well as both uppercase and lowercase letters
> - Don't have anything to do with the user (car, favorite food, spouse)
> - Are reasonably easy to remember through the use of mnemonic devices (so the user won't write 'em down!).
>
> The passwords *1st&10@the1* and *UR2Good2Me* are okay; *PASSWORD* and *myfiancebob* are bad.
>
> Companies who need better password security can turn to little devices called *token generators* that fit in a shirt pocket, and display a new password in a little LCD window every minute. Security software running on a network server can tie in with the token generator and authenticate the user. Token generators can also create non-time-based passwords that create a new password based on the last-used password. Even fancier systems use the server to generate a number which the user punches into a keypad on the token generator; the token generator then spits out another number, based on the server-created number, and that new number becomes the user's password (until the next time).

When configuring IIS, you can set *read* or *execute* permissions for each directory using the Internet Service Manager. All you have to do is choose the directory tab in the WWW Service Properties dialog box, click on a specific directory, and then click the Edit properties button.

Figure 15-2:
When configuring IIS, you can set *read* or *execute* permissions for each directory using the Internet Service Manager.

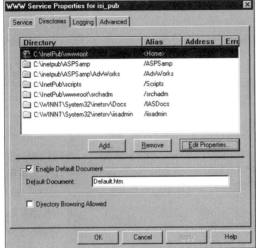

Figure 15-3:
Assigning group-level security to the anonymous account with Windows NT Server.

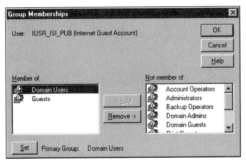

- **Smart intranetters disable web server applications that they don't use.** For example, if your intranet doesn't use Telnet or FTP, configure your web server so that it doesn't load those applications. If it isn't there, an intruder can't use it against you.

- **Another good idea is to set up your web server to disallow *directory browsing*.** If you accidentally forget to put a home page such as `default.htm` in a server directory, directory browsing lets the user see all the files in that directory. Not good, for example, if that's the directory that stores payroll files. And, as I suggest earlier in the "Yes, we're Internetted" section, you want to organize directories in a manner that reflects who should have access (payroll in one directory, company party announcements in another). Locking out directory browsing provides an additional safety net, in case one or two sensitive files slip into a nonrestricted directory.

Signed, Anonymous

Say, for example, that you want to make your intranet publishing application available to everybody on the network, and you don't even require them to have a valid Local Area Network (LAN) account. You can do this through something called *anonymous login*.

Anonymous login has been on the Internet for years. For example, File Transfer Protocol (FTP) sites that make files available to the general public let you log in with your user name as *anonymous*. Most Internet Web sites let users log in anonymously, too — an anonymous Web access is simply one that lacks a user ID and password in the HTTP message that the browser sends when it connects to the site.

Just because you want to provide anonymous login to your intranet doesn't mean that you want unauthenticated anonymous users to have access to system configuration files, or to be able to delete or move files around on the server. You need to, therefore, set up your web server with restrictions that apply to anonymous users. For example, Internet Information Server (IIS) sets up an NT Server account of the form IUSR_*computername*. (If the server's name is PUB1, the account would be IUSR_PUB1.) This special account enables you to assign restrictions that then apply to all anonymous logins (see Figure 15-3). In other words, every server login from a user who isn't already logged in as an NT user is considered anonymous, and uses the IUSR_*computername* account by default.

You don't *have* to use anonymous logins. You can set your web server to require every intranet user to be authenticated by the network before they can do anything. However, anonymous login is a convenient way to provide intranet access to people (for example, new employees) who may not have a network account, but who could still benefit from the information you publish.

Product-specific

You may be running other applications besides your web server program. For example, you may use a specialized publishing system that has its own programs to store and retrieve documents in a proprietary database. These sorts of applications often come with their own product-specific security features, and a wide variety of them exists. Just remember the following:

- **Security is cumulative.** Product-specific application security is in addition to whatever LAN-based or web server-based security you use.
- **Product-specific application security isn't a substitute for LAN-based or web server-based security.** Use it as an extra layer if you think you need it. Often, LAN- and web-based security is sufficient.
- **If your applications run programs via the Common Gateway Interface (CGI) or other mechanisms, you're best off keeping those programs in a single directory that you mark *execute-only* for all but intranet administrators.** For CGI scripts, for example, the directory is usually

named `cgi-bin`. You can enforce even tighter security by not using scripts at all, and instead using only standalone programs (EXE files in the DOS/Windows world). For more on CGI and web programs, see Chapter 12.

✔ **Take care to avoid rampant passworditis.** If every application you use has its own set of user IDs and passwords, in addition to whatever network and web server passwords you've set up, users are likely to write all those passwords down on sticky notes and paste them onto their computer monitors. Here's an old Chinese proverb: Too much security becomes no security.

If you're moving an existing system from a mainframe, minicomputer, or traditional client/server system onto your intranet, take care that the security provisions that the vendor built into those original systems move with the data and processing logic. Merely converting a database into a HyperText Markup Language (HTML) format, for example, with a product such as Lotus InterNotes Publisher, doesn't maintain the security features of the original database!

Some of your applications may publish information that must be kept private by law, such as some types of human resources data (who has a drug problem, for example), or information that may facilitate employer discrimination. Check with your legal counsel to identify information that requires strict access control by law, and then either slap tight security on that information and related applications, or don't publish the sensitive data on your intranet at all.

Java versus ActiveX security

Java and ActiveX programs can automatically download from a web server and run on the workstation. These applications have, therefore, generated hot debate among webheads as to their security. (Please see Chapter 12 if you're unclear on what Java and ActiveX programs are.)

At present, Java applets are usually considered to be somewhat safer than ActiveX components, for several reasons:

✔ Java programs can only connect to the server they came from — they can't connect to other computers without user authorization.

✔ The user's computer checks Java programs a line at a time to make sure that every command is kosher.

✔ Java programs, unlike ActiveX programs, can't access just any old directory on the user's machine, and are instead restricted to certain areas of disk and memory space — known as the *Java sandbox*.

Java and ActiveX programs don't present a huge security threat on most intranets, where web administrators can test them thoroughly before making them available to users. However, if Java and ActiveX programs flow from an external Internet server, those programs can do damage to data and programs on your intranet. You can limit Java and ActiveX programs to those originating on certain trusted servers on the Internet, but that's not necessarily a guarantee that those programs haven't been corrupted or modified on the trusted server. No convenient way exists to verify a program's source.

If your intranet is Internet-connected, you may want to play it safe and disable Java and ActiveX from public sites, at least until the technologies mature and the security issues are better understood. If your intranet doesn't use Java or ActiveX programs, you can configure user browsers to reject them all. For example:

- **In Netscape Navigator:** Choose Options⇨Network preferences⇨Languages and clear the Enable Java checkbox.
- **In Internet Explorer:** Choose View⇨Options⇨Security, and clear the buttons in the Active content box, as shown in Figure 15-4.

If your intranet *does* use Java or ActiveX, but you want to reject such programs if they come from the public Internet, you enable Java and ActiveX at the browser level, and use a *firewall* product, as I discuss in the "Remote Access Security" section, to block external Java or ActiveX programs.

Remote Access Security

In this section, I take a look at the various ways to prevent unauthorized users from connecting to your intranet from remote locations, whether via the public Internet or via modems that connect directly to your network.

Airwalls and firewalls

An *airwall* is nothing more than a complete physical separation between two networks. If your Internet server is completely separate from your intranet servers, with no interconnecting communications (cable, infrared, satellite, tin-can telephone) between them, you've got an airwall. You can entertain your server administrators next time you're in the server room by saying, "Hey, watch it! You bumped into the airwall!" They're sure to laugh heartily and invite you back real soon.

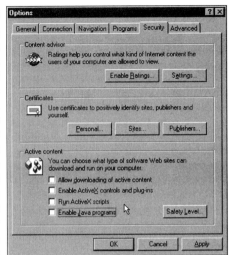

Figure 15-4: You can configure Internet Explorer to disable all Active content by clearing the four check boxes at the bottom of this Security dialog box.

A *firewall* is a mechanism for protecting a trusted network (usually, your intranet) from an untrusted network (usually, the Internet) to which it connects. You need a firewall if you have a *multinet* (if you have both internal and external network connections). Firewalls can usually restrict outbound communications by user ID, IP (Internet Protocol) address, or service.

A simple firewall may simply limit Internet communications to e-mail and deny all Web traffic in either direction. Another simple sort of firewall is a *packet-filtering router* that only permits communication between the Internet and a subnetwork within your organization (in which case, the subnetwork, and the applications that run on it, must apply their own security measures). A more complex firewall enables you to specify particular operations and data types that may flow between the networks, and lets you connect an Internet Web server (called a *bastion host*) to the firewall. The most complex, and effective, firewalls use something called a *proxy server*.

Proxy servers don't permit direct communication between the Internet and your intranet. Instead, they act as a store-and-forward repository. The proxy server examines incoming traffic from either direction, applies predefined criteria to see if that traffic is okay to pass on, and if so, passes it on. It acts as a proxy between two communicating computers that think they're connecting directly, but really aren't. Proxy servers hide your intranet IP addresses from the outside world — the proxy server has its own IP address, which is all that the external users see, and it can forward traffic to the appropriate internal IP addresses, which only the proxy server knows about.

Advanced proxy servers can provide different levels of access to different users. The most secure setups involve two servers. Figure 15-5 shows this kind of setup: a proxy server that evaluates and stores incoming traffic, and an intranet server that then requests that data from the proxy server, instead of receiving it automatically.

Proxy servers require browsers that are compatible with them (both Microsoft Internet Explorer 3 and Netscape Navigator 3 are). They also tend to slow system performance a bit.

Firewalls may be separate, standalone servers running firewall software, or add-on software that installs onto an existing web server. For example, Microsoft Internet Access Server (code name: Catapult) is a software-only firewall that plugs into the Internet Information Server (IIS) on a Windows NT Server machine.

Make sure that whatever firewall you buy supports *all* the TCP/IP services your network offers: HTTP for web access, SMTP for e-mail, FTP for file transfer, and so on. Firewalls tend to eat up administration time. When shopping, favor products with automated administration features and easy-to-read activity logs.

Modern firewalls provide options to disable Java and ActiveX content. Disabling this content doesn't stop your internal users from viewing applets and objects originating on your intranet, but does prohibit those applets and objects from crossing into your intranet from the outside world of the Internet. Be aware, too, that most firewalls have a hard time managing nonstandard data types, such as streaming audio and video. If your intranet users access or use such data types, check with the firewall vendor about what can and cannot be tracked and filtered.

The respected National Computer Security Association (NCSA) certifies firewalls through a standard test program. Some popular certified firewall products (see Appendix B for company details) include:

- FireWall-1 from Check Point Systems
- Eagle Firewall from Raptor Systems
- Borderware Firewall from Secure Computing Corp.
- Gauntlet from Trusted Information Systems

Dial-up security

Please feel free to skip this little section if your users never call into your intranet via modem from home, home office, customer location, or corporate ski condo.

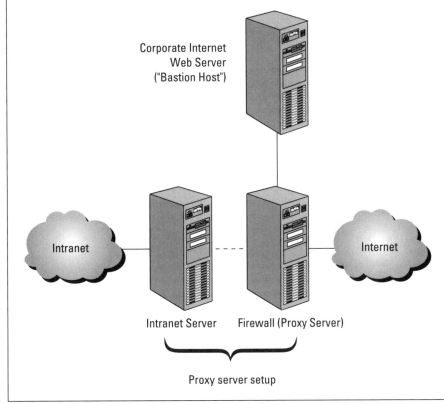

Figure 15-5: A proxy server firewall setup using two computers. This approach ensures that unwanted traffic doesn't cross the boundary between the computers.

Modern businesses are moving away from the idea that everyone has to be in a central office to get work done, thanks in large part to the availability of faster modems and of portable computers that now weigh less than barbells and don't require their own seats on an airplane. The more portable computing goes on in your business, the more you probably want to pay attention to dial-up security — it's often the weakest link in the intranet security chain, partly because dial-up modems can allow access *behind* the firewall (that is, straight into your network, bypassing firewall protection).

Here are three aspects of dial-up security worth considering:

- Power-on passwords
- Callback modems
- Encrypted sign-on

A *power-on password* is easy to create using a notebook computer's setup program, and it won't let an unauthorized user get past square one. When the computer is turned on, the user is asked for a user name and password. Without authentication, the computer won't do a thing. A thief may be able to simply disconnect the computer's battery, and the password vanishes. Today, some notebooks have soldered-in "lifetime" batteries that are tougher to switch off. In either case, thieves who hang around airport security checkpoints to purloin your portable, while a security agent scrutinizes your Texas-shaped belt buckle trying to figure out if it could be used as a lethal weapon, generally don't bother keeping laptops that have power-on password protection.

Callback modems work like this: A user dials up your intranet server, provides an identifying code, and then hangs up. The server looks up the user's phone number, which is cross-referenced to the identifying code, and calls the user back. Then the user's modem answers the phone, the user logs into the network, and then starts working. "But wait," you say. "What if the user doesn't know the phone number in advance?" One solution is for the traveling user to have a cellular modem with a fixed number.

Notebooks often use connection software that transmits unencrypted logon information (user ID and password). In theory, an electronic eavesdropper monitoring the dial-up line can sniff out that account information, and then gain access to the network by going to the office and posing as a copier repairperson. If the connection software has an option to encrypt logon passwords (for example, as Windows 95 Dial Up Networking does), enable this feature. You may also want to ask the phone company to assign an exchange prefix to your dial-up lines that differs from the office's regular prefix. A cracker has a tougher time guessing seven numbers than four.

One additional level of dial-up security encrypts all the communications between the remote user and the intranet, not just the login process. The technology that enables this security measure is called *Point-to-Point Tunneling Protocol*, or PPTP, as I discuss in the "Communications Security" section.

Communications Security

Communications security makes life tough on electronic eavesdroppers by coding, or *encrypting*, intranet traffic at the sending end, and *decrypting* it at the receiving end. Internet users never worried too much about communications security because the Internet was always basically a public network, but now that intranets are putting Internet technologies to commercial use, the industry has developed *add-on* technology to secure TCP/IP (Transmission Control Protocol/Internet Protocol) communications.

The U.S. government's Munitions Export Act has made using super secure encryption illegal in products sold internationally. The restriction stems from concern that international terrorists can use such encryption to make their communications uncrackable by the Feds. In my view, Uncle Sam has painted himself into a corner here, because the law doesn't stop U.S. companies from buying or licensing high-end encryption products from foreign companies. For now, if you buy high-end encryption products in the U.S., verify that they're legal so the vendor doesn't get hit with a federal lawsuit, file Chapter 11 bankruptcy, and leave you with products you bought but can't legally use. If you're an international organization, be careful about what intranet products you send outside North America, too — if you send to wholly owned subsidiaries, you may be okay because you're not selling to a foreign national company, but check anyway.

Secure HyperText Transfer Protocol

Secure HTTP (SHTTP) is one of the early intranet security technologies, and provides encryption for HyperText Markup Language (HTML) pages. Both browser and server must support SHTTP, and the browser must connect using the shttp:// prefix, instead of the standard http:// prefix.

Secure HTTP doesn't provide security for other intranet applications, such as File Transfer Protocol (FTP), and it hasn't been widely adopted on its own. Many of the features of SHTTP are being folded into a more popular technology called *Secure Sockets Layer (SSL)*.

Secure Sockets Layer (SSL)

Secure Sockets Layer (SSL) is a free, public technology developed for encrypting TCP/IP communications. SSL sits between a TCP/IP application (such as HTTP, FTP, Gopher, and so on) and TCP/IP itself, and requires support from both servers and browsers (most popular products in both categories work) to set up a secure link.

In an SSL session, a user connects with a server using the https:// Uniform Resource Locator prefix instead of the regular http:// prefix. (The s stands for "secure.") SSL authenticates the server's identity, and then automatically encrypts and decrypts communications between the two computers. SSL is a point-to-point security solution between two (and only two) computers.

Here's the general procedure for setting up SSL on your intranet:

1. **Generate a *key pair* using your web server software.** The process varies from server to server, but your server documentation should tell you how.

   A key pair consists of two numbers: a public key and a private key. The server and browsers use the key pair to encrypt and decrypt messages. The more digits your keys have, the more secure your SSL connection is. Assign a password to the key pair and *don't ever forget it!*

2. **Apply to Verisign, a central certificate authority, for a digital certificate in the form of a text file.**

   Verisign is at www.verisign.com. This step is required if you ever link your intranet to the public Internet, as no two certificates are identical. The certificate verifies the identity of the server to the browser.

3. **Using your web server utilities again, pop the certificate diskette Verisign sends you into the server's floppy drive, and install it to the server.**

4. **Make a backup copy of the key pair and the certificate, and store them in a *very safe place (fireproof vault, off-site lockbox).***

5. **Configure any web server directories that need this security to use SSL, for example, with Internet Information Server's Internet Service Manager program.**

6. **Ensure all user browsers are set up to use SSL security.**

   For example, in Netscape Navigator, choose Options⇨Security Preferences⇨General (see Figure 15-6).

7. **Modify links on your web pages to use the** https:// **prefix when referring to the secure directory on the web server.**

As you can imagine, encrypting and decrypting slows down computer-to-computer communication. For this reason, don't use SSL except for web server directories that you really need to keep secure. The best thing to do is to separate such secure areas from the public directories on your intranet server, so that you can use SSL only when necessary.

Netscape Navigator users can tell if they're connected to a secure site by looking at the little key in the lower left corner of the browser window. If the key is broken, the site isn't secure; if the key is unbroken, the site is secure.

Point-to-Point Tunneling Protocol

Point-to-Point Tunneling Protocol, supported by Microsoft Windows NT Server 4.0 and Internet Information Server 3.0, encrypts and packages

Figure 15-6:
Users must have the SSL options checked in Netscape Navigator to take advantage of Secure Sockets Layer.

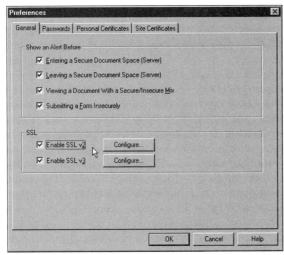

remote access traffic — for example, by users connecting to your intranet from home via a dial-up connection. The remote user needs to have a communication program, such as Windows 95 Dial-Up Networking, that supports PPTP.

PPTP isn't yet a formal standard, but the Internet Engineering Task Force is reviewing it, and the prospects are good for the computing community to accept PPTP widely.

Uptime Security

A secure system is not only unavailable to those you don't want to use it, but also easily available to those you do want to use it. Uptime security (that is, making your intranet available at all times to legitimate users) consists of two concerns:

- **Fault tolerance:** the system's ability to keep going and stay at least mostly functional, if a significant problem occurs
- **Fault resilience:** the ability to keep downtimes short if a really bad problem occurs

Faults can occur anywhere:

- In the server hardware, programs, or data files
- In the connecting network plumbing

- In client hardware, programs, and data files
- In the environment: power, phone, fire, flood, earthquake, roads

All client/server systems exhibit a three-way tradeoff between uptime, cost, and transparency to the user. Your intranet may not need to be available 100 percent of the time, and providing 100 percent uptime security is much more expensive than providing, say, 99 percent uptime. That last 1 percent is a killer: A wristwatch that works 100 percent of the time (Rolex) costs a hundred times as much as the one that works 99 percent of the time (Timex). Getting to the 99 percent level usually isn't horrifically more expensive or difficult than achieving 95 percent. In terms of transparency (the invisibility of security measure to users going about their daily tasks), users do put up with minor inconveniences, if they know the purpose of these is to increase system reliability.

Decide what level of availability you need, assuming that the downtime will occur at the most inconvenient possible moment. Then build in fault tolerance and fault resilience that provide that level of availability. You can't predict what a given network's uptime will be, especially because it depends not just on hardware, but also on which programs you run, and how reliable they are. You can monitor uptime over the months and years, see how well you're doing, and make adjustments if you need to.

Intranet fault tolerance

I don't have room to cover all the possible kinds of intranet fault tolerance, but to give you the flavor of the subject, this section discusses three: power backup, server redundancy, and antivirus technology.

Power backup

The simplest (and cheapest) fault tolerance comes in the form of a battery, specifically, an *Uninterruptible Power Supply (UPS)*, which connects between the AC wall outlet and the intranet server, hub, or other critical box.

Good power backup units actually do three things:

- **They provide battery power to run your intranet device for a while during a power outage.** I once taught a course in England and when I used the term *outage*, my students cracked up. "You mean a power *cut*?" they asked. Apparently they thought *outage* was a very pretentious and amusing term. I was about to point out that they say *dustbin* when they mean *trash can,* when 99.9 percent of what you put there isn't dust. At that moment, however, tea was served.

- **During normal operation, UPSs condition the AC power by filtering out electrical noise.**

Chapter 15: Intranet Security 285

✓ **They provide surge protection so that voltage spikes don't damage your equipment.** I came this close to calling these *uppages* in my seminar.

Proper UPS size is important. If the UPS isn't beefy enough to keep your server running, its circuit breaker trips, and instead of 10 minutes of protection, for example, you have zero minutes of protection. Remember that every time you add disk drives or other power-hungry devices to your intranet server, somebody who knows their amps from their volts needs to take another look at the UPS rating to see if it can handle the new load. You can also come in on a Saturday and yank the power cord out of the AC wall outlet, which is fun to do. If the server goes down, you need a bigger UPS.

Don't forget to put UPSs on every critical intranet component, not just the web server. Routers, hubs, and other network plumbing that must remain working for clients to use the intranet, also need power backup. So do the database servers with which your web servers may need to connect.

Some UPS vendors (see Appendix B for more company information) include:

✓ American Power Conversion
✓ Best Power Technology
✓ Panamax

Server mirroring and clustering

Power backup doesn't protect an intranet server from other sorts of faults, such as a memory module that suddenly develops amnesia. The next level of fault tolerance, therefore, provides for another server (or more) that can step into the breach when a primary server fails.

Mirroring (also called *hot standby*) is one approach. A mirrored server is basically a twin that mirrors everything on the primary server, by virtue of a high-speed connection between the two. Novell IntraNetware, for example, may use the vendor's System Fault Tolerance Level III (SFT III) software to achieve a mirrored setup. A less fault-tolerant system is a *warm standby* server, requires a technician to activate it if a primary server fails.

If you feel you don't need to mirror an entire server, you can still achieve a reasonable level of fault tolerance by mirroring the disk drives, which are the most likely components to fail. You can mirror disk drives on important client workstations, too, with programs from vendors such as Octopus Technologies. Disk *duplexing* takes things a step further by providing redundant disks, controllers, and power supplies. More sophisticated setups can use something called Redundant Arrays of Inexpensive Disks (RAID) instead of Single Large Expensive Disks (SLED). Honestly, I do *not* make up these acronyms.

Clustering is another approach to server fault tolerance. A server cluster is a group of servers that interconnect. If one server in the cluster fails, another picks up the slack. Servers in a cluster often share a single disk drive subsystem. Microsoft is working on clustering technology for Windows NT Server (code name: Wolfpack), but third-party solutions from companies like Vinca Corp. exist today for most network environments.

Antivirus technology

Computer viruses are great examples of how fault tolerance can be less expensive and more effective than fault resilience. Imagine that a virus infects a file. A good combination of server- and workstation-based antivirus software can detect the virus quickly, and alert administrators, who can then repair and disinfect the affected file before the virus spreads and forces a costly network shutdown.

I won't go into the dark and twisted world of the different kinds of computer viruses in great detail here — except to say that in the good old days, all you had to worry about was programs getting infected. Today, you have to worry about data files, too. The line is blurring between data and program. For example, a user downloads a word processing document from an intranet publishing server. Safe enough, right? Wrong, browser breath. When the user opens this data file in a word processing program, the data file may run a little program called a *macro* which (if it's a macro virus) can cause damage to other data files the user works with later.

This is bad, but the situation gets worse. Many intranet publishing applications rely on *helper programs* (*viewers* or *plug-ins*) that permit a user's browser to automatically run a certain kind of file, such as a word processing document. Helper programs make it super easy for users to activate data files that may be infected with a virus. Turning off the helper programs may not be a good solution if the helper program is necessary for a particular work task, so the burden falls on whoever's putting content up on your intranet to make sure that the documents don't contain viruses. Limiting who can publish on your intranet, therefore, makes a lot of sense.

Effective antivirus technology runs software on both servers and clients. Some of the questions to ask when shopping for antivirus software include:

- **How many different viruses can the software detect?** Thousands exist.
- **How frequently does the vendor issue updates so that the software can catch new viruses?** Evil, like rust, never sleeps.
- **How much of a pain is it to apply such updates?**
- **Can the software detect viruses it doesn't already know about?**
- **How prone is the software to false alarms?**

- ✔ **What ways can the software tell me about an alarm?** A Network message, a pager alert, and so on, are ways you can be alerted.
- ✔ **Can I tell the software to scan particular files or directories more often than others?**
- ✔ **What information does the software's log file provide? Can I understand it?**
- ✔ **Does the software kill my network in terms of speed?** Some software does.

Antivirus policies

Security consultants have preached for years that technology alone isn't enough to combat viruses effectively. They're absolutely right — you also have to have reasonable and widely followed antivirus *policies* in place. For example, how do users install software? Do they get it from a network server, out of a shrink-wrapped box, from a colleague who says, "This program's great, I got it from my wife's brother's car mechanic in Topeka," or from a guy working out of the back of a van in the company parking lot?

Other policies and procedures include:

- ✔ Scanning all new workstations for viruses
- ✔ Deciding whether computer games are allowed in the office
- ✔ Restricting users from booting workstations from diskette
- ✔ Assuring that those who report a virus won't be disciplined or held accountable, unless they are responsible for introducing it
- ✔ Educating users as to how to recognize viruses on their workstations
- ✔ Helping users protect their portable and home computers

Intranet fault resilience

Get a few computer people, managers, and users into a room and ask them this question: "What are the five worst things that can happen to our intranet, and how will we respond to them?" The answers will provide a starting point for designing a good fault resilience strategy. The first thing people think of is restoring damaged data and programs, by reverting to backup copies.

Data backup

Good data backups form the cornerstone of any intranet fault resilience program. Follow the steps and suggestions in this chapter, and chances are good that you'll never need a backup copy of any intranet data. Even so, a smart backup routine is like fire insurance for your home: You probably won't ever need the insurance, but if you do, you'll need it *badly*.

The good news is that if you keep all your intranet programs and documents on a web server or two, as is typical, you can focus on those machines and not worry too much about all those client workstations out there. If users store some data on their own systems, those users need a convenient method for duplicating the data, in case of disk failure (such as their own tape or cartridge drives). I personally prefer LAN-based solutions, in which a network server fetches workstation data automatically, usually at night, and dumps it to a tape drive.

For you Windows 95 shops, if users perform their own backups, for Pete's sake, don't use the Microsoft backup program. If a boot drive crashes, the user has to reinstall Windows 95 itself onto the new drive to be able to run the backup software and restore the disk files from tape (or cartridge disk, or whatever). A solution such as Cheyenne Backup is far more preferable — it can run off a diskette for much faster restores.

Web servers running on top of a network operating system, such as IntraNetware or Windows NT Server, can use the same backup programs for the web files as for the other files on the server. Here are some elements of a good data backup procedure:

- ✔ **Store at least one set of backups off-site, preferably in a different city if your business isn't solely local, but certainly in a different building.**

- ✔ **Back up frequently, preferably daily, and maybe even more often if the data changes frequently.**

- ✔ **Don't back up everything each time, if you don't need to.** *Differential* backups copy everything that changed since the last full backup.

- ✔ **Don't expect users to take a lot of responsibility for data backup.** The more automatic the backup procedures are, the better.

- ✔ **Consider the time it takes to restore the data.** Older tape drives can be very slow if you only need to recover a single file, and it happens to be at the end of the tape. Some organizations back up data to another hard drive for speedy recovery, as well as to tape or other removable media for off-site storage.

- ✔ **Be wary of data compression.** Compressed backups can be more sensitive to *media flaws* (physical glitches in the disk or tape).

- ✔ **Use redundancy options provided by your backup software, again to help protect against media flaws.** With redundancy, which writes error recovery data to the target media, you can often work around such flaws and reconstruct what the data should look like.

- ✔ **Occasionally perform test restores to make sure everything's working the way you think it is.** Do the test restores on a backup server (you do have a backup server somewhere, right?), in case they go haywire.

- ✔ **Consider media life.** Tapes, disk cartridges, and even optical disks all have finite lifetimes, although CD-Recordable (CD-R) disks last longer than most other media. Throw out old media well before the manufacturer's estimated lifetime. (Manufacturers are always optimistic!)

Disaster recovery

Disaster recovery planning certainly includes a solid backup strategy, but it goes beyond that. It deals with all the procedures and policies that pertain to any sort of disaster — fire, flood, earthquake, pestilence, and plague.

If your organization already has a disaster recovery plan, great — look it over and see if you need to do anything different or extra for your intranet publishing system. If not, grab a good book on the subject — I like Patrick Corrigan's *LAN Disaster Prevention and Recovery* (Addison-Wesley) — and sit down once a year with representatives from the management, technical, and user communities to evaluate whether you need a plan. If you decide that you do need a plan, decide what it should contain.

No people I know really *like* doing disaster planning, any more than they enjoy reviewing their personal insurance policies or writing their wills. Depending on how important your intranet is to your overall business, however, disaster planning can be a very worthwhile exercise.

Your security systems will pay you back handsomely by enabling you to spend more time improving your intranet systems, and less time dealing with expensive and damaging security breaches — breaches that can easily threaten management support for the intranet concept if the infractions are serious enough. Good security also helps users trust your intranet. Much like that month-old lasagna in the refrigerator: If they don't trust it, they won't use it.

Chapter 16
Publicity and Promotion

In This Chapter
▶ Understanding why you need to promote your intranet system
▶ Easing intranet access by choosing good network names
▶ Using existing corporate communications vehicles
▶ Planting intranet links on the desktop and in related documents
▶ Creating an intranet Public Relations demo
▶ Establishing a structure for continuous improvement
▶ Sharing your successes with your organization
▶ Cultivating key users and managers through special programs

Selling the initial project to receive budget approval is only the beginning. You need to sell the publishing system every day to users, managers, and content providers if you want to see its full productivity potential. As Sony discovered with the Beta consumer video format, doing a nice job on the technology isn't enough to ensure acceptance in the user community.

Nothing Sells Itself

Truer words were ne'er spake, and yet I've seen several excellent information system initiatives that didn't catch on, because no one was beating the bushes selling the systems to the user and management communities.

You can always take the approach of promoting your intranet information system by *requiring* employees to use it — that is, by not making the information available any other way. ("We'd like for you to use this new system, and by the way, you're fired if you don't.") Such an approach may backfire by making employees resent your new system, and it runs against the grain of the intranet culture, which has a grass-roots, ground-up history.

PREACH IT

If you're considering making intranet use mandatory, think about the more subtle approach of gradually phasing out traditional information access methods while continually pitching the benefits of your new system. You ultimately make the old ways so inconvenient that users choose to use your intranet on their own. This method is similar to the way IBM phases out old computer systems. The company doesn't tell the customer "You can no longer buy this model," at least not right away. It simply doubles and triples the cost of parts and maintenance contracts so that using the old systems becomes uneconomical. People appreciate being able to make their own decisions, even if the employer is obviously steering them in a certain direction.

I'm writing this little chapter because if you do a good job designing *and promoting* your intranet system, you don't have to require employees to use it — they'll use it because it makes sense to them. If using your intranet doesn't make sense to them, it may be time to go back to the drawing board (and Chapter 3, which presents project selection guidelines) to analyze the reasons why.

Encouraging users to take advantage of intranet resources is the primary reason to promote your publishing system. I can think of some others, too:

- To build a consensus of support among management, users, and content providers, so that the continued improvement and expansion of intranetting goes forward
- To familiarize users with your intranet system's organization and content
- To inform groups, teams, and departments of your activities, so that they can apply intranet publishing within their own organizations
- To lure new content providers to your intranet concept

Eight Ways to Promote Your Project

The following eight suggestions don't represent all the ways you can promote your intranet, but they give you a few concrete ideas, and get the gray cells firing so that you can come up with more ideas.

Pick an easy intranet address and name

This sounds trivial, I know, but if users can find your intranet easily, the easier you can promote it. A web system home page address, such as `http://www.independentsoftwareinc.com/intranet/publishing/humanresources/policiesandprocedures/index.html` **doesn't generate as much traffic or user-friendliness as the more obvious** `http://www.isi.com/policies/index.html`

If your business already has a public Internet presence, you're stuck with a domain name, but if your intranet comes first, you can choose the name. Also, consider coordinating with your marketing folks so that the name you choose for your intranet will also work for a public Internet site, if you set one up later. You can certainly create a separate public Internet server with a different domain name than your intranet, and many companies do, but you may find it more convenient and flexible to use the same domain name for both internal and external network users.

Having said that, hide these web site addresses where you can to make intranet access even easier, using various shorthand techniques. For example, you can make an icon on a user's desktop that says simply *Policies and Procedures* and the Uniform Resource Locator (URL — see Chapter 11 for more info) can be the long one in the previous paragraph. Nevertheless, from time to time your intranet users have to key the URL into a web browser.

Give the publishing project a catchy common name, and then use it often in documentation and promotional vehicles. A technical support system can be *SupportNet*, for example, as opposed to *The Acme Cognac Company Technical Support Document Publishing System* (*TACCTSDPS*). Avoiding acronyms is also good practice. The computer industry already has two thousand too many (TTTM) acronyms.

My favorite computer industry acronym has nothing to do with intranet publishing, but I'll tell it to you anyway. APL, a programming language with strong mathematical and statistical features, stands for *A Programming Language*. No kidding.

I'm no lawyer, but you may not be illegally infringing on trademarks, as long as your intranet is internal to your organization. A little advice from counsel is a good idea, though, especially if and when you link your intranet to the outside world.

I know you'll be smart, and register your intranet server domain names with the Internet Network Information Center (InterNIC) in Virginia, the Internet's central address authority. Doing so means that no name change is necessary if you ever link your intranet to the public Internet. See Chapter 9 for the details on checking existing domain names and registering new ones.

Use existing communications vehicles

Before rushing out and designing all sorts of new public relations vehicles for your intranet, take advantage of the company communications tools that already exist: newsletters, bulletin boards, and the *new-hire* book.

Print and electronic newsletters

Articles about the publishing project's features, goals, and benefits can appear in company or department newsletters. One attractive aspect of this promotional method is that you don't incur any new costs. Another is that your time investment is minimal: Someone else already handles printing and distribution.

Newsletter articles come to life if they present one or two real-life success stories. Poll your user community for cases in which the publishing intranet came in especially handy. ("CEO Napoleon Courvoisier resolves PowerPoint snag minutes before annual shareholder meeting — downloads bug fix from Help Desk intranet.")

Newsletters are also good places to post short articles on how to use the new intranet system. Chances are that not everyone in your target user community knows how to use a web browser, or even link to a Uniform Resource Locator (URL). You may want to consider a series of articles on using the publishing system, starting with beginner's topics and moving to more advanced tips.

Watch out for the common mistake of including *only* novice information in newsletter articles. The techies in your user universe may appreciate the occasional article on Java or ActiveX.

A great technique for print and electronic newsletters is to point readers to intranet locations for more information, or examples of a particular topic in action. You may also want to work out a way to put any existing corporate or departmental newsletters onto your intranet system (see Chapter 4 for suggestions on how to do so).

Real and virtual bulletin boards

You may have forgotten about the *real* bulletin board (you know, cork and pushpins?) in the hallway just outside the cafeteria, or wherever you have one. You can use good old-fashioned posters to promote your publishing project as well as any intranet bulletin board.

A nice color screen snapshot of your intranet home page can grab the attention of passersby better than a boring black-and-white laser-printed page. If you don't have a good color printer, you can take a file on diskette to the local full-service print shop, where you can have a fancy, dye sublimation printout made for $10 or so (dye sublimation prints look much cooler than inkjet or thermal wax prints). Color laser prints are cheaper at about two bucks, but don't look quite as cool.

If your organization maintains a virtual bulletin board system (BBS) on an existing computer network, consider posting a press release about the new project in its *What's New* section and continuing to post notices as you expand your intranet's capacity or features. You may even want to post a demo program that users can download and run to get the feel of your intranet system, as I discuss a little later in this chapter.

Get into the new-hire book

Every new employee in a medium to large organization gets some sort of *new-hire* book, usually a three-ring loose-leaf binder with multiple sections. Human Resources generally assembles the material, which includes everything from the mundane (retirement benefits) to the vital (holiday schedules). Most new-hire books also contain a section on using and abusing the information system.

How your intranet systems appear in the new-employee manual varies greatly. Some intranetters like to put together a separate brochure, such as a letter-sized sheet folded into thirds, and tuck it away somewhere in the package. This has the advantage that you can use the brochure elsewhere also, casually leaving copies lying around in the cafeteria, parking garage, conference rooms, and so forth. The brochure can not only inform readers about your intranet, but include quick tips and steps explaining how to connect to it as well. I know one Information Services manager who was rolling out a new system and convinced bookkeeping to slip a brochure about the new intranet in with everyone's paycheck.

Even though a brochure may be a good idea on its own, I prefer formatting your intranet system information to be an integral part of the new-hire book's computer section. Inserted brochures have an air of impermanence. Work with Human Resources: Ask them to include intranet material using the same word processing or desktop publishing system they used to create the main body of the book. Eventually your intranet may replace the printed HR dust collector, but meanwhile, you may as well take advantage of the paper document to help encourage its own demise.

Place links everywhere

The more ways you provide for users to find your intranet publishing system, the more likely they are to try it out initially, and to use it regularly.

Remember the first few years of *USA Today*? If you traveled on business, you just couldn't avoid this newspaper. Free copies were everywhere: in the airport, on the plane, under your hotel room door. After ignoring it for the fiftieth or sixtieth time, you picked up a copy. Before long, you got used to its organization, and you quickly found the parts you wanted to read. *USA Today* is rarely the best newspaper in whatever town you happen to find yourself, but like a McDonald's hamburger, it's always convenient, always consistent, always a known quantity.

You want to make your intranet as convenient, consistent, and comfortable to use as *USA Today* (just don't make it as ugly). A great way to do so is to place hyperlinks to your intranet home page everywhere you can. The two areas to target are the *desktop* and *related documents*.

On the desktop

The *desktop* is what the user sees on the screen after turning on the computer: file folders, program menus, little icons representing particular data files, screen *wallpaper* with nature scenes photographed by people with better jobs than we have, and so on. Possible locations for intranet links on the desktop include:

- ✔ **An icon on the desktop:** If you just have one intranet publishing system
- ✔ **A file folder on the desktop:** The file folder can contain icons for each of the various corporate intranet publishing systems, if you have more than one
- ✔ **An entry on the main list of programs:** For example, in Windows 95, you can have Start⇨Programs⇨Super Duper Intranet

Creating these links, icons, and file folders doesn't have to be a tedious, one-at-a-time project. Your network administrator can probably create a slick little login script that automatically copies the links onto users' desktops when they log in to the network. For example, on a Windows 95 PC, desktop icons reside in `C:\Windows\Desktop`, and the main list of programs resides in `C:\Windows\Start Menu\Programs`.

If your organization uses a standard setup routine to configure a new user workstation, customize that routine so that it sets up your intranet icons, folders, and programs automatically. (For example, if you install Windows 95 onto new PCs from network servers, customize the file `msbatch.inf` on the server. The details are in Appendix D of the Microsoft *Windows 95 Resource Kit*.)

Within other documents

Many network e-mail systems nowadays (such as Microsoft Exchange) permit the message-sender to embed a web page hyperlink inside a mail message. ("Bookkeeping introduces a new network-based expense report form you can fill out on the road from your notebook and submit by modem. Check it out at `http://acme.pub.com/expense.html`.") The message recipient can then simply click the underlined text (it often also appears in a different color) to activate a web browser and connect to the specified page.

You may have to use the full and proper Uniform Resource Locator (URL) format (starting with `http://`) to get embedded hyperlinks to work inside e-mail messages.

Include embedded intranet links in other online documents that may relate to your intranet, if the document format supports such linking. The list of possibilities includes:

- Electronic newsletters
- BBS files
- Any intranet demos you create
- User help files, word processing forms
- Document templates

Provide a demo

Computer users like demos of new products. For one thing, the demo takes the user step by step through a new system. Turning a user loose on a live system can be a little bit like putting a landlubber into a one-person sailboat on a windy lake and saying, "Have fun and sail around!" When running a demo, the user also has less fear of making a mistake and somehow accidentally bringing the network to a crashing halt. Demos can use animations (for example, created using Lotus Screencam) to demonstrate intranet navigation, even though your live intranet may avoid these bandwidth-intensive files for speed reasons. Finally, the demo doesn't require that the user already have a network connection.

You can create an intranet demo various ways:

- **Build a set of HTML pages, which has the advantage of being easy to assemble and looking just like the live system.** If the user doesn't yet have a web browser, however, this approach doesn't do much good.
- **Create a demo using a tool that you know nearly everyone has, so that you can reach a wider variety of users.** For example, if your organization mainly uses PCs, and the standard office suite is Microsoft Office 97, build a slideshow demo using PowerPoint 97 (for tips on building slick slideshows, check out *Creating Cool PowerPoint 97 Presentations* by Weadock and Weadock, IDG Books Worldwide, 1997).
- **Create a standalone program that doesn't need any other software to run.** This is a more labor-intensive, but impressive, approach. You can build such a demo with a sophisticated authoring program like Asymetrix Toolbook or Macromedia Director, if you have people on staff who are already familiar with these tools.

Design your demo to be modular, so you can change bits and pieces around as necessary, to customize the software for different departments.

Here are some topics to consider including when creating your demo modules:

- Internet and World Wide Web background information
- The definitions of server and browser
- The definitions of hypertext and HyperText Markup Language (HTML), with examples
- How to type in a Uniform Resource Locator (URL)
- How your corporate intranet differs from the Internet
- How your corporate intranet differs from traditional Local Area Networks (LANs)
- One-way and two-way intranet information
- Intranet business benefits and costs
- Types of data the user may encounter on the corporate intranet (text, formatted text, forms, graphics, software files, and so on)
- Sample applications that are relevant for the specific audience
- Security and virus concerns

This book contains a lot of information to get you started on each of these topics.

Make continuous improvement

One of the better ways to promote an intranet project is to keep improving it. The management catch phrase is *continuous improvement*. Enhancing your intranet system is usually easier than enhancing traditional client/server applications, so continuous improvement is a realistic goal.

If a user notices something new and useful every few times he or she connects to your intranet, that user is likely to keep connecting. Any salesperson knows that existing customers are the best future prospects, and sharp intranetters keep current users' loyalty by making their products better over time.

A true story

Grab a hot chocolate and gather 'round the fireplace, because I'd like to tell you a little story about a company called Satellite Software International (SSI). Back in the mid-'80s, this company had an idea for a new PC word processing package. Many commentators in the industry press scoffed, because several serviceable microcomputer word processors already existed. What was the point of one more?

But SSI went ahead anyway. The first version of their product was hard to use, and it certainly didn't displace its competitors. SSI offered a toll-free number, however, for customers to suggest new features. The company listened, and soon the next version was out, incorporating most of the features users said they wanted. After two more cycles of suggestions and enhancements, the company's product was the market leader, and it remains popular to this very day, even if SSI's successors have allowed the product's luster to fade. That product's name — if you haven't guessed by now — is WordPerfect. The moral to this story is that listening to users pays off.

User suggestion box

Give your users an easy way to tell you how you can improve your intranet system by providing an online, anonymous suggestion box.

The old story about the small business owner who told any employee with a complaint to "drop a note in the suggestion box," after having placed the suggestion box in a utility closet, makes a valid point! Put an e-mail link to the project manager on the publishing system's home page.

If you find that the suggestions you receive are too vague to be truly helpful ("Make the system better!" and so on), you may want to structure a HyperText Markup Language (HTML) form for users to complete.

See Chapter 5 for tips on form design.

Continuing education

Getting suggestions from users is wonderful, but you have to know how to act on the suggestions, and that takes expertise. An information system continues to improve if the people involved with it have brains that continue to improve. Part of a continuous improvement strategy includes *ongoing intranet education* for users, content providers, and intranet designers.

These groups have different educational needs: Users need information on access, navigation, and available features; content providers need details on formatting options and updating procedures; and designers need, well, everything.

Intranet technologies are evolving so fast that companies need to figure on spending a few days a year for key people to catch up with the latest developments. Topics for ongoing intranet designer education include:

- State of the standards (HTML, Java, and so on — see Chapter 19 for more on these standards)
- Web management tools (see Chapter 13)
- Document formatting options (see Chapter 10)

- Search engine technology (see Chapter 11)
- Browser technology (see Chapter 3)
- Programming tools and techniques (see Chapters 5 and 12)
- GUI design classes, including user psychology, color theory, and so on

Trumpet your success

According to an old folk saying, you don't want to hide your light under a bushel basket. I'm not quite sure what that means exactly, but it is fun to say *bushel basket*. Don't be modest! Send out the occasional e-mail to announce aspects of your intranet system's ongoing success:

- Site activity
- Anecdotes about the system meeting business needs
- Capacity expansion
- New features
- New team members
- Spin-off projects

If you use corporate e-mail systems for promotion, follow good *netiquette*: Keep the messages brief and to the point. These are teasers and you only turn off readers by providing the lurid system details. Point users to intranet sites so they can get the details if they want 'em.

Another bit of netiquette is to restrict e-mails to users who are likely to find them relevant. Human Resources publishing systems probably interest everybody, but a new blueprint publishing system probably doesn't — you'd probably want to restrict that message to those in the engineering, art, or design groups. If you work in an organization with more than 30 people, and you haven't yet set up e-mail groups for targeted distribution, you may be wise to do so. You don't want to contribute to information overload.

You can trumpet your successes in other ways than e-mail. For example, you may consider emulating J.C. Penney and hold an annual one-day intranet fair, where employees can drop by a central location, see examples of your intranet systems up and running, and ask questions of the intranet developers and content providers.

Cultivate key users

Every organization has a select few computer users who seem to have unusual influence over their colleagues when it comes to all things cyber. These people may be (in larger organizations) Help Desk liaisons, or just informal support people who answer user questions in the field. If you're new to the organization and aren't sure who these people are, ask around.

You can cultivate the key users in your organization in the following ways:

- Make sure they understand your project's goals and benefits.
- Involve them in the initial design and the ongoing enhancement of the project.
- Ask their opinions about the publishing system, and then take their suggestions seriously.
- Get their ideas for how you can better promote the system to other users.

Don't forget the managers!

Promoting your publishing system to the user community is great, but you also need to build a broad base of management support for it. Chapter 9 discusses involving managers in the early stages of a project — but don't stop there! Keep managers informed of the system's progress and acceptance as it evolves.

Senior managers are often the most hesitant to embrace intranet publishing, because it represents a shift of information — and, therefore, power and responsibility — within the organization.

Recognize that managers in any organization have somewhat different needs for information than typical users.

One way to reach managers on an ongoing basis is to hold periodic *technology briefings*. Managers like attending *briefings* because they sound managerial. Managers hate attending *training sessions* because they *don't* sound managerial. I've suggested this approach for years to Help Desk managers, and they report good success with it. Keys to technology briefing success are as follows:

- Schedule it at a time when managers are less likely to have conflicts, such as an early morning or late afternoon. Even better, shoot for a Wednesday or Thursday; Monday and Tuesday are typically catch-up days, and people tend to drift a bit on Fridays. You also minimize the risk of losing people taking three-day weekends.

- Keep it brief — 90 minutes, tops.
- Keep it high-level. These people rarely want, or even need, the technical details. Have the techie stuff available in case someone asks, but don't make these details part of the main presentation.
- Focus on benefits (which Chapter 1 details), but disclose costs, too.
- Close with thoughts about the future: how you plan to make the current system even better, other publishing possibilities, any way to leverage the technology you've demonstrated for the good of the organization.

The best advice I can pass along was given to me years ago by a programming professor. She told me that if I wanted to succeed as a computer consultant, I should always spend 25 percent of my time on promotion and publicity, even if I'm swamped with work. Time and experience have borne her out. Skipping the public relations is tempting when you're up to your eyeballs in rolling out a new system, but if you conscientiously promote your intranet project, it stands a much better chance to gain wide acceptance, and to bring your organization the benefits that I discuss in Chapter 1.

Part V
The Part of Tens

The 5th Wave By Rich Tennant

In this part...

The "Part of Tens" is a standard feature of the ...*For Dummies* series, and this book is no exception. If you want a quick overview of the book's key points, read the ten "P's" of intranet publishing success. I throw in a list of ten standards to keep an eye on, for two reasons: they're evolving rapidly; and the closer you can adhere to them, the easier time you have maintaining and expanding your project.

Please don't forget to take a look at the appendixes, which are really useful, and the CD-ROM, which is not merely an attractive and durable coffee mug coaster but also a valuable resource including hundreds of megabytes of cool software. (You even get to see the Acme Cognac sample intranet pages in full color.) As a parting note, I wish you great success with your intranet publishing projects, and I hope this book helps you along the way. See you on the other side of the firewall.

Chapter 17
Ten Ps of Intranet Publishing Success

In This Chapter
- Matching an intranet project to your organization
- Planning up front to minimize life-cycle costs and maximize benefits
- Keeping system speed and user productivity uppermost in your mind
- Thinking in terms of computer screens, not printed pages
- Maintaining your project and demonstrating its value over time

If you find yourself hanging on my every word in the 16 chapters preceding this one (or at least on every other word), this little section reinforces the keys to intranet publishing success those chapters present. If you're starting at the end of this book and working your way to the front (the way many people do their taxes), that's a valid approach, too, and I give you navigational icons to take you back to the relevant chapters.

Pick Your Projects

When you hit your late thirties, you begin to realize that you're not going to be able to do everything in life that you planned to do when you were in your early twenties. For example, it seems unlikely now that I will write a great violin concerto, bring integrity back to the U.S. presidency, write a technothriller that will blow Michael Crichton into the weeds, and win Wimbledon. The wisdom that comes with age forces me to admit that I may only be able to achieve three out of four.

My point is that you need to pick your projects carefully, because you only have so much time and energy for each one. Every new venture you undertake rules out a thousand other possibilities. I don't mean to suggest that you will only roll out one or two intranet publishing projects in your career, or that you will hit the ball out of the park on the first swing. Both are possible, however, so make every effort to make the first intranet system you're involved with a successful one. Here are some tips that can increase your chance of success:

- **Cut your teeth on a simple one-way, one-to-many, plain text, basic-technology system.** A read-only publishing system without fancy graphics, multimedia, or database connectivity is a good place to start.

- **Start with a project that doesn't extend beyond your organization's boundaries.** That is, don't bring customers and suppliers on board your intranet until you have some experience with the technology.

- **Match your intranet publishing project to the technology you already have, in terms of servers, clients, and network infrastructure.** You can add new technology for fancier applications later, but keeping the cost down for the first project increases your management's comfort level.

- **Pick a project that allows you to quantify your success in an easily understandable way.** For example, favor a project that reduces paper publishing and distribution costs by a measurable amount.

- **Don't get caught up in a legal tangle because you didn't take care of determining your rights and obligations with respect to the information you publish.** Trademarks, copyrights, and trade secrets must concern all publishers, even electronic ones.

Chapter 3 deals with these intranet project selection issues.

Play with Possibilities

Information system professionals tend to focus on one answer to a problem, rather than considering the whole range of possibilities. They concentrate their efforts on business problems that seem to fit the tools at hand, and ignore problems that they don't already know how to solve. At various times in the evolution of computing, the industry responded to every business problem with one of the following stock answers: "You need a (*pick one:* mainframe, minicomputer, PC, desktop publishing, network, client/server system, multimedia, intranet)."

Focusing too much on the tool, and too little on the possible ways to use the tool, is a mistake with a long, proud tradition. Break from that tradition and spend a little time letting your mind range over the possibilities of intranet publishing. You don't need to rush off and put your policies and procedures manuals on the system, just because everyone else is doing it. Consider these possibilities of what to include on your intranet:

- Employee directory and organizational charts
- Human resources manuals and benefits information
- Newsletters, schedules, and project status reports
- Emergency and disaster plans
- Purchase requisitions, expense reports, and budgets
- Collaborative document editing
- Design and manufacturing drawings
- User surveys
- Product sales sheets and specifications
- Customer information for sales support
- Technical support (troubleshooting knowledge base, common problems and solutions)
- Software distribution
- Searchable product documentation
- Online training courses — Intranet Based Training (IBT)

Chapters 4 through 8 present dozens of possible intranet publishing applications, some of which you may not have thought of.

Plan for Success

Those little inspirational books filled with nuggets of wisdom about life can be unbearably frustrating:

"Fools rush in where angels fear to tread."

"He who hesitates is lost."

"Nothing ventured, nothing gained."

Everyone knows of stories where opportunities have vanished due to excessive analysis and planning, and the temptation to jump right into intranet publishing without much planning is a big one. Planning for intranet success, however, doesn't have to be a paralyzing, years-long process. You can probably do all the planning you need for a small intranet in a couple of weeks. This planning requires a lot of gray cell activity, and the ability to communicate the benefits of planning to your superiors.

You may be in a position where your boss wants an intranet up and running yesterday. My experience has been that caving in to that sort of pressure never works out very well for anyone. You can do your boss a great service by asking (diplomatically, of course), "Do you want it done tomorrow, or do you want it done right?" If you try this and get fired, please feel free to complain to me directly at 976-555-1234.

Chapter 9 addresses the key planning issues for intranet publishing.

Pinclude Everyone

Computer professionals use the term *cooperative processing* to mean information systems that use multiple computers to address a business need. In a larger sense, cooperative processing means information systems that all major constituencies have a hand in designing and implementing. I guess the opposite of this term is *adversarial processing*, in which managers shove computer systems down the throats of unwilling and resentful users. I've seen a lot of those systems, and you don't want one.

The more the key groups are involved in your intranet publishing project, the greater your chances for satisfying them. These groups include:

- **The technologists** who create the system (including your webmaster, hardware experts, programmers, and so on)
- **The users** who work with it every day
- **The managers** who must understand and approve the system
- **The content providers** who contribute the documents you publish

You must have certain safeguards against the paralysis of democracy, in which nothing happens because you can't get a unanimous vote on anything. By asking the key intranet constituencies to prioritize their concerns and wishes, instead of merely listing them, you can approach the goal of an intranet that everyone supports — and in which everyone has a stake. Also recognize, and address, the legitimate turf and career concerns that many groups have when you start repackaging information for your intranet and altering jobs either to include new intranet tasks, or to remove tasks that your intranet may make obsolete.

Chapter 3 discusses using surveys to involve all four groups at the design stage, while Chapter 16 offers suggestions for ongoing communications with these groups after the system is up and running.

Put Performance on a Pedestal

Digital video has long been an interest of mine, and I remember when the first versions of QuickTime and Video for Windows appeared on the microcomputer scene. I thought those postage-stamp-size windows of slow, jerky video were the bee's knees, because I knew that nothing so fancy had ever been remotely possible before. (Heck, I thought it was cool when I bought my company's first PC in 1985 for $7000, and it could display *four different colors!* All four were really ugly, but that didn't matter at the time.) However, when other, non-technical colleagues looked at these early implementations of digital video, their reaction was "Gee, it's really lame compared to TV, isn't it?" Of course, they were right, within their own frame of reference.

Users judge any network information system's speed against what they're used to experiencing on a standalone workstation. An intranet developer may be thrilled that a user can view a complex document over the network with only a ten-second delay, but the user compares that to the one-second delay of viewing the same document when it resides locally on the user's own hard drive.

Speed isn't only important because users expect it. Speed is important because it helps people work productively. The two-second delay associated with an intranet hyperlink is just enough to allow the human mind to wander afield to thoughts of last night's elaborate date, this morning's hangover, or next week's credit card bill. A computer system that doesn't require users to refocus their thoughts after every keystroke is one that allows users to really cook, and get some serious work done.

Chapter 14 is all about making your intranet burn rubber, and Chapter 11 discusses how to make navigating your intranet quick and efficient.

Put Productivity on a Higher Pedestal

A charming little book called *Cheaper by the Dozen* (Gilbreth and Carey, Bantam Starfire) is about a large family whose father worked as a time-and-motion study consultant. He helped manufacturing businesses improve efficiency by streamlining the physical motions involved in product assembly. He carried his work home, to the extent of advising his offspring about the most efficient way to towel off after a shower, which, of course, made his family members want to bludgeon him with a baguette in one swift, efficient swing.

These days, it's fashionable to pooh-pooh those early efforts at improving efficiency, on the grounds that they view human beings too much as machines. The underlying question those time-and-motion experts asked, however, is, "How much are you getting done in how much time?" This question is one that intranet publishers are foolish to dismiss out of hand. User productivity is the goal of any intranet system, so examine your intranet with the following questions in mind:

- **How many operations (keystrokes, mouse clicks) and intranet pages stand between users and the documents they need?**

- **Do you see opportunities to combine intranet publishing with business process reengineering (BPR)?** Intranets help overcome key BPR obstacles, such as incompatible computer platforms and employee cross-training requirements.

- **Do security measures slow users down to the point that they must jump through too many hoops to get the information they need?** Should you change your thinking about information security from a *need-to-know* basis to a *need-to-withhold* basis?

- **Is your intranet up and running above 99 percent of the time?** If users depend on the system for information, it must demonstrate both *fault tolerance* (staying running when a problem occurs) and *fault resilience* (recovering quickly from faults that shut down the system).

Chapter 3 discusses Business Process Reengineering (BPR) and intranets in more detail, while Chapter 15 presents techniques for implementing security and ensuring uptime without adding too many productivity-sapping steps for users.

Publish for the Screen

The author of a print document must pay attention to the physical form the document ultimately assumes. Intranet publishers must become as intimately familiar with the dynamics of computer screens as print publishers are with the paper page. The tremendous importance of the user interface to any information system project suggests that you may want to bring in a user interface design specialist. Have this person spend a day reviewing your intranet screens, and suggest ways to improve design and layout. Most major computer consulting firms have user interface specialists on staff, and entire companies exist that consult solely on interface design. Try to find someone who has intranet rather than (or in addition to) Internet experience — form must match function, and internal workaday business systems have different functions than external promotional sites.

Chapter 12 presents specific web page design techniques, and Chapters 4 through 8 discuss a variety of formatting tools (tables, forms, and so on) to deliver information in screen-friendly ways.

Promote the Site

If your organization's users don't know about your intranet, they won't use it, and your efforts to cut document distribution costs and boost employee productivity are stymied. Promote and publicize your intranet the following ways:

- ✔ Take advantage of existing company communications vehicles, such as newsletters, to announce your intranet's debut as well as significant enhancements you make to it over time.

- ✔ Take advantage of hypertext links to make jumping over to your intranet from a standard desktop, from e-mail messages, and from online help files easy.

- ✔ Create a software demo that computer users can download to learn the benefits of your intranet, and get comfortable with its structure and navigational tools before actually getting online.

- ✔ Put procedures in place to gauge user opinions and collect intranet improvement suggestions, which you can use for continuous improvement.

Chapter 16 offers several tips for publicizing your intranet within the organization to ensure widespread awareness, and promote intranet use.

Prepare for the Future

Intranets tend to take off, exceeding everyone's expectations for usage and acceptance. If you aren't ready for this situation, your intranet can quickly become SAD: Slow, Anarchic, and Disorganized. And you can therefore become a SAP: Searching for Another Position. Make sure success doesn't catch you off guard by addressing these issues early:

- ✔ **Create organizational structures and roles that can handle intranet growth.** An advisory board, a webmaster, designated content providers and managers, user community liaisons, and so on, need to be part of the team.

- ✔ **Bring internal technical support staff up to speed on intranet technology.** They can handle user questions and problems.

- ✔ **Make design decisions that can support growth and expansion.** For example, deploy software utilities that can manage IP addresses automatically, and favor portable programming solutions that don't lock you in too tightly to a single vendor.

- ✔ **Put procedures and programs in place to handle routine network management chores, and intranet-specific chores.** Making server backups and verifying hyperlinks are but two examples.

Chapter 13 lays out the key aspects of ongoing intranet maintenance.

Prove the Value

The great salespeople don't vanish when the sale closes. They follow up with the customer at appropriate and non-annoying intervals. They find out how the product is working out for the customer, and reinforce the idea that buying that product was a good decision. The salesperson's hope is that the customer will buy another product from him or her at some point in the future. The risk is that the product has fallen apart and the customer regrets ever listening to the salesperson in the first place.

Selling an information system to business managers isn't much different. Even after you receive budget approval — even after your intranet system is zapping electronic documents far and wide — reinforce the value of the system in the minds of your business decision-makers by demonstrating savings and productivity gains on an ongoing basis. You can do this via intranet pages, company newsletters, or periodic management briefings. You can, for example, conduct a semiannual *State of Our Intranet* address, which should be about one-tenth the length of Bill Clinton's *State of the Union* addresses.

Chapters 1 and 2 present the benefits and costs of intranet publishing systems, and can get you started creating your own plan to assure managers that your intranet was a good idea, and that enhancing and expanding it also makes sense.

Ponder the preceding pertinent, practical points and proceed to present productive, profitable, pleasing publishing projects.

Chapter 18
Ten Standards to Watch

In This Chapter
- Following HTML as it evolves to meet business needs and reflect current technology
- Understanding why Java standardization is still far from complete
- Tracking the powerful ActiveX technology as it (possibly) migrates to other platforms
- Exploring important upcoming typeface and printing enhancements for intranet users
- Keeping abreast of multimedia developments such as RealAudio
- Why gigabit Ethernet may be your ticket to new intranet publishing possibilities

*T*he world of intranet standards is a fluid one (you could liken it to quicksand). This chapter presents ten standards to keep a close eye on, to ensure that your publishing projects work well together, and remain robust and flexible over time.

Mention the word *standards* to a computer professional, and you're sure to elicit a dramatic reaction, from gung-ho enthusiasm ("Yes, we follow *all* the standards! We *love* standards!") to migraine-faced dismay ("Sheesh, those things change on a daily basis. We can never keep up."). Especially in the quickly mutating world of intranet technology, standards come and go with frustrating speed, some making the cut and others falling by the roadside. Don't dismay: Adhering to the more pervasive and long-lived standards is a huge key to intranet publishing success over the long haul.

One of the great things about intranets is that their technologies and standards are really the same as Internet technologies and standards, and the Internet is a place where openness and interoperability traditionally carry great weight. The good news, therefore, is that the standards most likely to succeed are those that accommodate a wide variety of hardware and software (case in point: Java programs, which can run on almost any kind of computer). If a proprietary standard succeeds, it has to deliver big benefits compared to open solutions, and the net result is more choices for customers.

Nobody in their right mind suggests that any organization blindly adopt every new standard (or every new revision of a standard) as soon as the standard hits the market. I *do* suggest, however, that you watch the more significant standards (such as the ten I discuss here) carefully, so that you can implement them when they reach a certain level of maturity and acceptance, and are likely to deliver tangible benefits. You need to compare open standards, which no single company controls, against proprietary technologies that may be faster or more rich with features, but are probably less portable to different servers and more limiting in terms of the products with which they work.

HTML and Dynamic HTML

As you may already know, HyperText Markup Language (HTML) is a *huge* issue for intranet publishers because it's the core language of web pages. The World Wide Web Consortium (W3C for short) and the Internet Engineering Task Force (IETF) manage the HTML standard and its evolution. To be honest, W3C now tends to follow the commercial market leaders (Netscape, Microsoft) rather than lead them. Think of HTML standards as slightly outdated, but widely accepted specs as to what a browser on any platform should be able to do.

Hop on back to the HTML sidebar in Chapter 1 if you're not sure what HTML means, or why it's important.

Standard HTML has several versions, both in use and under development.

- **HTML 1.0 is plain vanilla HTML with no chocolate syrup.** All the *tags* (commands) in HTML 1.0 are supported in newer versions so modern browsers can successfully read older web pages. Nobody thinks very much about HTML 1.0 these days, but hey, a list should be thorough.

- **HTML 2.0 is the safe choice for intranet publishers who must deal with a variety of workstation and browser versions.** This version adds forms and menu capabilities to the basics in HTML 1.0, but lacks most of the goodies Microsoft and Netscape have added in recent years.

- **HTML 3.0 is a catch-up standard that didn't catch on.** This version adds support for tables and new layout features, such as text flowing around graphics, as well as scientific and mathematical notation formats.

- **HTML 3.2 supports most of the HTML extensions that Microsoft and Netscape have added on their own.** The industry has adopted 3.2 much more widely than 3.0. Version 3.2 is currently the most important version: Both Navigator and Internet Explorer support HTML 3.2 in their 2+ versions. Tim Berners-Lee, creator of the Web, proclaimed in early 1997 that HTML 3.2 offers the best assurance of compatibility across platforms and over time.

Chapter 18: Ten Standards to Watch

Check out all the details of the HTML 3.2 spec at `www.w3.org/MarkUp/Wilbur`. Key elements (and non-elements!) of HTML 3.2 include:

- Support for tags that locate a Java applet on a page and that permit sending data to a Java applet.
- Support for *alternate tags* that allow a non-Java browser to at least display a description of the program that it can't actually run.
- Support for subscripts and superscripts, so you can now include statements on a web page such as "Bill Gates has 3×10^9 dollars."
- No support for Netscape frames, which divide a browser window into multiple sub-windows, popular though they've become for sites requiring complex navigational abilities.
- No mention of ActiveX, either — Microsoft's popular programming standard. The standard always lags the market-leading technology.

Upcoming versions of HTML (the next one is code-named *Cougar* for no apparent reason) are likely to contain support for some or all of the following elements:

- Netscape frames
- Microsoft ActiveX controls
- JavaScript and VBScript (programming languages to run from the browser on user computers)
- Extrasensory thought transference (oops, sorry, that's a future version)
- Precise object placement
- Cascading Style Sheets (see the "Cascading Style Sheets" section for more information)

New versions of HTML may also support something called *dynamic HTML*, with which users can change web page cosmetics and reveal hidden content with clicks and passes of the mouse. Microsoft and Netscape have both submitted proposals to W3C for dynamic HTML.

Microsoft has made a point of announcing that it won't include any features in its web browser that aren't either part of the W3C standards or under consideration by W3C. So Microsoft's dynamic HTML will probably use style sheets in some way, whereas Netscape's dynamic HTML may use a different approach. Both vendors say they'll abide by W3C decisions.

Watch out for technologies that depend on custom HTML extensions, only supported by one particular browser. If a document works with Navigator but not with Internet Explorer, it may not work with Windows 98, which integrates the browser with the operating system. If a document works with

Internet Explorer, but not with Navigator, it may disenfranchise the bulk of browser users (Navigator still has the largest installed user base). Generally, if a feature is part of HTML 3.2, both popular browsers support the feature.

My advice is to use your knowledge of HTML standards not as a substitute for application testing, but as a way to determine which features your publishing applications and browsers need to support, and where potential compatibility problems may lurk. For example, look for mismatches, such as an application that supports HTML 3.2, but a browser that only supports HTML 2.0.

Cascading Style Sheets

For years, word processors and desktop publishing programs have used *style sheets* to simplify life for people creating consistently formatted documents.

A *style sheet* is nothing more than a named collection of attributes describing a chunk of a document. For example, a style sheet may dictate that a document's title page be vertically centered, with 1-inch margins all around, using the Helvetica font in a 24-point size for the title and Helvetica 14-point for the author's name. With a well-designed application, you can be able to apply such a title page style to the first page of a new document in one fell swoop, without having to specify every little detail all over again.

The *Cascading* part of Cascading Style Sheets (CSS) just means that you can create *child* style sheets that inherit properties of *parent* style sheets while adding one or more wrinkles of their own. I guess the parent style sheet characteristics cascade down to the child, but a better metaphor must exist. In the meantime, we're stuck with this one.

CSS promises to bring the convenience of style sheets to web authors. Instead of having to worry about dozens of different HTML tags, you can simply specify a style sheet using a single tag, and automatically apply all the desired formatting to a web page. Changing the formatting becomes easier, too, because there's less to change. You can store CSS formatting information in a text file with a .CSS extension.

Some of the document publishing applications I mention in other chapters (mainly Chapter 12) can do this sort of thing today, but in a proprietary way that ties you to their software. If and when CSS becomes a bona fide standard, your formatting conventions will hold true, regardless of the software you use.

CSS represents a shifting of responsibility for document formatting from the server to the browser, because the browser applies the style sheet at the client side. Intranet publishers who want to maintain stricter control over document appearance may find CSS as frustrating as HTML font size limitations. The moral of this story is that you may not want to use CSS for web navigation pages or home pages, but it can be a boon for more straight-forward documents.

You can watch the development of CSS at www.w3.org/pub/TR/REC-CSS1-961217

eXtensible Markup Language (XML)

If you want to do something really fancy or tricky with HyperText Markup Language (HTML) that you can't do with standard tags, such as create a *dynamic table of contents* that changes automatically when you add or remove documents, you typically wind up using comment tags and buying (or writing) a special program to interpret the contents of those comments. You may also use a Java applet to view web page attachments that contain special formatting. These approaches can certainly work, but none is exactly elegant or efficient.

The World Wide Web Consortium (W3C) is working on an extension to HTML called *XML*, which is short for eXtensible Markup Language (XML must have looked cooler than EML to some authority at W3C). XML will allow web publishers to create their own custom HTML tags in a consistent way. Much like the CSS standard I describe in the previous section, XML will take some of the things intranet publishing tool vendors are already doing with proprietary techniques and slap some standardization on them for better compatibility between programs.

Many industry heavy-hitters, including Microsoft, seem to support the XML effort, with the notable exception, so far, of Netscape. XML has a better chance of success than Standardized General Markup Language (SGML), HTML's daddy, which is a much more complex and lengthy standard. Whether XML will take root without Netscape support is a big question, but if the standard gathers enough momentum, Netscape may well jump on the bandwagon.

You can follow XML development progress at the Graphics Communication Association Web site: www.gca.org

Java

Java is developing faster, perhaps, than any programming language in the history of computing because of its ability to run on so many different kinds of computers and because of its similarity to today's most popular programming language, C++. At this stage in its life cycle, you're very likely to run into Java compatibility problems even though Java is supposed to be a language that is platform-independent, and fully portable (all of which means that any Java program is supposed to run properly, unmodified, on any computer that can run Java programs). Attention to evolving Java standards is essential for trouble-free intranet implementation.

The few standards that do exist are in rapid flux. Sun Microsystems JavaSoft operating unit develops and manages the primary language standard by producing and supporting the Java Development Kit (JDK). New versions, subversions, and beta releases of JDK come out every few months.

Many companies, including IBM, Microsoft, and JavaSoft, are creating Java *virtual machines* (software programs that enable Java programs to run on a particular computer). Even more companies are creating Java *compilers*, which speed Java performance on specific hardware by converting Java programs to speak the "native tongue" of a particular processor, such as an Intel Pentium.

For example, both Internet Explorer and Navigator incorporate *Just-In-Time* Java compilers. These compilers don't necessarily work with all the Java programs out there, in part because no standards or specifications currently exist for Java compilers.

The International Standards Organization has been putting pressure on the key players in the Java industry (I won't mention any names, but I hope executives of *Microsoft* and *Sun* are reading this) to stop sniping at each other, and start cooperating to develop solid standards for the language, the virtual machines, and the compilers.

Intranetters, unite! If you work with Java technologies, send letters to your product vendors and urge them to cooperate with their competitors in developing good standards. No one wants to see Java disintegrate into dozens of semi-compatible variants.

ActiveX

ActiveX is a set of technologies that helps programmers create custom software that can run "inside" other programs, such as intranet web browsers. (For an intro to ActiveX, check out Chapter 12.)

ActiveX isn't a lean, mean, tightly-written specification (some people question whether the whole thing is written anywhere at all). Rather, it is a hugely complex and ambitious set of standards. ActiveX has its critics, but the fact remains that Microsoft is the 800-pound gorilla in the computer industry these days, and Microsoft is banking big time on ActiveX.

In an effort to quell criticism of ActiveX as yet another proprietary set of standards, Microsoft enlisted Massachusetts-based Open Group to be the standard-bearer (pun intended) and help ensure that the technology spreads to multiple platforms — mainly UNIX. The Open Group's ActiveX committee is called the Active Group — I love that name! — and consists of several major industry players (Adobe, DEC, and Hewlett Packard, among others).

You may want to keep tabs on another related standard: *Component Object Model* (COM). ActiveX is supposed to be compatible with COM, which helps standardize how various programs get along in a network environment like intranets.

If you're a Windows shop, make sure that you keep up with ActiveX. Follow its evolution at the Microsoft Web site, www.microsoft.com, and the Open Group's Active Group at www.activex.org.

PostScript Level 3

Many network printers (the exact number is zillions) run Adobe Systems PostScript software as their native language. You can think of a printer as just a special purpose computer, and it has to receive and process commands in a certain language. From the original Apple LaserWriter to today's newest Hewlett Packard LaserJet, most laser printers on computer networks follow PostScript commands to format documents correctly for output.

I know you're curious, so here's an example of the sort of commands a computer issues to a PostScript printer to print a document:

```
/Win35Dict 290 dict def Win35Dict begin/D/def load def/
    bd{bind D}bindD/in{72 mul}bd/ed{exch D}bd/ld{load D}bd/
    tr/translate ld/scl{in 100
div}bd/rlt/rlineto ld/spg/showpage ld/NupSpg/showpage ld/
    gs/gsave ld
```

Trust me; the printer knows what all that means.

- **PostScript Level 1 is still probably the version with the largest user base.** It was the first printer Page Description Language (PDL) to handle graphics well (good half-toning capabilities that could render a reasonably good-looking image on a device such as a laser printer).

- **PostScript Level 2 is what today's top-line printers use.** It offers better color matching support for color printing, and several speed enhancements.

In spite of very wide market acceptance, neither PostScript Level 1 nor Level 2 has a clue how to print a HyperText Markup Language (HTML) page directly — that is, without being translated into PostScript, for example, by a Windows 95 printer driver. The translation step takes time and, therefore, slows things down. Translating the document can also introduce inaccuracies, so that a printed HTML page may not look precisely like the one on the user's screen.

PostScript Level 3 addresses some of these problems by making printers more web-savvy, as follows:

- A PostScript Level 3-equipped printer can read and understand HTML without a translation step.

- It can also recognize web-page graphics formats, and massage them so that they look better on the printed page, with something Adobe calls Enhanced Image Technology (EIT — gotta have a three-letter acronym for everything these days!).

- Beyond HTML support, PostScript Level 3 provides better support for documents formatted in Portable Document Format (PDF — see Chapter 10). Right now, to print page 99 of a big PDF file, the printing computer has to mentally flip from pages 1 through 98 to know just how page 99 should appear. PostScript Level 3 is advertised to help alleviate this *big* PDF speed problem.

- Level 3 printers can have their own home pages, which an intranet manager can access to set printer options for the entire network without having to punch buttons on the front of the printer.

- You can even set up a web page that will enable users to print over an intranet to specialty PostScript devices, such as very expensive color PostScript printers.

- For organizations with international intranets, the Level 3 PlanetReady printing feature does a better job handling print jobs in non-English languages than previous versions.

Adobe hasn't upgraded PostScript very often (it introduced PostScript Level 2 in 1991, the Jurassic era, as far as Internet technologies go), and technicians can't usually upgrade a printer's programming language in the field. Currently, no one is sure how PostScript Level will be able to keep pace with HTML, a standard that keeps evolving rapidly. Intranet publishing systems that take advantage of the very latest HTML formatting capabilities will probably still require printer drivers to translate them to PostScript.

If Adobe delivers on half of these promises, PostScript Level 3 is a definite standard to watch. Stay tuned to `www.adobe.com` for developments.

OpenType and TrueDoc

HTML separates form and content, but often an intranet publisher wants to specify both. A common example is the fonts users see on their screens. In most intranet systems, the designer can't specify what typeface the user sees: Users have different fonts installed on their local workstations, and no convenient way exists to send a font with the document.

Today, if an intranet publisher jumps up and down and flat-out *insists* that all users see a specific font, the only solutions are partial ones:

- ✔ The Adobe PDF format embeds fonts with documents, but requires a browser plug-in.
- ✔ Some Microsoft Office products also use font embedding, but the feature only works with certain fonts.
- ✔ Sending data as a graphic instead of text is practical only for small snippets of text, and it's sloooow.

Thankfully, technology marches on. Two potential standards offer different approaches for bringing font fidelity to web systems: *OpenType* and *TrueDoc*.

Microsoft and Adobe have, for years, positioned themselves on opposite sides of the font technology fence — Microsoft espousing its TrueType specification, and Adobe evangelizing the Type 1 PostScript font specification (which is not a printer language despite the similar name to other PostScript protocols). However, these companies appear to have buried the silicon hatchet and have cooperatively developed a standard called OpenType. Microsoft is publicly positioning OpenType as the successor to TrueType, but OpenType actually includes Adobe's Type 1 technology.

Bitstream, a company with a long history of expertise in digital type, beat the Microsoft-Adobe partnership to the punch with a competing standard it calls *TrueDoc*. Oracle, Macromedia, Netscape, Novell, and Common Ground, among others, have licensed TrueDoc technology, giving Bitstream a fighting chance to prevail against the Microsoft-Adobe alliance.

The main characteristics that OpenType and TrueDoc share are as follows:

- They work with existing TrueType and PostScript Type 1 fonts.
- They use compression to reduce download times.
- They use *read-only* embedding, so that users can view a particular document correctly, but can't use the font to create or edit their own documents.
- They send only the characters that a particular document uses (tech term: *subset*), again to reduce delays.

Here are the differences between the products:

- OpenType sends the actual font file to the browser, but TrueDoc builds outline images of the fonts on the fly, and then sends those to the browser.
- TrueDoc files are smaller and download faster than OpenType.
- TrueDoc supports non-Latin fonts such as those used by eastern European languages like Czech; OpenType doesn't.
- TrueDoc is available as a set of Java classes for inclusion in products (such as Coda from Randomnoise, discussed in Chapter 10) written in Java.
- OpenType provides more accurate font fidelity.

You can visit the Microsoft digital-type Web site at `http://207.68.137.40:80/truetype/` Bitstream is at `www.bitstream.com`

RealAudio

Most intranet publishers don't concern themselves with sound bites, largely because most sound files require that the user first download and then play the file — an operation that takes a while. Seattle-based Progressive Networks Inc. is doing everything in its power to change that by working on *streaming audio,* which starts playing as soon as the file starts downloading to the browser.

Progressive Networks streaming RealAudio technology, already in version 4.0, may not be quite ready for prime time, except in intranets with a fast network infrastructure. RealAudio also has strong competitors (such as the audio support in Macromedia's Shockwave). However, as the technology evolves, it's likely to become a *de facto* standard.

Sound files can liven up an otherwise tedious intranet site ("Click here to hear the voice mail Deidre left for Bob after the Christmas party."). Be aware, though, that streaming audio may not work with some security systems that protect intranets from the public Internet (see Chapter 15 for more details).

Track RealAudio's progress at www.realaudio.com.

Object-Relational DBMS

For years, the computer industry has been singing the praises of *relational databases*. These databases structure information in tables, and allow you to quickly look up information based on any criteria you want to include in your database entries. Even today, most large organizations still haven't converted all their older databases to relational databases, but most agree that the goal is desirable, and one which they're working hard to achieve. Relational databases are flexible and relatively easy to modify compared with older types.

A big problem with relational databases is that they have a hard time coping with graphics and multimedia. For example, an intranet newsletter editor looking for a cute image to add to a meeting announcement can't easily ask a traditional database of graphic files for a list of all the clip art images pertaining to meetings.

The major database companies are racing to see who can solve this sort of problem fastest and most effectively. Most are working with something called *object-relational* technology, which treats data elements (like images) as objects that database programs can store, categorize, and retrieve easily, no matter what type they are.

Object-relational database servers often go by the modest and unassuming name of *universal servers*. In the Informix system (Informix is a major database vendor), *datablades* are specialized software tools that you can use with a database and deal with data types other than text; Oracle, another heavy-hitter in the database industry, calls such tools *data cartridges*.

If you're an intranet publisher with large document repositories, including graphics or other non-text data types, object-relational technology is definitely worth watching, even though no formal standards yet exist.

Gigabit Ethernet

Many organizations are just now moving their network communications standard from regular old Ethernet to fast Ethernet, with a maximum speed ten times greater, or switched Ethernet, which sets up short-term, high-speed connections between specific computers. (For more on these technologies, see Chapter 14.) Nevertheless, a new kid is already in town, and its name is *gigabit Ethernet*. Gigabit Ethernet runs at a gigabit per second — ten times faster than Fast Ethernet, and a hundred times faster than plain vanilla Ethernet.

You probably won't connect user workstations to a network using gigabit Ethernet — it requires fiber-optic cable to achieve its speed gains, at least at the time I write this, and the cost of fiber connections is prohibitive for workstations — but you may consider it today for network backbone connections and server-to-server links. Gigabit Ethernet can deliver more bang for the buck than Asynchronous Transfer Mode (ATM), and products are already appearing on the market. Further, gigabit Ethernet using standard Category 5 twisted-pair cable (the kind of cable you probably already run to desktop workstations) is almost sure to follow.

Those multimedia intranet publishing applications you can't deploy today may just be possible with gigabit Ethernet. Actually *show* people how to change a laser printer toner cartridge over the Help Desk intranet! Publish digitized videos that teach sales staff how to hone their persuasive skills! Have the CFO explain the ridiculously complex budgeting process in full-color, full-screen, full-motion! (I can go on, but I'm running out of pages here.)

So who's minding the standard? The International Association of Electrical and Electronic Engineers (IEEE) created a gigabit Ethernet task force in mid-1996, and has published a draft standard called 802.3z. The market won't wait for a formal standard, but the products now on the market generally support the draft standard. You can track the gigabit Ethernet standard in early 1998. Watch developments at the IEEE site, www.ieee.org.

Part VI
Appendixes

Appendix A: Glossary

*T*his glossary defines most, if not all, of the technical terms in this book. Because you're more likely to know an acronym than what it stands for, definitions appear with the acronyms rather than with the expanded term. Cross-referenced terms are in *italics*.

ActiveX. An evolution of the Object Linking and Embedding (OLE) technology in Windows, *ActiveX controls* are bits of software that let a web browser do things like run ActiveX-compatible applications, such as the Microsoft Office suite, "inside" the browser window. ActiveX also enables programmers to create Windows-based client/server applications for an intranet. ActiveX is so closely tied to Windows that it doesn't do much for non-Windows platforms.

ActiveX control. A web page component that provides for dynamic, interactive behavior. See also *ActiveX* and *Applet*.

Add-in. A program that gives another program new or extended capabilities. See also *helper program*.

Airwall. A physical separation between two computer networks, such as a company intranet and a company Internet server. An airwall makes it just about impossible for an Internet *cracker* to penetrate your intranet.

Anonymous login. A login to a server in which the user does not specify a network user name, or specifies the user name `anonymous`. Often used for *FTP* download sites on an intranet.

API (Application Program Interface). A defined set of commands or "calls" that application programs use to communicate with underlying services, software, or devices. *ISAPI (Information Server API),* for example, allows applications to interact with Microsoft Internet Information Server.

Applet. 1) A small, single-purpose program, often designed to run "inside" another program; usually refers to Java programs that run inside a web browser. 2) A runt apple.

Archie. A service that can help you find a specific file on an *FTP* site somewhere — as long as you know the exact file name.

ATM (Asynchronous Transfer Mode). A network data transmission system that offers high speed and the ability to prioritize traffic. ATM is too expensive to bring to desktop workstations, but many organizations are using it for network *backbone* communication.

Attachment. A data file or program sent along with an e-mail message.

Authentication. Validating that a user who supplies a given name and password is, in fact, a legitimate network user. Intranet servers handle authentication either by using an existing security database or by checking their own internal one.

Backbone. The part of a large network, typically a communications channel connecting servers, that manages most of the traffic and links *Local Area Networks (LANs)* together.

Back-end. The part of a computer system that administrators, rather than users, work with directly. Just as a business may have a front office that customers see and a back office where the daily work gets done, computer systems can have a front-end (such as a user's web browser) and a back-end (such as a server running *CGI scripts* or connecting to databases).

Bandwidth. The data-carrying capacity of a data channel.

Bastion host. A server computer that connects to the public Internet, with security mechanisms in place to protect any internal networks (such as intranets) from Internet *crackers*. See also *firewall*.

Bookmark. 1) An entry in a user's "favorite places" browser list that lets the user go directly to a specific web page without having to type the *URL* all over again. 2) A hyperlink at the top of a long web page that takes the user directly to a spot further down the page without making the user scroll down to it.

BootP (Bootstrap protocol). Technology from the *Unix* world that allows the system to make on-the-fly *IP* address assignments from a predefined pool of addresses as users connect to the intranet. See also *DHCP*.

BRI (Basic Rate Interface). The most common type of *ISDN* connection, consisting of two digital voice-and-data channels and one digital signaling channel. The BRI is designed for an individual line connection over standard copper telephone lines.

Bridge. A device that connects one network to another and passes data between the two — usually, a computer with two network boards in it (but not necessarily the same cable type).

Browser. The software tool users run to "browse" intranet and Internet web servers. Browsers speak *HyperText Transfer Protocol (HTTP)* and present web documents in a *Graphical User Interface (GUI)*. They provide some navigation controls and may offer security and performance features. Netscape Navigator and Microsoft Internet Explorer dominate the browser market.

Bus. A data highway inside a computer. Traffic flows on buses between all the computer's component parts: processor, memory, storage devices, keyboard, screen, and network interface card.

Bus mastering. A feature of high-performance computer circuit boards that allows them to temporarily take control of the computer and shuttle data around without processor intervention. Bus mastering is generally used by disk controllers, network adapters, and video cards, and also improves web server performance.

Cache. An area on disk that stores data recently read or considered likely to be read again soon. Web browsers use a special cache to store recently accessed web sites and graphics for faster performance.

CAD (Computer-Aided Design or Computer-Aided Drafting). Software (such as AutoCAD) and hardware (such as powerful graphics workstations and graphics tablets) that handle traditional product design and drafting functions on the computer.

Callback modem. A security modem that returns a call. You first call the callback modem, and then it calls you back at a predetermined number, based on a password you enter on the first call.

CBT (Computer-Based Training). Applications that offer interactive, self-paced user training by providing information in either text or graphical form and then providing a way for the user to validate the training, for example, by passing a self-paced test.

Certificate. A digital, encrypted document that verifies that a computer is who it says it is, and provides the public key for that computer. Obtaining a digital certificate (from a central authority, such as Verisign) is part of implementing *SSL* security on an intranet. See also: *public key encryption, SSL*.

CGI (Common Gateway Interface). A standardized method for a web server to pass instructions and data along to an external program (such as a mail *router*, database connector, or *search engine*) and for that program to return information to the user via *HTML*. CGI works with nearly all browsers and servers, but may be slow compared to other intranet programming methods.

CGI script. A program, usually written in a scripting language such as *PERL*, invoked by a web server at the request of an intranet browser — for example, to process the data in a user-submitted form.

CHAP (Challenge-Handshake Authentication Protocol). A password *encryption* technique that makes it virtually impossible for an eavesdropper to pick the password off the data stream.

Client. 1) A workstation that connects to a shared resource on a server (in a client/server network). An intranet client, for example, can be a user workstation running Windows 95, OS/2, Unix, or Macintosh software. 2) An application running on a client workstation, such as a web browser. 3) The combination of client hardware and software.

Client/server network. A network (such as NetWare, or Windows NT Server) in which a dedicated PC running a Network Operating System handles resource-sharing responsibilities, such as file- and printer-sharing, for client computers (user workstations). Intranets often run on top of an existing client/server network.

Client/server computing. A type of processing based on a simple, stable control relationship between two cooperating programs, which may be running on two separate computers. Intranets are examples of client/server computing.

Communication buffers. Server memory devoted to *caching* network interface card read and write activity. Servers with too little memory and too few communication buffers don't work well.

Control. Usually, a programmed action button, multiple choice button, or on-off button that a software user can select to perform a predefined procedure. Custom *ActiveX* controls can get much fancier than simple buttons, however, and allow programmers to add special features to web pages viewed with Microsoft Internet Explorer (as well as to other programs). Many companies have libraries of controls that were developed for other programs and that the companies can now use with intranet browsers.

CPR (Computer Pulmonary Resuscitation). Attempting to revive a crashed computer by alternately forcing air in through the vent holes and violently hitting the cover.

Cracker. Someone who attempts to gain unauthorized access to a computer or network with ill intent. The Internet is to a cracker like a bank is to a thief. A big advantage of intranets is that you can insulate them from crackers more easily than you can insulate your Internet servers (if you have any).

Crawl. What an intranet search engine does to build an index of existing web sites. To move from page to page, noting the text and key words used in each page, and incrementally create a catalog that users can later search to find the pages they need.

Database server. A specialized server that accepts requests from clients or from web server programs, and selects data for sending across the network to satisfy those requests. Larger intranets often communicate with database servers for document storage, retrieval, and searching.

Data warehouse. A database for data retrieval, analysis, and presentation only — not updating. Data warehouses are separate from the databases which get updated regularly in the course of business, however, data warehouses must be refreshed and updated by those systems at regular intervals. Companies use data warehouses to reduce traffic on their day-to-day transaction processing systems.

DBMS (Database Management System). An application that handles data entry, validation, updating, querying, reporting, and archiving.

Decryption. The process of decoding an encrypted file or message.

DHCP (Dynamic Host Configuration Protocol). A Windows-compatible software utility that allows the system to make on-the-fly *IP* address assignments from a predefined pool of addresses as users connect to the intranet. See also *BootP*.

Directory Services. Network software that makes resource information (such as user names and addresses) available to everyone on the network. *NDS* (*Netware Directory Services*) is an example; the NetWare Web Server works hand in hand with NDS.

DNS (Domain Name Service). A software program for matching up computer IP addresses such as `207.68.137.40` with easier-to-remember English-like names, such as `acme.pub.com`.

Download. 1) To copy a file from one computer to another, in the direction toward the user initiating the copy. 2) In Silicon Valley, to chug a beer. See also *upload*.

DUN (Dial-Up Networking). Microsoft's Windows 95 and NT remote access software, allowing remote PCs to connect to an intranet or *Local Area Network (LAN)* over phone lines.

Duplexing. A network server reliability technique using redundant disk controllers and drives to protect against the failure of either component. Each drive has the same data as all the others so that if one crashes, another drive still has your data.

EDI (Electronic Data Interchange). Intercompany standards for exchanging information such as orders and inventory.

EIDE (Enhanced IDE). An extension to the Integrated Drive Electronics standard permitting larger disk drive sizes, more devices per connector, and faster data transfer rates.

EIS (Executive Information System). A read-only computer system or application providing access to corporate data, usually in a summarized and graphical form. Intranets can work well as EISs.

Encryption. The mathematical massaging of data characters to make them unintelligible to unauthorized viewers. Most encryption schemes rely on keys to decode encrypted data at the receiving end. See also *public key encryption, private key encryption*.

Enterprise. A whole business: branch offices, wholly-owned subsidiaries, offshore tax shelters in the Caymans, and all. Often used to denote the most expensive and powerful versions of software applications, as in Netscape Enterprise Server.

Ethernet. A very popular 10 megabit per second networking standard using either thick coaxial, thin coaxial, or twisted-pair cable. Ethernet handles network traffic using a data collision-detection scheme.

eXtensible Markup Language. See *XML*.

FAQ (Frequently Asked Questions). A document, such as an intranet web page, featuring a list of common questions and their answers. FAQs are excellent ways to avoid having experts take time to answer the same question over and over.

Fast Ethernet. 100 megabit per second *Ethernet* that can run on standard twisted-pair cables, but requires updated network hardware. Multimedia intranets run better over fast Ethernet.

Fault tolerance. Said of computer systems that can operate without interruption during a component failure, either in hardware or software.

FEP (Frequently Encountered Problems). A document, such as an intranet web page, featuring a list of common problems and their solutions.

File system buffers. Server memory devoted to *caching* disk read and write requests. Intranet servers with too little memory and too few file system buffers don't work well.

Firewall. Any system or group of systems that implements and enforces an access control policy between two networks. Firewalls can run on their own special computer, or on the same computer as a web server.

Footer. Information that appears at the bottom of every intranet web page.

Form. In intranetting, a form is a part of a web page with various places for the user to enter information. *HTML* offers several form tools, such as checkboxes and drop-down lists; other companies, such as Caere and Adobe, provide additional features through their own software.

Frame. A browser extension popularized by Netscape that allows more than one *HTML* page to appear in the same browser window. Internet Explorer now supports frames.

Front-end. The part of a computer system that users work with directly. In intranetting, the front-end usually refers to the user browser and any associated helper programs. See also *back-end*.

FTP (File Transfer Protocol). A *TCP/IP* application designed for copying files of various types between computers. Intranetters may use FTP, when designing a software *download* page, or when updating a web server from a remote site. Most browsers support FTP and its use can be made transparent to the user, at least for downloading.

Gateway. 1) A *router* that interconnects completely different networks, or networks and mainframes, by translating protocols. 2) A software tool that provides access to other enterprise mail systems.

GIF (Graphics Interchange Format), pronounced "jif." A compressed graphics file format developed by CompuServe and characterized by small file sizes and a maximum palette of 256 colors. One of two graphics file formats typically used on intranets and in *HTML* documents. See also *JPEG* and *Transparent GIF*.

Gigabit Ethernet. Gigabit Ethernet runs ten times faster than *Fast Ethernet,* or a hundred times faster than plain vanilla *Ethernet*. Gigabit Ethernet is worth considering for network *backbone* connections and server-to-server links — it could in the future deliver more bang for the buck than *Asynchronous Transfer Mode (ATM)*.

Gopher. An information search-and-retrieval application that started at the University of Minnesota. Gopher servers around the world (usually at academic institutions) help Internet users find data they need, but it's a text-only service (no graphics). Gopher can also run on intranets, although small web servers (such as Microsoft Personal Web Server) don't all support it.

Groupware. Software designed to facilitate the cooperative, collaborative efforts of multiple people working on the same project.

GUI (Graphical User Interface), pronounced "gooey". Software such as Microsoft Windows that presents a graphical "face" to the user, as opposed to a text-mode interface such as the DOS command line or a simple text mainframe terminal. The GUI is a big part of what makes intranet browsers able to handle images as well as text.

Header. Information that appears at the top of every intranet web page.

Help Desk. An organizational unit responsible for answering users' technical questions and helping with computer problems in order to maximize employees' productivity and minimize downtime. Intranets offer many benefits for the Help Desk.

Helper program. Also called *plug-in*, a program that an intranet browser can call upon to process a particular type of data. For example, you may use a helper program to decode and play a sound file or video clip that the browser by itself doesn't know how to display. This term is used loosely in the trade press, but some prefer to use *helper program* for separate programs that run in their own memory space, and *plug-in* for programs that run in the browser's memory space.

Hit. A file access on a web page. A single visitor may generate several hits, because each displayed graphic file counts as another hit. See also *visit*.

Home page. An HTML web page that serves as a jumping-off point for a user's intranet excursion, usually presenting a table of contents with links to other pages or systems. A corporate intranet may have a single home page, or several home pages for each department, division, team, and so on.

HTML (HyperText Markup Language). The most popular coding method for defining documents on intranets and on the World Wide Web, HTML permits the web page author to specify approximately where text, graphics, and links should appear, and what they should do (if anything). Based on *SGML*.

HTML Help. A Microsoft standard for providing online help via a web server. HTML Help initially supports only Windows 95 and Windows NT. It relies on *ActiveX* controls to provide help features such as index, table of contents, and pop-up windows.

HTTP (HyperText Transfer Protocol). The client/server *protocol* that manages *links* between pages on a web server. Intranet servers and browsers "speak" HTTP, which underpins the World Wide Web and corporate intranets.

Hub. A device at a central location to which two or more cables connect in a star configuration. Hubs may be separate devices or plug-in circuit boards; they also may include network management software (*intelligent* hubs) or not. So-called *switching hubs* can provide better intranet performance. The upper component of a hub enclosure is called a "hub cap." (joke)

Hyperlink. A highlighted text area or graphic that takes the user to a different place in the same document, or to another document, when clicked with a mouse.

Hypertext. A document, such as an online help file or a web page, that contains *hyperlinks,* or jumps, that take the user to other places in the same document or to other documents. As the term is traditionally used, hypertext links and targets are both text.

Hypermedia. The extension of the *hypertext* concept to multimedia data types. Hypermedia links can be graphical, like little button icons or image maps. Hypermedia targets can be text, sound, graphics, or video.

IBT (Intranet-Based Training). Computer-based training designed for the intranet, using *HTML, GIF, JPEG, Java* and/or *ActiveX* technologies. See also *CBT*.

IETF (Internet Engineering Task Force). An Internet management committee that recommends standards.

Image map. A web page graphic that may have multiple "clickable" regions on it, each of which acts as a *hyperlink*. Client-side image maps are handled by the user's browser; server-side image maps are handled by a web server and add to server overhead.

Internet. The world's largest computer network, the Internet was originally just for military and academic use but has now grown to include all manner of private, public, and commercial uses. Physically, the Internet is a collection of millions of computers that each has its own unique network address to identify it to other computers, and that each speak the same basic communications language *(TCP/IP)*. These computers connect to each other via a complex network of communication links managed by computerized traffic *routers,* for the purpose of exchanging information.

InterNIC (Internet Network Information Center). A federally-funded organization in Virginia that registers and keeps track of the domain names for computers that connect to the Internet, and provides Internet-related information to the public.

Intranet. A *TCP/IP* computer network that shares information to corporate employees, using tools such as electronic mail and web pages. Intranets can include formatted, structured information, as well as unformatted or loosely structured information. They use Internet technologies such as *HTTP, HTML,* and *FTP,* but usually forbid or restrict access to the public Internet.

IP (Internet Protocol). The part of the TCP/IP networking protocol set that handles addressing and routing.

IP address. The numerical address of a particular computer on the Internet or an intranet, consisting of four numbers separated by periods. Each computer on a TCP/IP network must have a unique IP address. See also *BootP, DHCP, DNS,* and *WINS*.

IPX (Internet Packet eXchange). A message routing protocol used by NetWare networks. See also *TCP/IP*.

ISAPI (Internet Server Application Program Interface). The set of programming tools offered by Microsoft's Internet Information Server and Personal Web Server. See also *NSAPI*.

ISDN (Integrated Services Digital Network). Allows voice, fax, data, and video on the same network, and much higher speeds than regular voice lines. Telephone companies in major U.S. metropolitan areas offer ISDN connectivity, although it's still more popular in Europe.

ISP (Internet Service Provider). An organization that offers Internet connectivity, usually for a monthly fee. ISPs offer web hosting services for both Internet and intranet use.

Java. A programming language developed by Sun Microsystems to be platform-independent, secure, portable, and familiar (it's based loosely on the C++ language). Java is becoming popular on intranets because it offloads processing chores from servers to clients, and because it works on many different kinds of computers.

JavaScript. A programming language that uses "scripts" embedded in an *HTML* document. The browser reads (interprets) the script and acts on it when it encounters a web page that includes a script. Despite the similar name, JavaScript is not the same animal as *Java;* JavaScript is both easier and more limited. See also *VBScript*.

JDBC (Java DataBase Connectivity). An Application Program Interface, or *API,* that permits *Java* programs to communicate directly with database management systems that adhere to the *Open DataBase Connectivity* standard. JDBC allows intranet clients to bypass the web server and access back-end databases more directly.

JPEG (Joint Photographic Experts Group). A graphic file type featuring adjustable compression and the ability to display millions of colors. JPEG is one of two graphic file formats used on intranets and the Internet. Best suited for compressing photorealistic images rather than images with precise lines and curves, JPEG compression can cause some loss of fidelity in order to achieve small file sizes. See also *GIF*.

Jump. As a noun, "jump" means the same as *hyperlink*. As a verb, it means "to click on a hyperlink."

LAN (Local Area Network). A network containing servers, workstations, cable, and software all connected together within a relatively small geographical area.

Legacy system. An old system.

Link. See *hyperlink*.

MCI (Media Control Interface). A language for controlling multimedia devices in Windows and in some IBM systems.

Middleware. In a client/server system, software that mediates and standardizes the connections between different parts of the system's communications pathways. Intranets are middleware, especially if they link users to existing computer programs or databases.

MIME (Multipurpose Internet Mail Extensions). A set of extensions to the original Internet e-mail standards so that users can send and receive data types other than text. Intranetters publishing unusual file types may have to register new MIME types at the web server and at the browser.

Mirroring. A network reliability technology that uses redundant disk drives (each disk drive has the same data on it) with the same controller. Protects against drive failure but not controller failure. See also *duplexing*.

MPEG (Motion Picture Experts Group). A compressed file format, popular on the Internet and used in some intranets, designed for video and audio data types. Like *JPEG*, MPEG compression can result in some loss of fidelity as a tradeoff for smaller file sizes.

NDS (NetWare Directory Services). A domain naming system for NetWare 4.*x* networks.

NetBIOS name. The name of a computer in the Microsoft networking scheme.

NetHelp. Netscape's approach to providing online help via the Navigator browser family. NetHelp's current strength is its support for many types of computers.

Network. Two or more computer systems connected to enable communication or resource sharing; the sum total of clients, servers, and interconnecting infrastructure. Often informally used as a synonym for *Local Area Network* (*LAN*).

Network computer. A computer with no local disk space, that loads all programs and data over the network.

NIC (Network Interface Card). A plug-in circuit board that connects a computer to a network and manages data transfers between the two. The speed (such as 10 or 100 megabits per second) and width (such as 8 or 16 bits) of the connection help determine an intranet's perceived performance.

NSAPI (Netscape Server Application Program Interface). The set of programming tools offered by Netscape web servers, both Enterprise Server and FastTrack Server. A program could use NSAPI to take a user-submitted *HTML* form and update a database, for example.

NT. Windows NT, for New Technology, the high end of the Windows product line, targeted for *LAN* servers (NT Server) and high-end Windows workstations (NT Workstation).

OCR (Optical Character Recognition). The process of converting a scanned document from a collection of tiny dots into a text document that a computer word processor or editor can understand.

ODBC (Open DataBase Connectivity). The most widely supported standard for open database *middleware*, initially developed by Microsoft. All major relational DBMSs support ODBC — *DBMS* vendors supply their own ODBC software. See also *JDBC*.

OLE (Object Linking and Embedding), pronounced "oh-LAY." A Windows technology that allows not only the creation of compound documents with data originating in more than one program, but also the editing of pasted data using its originating application without leaving the host application. OLE has now evolved into *ActiveX*.

OpenType. A font specification, developed jointly by Microsoft and Adobe, that uses data compression to make it practical for web pages to use specific, downloaded typefaces.

Operating system. The basic software that allows a computer to interact with users, manage files and devices, and communicate over a network. Windows 95, UNIX, MacOS, and OS/2 are all operating systems. Those designed for network servers, such as NetWare and Windows NT Server, are called network operating systems.

Page. On an intranet system, one *HTML* text file and its associated graphics, *form* elements, and programs.

Patch. A modification to software that corrects a problem. Intranets are good for distributing software patches.

PCI (Peripheral Component Interconnect). An Intel-developed high-performance local *bus* used for video, disk, and network interface cards.

PDF (Portable Document Format). Adobe's file format standard for document interchange, and one of the more popular document formats on the Internet and intranets. Unlike *HTML*, PDF precisely defines a document's appearance, including typefaces and object positioning. It also supports video and sound files.

PERL (Practical Extraction and Report Language). A programming language used frequently in *CGI scripts*. PERL has roots in the *Unix* world and contains several commands for handling text, making it suitable for processing *HTML forms*.

Platform. A computer *operating system,* or the combination of the operating system and underlying hardware. For example, Microsoft Internet Information Server runs on the Windows NT Server platform.

Plug-in. See *helper program*.

PostScript. A device-independent page description language from Adobe Systems, used to control printers and (on some workstations) displays; known for sophisticated graphics-handling.

Power conditioning. Usually, line voltage surge suppression, waveform regulation, and backup capability, all rolled into a single box. Power conditioning "cleans" the electricity that comes from the power plant so that your computers run more reliably. Intranet servers should have power conditioning.

PPP (Point-to-Point Protocol). A standard for communications across relatively slow links (such as dial-up phone lines), and the usual protocol for Windows 95's *Dial-Up Networking* (*DUN*) facility.

PPTP (Point-to-Point Tunneling Protocol). Supported by Windows NT Server 4.0 and IIS 3.0, PPTP encrypts and packages remote access traffic — for example, by users connecting to your intranet from home via a dial-up connection.

PRI (Primary Rate Interface). A commercial *ISDN* installation consisting of 24 digital channels in the U.S., and 31 in Europe. In the U.S. version, 23 of the channels carry data and the 24th is used for commands.

Private key encryption. Also known as *symmetric* encryption; a cryptography scheme in which each individual has a private secret key that is used for both encryption and decryption. See also *public key encryption*.

Protocol. A set of rules, specifications, or standards that control and manage the creation, maintenance, and termination of data transfer between computers.

Proxy server. A server that permits no direct traffic between one network and another, but, for security reasons, acts as a store-and-forward device for data or messages meeting predefined criteria. If, for instance, you are on a network with a proxy server and you browse to a web page, the proxy server actually picks up the web page, checks it to see if it meets security needs, and then sends it down the network to you. Proxy servers may forward permitted data or messages automatically, or only on request from another computer. See also *Firewall*.

Public key encryption. Also known as *asymmetric* encryption, a cryptography scheme in which each individual has a private secret key and a published, public key. A sender looks up the recipient's public key and uses it to encrypt a message, and the recipient uses the private key to decrypt it. See also *private key encryption*.

QuickTime. A digital video-and-audio standard developed by Apple and popular for intranet use.

RAM (Random Access Memory). Chip-based memory in a computer, which is both faster and more expensive than disk-based memory (hard drives). A computer's RAM contains the currently active programs and data files, and its contents starts empty every time the computer restarts. Intranet servers need more RAM than user workstations do.

Router. A network device, more sophisticated than a *bridge*, that can send or redirect data traffic to the least crowded routes by examining data packet destination addresses. *LANs* connected by routers form internetworks.

RTF (Rich Text Format). A text file format that permits more features (multiple fonts, graphics) than plain old text, but fewer features than a word processor's native file format. A common format for converting documents between programs and the base format for creating traditional Windows "help" files.

SCSI (Small Computer Systems Interface). A high-performance device connection system (such as for hard drives) commonly used in network servers. See also *EIDE*.

Search engine. A web site or document publishing utility that allows users to search for content by specifying key words or phrases. Search engines may be layered on top of a web server and simply go out and index the contents of the server, or they may be an integral part of a document system such as a Folio infobase.

Segmentation. Dividing a local area network into multiple segments, or subnets, usually to increase performance. Segmentation or "subnetting" may increase the administration burden for the overall network.

Server. 1) A computer that provides network services, such as web, file, print, communication, name space, directory, security, or application services. 2) A program providing services to a client application, for example, a database server. 3) The combination of server hardware and programs.

SGML (Standard Generalized Markup Language). A document design system used in high-end publishing applications, and the parent of *HTML*. SGML imposes a stricter separation of form and content than HTML, and offers capabilities such as dynamic tables of contents, customized views, and precision searching. Some intranet products incorporate SGML features.

Shockwave. A compression technology for animations and multimedia presentations created with Macromedia Director and Flash. The Shockwave "helper" program allows a browser to view web pages containing "shocked" content.

SHTTP (Secure HyperText Transfer Protocol). An early intranet security scheme, SHTTP provides encryption for *HTML* pages. Both the browser and server must support SHTTP, and the browser must connect using the "shttp://" prefix. Many features of SHTTP are folded into a more popular scheme, Secure Sockets Layer. See also *SSL*.

Site map. A visual representation of an intranet site, showing home pages, content pages, and links.

SMTP (Simple Mail Transport Protocol). The basic TCP/IP protocol for e-mail exchange.

SNMP (Simple Network Management Protocol). A popular standard, which developed in the *UNIX* world, for managing local area networks. SNMP specifies a protocol for communication between a management console and network devices.

SQL (Structured Query Language). A set of commands for interrogating databases; very popular among database management system vendors in client/server networks.

SSL (Secure Sockets Layer). A standard method of providing encrypted data transmission between an intranet browser and web server, both of which must support SSL (most do).

Stream. To begin playing as soon as a download operation begins, instead of only after it's completed. For example, streaming audio starts playing as soon as the user opens a web page containing a sound file.

Structured Query Language. See *SQL*.

Style sheet. A named collection of attributes describing a chunk of a document. For example, a style sheet might define a document's title page to be vertically centered, with 1-inch margins all around, using the Helvetica font in a 24-point size for the title, and Helvetica 14-point for the author's name.

Switching hub. An intelligent device that establishes dedicated, real-time connections between individual computers on a local area network, instead of forcing all computers on the *LAN* to share a single connection.

Table. In *HTML,* a data structure that allows web page designers to have more control over the appearance of information by placing it in row and column formats. Designers can use tables to format any kind of data, including form check boxes and graphic images.

Tag. In *HTML,* a statement, denoted by angle brackets <>, that gives the browser formatting instructions.

TCO (Total Cost of Ownership). What computer systems really cost, as opposed to their price tags. The *network computer* is an attempt to reduce TCO.

TCP/IP (Transmission Control Protocol/Internet Protocol). A set of network protocols for file transfer, network management, and messaging — intranets use TCP/IP. TCP/IP is popular in the educational, engineering, and governmental areas; it was developed in the early '70s by the Defense Advanced Research Projects Agency. TCP breaks apart and reassembles packets in the correct order, and resends if errors occur; IP handles routing and transmission. For more on TCP/IP, see the sidebar in the Introduction.

Template. A sample web page that a designer uses as a starting point. Templates offer intranet designers a convenient way to create and maintain a standard look-and-feel for a single intranet or several intranets within the same organization.

Thin client. A type of client/server system that puts only the user interface component on the client, keeping all the process logic and data storage on the server.

TIFF (Tagged Image File Format). A bitmap graphic standard. TIFF images are commonly used in desktop publishing programs, but must be converted to *GIF* or *JPEG* for intranet use.

Tile. A small graphic that a browser can use as a web page background by repeating it to fill the page space. Tiles are faster, smaller, and more flexible than full-page background images.

Transmission Control Protocol/Internet Protocol. See *TCP/IP*.

Transparent GIF. A *GIF* graphics file with a see-through background, so the foreground appears to float over the page on which it appears.

True color. Photorealistic color in a computer graphic, having a palette of about 17 million different colors (that's even more than the human eye can differentiate). *GIF* files don't offer true color, but *JPEG* files can.

TrueDoc. A font technology from Bitstream that sends font outlines on the fly over the network along with a requested web page, so users can see pages in specific typefaces. See also *OpenType*.

TWAIN. A standard put together by scanner manufacturers to allow all compliant scanning programs to work the same way as far as the user is concerned.

Unix. The computer operating system on which most Internet and intranet technologies developed, and a popular operating system for high-performance intranet servers.

Upload. 1) To copy a file from one computer to another, in the direction away from the user initiating the copy. 2) In Silicon Valley, to regurgitate a beer. See also *download*.

UPS (Uninterruptible Power Supply). A backup device that provides power to a server, workstation, or other device continuously from its battery, which is constantly being recharged from AC line power. If you experience a power outage, the UPS kicks in and lets you shut down your computer gracefully.

URL (Uniform Resource Locator). The address that points users to a specific intranet service (usually *HTTP* or *FTP*) and location (web page, file to download). Every link on a web page has an associated URL. Example: http://acme.pub.com/index.html is a fictitious URL for the home page of Acme Cognac's intranet web site.

VBScript. A programming language, based on Microsoft's Visual BASIC for Applications, that uses "scripts" (little programs) embedded in an *HTML* document. The browser reads (interprets) the script and acts on it when it encounters a web page that includes a script. See also *JavaScript*.

Vector graphics. Also *object-oriented* graphics; graphics interpreted or manipulated as objects or elements rather than dots. For example, a *CAD* drawing uses vector graphics.

Veronica. An Internet search service; stands for Very Easy Rodent-Oriented Net-wide Index to Computer Archives.

Visit. A web-page user session. A user who visits an intranet site with a single HTML file and four graphics files has generated one visit but five hits. See also *hit*.

VRML (Virtual Reality Modeling Language), pronounced "VER-mal". An evolving standard defining how web pages can display, and browsers can view, three-dimensional models over an intranet or the Internet.

WAIS (Wide Area Information Server), pronounced "ways". An Internet application for locating documents with key words, usually more convenient than *Gopher*.

WAN (Wide Area Network). *Local area networks* (*LANs*) connected across large distances, usually via communications protocols running on satellite, microwave, or Internet links.

Webmaster. An individual primarily responsible for the design and management of a web site.

Welcome page. See *home page*.

WINS (Windows Internet Naming Service). Software that matches up IP addresses with computer names, called *NetBIOS names,* in the Microsoft network system.

World Wide Web Consortium. Also known as W3C, an industry group that tracks and formalizes standards for Internet technologies such as *HTML*. For more information, connect to http://www.w3.org.

WWW (World Wide Web). Born in 1993, the multimedia face of the Internet. Web pages can include color graphics, and even sound and video. They can also include convenient and automatic links to other Web pages. The Web is based on the *TCP/IP, HTTP,* and *HTML* standards.

WYSIWYG (What You See Is What You Get). The goal of matching printed documents precisely with their screen appearance. *HTML* isn't yet very good at WYSIWYG printing.

XML (eXtensible Markup Language). A proposed extension to *HTML* that would bring some *SGML* capabilities, such as dynamic table of contents generation, to web pages.

Zip file. An archive created with the PKZIP or Win Zip compression utility and that a user may decompress with PKUNZIP or Win Zip. Commonly used on intranet download pages to save time and reduce network traffic.

Appendix B: References & Resources

In This Chapter
- Info on companies and products mentioned in this book
- Books
- Magazines
- CD-ROMs
- Links to useful Internet sites

Books like this one are by nature introductory, but any good introduction should point you to other materials that can take you further in your journey to becoming a successful intranet publisher. Ergo, this appendix!

Companies Mentioned in This Book

This section provides Internet addresses, phone numbers (both the free-in-the-USA 800/888 variety and toll numbers for the convenience of my international readers), and physical addresses for the companies I mention in the book, plus product names where I could fit them in.

I'm a travelin' man, and I've seen a lot of software. But I don't have firsthand experience with every product or company listed, so appearance in this list is not a purchase recommendation! Nevertheless, these are companies and products I think are worth some investigation at least. If I've left out one of your favorite companies or products, please 1) forgive me! and 2) let me know by dropping me an e-mail at gweadock@i-sw.com.

Adobe Systems, Inc.
www.adobe.com
800-833-6687 (main), 800-272-3623
(Acrobat), 415-961-4400, 408-536-6000
1585 Charleston Road
Mountain View, CA 94039-7900
Acrobat, FrameMaker, PageMaker, Photoshop, Premiere

Aimtech Corporation
www.aimtech.com
800-289-2884, 603-883-0220
20 Trafalgar Square, Nashua, NH 03063-1987
Jamba

Allaire Corp.
www.allaire.com
888-939-2545, 617-761-2000
One Alewife Center, Cambridge, MA 02140
Cold Fusion

American Power Conversion Corp.
www.appc.com
800-800-4APC, 401-789-5735
132 Fairgrounds Road
West Kingston, RI 02892-9906
Power backup products

American Tech, Inc.
670 N. Beers Street, Colonial Commons, P.O. Box 320, Holmdel, NJ 07733-0320
908-946-8844
Purchasing software

The Apache Project
www.apache.org
Freeware web server software (the Internet's most popular server)

askSam Systems Inc.
www.asksam.com
800-800-1997, 904-584-6390
119 S. Washington Street
Perry, FL 32347-9968
askSam Web Publisher

Astea International Inc.
www.astea.com
800-347-7334, 215-682-2590
455 Business Center Drive, Horsham, PA 19044
PowerHelp

Astrobyte, LLC
www.astrobyte.com
303-534-6344
1800 15th Street, Suite 104, Denver, CO 80202
BeyondPress

Asymetrix Corp.
www.asymetrix.com
800-448-6543, 206-462-0501
110 110th Avenue, NE, Suite 700
Bellevue, WA 98004-5840
Toolbook II Instructor, Toolbook II Assistant, Neuron plug-in

BackWeb Technologies Inc.
www.backweb.com
800-863-0100, 408-437-0200
2077 Gateway Place, Suite 500, San Jose, CA 95110

Best Power Technology
www.bestpower.com
800-356-5794, 608-565-7200
P.O. Box 280, Necedah, WI 54646
Power backup products

Bitstream Inc.
www.bitstream.com
800-522-FONT, 617-497-6222
215 First Street, Cambridge, MA 02142-1270

Blue Sky Software Corp.
www.blue-sky.com
800-677-4946, 619-459-6365
7777 Fay Avenue, Suite 201, La Jolla, CA 92037
Help-to-HTML, RoboHelp

BMC Software, Inc.
www.bmc.com
800-841-2031, 713-918-8800
2101 CityWest Boulevard, Houston, TX 77042-2827
Network performance monitors

Borland International, Inc.
www.borland.com
800-932-9994, 408-431-1000
100 Borland Way, Scotts Valley, CA 95066-3249
IntraBuilder, Visual dBase Professional

Cabletron Systems, Inc.
www.ctron.com
800-332-9401, 603-332-9400
35 Industrial Way, Building 36, P.O. Box 5005
Rochester, NH 03866-0505
Spectrum network management system

Caere Corp.
www.caere.com
800-535-SCAN, 408-395-7000
100 Cooper Court, Los Gatos, CA 95030
OmniPage Pro, Omniform Interactive Publisher, PageKeeper

Appendix B: References & Resources

Checkpoint Software Technologies, Ltd.
www.checkpoint.com
800-429-4391, 617-859-9051
1 Militia Drive, Lexington, MA 02173
FireWall-1

Cisco Systems, Inc.
www.cisco.com
800-553-6387, 408-526-4000
170 W. Tasman Drive, San Jose, CA 95134-1706
DNS/DHCP Manager, CiscoWorks network management system

Claris Corp.
www.claris.com
800-544-8554, 408-987-7000
P.O. Box 58168, 5201 Patrick Henry Drive
Santa Clara, CA 95052-8168
Home Page

Computer Associates International, Inc.
www.cai.com
800-225-5224, 516-342-5224
One Computer Associates Plaza
Islandia, NY 11788-7000
Network performance monitors

Concord Communications Inc.
www.concord.com
800-851-8725, 508-460-4646
33 Boston Post Road West
Marlborough, MA 01752
WAN monitoring/testing tools

Corel Corp.
www.corel.com
800-772-6735, 613-728-8200
1600 Carling Avenue, The Corel Building
Ottawa, Ontario, CANADA K1Z 8R7
Photo-Paint, WordPerfect Suite

CrossComm Corp.
www.crosscomm.com
800-388-1200, 508-481-4060
450 Donald Lynch Boulevard
Marlborough, MA 01752-4728
ExpertWatch (performance monitoring service)

Design Intelligence, Inc.
www.design-intelligence.com
206-343-7797
1111 Third Avenue, Suite 2650, Seattle, WA 98101
ipublish, ipublish-enterprise

Digital Equipment Corp.
www.dec.com
www.digital.com
800-344-4825, 508-493-5111
146 Main Street, Maynard, MA 01754-2571
AltaVista (search engine), PolyCenter (network management system)

e. g. Software, Inc.
www.egsoftware.com
503-294-7025
621 SW Morrison Street, Suite 1025
Portland, OR 97205
WebTrends

Electronic Book Technologies, Inc.
www.ebt.com
401-421-9550
One Richmond Square, Providence, RI 02906
DynaBase

Eloquent, Inc.
www.eloquent.com
415-655-2500
1710 S. Amphlett, Suite 200
San Mateo, CA 94402-2703
Infomedia

Enigma Information Retrieval Systems, Inc.
www.enigmainc.com
888-364-4624, 617-239-8279
70 Walnut Street, Suite 206, Wellesley, MA 02181
Insight into Information

Equilibrium Technologies
www.equilibrium.com
800-524-8651, 415-332-4343
3 Harbor Drive, Suite 111, Sausalito, CA 94965
DeBabelizer (graphics toolkit)

Excite, Inc.
www.atext.com
415-934-3611
1091 N. Shoreline Boulevard, 2nd Floor
Mountain View, CA 94043

Extensis Corp.
www.extensis.com
800-796-9798, 503-274-0539
1800 S.W. First Avenue, Suite 500
Portland, OR 97201
CyberPress

Folio (a division of Open Market, Inc.)
www.folio.com
800-543-6546, 801-229-6700
5072 North 300 West, Provo, UT 84604
Folio Builder, Folio Views, Folio SiteDirector

Fractal Design Corporation (now MetaCreations)
www.fractal.com
800-297-2665, 408-688-5300
5550 Scotts Valley Drive, P.O. Box 66959
Scotts Valley, CA 95067-6959
Painter

Frontier Technologies Corp.
www.frontiertech.com
800-929-3054, 414-241-4555
10201 N. Port Washington Road
Mequon, WI 53092
Intranet Genie

Fulcrum Technologies Inc.
www.fulcrum.com
800-385-2786, 613-238-1761
785 Carling Avenue
Ottawa, Ontario CANADA K1S 5H4
Fulcrum Find!, Fulcrum Knowledge Network

Ganymede Software Inc.
www.ganymedesoftware.com
888-GANYMEDE, 919-469-0997
1100 Perimeter Park Drive, Suite 104
Morrisville, NC 27560
Chariot (WAN performance simulation/testing tool)

Haht Software, Inc.
www.haht.com
800-438-4248, 919-786-5100
4200 Six Forks Road, Raleigh, NC 27609
HAHTsite

Hewlett-Packard Company
www.hp.com
800-752-0900, 415-857-1501
3000 Hanover Street, Palo Alto, CA 94304
OpenView network management system

Hummingbird Communications Ltd.
www.hummingbird.com
800-598-3821, 415-917-7300
480 San Antonio Road, Suite 100
Mountain View, CA 94040
Common Ground Publisher

IBM Corporation
www.ibm.com
800-426-3333, 914-765-1900
Old Orchard Road, Armonk, NY 10001-3782
NetView network management system

InContext Corp.
www.incontext.com
800-263-0127, 416-922-0087
2 St. Clair Avenue, W, 16th Floor
Toronto, Ontario, CANADA M4V 1L5
WebAnalyzer

InfoAccess, Inc.
www.infoaccess.com
800-344-9737, 425-201-1915
15821 NE 8th Street, Suite 200, Bellevue, WA 98008
HTML Transit, Transit Central

Informix Software Inc.
www.informix.com
800-331-1763, 415-926-6300
4100 Bohannon Drive, Menlo Park, CA 94025

Intel Corp. (Personal Computer Enhancement Division)
www.intel.com
800-538-3373, 503-629-7354
5200 NE Elam Young Parkway
Hillsboro, OR 97124-6497
LANDesk Manager

Internet Resources Group
www.redalert.com
972-422-6364
821 Ashburn Place, Plano, TX 75075
Red Alert monitoring service

Intrusion Detection Inc.
www.intrusion.com
800-408-6104, 212-348-8900
217 East 86th Street, Suite 213
New York, NY 10028
Kane Security Analyst

Isotro Network Management, Inc.
www.isotro.com
800-ISOTRO-2, 613-722-1921
875 Carling Avenue, Suite 200
Ottawa, Ontario, CANADA K1S 5P1
NetID (IP address management)

JASC, Inc.
www.jasc.com
800-622-2793, 612-930-9800
11011 Smetana Road, Minnetonka, MN 55343
PaintShop Pro

JetForm Corp.
www.jetform.com
800-JET-FORM, 613-230-FORM
560 Rochester Street
Ottawa, Ontario, CANADA K1S 5K2
JetForm

KnowledgePoint
www.knowledgepoint.com
800-727-1133, 707-762-0333
1129 Industrial Avenue, Petaluma, CA 94952-1141
Policies Now!

Lotus Development Corp. (a division of IBM)
www.lotus.com
800-346-1305, 617-577-8500
55 Cambridge Parkway
Cambridge, MA 02142-1295
Domino, InterNotes Publisher, Notes, ScreenCam

Macromedia, Inc.
www.macromedia.com
800-457-1774, 415-252-2000
600 Townsend Street, Suite 310 W
San Francisco, CA 94103-4945
Authorware, Backstage Internet Studio, Director, Flash

Magic Solutions
www.magicsolutions.com
800-96-MAGIC, 201-587-1515
10 Forest Avenue, Paramus, NJ 07652-5242
SupportMagic, WebMagic

Marimba, Inc.
www.marimba.com
415-328-5282
445 Sherman Avenue, Palo Alto, CA 94306
Castanet

MetaCreations (see Fractal Design Corporation)

Microsoft Corp.
www.microsoft.com
800-426-9400, 206-882-8080
One Microsoft Way, Redmond, WA 98052
FrontPage, Internet Information Server, Project, SiteServer, Systems Management Server, Windows NT Server, Windows 95, Word

Molloy Group
www.molloy.com
201-540-1212
Four Century Drive, Parsippany, NJ 07054
Internet Knowledge Kiosk, Top of Mind

Net-It Software Corporation
www.net-it.com
888-638-4866, 415-551-0600
1550 Bryant Street, 2nd Floor
San Francisco, CA 94103
Net-It Central, Net-It Now!

NetObjects, Inc.
www.netobjects.com
888-449-6400, 415-482-3200
2055 Woodside Road, Suite 250
Redwood City, CA 94060
NetObjects Fusion

Netscape Communications Corp.
home.netscape.com
800-638-7483, 415-254-1900
501 East Middlefield Road
Mountain View, CA 94043
Communicator, Enterprise Server, Fastrack Server, Navigator Gold

NetSolve, Inc.
www.netsolve.net
512-795-3000
9130 Jollyville Road, Suite 200, Austin, TX 78759
Contract fault monitoring

Novell, Inc.
www.novell.com
800-453-1267, 801-222-6000
1555 North Technology Way, Orem, UT 84757
IntraNetware, ManageWise, NetWare

O'Reilly & Associates, Inc.
www.ora.com
800-998-9938, 707-829-0515
103 Morris Street, Suite A, Sebastopol, CA 95472
WebSite, WebSite Professional

Octopus Technologies, Inc.
www.octopustech.com
800-919-1009, 215-579-5600
1717 Langhorne Newtown Road, Suite 402
Langhorne, PA 19047
Workstation disk mirroring

Open Text Corp.
www.opentext.com
800-507-5777, 519-888-7111
185 Columbia Street West
Waterloo, Ontario, CANADA N2L 5Z5
LiveLink Search 64, LiveLink Intranet Suite
(server, search engine, workflow, library)

Optimal Networks Corp.
www.optimal.com
415-845-6333
1507 East Meadow Circle, Palo Alto, CA 94303
Optimal Internet Monitor

Oracle Corp.
www.oracle.com
800-633-0596, 415-506-7000
500 Oracle Parkway, Redwood Shores, CA 94065
Career Management

Packeteer
www.packeteer.com
408-364-0193
307 Orchard City Drive, Suite 305
Campbell, CA 95008
PacketShaper

Panamax
www.panamax.com
800-472-5555, 415-499-3900
150 Mitchell Boulevard, San Rafael, CA 94903-2057
Power battery backup

PeopleSoft, Inc.
www.peoplesoft.com
800-947-7753, 510-225-3000
4440 Rosewood Drive, Pleasanton, CA 94588
PeopleSoft 7 (company information system)

Platinum Technology, Inc.
www.platinum.com
800-378-7528, 630-620-5000
1815 South Meyers Road
Oakbrook Terrace, IL 60181-5241
WireTap

Pointcast, Inc.
www.pointcast.com
800-548-2203, 408-253-0894
10101 North De Anza Boulevard, Suite 400, 4th Floor, Cupertino, CA 95014

Primavera Systems, Inc.
www.primavera.com
800-423-0245, 610-667-8600
Two Bala Plaza, Bala Cynwyd, PA 19004
Primavera Project Planner, SureTrak Project Manager

Progressive Networks, Inc.
www.prognet.com
206-674-2700
1111 3rd Avenue, Suite 500, Seattle, WA 98101
RealAudio, RealVideo

Quadralay Corporation
www.quadralay.com
512-719-3399
9101 Burnet Road, Suite 105, Austin, TX 78757
WebWorks

Quark, Inc.
www.quark.com
800-788-7835, 303-894-8888
1800 Grant Street, Denver, CO 80203
Quark XPress

Quintus Corp.
www.quintus.com
800-337-8941, 510-624-2800
47212 Mission Falls Court, Fremont, CA 94539
ImpaQ

RandomNoise, Inc.
www.randomnoise.com
888-GET-CODA, 415-437-0321
550 15th Street, 2nd Floor, Suite 24
San Francisco, CA 94103
Coda

Raptor Systems Inc.
www.raptor.com
800-9-EAGLE-6, 617-487-7700
69 Hickory Drive, Waltham, MA 02154
Eagle Firewall

Remedy Corp.
www.remedy.com
415-903-5200
1505 Salado Drive, Mountain View, CA 94043
ARWeb

RSA Data Security, Inc. (a division of Security Dynamics, Inc.)
www.rsa.com
800-782-5453, 415-595-8782
100 Marine Parkway, Suite 500
Redwood City, CA 94065-1031

SAP America, Inc.
www.sap.com
800-USA-1SAP, 610-725-4500
701 Lee Road, Wayne, PA 19087

Scitor Corp.
www.scitor.com
800-533-9876, 415-462-4200
333 Middlefield Road, 2nd Floor
Menlo Park, CA 94025
Project Scheduler

Scopus Technology, Inc.
www.scopus.com
510-597-5800
1900 Powell Street, Suite 700
Emeryville, CA 94608-1819
WebTEAM

Seagate Software (Information Management Group)
www.seagatesoftware.com
800-877-2340, 800-663-1244 (Canada), 604-681-3435
1095 West Pender Street, 4th Floor, Vancouver
British Columbia, CANADA V6E 2M6
Crystal Reports Professional

Secure Computing Corp.
www.borderware.com
800-692-LOCK, 612-628-2700
2675 Long Lake Road, Roseville, MN 55113
Borderware Firewall

Security Dynamics
www.securid.com
800-SECURID, 617-547-7820
20 Crosby Road, Bedford, MA 01730

Appendix B: References & Resources

Sequel Technology, LLC
www.sequeltech.com
800-881-2465, 206-646-6780
3245 146th Place, SE
Lincoln Executive Center
Bellevue, WA 98004
Net Access Manager

ServiceSoft Corp.
www.servicesoft.com
800-737-8738, 617-449-0049
50 Cabot Street, Needham, MA 02194
Knowledge Builder, Web Advisor

ServiceWare, Inc.
www.serviceware.com
800-KPAKS-4U, 412-826-1158
333 Allegheny Avenue, Oakmont, PA 15139
Knowledge Paks

Silicon Graphics, Inc.
www.sgi.com
800-800-7441, 415-960-1980
2011 North Shoreline Boulevard
Mountain View, CA 94043-1389

SoftQuad, Inc.
www.softquad.com
800-387-2777, 416-544-9000
20 Eglington Avenue West, 12th Floor
Toronto, Ontario, CANADA M4R 1K8
HotMeTaL, HotMeTaL Intranet Publisher

Stanford Testing Systems, Inc.
www.testprep.com
800-233-4728, 509-468-5100
P.O. Box 28160, Spokane, WA 99228
IBTauthor

Sun Microsystems, Inc.
www.sun.com
800-821-4643, 800-821-4642 (CA),
415-960-1300
2550 Garcia Avenue
Mountain View, CA 94043-1100
Firewall products, Java, SPARC servers and workstations

SunSoft, Inc.
www.sun.com/sunsoft
800-SUN-SOFT, 512-345-2412
2550 Garcia Avenue
Mountain View, CA 94043-1100

Sybase Inc.
www.sybase.com
800-879-2273, 510-922-3500
6475 Christie Avenue, Emeryville, CA 94608

Symantec Corp.
www.symantec.com
800-441-7234, 408-253-9600
10201 Torre Avenue, Cupertino, CA 95014-2132
Norton Administrator for Networks, Visual Café Pro

Tally Systems Corp.
www.tallysys.com
800-262-3877, 603-643-1300
P.O. Box 70, Hanover, NH 03755-0070
NetCensus

Tivoli Systems, Inc. (subsidiary of IBM)
www.tivoli.com
800-2TIVOLI, 512-436-8000
9442 Capital Of Texas Highway North
Arboretum Plaza One, Austin, TX 78759
Network performance monitors

Trusted Information Systems Inc.
www.tis.com
888-FIREWALL, 301-854-6889
3060 Washington Road, Route 97
Glenwood, MD 21738
Firewall products

Tumbleweed Software Corporation
www.tumbleweed.com
800-696-1978, 415-369-6790
2010 Broadway, Redwood City, CA 94063
Posta, Tumbleweed Publishing Essentials

The Vantive Corp.
www.vantive.com
800-582-6848, 408-982-5700
2455 Augustine Drive, Santa Clara, CA 95054
Vantive Help Desk

VDONet Corp.
www.vdo.net
415-846-7700
4009 Miranda Avenue, Suite 250
Palo Alto, CA 94304
VDOLive

Verity, Inc.
www.verity.com
800-424-3682, 408-541-1500
894 Ross Drive, Sunnyvale, CA 94089
Search '97

Vinca Corp.
www.vinca.com
800-934-9530, 801-223-3100
1815 South State Street, Suite 2000
Orem, UT 84058
Network clustering technology

Visio Corp.
www.visio.com
800-446-3335, 206-521-4500
520 Pike Street, Suite 1800
Seattle, WA 98101-4001
Visio Professional

Visual Networks
www.visualnetworks.com
301-208-6784
2092 Gaither Road, Rockville, MD 20850
Wide-area network testing tools

VXtreme Corp.
www.vxtreme.com
800-501-4689, 408-617-2330
675 Almanor Avenue, Sunnyvale, CA 94086
Web Theater

Xing Technology Corp.
www.xingtech.com
800-294-6448, 805-473-0145
1540 West Branch Street
Arroyo Grande, CA 93420-1818
StreamWorks

Books

One cliché I truly agree with is that if a book contains one really good idea, it's worth the purchase price. I'm happy to report that the two dozen or so books in this section contain many good ideas, covering intranets, intranet publishing, web server technology, workstation software, general networking, and client/server computing. Each one is worth a look next time you find yourself lost among the rows of computer books at your local bookstore-slash-coffee house — or wandering cyberspace bookstores such as www.amazon.com.

Build an Intranet on a Shoestring: Maximum Technology at Minimum Cost
Paul Youngworth
Ventana
415 pages, $34.99 (includes CD-ROM)

Building an Intranet For Dummies
John Fronckowiak
IDG Books Worldwide
384 pages, $29.99 (includes CD-ROM)

Building the Corporate Intranet
Steve Guengerich, Douglas Graham, Mitra Miller, and Skipper McDonald
John Wiley & Sons, Inc.
440 pages, $39.95

Building Windows NT Web Servers
Ed Tittel, Mary Madden, and David B. Smith
IDG Books Worldwide
665 pages, $44.99 (includes CD-ROM)

Bulletproofing Client/Server Systems
Richard J. Martin and Glenn E. Weadock
McGraw-Hill
332 pages, $34.95

Bulletproofing NetWare
Mark Wilkins and Glenn E. Weadock
McGraw-Hill
336 pages, $34.95

Bulletproofing Windows 95
Glenn E. Weadock
McGraw-Hill
350 pages, $34.95

Client/Server Computing For Dummies
Doug Lowe
IDG Books Worldwide
396 pages, $19.99

Client/Server Technology for Managers
Karen Watterson
Addison-Wesley
235 pages, $17.95

Creating Cool FrontPage Web Sites
Paul M. Summitt and Mary J. Summitt
IDG Books Worldwide
360 pages, $29.99 (includes CD-ROM)

Creating Cool Web Pages with HTML
Dave Taylor
IDG Books Worldwide
294 pages, $24.99 (includes diskette)

Firewalls and Internet Security
William R. Cheswick and Steven M. Bellovin
Addison-Wesley
306 pages, $35.45

HTML For Dummies, 2nd Edition
Ed Tittel and Steve James
IDG Books Worldwide
450 pages, $29.99

Internet Security SECRETS
John Vacca
IDG Books Worldwide
758 pages, $39.99 (includes CD-ROM)

Intranet Bible
Ed Tittel and James Michael Stewart
IDG Books Worldwide
854 pages, $49.99 (includes CD-ROM)

Intranet Business Strategies
Mellanie Hills
John Wiley & Sons
396 pages, $29.95

Intranet Resource Kit: Everything You Need to Create Your Intranet Today
edited by Dr. Prakash Ambegaonkar
Osborne/McGraw-Hill
498 pages, $39.99 (includes CD-ROM)

Intranets: The Surf Within
James D. Cimino
Charles River Media, Inc.
338 pages, $39.95 (includes CD-ROM)

LAN Disaster Prevention and Recovery
Patrick H. Corrigan
PTR Prentice-Hall
310 pages, $29.95

Mastering Intranets (Windows 95/NT Edition)
Pat Coleman and Peter Dyson
Sybex
793 pages, $49.99 (includes CD-ROM)

The Mythical Man-Month
Frederick P. Brooks, Jr.
Addison-Wesley
322 pages, $25.77

Networking For Dummies, 2nd Edition
Doug Lowe
IDG Books Worldwide
384 pages, $19.99

Running Microsoft Windows NT Server 4.0
Charlie Russell and Sharon Crawford
Microsoft Press
615 pages, $39.95

TCP/IP For Dummies, 2nd Edition
Marshall Wilensky
IDG Books Worldwide
432 pages, $24.99

Webmaster Strategies
Michael Sullivan-Trainor
IDG Books Worldwide
400 pages, $29.99

Magazines

In the fast-mutating intranet world, magazines should supplement your book diet. Here are a few you should consider that cover intranet-related technology. Even if you truly don't have time to read ONE MORE DADBLASTED MAGAZINE, many of these periodicals can keep you up to date on current trends after a quick skim of each issue.

Byte: The Magazine of Technology Integration
www.byte.com
One Phoenix Mill Lane
Peterborough, NH 03458
603-924-9281

CIO
www.cio.com/CIO
492 Old Connecticut Path, P.O. Box 9208
Framingham, MA 01701-9208
508-872-0080

Client/Server Computing
www.sentrytech.com
One Research Drive, Suite 400B
Westborough, MA 01701
508-366-2031

Computerworld
www.computerworld.com
500 Old Connecticut Path
Framingham, MA 01701
508-879-0700

Information Week
www.techweb.cmp.com/iw
600 Community Drive
Manhasset, NY 11030
516-562-5051

Infoworld
www.infoworld.com
P.O. Box 1172, Skokie, IL 60076
800-457-7866

Internet Magazine
www.zdimag.com
One Park Avenue
New York, NY 10016-5802
800-825-4237

Internet World
www.iw.com
20 Ketchum Street, Westport, CT 06880
800-573-3062

LAN Magazine
600 Harrison Street
San Francisco, CA 94107
800-234-9573

LAN Times
www.lantimes.com
1900 O'Farrell Street, Suite 200
San Mateo, CA 94403
800-525-5003

Network Computing
techweb.cmp.com/nc
600 Community Drive
Manhasset, NY 11030
516-562-5882

Network World
www.networkworld.com
151 Worcester Road
Framingham, MA 01701-9524
800-643-4668, 508-875-6400

PC Magazine: The Independent Guide to Personal Computing
www.pcmag.com
One Park Avenue
New York, NY 10016-5802
212-503-5255

PC Week
www.pcweek.com
10 Presidents' Landing
Medford, MA 02155
617-393-3700

Software Magazine
www.sentrytech.com
One Research Drive, Suite 400B, Westborough, MA 01581
508-366-8104

Web Developer (now online only)
www.webdeveloper.com
20 Ketchum Street, Westport, CT 06880
800-573-3062

Windows Magazine
www.winmag.com
One Jericho Plaza, Jericho, NY 11753
516-733-8300

Windows NT Magazine
www.winntmag.com
PO Box 447, Loveland, CO 80539-0447
800-621-1544, 970-663-4700

CD-ROMs

CD-ROMs are great because of their keyword search capability. Two CD-ROM references that I know of are especially useful for intranet publishers: Computer Select, and Microsoft TechNet.

Computer Select
Information Access Company
800-419-0313, 212-503-4400
$1,250/year (standalone CD), $8,995/year (up to six concurrent users)
The Computer Select CD contains a year's worth of about 100 periodicals, either in full-text or abstract, updated monthly and with its own easy-to-use search engine. The product also includes the Data Sources directory of computer companies, software, and hardware products, plus a glossary of techie terms. A great research tool.

TechNet
Microsoft Corporation
800-344-2121
$295/year
TechNet has grown into a remarkably useful resource for Microsoft shops. It includes the Microsoft knowledge base of tech support notes; system software updates, resource kits, and service packs; and white papers. But wait, you also get 25 percent off all Microsoft Press books. A bargain at twice the price.

Useful Links

You can find a few useful Internet links to point you to some online sites that deal with various aspects of intranet publishing on the enclosed CD-ROM (as LINKS.HTM) for point-and-click access from a PC with an Internet connection. The Internet is an ever-changing place, so please forgive me if any of the links are dead-ends by the time you read this book! I tried every one during the writing of this book, and they all worked. If you hit a snag, feel free to e-mail me at gweadock@i-sw.com and I'll try to find the updated link for you if it exists. But before you do, please double-check your capitalization. UNIX web servers can be nit-picky that way.

Appendix C: About the CD-ROM

System Requirements

Make sure your computer meets the minimum system requirements listed below. If your computer doesn't match up to most of these requirements, you may have problems in using the CD.

- A PC with a 486 or faster processor, a Mac OS computer with a 68030 or faster processor, or a computer running UNIX.
- Microsoft Windows 3.1 or later, Mac OS system software 7.5 or later, or some version of UNIX.
- At least 8MB of total RAM installed on your computer. For best performance, we recommend that Windows 95-equipped PCs and Mac OS computers with PowerPC processors have at least 16MB of RAM installed.
- At least 200MB of hard drive space available to install all the software from this CD. (You need less space if you don't install every program.)
- A CD-ROM drive — double-speed (2x) or faster.
- A monitor capable of displaying at least 256 colors or grayscale.
- A modem with a speed of at least 14,400 bps.

If you need more information on the basics, check out *PCs For Dummies,* 4th Edition, by Dan Gookin; *Macs For Dummies,* 4th Edition, by David Pogue, *Windows 95 For Dummies* by Andy Rathbone; or *Windows 3.11 For Dummies,* 3rd Edition, by Andy Rathbone (all published by IDG Books Worldwide, Inc.).

What You'll Find

The CD-ROM that comes with this book contains a variety of software for you to experiment with as you develop your intranet publishing projects. It includes freeware, shareware (which you need to pay for and register if you decide to continue using it after an evaluation period), tryout versions of commercial software, and sample web templates for some of the applications in the book. It also includes a list of useful Web links for more intranet information and resources.

This appendix lists the CD-ROM's contents by category. Much of the freeware, shareware, and tryout software works only after you run an installation program. Installation instructions may appear in a "README.TXT" file, or all you may have to do is double-click on a file named "SETUP.EXE" or something similar.

The publisher and I have taken all reasonable precautions to ensure that these files are good and true and neither damaged nor infected by a computer virus. Even so, I recommend that you take the usual precautions before installing any software: Make sure you have a current backup of your hard drive, and scan any program files for viruses before running them.

The CD-ROM is formatted so that you can access it from most PCs, UNIX systems, Macintoshes, and so forth. However, many of the programs require a PC to run, and some require a 32-bit operating system (Windows 95 or Windows NT). Note that out of courtesy to those offices that don't like programs running automatically, this CD-ROM is NOT formatted as a Windows 95 "autoplay" disk, so just popping it into your system and waiting for something to happen isn't going to work!

For the Windows 95 and NT instructions, the Run command assumes that your CD-ROM drive is letter D: on your computer. If your drive has a different call letter, substitute that letter for D:.

For all Windows 95 and NT machines, click Start⇨Run, then type the run command included with each of the following software descriptions. In the case of documents, you must run the appropriate application and open the document from the location indicated in the following descriptions.

For Windows 3.1 machines, go to the File Manager and click File⇨Run and then enter the appropriate run command included with the following software descriptions. In the case of documents, you must run the appropriate application and open the document from the location indicated in the following descriptions.

For Macintosh and UNIX machines, follow the appropriate instructions. In the case of documents, you must run the appropriate application and open the document from the location indicated in the following descriptions.

Document Publishing Applications

Adobe's PageMaker 6.5 Tryout is a trial version of the classic desktop publishing application with new web-enabled functionality.

Windows 95 and NT: d:\PUBAPPS\ADOBE\PAGEMAKR\SETUP.EXE

Mac OS: Open the PubApps, Adobe, and Adobe PageMaker 6.5 Tryout folders, and double-click the Install PM6.5 Tryout icon.

askSam 3.0 and askSam Web Publisher 3.0 are demos of askSam Systems' document management and intranet publishing solutions.

askSam 3.0 on a Windows 95 or NT machine:
d:\PUBAPPS\ASKSAM\ASKSAM3\SETUP.EXE

askSam Web Publisher on a Windows 95 or NT machine:
d:\PUBAPPS\ASKSAM\WEBPUB3\SETUP.EXE

Asymitrix Toolbook II Assistant is a demo version of this intranet-based training development tool (Windows 95/NT). d:\PUBAPPS\ASYMITRIX\SETUP.EXE

Blue Sky Software's book, *Mastering HTML-Based Help*, is included free (folder: PUBAPPS\BLUESKY\BOOK) along with a white paper on HTML Help and NetHelp (folder: PUBAPPS\BLUESKY\WHITPAPR), and information on the WinHelp Inspector utility (folder: PUBAPPS\BLUESKY\INSPECTR) and information on WinHelp Office and RoboHelp (folder: PUBAPPS\BLUESKY\PRODUCTS). These folders contain Zip archives or Word documents that must be opened with WinZip (included on the CD-ROM) or Microsoft Word 95.

Design Intelligence's iPublish is a free 60-day "test drive" version of the intelligent-layout document publishing application. (9.3 megabytes)

Windows 95 and NT: d:\PUBAPPS\DESIGNIN\LFN\SETUP.EXE

InfoAccess' HTML Transit is a free evaluation version of this highly rated conversion utility.

Windows 95 and NT: d:\PUBAPPS\INFOACCS\EVALTRAN.EXE

The following Microsoft "Internet Assistants" are add-ins to Windows Office 95 or Office 4.2.*x* for Macintosh programs. You do *not* need these files if you run Office 97 programs, which all have the Internet Assistant capabilities built in.

Microsoft's Internet Assistant for Access is free software that includes an HTML export command. (849K)

Windows 95: d:\PUBAPPS\MICRSOFT\IA95.EXE

Microsoft's Internet Assistant for Excel (files: HTML.XLA, README.TXT) is free software that allows you to create HTML tables from Excel spreadsheets. (224K)

For Windows, copy d:\PUBAPPS\MICRSOFT\HTML.XLA to Excel's LIBRARY folder on your hard drive.

For Mac OS, copy HTML.XLA from the PubApps\Microsoft folder to Excel's Macro Library folder on your hard drive.

Microsoft's Internet Assistant for PowerPoint 95 is free software that includes an HTML export command to create "stills" of PowerPoint slideshows. (235K)

All versions of Windows: d:\PUBAPPS\MICRSOFT\PPTIA.EXE

Microsoft's Internet Assistant for Schedule + is free software that publishes Schedule + information in HTML format. (1.42 megabytes)

All versions of Windows: d:\PUBAPPS\MICRSOFT\SCHIA.EXE

Microsoft's Internet Assistant for Word is free software that allows you to create HTML files from Word 6.0a or greater documents. (1.06 megabytes)

All versions of Windows: d:\PUBAPPS\MICRSOFT\WORDIA.EXE

Mac OS: Open the PubApps and Microsoft folders, and double-click the Macintosh IA Word 2.0z.sea icon.

Net-It Software's Net-It Now! and Net-It Central (Windows95)

This demo comes as a web page. Run your web browser and open the file Start Here.html, located in d:\PUBAPPS\NET_IT\LFN.

Document Viewers and Utilities

Adobe's Acrobat Reader 3.0 is free software that lets you view documents in Adobe's PDF format. The provided files can install an ActiveX control for Microsoft Internet Explorer (PDF.OCX), a plug-in for Netscape Navigator (NPPDF32.DLL), and the standalone viewer program. (3.9 megabytes)

Windows 95 or NT: d:\DOCUTILS\ADOBE\WIN95_NT\AR32E30.EXE

Windows 3.1: d:\ \DOCUTILS\ADOBE\WIN3\AR16E30.EXE

UNIX: Extract the appropriate gzip archive in the \DOCUTILS\ADOBE\UNIX directory on the CD-ROM.

Mac OS: Open the Docutils, Adobe, and Adobe Acrobat Reader folders, and double-click the Reader 3.0 Installer icon.

Note: Acrobat Reader 3.0 may have problems running under Mac OS 8, the latest version of the Mac operating system at the time of this writing. For an updated version of the program, visit the Adobe home page at www.adobe.com.

Macromedia's Shockwave is free software for both Netscape Navigator and Internet Explorer. The version we include on the CD-ROM also includes the capability to play "Flash" vector animations. (about 2 megabytes)

Windows 95/NT: d:\DOCUTILS\MACROMED\SHOCK32.EXE

Windows 3.1: d:\DOCUTILS\MACROMED\SHOCK16.EXE

Mac OS: Open the Docutils and Macromed folders, and double-click the Shockwave installer icon that is appropriate for your kind of Macintosh computer (680x0 or PowerPC processor).

Microsoft's ActiveMovie 1.0 for Windows 95 and NT installs support for streaming video, including MPEG, QuickTime and AVI.

ActiveMovie is included on the CD as part of the installation for Internet Explorer 3.0.2 for Windows 95 and NT. If you already have Internet Explorer installed, check for AMOVIE.OCX in the Windows\System directory to see if ActiveMovie is installed. (635K)

The following Microsoft "Viewers" allow users who do not have the full version of a particular Office program to view, but not edit, documents created in that program. In each case, the viewer installation program automatically sets up the viewer as a Netscape Navigator or Internet Explorer "helper" program.

Microsoft's Viewer for Excel permits viewing of Excel files from Version 2.0 and up. (3.7 megabytes)

Win95: d:\DOCUTILS\MICRSOFT\VIEWER.EXE

Microsoft's Viewer for PowerPoint 97. (2.8 megabytes)

Win95: d:\DOCUTILS\MICRSOFT\PPVIEW97.EXE

Microsoft's Viewer for Word permits viewing of documents created with Word for Windows. (2.12 megabytes)

Win 95: d:\DOCUTILS\MICRSOFT\WD95VW71.EXE

StuffIt Lite 3.6, from Aladdin Systems is a shareware document compression/decompression utility for the popular StuffIt archive format used on Mac OS computers.

Mac OS: Open the Docutils and Aladdin folders and double-click the StuffIt Lite 3.6 Installer icon.

WinZip 95 v6.1, from Nico Mak Computing is a shareware document compression/decompression utility for the popular zip archive format that can help you reduce file transfer times over the intranet.

Windows 95/NT: d:\DOCUTILS\NICOMAK\WINZIP95.EXE

Graphic Images and Utilities

Adobe's Photoshop 4.0 Tryout is a trial version of this classic image editing program.

Windows 95/NT: d:\GRAPHICS\ADOBE\PHOTOSHOP\DISK1\SETUP.EXE

Mac OS: Open the Graphics, Adobe, and Adobe Photoshop 4.0.1 Tryout folders, and double-click the Install Adobe Photoshop Tryout icon located in the Install - Disk 1 folder.

GraphicConverter 2.9.1 for Mac OS from Lemke Software is a powerful shareware graphics utility that can view and convert many graphic formats.

Mac OS: Open the Graphics and Lemke folders, and double-click the GraphicConverter 2.9.1 (US) installer icon.

LView Pro v1.D2 from Leonardo Loureiro is a shareware graphics file viewer that's handy for creating thumbnail contact sheets. LView Pro software is copyright 1993-1996 by Leonardo Haddad Loureiro. For more information on this software, visit the LView home page at `www.lview.com` on the World Wide Web.

Windows 95: d:\GRAPHICS\LVIEWPRO\LVIEWPRO.EXE

Paint Shop Pro from JASC may just be the most popular shareware graphics utility ever.

Windows 95: d:\GRAPHICS\JASC\SETUP.EXE

Multimedia Utilities

Adobe Premiere 4.2 Tryout is a free trial version of the popular video clip editing program for Windows 95 and NT. Premiere can edit and export clips in AVI and QuickTime formats for distribution over the intranet.

Windows 95/NT:
d:\MULTIMED\ADOBE\PREMIERE\WIN95&NT\DISK1\SETUP.EXE

Windows 3.1: d:\MULTIMED\ADOBE\PREMIERE\WIN3X\DISK1\SETUP.EXE

Macromedia's Flash 2 Tryout

Windows 95: d:\MULTIMED\MACROMED\FLSH2TRY.EXE

Mac OS: Open the Multimed and Macromed folders, and double-click the Flash 2 Installer icon that is appropriate for your kind of Macintosh computer (680x0 or PowerPC processor).

Sound Forge XP demo from Sonic Foundry is a limited trial version of the market-leading sound file editing utility. This version cannot save, record, or use the Windows clipboard. (3.1 megabytes)

Windows 95/NT: d:\MULTIMED\SONIC\SFD4BX86.EXE

Templates

Various templates illustrating concepts in this book are available free for your use in the \BOOK\Templates directory.

Web Browsers

Microsoft's Internet Explorer 3.0 is free and one of two major players in the browser market. The CD-ROM contains versions for Windows 95 (10.3 megabytes), Windows NT (8.5 megabytes), and Mac OS (9 megabytes).

Windows 95: d:\WEBBROWS\IE302M95.EXE

Windows NT: d:\WEBBROWS\IE302MNT.EXE

Mac OS: Open the WebBrows folder, and double-click the IE 3.01 Full Installer icon.

AT&T WorldNet(sm) Service with Netscape Navigator is a way to get an ISP and a copy of the king of web browsers all in one.

Windows (all versions): d:\WEBBROWS\WORLDNET\NNSETUP\SETUP.EXE

Mac OS: Open the Webbrows and Install AT&T WorldNet Service folders, then double-click the Install AT&T WorldNet icon.

Web Page Design Programs

Adobe's PageMill 2.0 Tryout is a trial version of Adobe's WYSIWYG page design tool.

Windows 95: d:\WEBPAGE\ADOBE\INSTALL.EXE

Mac OS: Open the WebPage, Adobe, and Adobe PageMill folders, and double-click the Install PageMill Tryout icon.

HTML Assistant Pro 97 from Brooklyn North Software Works

Windows 95: d:\WEBPAGE\BROOKLYN\Pro97dem.exe

Macromedia's Backstage Internet Studio Tryout

Windows 95: d:\WEBPAGE\MACROMED\BIS2TRY.EXE

HoTMetaL Light 3.0 from SoftQuad is a restricted freeware version of the popular page design tool.

Windows 95: d:\WEBPAGE\SOFTQUAD\SETUP.EXE

Web Sites

LINKS.HTM, located in the BOOK folder, contains links to the various Internet Web sites mentioned in the book's main text and in Appendix B. You need a web browser to load LINKS.HTM, so if you don't already have one, see the "Web Browsers" heading earlier in this list.

Miscellany

Sun Microsystems Java Development Kit is a powerful application for the development of Java applets to include in your intranet web pages. Copyright 1997 Sun Microsystems, Inc., 901 San Antonio Road, Palo Alto, CA 94303-4900 USA, All rights reserved. (Windows version: 8.74MB; Mac OS version: 2.7MB). Visit the Java home page at www.javasoft.com for the latest updates.

JDK Version 1.1.3 for Windows 95: d:\MISC\JDK113.EXE

JDK documentation for Windows 95: d:\MISC\DOCS.EXE

JDK Version 1.0.2 for Mac OS: Open the MISC folder and double-click the JDK_1_0_2-MacOS.sea icon.

JDK documentation for Mac OS: Open the MISC folder and double-click the JDK API Documentation.sea icon.

If You've Got Problems (Of the CD Kind)

I've done my best to compile programs that work on most computers with the minimum system requirements. Alas, your computer may differ, and some programs may not work properly for some reason.

The two likeliest problems are that you don't have enough memory (RAM) for the programs you want to use, or you have other programs running that are affecting installation or running of a program. If you get error messages like `Not enough memory` or `Setup cannot continue`, try one or more of these methods and then try using the software again:

- Turn off any anti-virus software that you have on your computer. Installers sometimes mimic virus activity and may make your computer incorrectly believe that it is being infected by a virus.

- Close all running programs. The more programs you're running, the less memory is available to other programs. Installers also typically update files and programs. So if you keep other programs running, installation may not work properly.

- Have your local computer store add more RAM to your computer. This is, admittedly, a drastic and somewhat expensive step. However, if you have a Windows 95 PC or a Mac OS computer with a PowerPC chip, adding more memory can really help the speed of your computer and allow more programs to run at the same time.

If you still have trouble with installing the items from the CD, please call the IDG Books Worldwide Customer Service phone number: 800-762-2974 (outside the U.S.: 317-596-5261).

Index

• Symbols •

<!-- and --> tag pair, adding comments to HTML code, 240
®, 71

• A •

absolute links, 239
Access, Internet Assistant for, 357
accessibility of documents, 23
accommodation of documents, 171
Account Policy dialog box, 270
Acrobat Reader 3.0, 358–359
Acrobat. *See* Adobe Acrobat
Active Movie 1.0, 359
Active Server Pages (ASP), 65
ActiveMovie control of Internet Explorer, 216
ActiveX, 222, 278, 318–319, 327
  controls, 68, 132, 222, 327
  programs, configuring browsers to reject all, 276, 277
  security, versus Java, 275–276
actors in Macromedia Director, 219
add-in program, 327. *See also* helper programs
addresses, assigning to each computer, 11
Adobe Acrobat, 178, 188–190
  cost of, 44
  extending HTML forms capabilities, 91
Adobe FrameMaker 5.1, HTML conversion capabilities of, 184–185
Adobe PageMaker 6.5, HTML conversion capabilities of, 184
Adobe PageMill, 227, 228
Adobe Premiere 4.2 Tryout, 360–361
Adobe Premiere
  editing and storing videos to web servers, 219–220
  editing video clips, 136

Adobe's Acrobat Reader 3.0, 358–359
Adobe's PageMaker 6.5 Tryout, 356–357
Adobe's PageMill 2.0 Tryout, 362
Adobe's Photoshop 4.0 Tryout, 360
advanced technology intranets, 61
advanced text and graphics publishing system, 58
advertisements, placing on intranets, 261
advisory board, 232
Afterburner, compressing Director movies, 219
AIFF (Audio Interchange File Format), 215
Aimtech IconAuthor 7.0, 142
airwalls, 276, 327
Allaire Cold Fusion database toolkit, 66
AltaVista, 203
alternate tags, support for, 315
ambiguous design elements, 177
anchors. *See* bookmarks
animated GIFs, 217
animation on an intranet, 216–219
Animation Publisher. *See* Internet Animation Publisher
annotations in SGML documents, 101
anonymous logins, 271, 274, 327
  setting up an FTP directory for, 126
  special account for in IIS, 271, 273
antivirus policies, 287
antivirus technology, 286–287
Apache web server, 64
API (Application Program Interface), 94, 327
applets, 52, 220, 327
  in HTML Help, 132
  in IBT, 149
Application Program Interface (API). *See* API

application-level security, 271–274
applications, maintaining, 240–243
Archie, 8, 327
askSam 3.0, 357
askSam document database system, 187
askSam Web Publisher, 187, 357
Astra SiteManager from Mercury Interactive, 240
Asymetrix Toolbook II Assistant, cost of, 44
Asymetrix Toolbook II Instructor 5.0, 145
Asymetrix Web3D, 217
asymmetric encryption. *See* public key encryption
Asynchronous Transfer Mode (ATM). *See* ATM
AT&T WorldNet(sm) Service with Netscape Navigator, 361
ATM (Asynchronous Transfer Mode), 327
  for network backbones, 255
attachments, 128, 328
AU format, 215
authentication, 328
author of this book, Internet address for e-mail, 18
Authorware, 143
Auto Load Images option, disabling, 197
AutoAdmin, 69
Autodesk AutoCAD file format (DWG), 100
Autodesk Whip, 100, 213
automatic indexing of search engines, 203
AVI (Audio-Video Interleave) format, 136, 220

• B •

back-end database system, 60
back-end technologies, maximizing for performance, 262
back-end, 328
backbone, 255, 328
background graphics, optimizing, 261

background tiles, making more text-friendly, 212
backgrounds, in an intranet publishing system, 211–212
Backstage Internet Studio from Macromedia, 43, 227–228
Backstage Internet Studio Tryout, 362
BackWeb Technologies, 206
bandwidth, 143, 328
banner graphics, 195
basic login in IIS, 270
basic technology intranets, 60
bastion host, 277, 279, 328. *See also* firewalls
batch process, 188
batch-processing utilities from portable document format vendors, 178
battery power backup, 284
benefits information, posting, 80–81
BeyondPress from Astrobyte, 184
Big I Internet. *See* Internet
bitmap formats, 110, 185, 213
bitmap graphics, dropping onto web pages, 186
Blue Sky Software's *Mastering HTML-Based Help*, 357
bookmarks, 78, 197, 328
  adding to long pages, 259
  in PDF documents, 199, 200
books, list of recommended, 350–351
Boolean operators, 201
BootP (Bootstrap protocol), 236–237, 328. *See also* DHCP
bots, 224
bottom line, improving with Internet technology, 17
bottom-up projects, 156
BPR (Business Process Reengineering), 104–105, 310
bridge, 328
broken links, 241–242
browsers, 9, 328
  configuring to reject all Java or ActiveX programs, 276
  disabling graphics in, 197
  evaluating and testing new versions of, 248
  graphics files supported by, 213
  on the CD-ROM with this book, 361

printing to your own computer from, 28, 29
budget processing, placing on an intranet, 98, 99
buffering in memory, 252
Builder and SiteDirector from Folio, cost of, 44
bulletin boards
  creating cyberspace, 73–86
  publicizing on real and virtual, 294–295
bus, 328
bus mastering, 253, 328
business managers. *See* managers
business plan for intranet publishing, 159
Business Process Reengineering (BPR). *See* BPR
business processes, streamlining, 104
businesses, improving with information publishing systems, 16–17
byte serving, 179

• C •

cache, 329
  tuning, 257
caching, 256–257
  look-ahead, 258
  setting, 257
CAD (Computer-Aided Design or Computer-Aided Drafting), 329
Caere OmniForm Internet Publisher, extending HTML forms capabilities, 91
Calendar, 69
calendars, creating web-based, 85
call avoidance applications, 134
call support, intranet publishing systems for, 123–137
call support applications, 134
callback modems, 280, 329
calls, 94
canned knowledge bases, 121
capacity planning capability of NMS software, 244
Capture program, 188
career management applications, 81–82
Cascading Style Sheets (CSS), 316–317
case sensitivity of intranet servers, 239

case sensitivity of JavaScript, 223
Castanet from Marimba, 206
casual web servers, 66–67
Catalog program, 189
CBT (Computer-Based Training), 329
  plug-ins, drawbacks of, 145
  products, publishing on an intranet, 142–145
  programs, plug-ins or helper programs for, 144–145
CD-ROM with this book, 355–356
  browsers, 361
  document publishing applications, 356–358
  document viewers, 358–359
  graphic images, 360
  graphic utilities, 360
  installation instructions, 356
  multimedia utilities, 360–361
  not formatted as Windows 95 autoplay, 356
  problems with, 363
  system requirements for, 355
  templates, 361
  useful links, 353
  utilities, 358–360
  web page design programs, 362
  web sites, 362
CD-ROMs, recommended for reference, 353
cells, 74
central sites for intranets, 263
CERN, 91
certificates, 282, 329
CGI, 91–93, 329
  programming gotchas, 92–93
  programs, portability of, 238
  scripts, 92, 329
  scripts, prewritten, 224
  system for HTML forms, 92, 93
CGI-BIN directory, 92
champions, finding for intranet projects, 157
Champy, James, 105
channels of content, 205
CHAP (Challenge-Handshake Authentication Protocol), 329
Chariot from Ganymede Software, 264
check boxes in HTML forms, 88, 89
child style sheets, 316
client computer, 13
client-side form data validation, 223

Index

client-side image maps, 196, 334
client workstations
  compatibility with intranet publishing systems, 30–31
  tuning, 250, 251, 256–258
client/server computing, 329
client/server network, 329
client/server systems, 13–14
  intranets as, 13–14
  tradeoff between uptime, cost, and transparency, 284
clients, 8, 329
  intranet capabilities of, 67–70
  maintaining, 247–248
  performance bottlenecks of, 69–70
  tuning, 250, 251, 256–258
clustering, 286
  of search engines, 202
Coda program from Randomnoise, 179–180
collaboration functions, 16
collaborative document management, 98
Collabra newsgroup reader, 69
color depth, 260
colors, reducing the number of, 260
combo cards, replacing NICs with, 255
combo GIF, 148
combo tiles, 211
comments, embedding in programs and HTML documents, 240
commercial software, publishing documentation for on an intranet, 132–133
Common Gateway Interface. *See* CGI
Common Ground Web Publishing System, 178
communication buffers, 329
communications security, 280–283
Communicator package, 68–69
companies, mentioned in this book, 343–350
company information, posting on the network, 73–86
company timetables. *See* schedules
competitive analyses, providing, 112
competitive weapons, intranets as, 40

compiled programs, compared to interpreted, 94
Component Object Mode (COM), 319
Composer, 68
computer animation on an intranet, 216–219
computer-based presentations, on an intranet, 111
Computer-Based Training. *See* CBT
computer slide shows, downloading from an intranet, 111
computer video on an intranet page, 219–220
computer viruses, 286
computers, assigning unique addresses to, 11
configuration data
  Help Desk access to, 119–120
  providing over an intranet, 108–109
connectionless protocol, 254
consensus, building for intranet projects, 155–160
constituencies, including all, 308
consultants, designing intranet projects with, 164–165
content
  searching for by date, 243
  setting guidelines about who can publish, 166–167
content areas, assigning responsibility for, 243
content delivery. *See* push publishing
content development, cost of, 43
content pages, versus link pages, 259
content providers, 159
  as a constituency, 157, 158
  defining formatting guidelines for, 243
  ongoing intranet education for, 299
  support of intranet projects, 159–160
continuing education, 299–300
continuous data transfer speed for sound, 216
continuous improvement of intranet projects, 298–300
controls, 330

conversion of documents, 171
conversion templates, 177
conversion utilities to HTML, 175
cooperative processing, 308
copyrights, 71
cost savings, 17, 170
costs of intranet publishing, 41–48
courseware designed for an intranet, publishing, 145–146
courseware development tool, 60
cracker, 330
crawling capability of search engines, 203
credit information, providing, 114
custom HTML, delivering documents with, 177–179
custom knowledge bases, 122
custom software, publishing documentation for, 133–134
customer information, providing, 113–114
customer testimonials and references, 111–112
customers
  measuring the number of satisfied, 170
  tracking, 114
cyberbolic view, 240
CyberPress from Extensis, 184

data
  passing from one intranet page to another, 228
  simple, 58
data backups, 287–289
data bus speed, 252
data cartridges, 323
data flows, simple, 58–60
data inaccuracy in intranet publishing, 53
data processing in intranets, 91–96
data transfer speed, continuous for sound, 216
data types
  indexed by search engines, 201
  published by intranet publishing systems, 58
data validation in forms, 95
data warehouse, 330
database, 22

database connections with Backstage Internet Studio, 227–228
database documents, converting to intranet, 186–188
database publishing with intranets, 15
database server, 330
database-to-intranet integration, 114
datablades, 323
DBMS (Database Management System), 330
DeBabelizer
  converting groups of graphics files, 186
  performing color-depth reduction for groups of files, 260
decryption, 280, 330
definition screens in IBT, 147, 148
defragmenting disks, 253
delivery strategy for intranet publishing, 175
demand-driven publishing, 205
demos, providing, 297–298
department-level intranet schedules, 84–85
dependent file syndrome, 242
design consistency, 234
design elements, ambiguous, 177
Design Intelligence's i publish, 357
design manual, creating and maintaining, 240
design principles for web sites, 207–212
design tasks, streamlining with intranet publishing, 100–102
desktop databases, 114
desktop publishing programs, web publishing capabilities of, 183
desktop publishing software. *See* DTP
desktop publishing-type documents, creating and reformatting for print or intranet, 173
desktops, placing links on, 296
development speed, of intranets, 24–25
DHCP (Dynamic Host Configuration Protocol), 237, 330. *See also* BootP (Bootstrap protocol)

dial-up communications, adding equipment for, 46
dial-up modem connection, 9
Dial-Up Networking (DUN), 331
dial-up security, 278–280
differential backups, 288
digital certificates, 282, 329
digital video clips, 219
DigitalPaper (DP) format, 178
dilettantes, dangerous, 51
direct leased line connection, 9
direct messaging. *See* push publishing
directory browsing, disallowing, 273
directory services, 330
disaster recovery plans, 85, 289
disk drives. *See also* hard drives
  mirroring, 285
  redundant, 335
distance learning, 16
Distiller program, 188
distribution speed of intranet publishing, 25
DNS (Domain Name Service), 330
DNS server, 237
DNS/DHCP Manager, 237
DOC file suffix, 171
document
  accommodation, 171
  annotations in SGML, 101
  conversion, 171
  publishing, 15
  publishing applications on the CD-ROM with this book, 356–358
  updating, 240
  viewers on the CD-ROM with this book, 358–359
documentation
  of intranets, 239–240
  publishing searchable on an intranet, 130–134
documents
  editing on an intranet, 98–99
  printing to a virtual printer, 178
  publishing many types of, 32–33
  publishing on intranet, 22
  verifying for changes in Netscape Navigator, 257, 258
Domain Name Service. *See* DNS

domain names, 238
  matching IP addresses to, 237
  registering, 167, 293
  selecting for servers, 167
Domino.doc, 98, 99
double-spaces after periods, replacing with single-spaces, 185
download, 330
download site, setting up with FTP service, 124
downloading files, effect on performance, 262
drill-down documents, creating graphics-based, 197
drop-down selection lists in HTML forms, 89
DTP documents, converting into HTML, 183–185
DUN (Dial-Up Networking), 331
duplexing, 285, 331
duplication of effort, avoiding, 49
DWF (Drawing Web Format) files, 100
DWG files, 100
dynamic documents, 58
dynamic HTML, 315
dynamic table of contents, 101, 225, 317

EDGAR database, 113
EDI (Electronic Data Interchange), 331
educational opportunities, posting on an intranet, 82
EIDE disk drives, 331
  compared to SCSI, 253
EIS (Executive Information System), 331
electrical noise, filtering, 284
electronic lies, 53
e-mail, attachments to, 128
emergency and disaster plans, 85–86
emergency intranet systems, 86
employee directory, 76–77
employees, surveying, 102
encrypted login in IIS, 270
encrypted signon, 280
encryption, 331
  effect on performance, 282
end-to-end transmission performance, testing, 264
end-user training, costs of, 47
Enhanced IDE. *See* EIDE

Index   369

Enhanced Image Technology (EIT), 320
enterprise, 331
Enterprise Server, 65
Envoy format, 178
Error 404, 241
Ethernet, 255, 331
evaluation criteria for search engines, 201–203
Event Viewer, running over a LAN connection, 247
Excel
  Internet Assistant for, 357–358
  viewer for, 359
Exchange program, 189
Excite for Web Servers, 203
execute permissions, assigning in IIS, 271, 272, 273
Executive Information System. See EIS
expectations, conditioning, 62–63
expense reports, 97–98
eXtensible Markup Language. See XML
extranets, 16, 35, 167

• F •

Fair Use Doctrine, 71
fancy HTML forms, 90–91
FAQ (Frequently Asked Questions), 129, 331
FAQ home page, creating, 129, 130
fast Ethernet, 255, 331
FastTrack Server, 66
fat server-thin client model, 24
fatware, 38
fault resilience, 283, 310
fault tolerance, 283, 310, 331
favorites, 78
FEP (Frequently Encountered Problems), 129–130, 331
fields in HTML forms, 89
file compression software, 124
file distribution effect on performance, 262
file folders, placing on desktops, 296
file formats. See also formats
  for intranet video publishing, 220
  viewing in Windows 95 or Windows NT, 171–172
file system buffers, 331
File Transfer Protocol (FTP). See FTP (File Transfer Protocol)

files
  buffering in memory, 252
  compressing for faster downloads, 262
  separating internal-only into their own directories, 268
  using lowercase letters for all, 239
firewalls, 277, 278, 332. See also bastion host
  bypassing with modems, 279
  certifying, 278
  cost of, 43
  listing of, 278
  streaming audio and video and, 278
first project, planning, 161–165
Flash 2 from Macromedia, 218–219
Flash 2 Tryout, 361
Flash vector animations, playing, 359
flatbed scanner, cost of, 45
flipbook animation, 217
floating GIF, 214
flowcharting tools, site maps and, 241
Folio infobase system, 187–188
footer, 209, 332
  linking to the home page in, 195
form data validation, 223
form tools, 332
formats, 171. See also file formats
formatting guidelines
  defining for content providers, 243
  publishing for intranet projects, 166
forms, 332
  HTML, 88
FrameMaker 5.1, HTML conversion capabilities of, 184–185
frames, 197–198, 208, 332
Frequently Asked Questions. See FAQ
Frequently Encountered Problems. See FEP
front-end, 328, 332. See also back-end
FrontPage 97, 224–225
FrontPage
  bundled with Internet Information Server, 64
  frame design in, 197–198
FrontPage Editor, 224
FrontPage Explorer, 224, 225
FrontPage kit from Microsoft, cost of, 43

ftp:// prefix, 126
FTP directory, 126, 127
FTP (File Transfer Protocol), 8, 124, 125, 332
FTP software download site, creating on a Help Desk intranet, 125–127
Fusion product from NetObjects, cost of, 43
FutureSplash. See Flash 2 from Macromedia

• G •

gateway, 332
gateway products, 11
Get method, 92
GIF files
  animating, 217
  creating, 213
  interlacing, 214
  with a see-through background, 340
GIF format, 214, 332
  reducing the number of colors in, 260
gigabit Ethernet, 255, 324, 332
Gopher, 8, 332
government regulations, accessing through an intranet, 84
graphics-based drill-down documents, creating with image maps, 197
Graphic Converter 2.9.1 for Mac OS from Lemke Software, 360
graphic images
  for intranet pages, 213
  on the CD-ROM with this book, 360
graphic utilities on the CD-ROM with this book, 360
graphical data, publishing, 254
graphics
  optimizing, 260–261
  storing and loading two versions of, 261
graphics files, converting for an internet, 185–186
Graphics Interchange Format. See GIF
graphics tools, cost of, 43
grass-roots intranets, 203
grids, placing over pages, 75
groupware, 16, 60, 332
groupware applications, 98
GUI (Graphical User Interface), 332

• H •

H.i.P. Editor, 226
H.i.P. Information Manager, 226
H.i.P. Monitor, 226
H.i.P. Viewer, 226
Hammer, Michael, 105
hard drives. *See also* disk drives
  defragmenting, 253
  duplexing, 285
  replacing or adding faster, 253
hardware
  costs for intranet publishing, 45–46
  publishing documentation for, on an intranet, 132–133
hardware guidelines for intranets, 235–236
hardware inventory capability of NMS software, 244
header section of intranet pages, 209, 332
Heisenberg Uncertainty Principle, 263–264
Help-2-HTML, 132–133
Help Desk Institute Web site, 138
Help Desk support for intranet systems, 234–235
Help Desks, 117–118, 333
  access to inventory and configuration data, 119–120
  creating an FTP download site on an intranet, 125–127
  Internet access for, 118–119
  knowledge bases from an intranet, 121–122
  network maps from an intranet, 121
  software distribution from an intranet, 123–129
  systems for internal use, 118–122
  user information from an intranet, 120
help files, converting into HTML format, 132–133
helper programs, 39, 333. *See also* plug-ins
  for CBT programs, 144–145
  running on workstations, 67
high color, 260
high-end encryption products, verifying the legality of, 281

high uptime intranet, 45
hired partner, educating employees with, 164
hit counter program, 62
hit parade list of FAQs and FEPs, publishing on an intranet, 129–130
hits, tracking the number of, 169–170
home page, 194–196
  linking to, 194–195
HOSTS file, 237
hot standby, 285
HoTaMaLe plug-in, bundled with Adobe FrameMaker 5.1, 185
HoTMetaL Intranet Publisher (H.i.P.), 225–227
  cost of, 43
  table of contents viewer plug-in, 199
HoTMetal Light 3.0, 362
HTML, 333
  charting and, 77–78
  converting to stock, 175–177
  delivering documents with custom, 177–179
  delivering documents with stock, 175–177
  encryption for, 281
  page breaks in, 52
  tabular data and, 73–75
  versions of, 314–315
HTML Assistant Pro 97 from Brooklyn North Software Works, 362
HTML code, adding comments to, 240
HTML commands, viewing the underlying, 26–27
HTML Converter add-on utility, 102
HTML documents, printing, 52
HTML extensions, 67, 315–316
HTML forms, 88
  building, 90
  drawbacks of, 95
  fancy, 90–91
  multiple on the same page, 90
  standard, 88–90
  submitting problem reports on, 134–135
HTML Help, 132, 133, 134
HTML Layout, ActiveX control, 222
HTML tables, 73–75
  presenting competitive analyses, 112
HTML Transit, 175, 176, 357
http:// prefix, 9

HTTP (HyperText Transfer Protocol), 9, 333
https:// prefix, 281
hubs, 333. *See also* intelligent hubs; switching hubs
humor in an intranet publishing system, 212
hyperlink navigation, search engines as an alternative to, 200–201
hyperlinks, 193–194, 333
hypermedia, 333
hypertext, 25, 333
hypertext link, 25
HyperText Markup Language. *See* HTML
HyperText Transfer Protocol. *See* HTTP

• I •

i publish software, 173–174
IBT Author from Stanford Testing Systems, 145
IBT (Intranet Based Training), 139, 334
  computer-related courseware possibilities for, 141
  creating your own, 145–146
  defining terms using hyperlinks, 147, 148
  design guidelines for, 146–152
  inappropriate educational material for, 141–142
  keys to successful publishing of, 152
  noncomputer education applications, 141
  tips for designing successful, 152
  topics for, 140–142
IconAuthor 7.0, 142
icons
  placing on desktops, 296
  in this book, 5–6
IETF (Internet Engineering Task Force), 334
IIS (Internet Information Server), 64, 270, 271
Image Composer graphics utility, 224
image maps, 196, 334
images
  compressing into JPEG, 214
  compressing nonphotographic with JPEG, 215

Index

Independent Computer Consultants Association, 165
Index Server, 203
  bundled with Internet Information Server, 64
Indexed Color command in Photoshop, 260
indexing, automatic by search engines, 203
industrial web servers, 64–66
InfoAccess' HTML Transit, 357
infobase in Folio, 187
information ball of yarn. *See* Internet
Information Dimensions Basis V8, cost of, 44
information publishing systems, improving businesses with, 16–17
Information Services (IS) department, assigning IP addresses centrally, 236
Information superhighway, 8
information systems, impact of intranets on existing, 36–37
Information Technology (IT) education markets, for professionals and users, 140
infrastructure, 250
  as a factor in intranet publishing, 70
  tuning, 251, 254–256
  upgrading for intranets, 46
in-house developers, effect of Network PCs on, 39
insurance plan data, posting, 80–81
integration of intranet publishing, 28
intellectual property law, 71–72
interactive design techniques for IBT, 148–150
interactive documents, 22
interactive education, 16
interactivity, providing to a web site, 220–224
interface, compared to a programming language, 91
interlaced GIF files, 214
Internet, 6–8, 334
  building a private, 10–12
Internet access
  for Help Desks, 118–119
  limiting, 268

Internet Animation Publisher, retrofitting PowerPoint 95, 146
Internet Assistant for Access, 357
Internet Assistant for Excel, 98, 357–358
Internet Assistant for PowerPoint 95, 358
Internet Assistant for Schedule+, 358
Internet Assistant for Word, 183, 358
Internet Database Connector (IDC), 65
Internet Engineering Task Force. *See* IETF
Internet Explorer, 69, 361
  rejecting all ActiveX programs, 276, 277
  setting caching, 257
Internet Explorer Administrator Kit, presetting browser options, 210
Internet Information Server (IIS). *See* IIS
Internet links on the CD-ROM with this book, 353
Internet Network Information Center. *See* InterNIC
Internet Packet eXchange. *See* IPX
Internet Protocol. *See* IP
Internet Server Application Interface. *See* ISAPI
Internet servers, assigning addresses to, 11
Internet Service Manager, running, 64
Internet Service Provider (ISP). *See* ISP
Internet technologies, printing and, 13
Internet technology, improving productivity with, 17
Internet Web sites. *See* Web sites
InterNIC (Internet Network Information Center), 11, 293, 334
InterNIC registration authority, 167
InterNIC Web site, 167
interpreted programs, compared to compiled, 94
intranet address, selecting for ease of use, 292–293
intranet advisory board, 232

intranet-based technical support, 123
Intranet Based Training. *See* IBT
intranet browsers, supporting both, 68
intranet client, 329
intranet content, guidelines about, 166
intranet data processing, 91–96
intranet demos, creating, 297–298
intranet designers, ongoing intranet education for, 299–300
intranet documents, sources of, 181–188
intranet education, ongoing, 299–300
intranet fair, 300
intranet fault resilience, 287–289
intranet fault tolerance, 284–287
intranet icons, setup routines for, 296
intranet images, list of programs to consider for creating, 213
intranet maintenance plan, people issues of, 232–235
intranet market, 11
intranet-only publishing strategy, 172–173
intranet pages
  compared to printed pages, 208–209
  cosmopolitan qualities of, 209
  graphic images for, 213
  hidden sections of, 208–209
  independence of, 209
  resizing, 208
  text formatting of, 210–211
intranet plumbing, 34
intranet-plus publishing strategy, 173–174
intranet project teams, 157
intranet projects
  announcing the success of, 300
  mandatory use of, 291–292
  outsourcing, 163–164
  partnering, 164
  planning, 307–308
  publicizing, 311
  using consultants to design, 164–165
  ways of promoting, 292–302

intranet publishing, 22
  benefits of, 23–34
  business plan, 159
  compared to paper
    publishing, 33–34
  cost of hardware for, 45–46
  cost of software for, 42–45
  costs of, 41–48
  distribution speed of, 25
  enabling the Network PC
    concept, 39–40
  examples of, 21–22
  higher front-end costs of, 34
  integration of, 28
  overcentralized
    development of, 51
  people costs of, 46–48
  potential impact of, 35–36
  risks of, 48–54
  standardized user interface
    of, 28–30
  when not to use, 34
intranet publishing projects
  constituencies of, 157, 158
  list of possibilities, 306–307
  measuring the success of,
    70–71, 168–170
  planning for success, 165
  selecting, 305–306
intranet publishing systems
  compatibility with client
    workstations, 30–31
  data types published by, 58
  designing two-way, 87–88
  ease of development of, 31
  ease of upsizing, 32
intranet security, 267
intranet servers
  budgeting a dedicated
    machine for, 45
  clustering, 286
  installed base of, 10
  mirroring, 285
intranet sites
  organizing for easy
    navigation, 192–200
  providing interactivity to,
    220–224
  structuring, 191–206
intranet systems
  enhancing continuously,
    298–300
  maintaining, 243–248
  maintenance required by,
    231–232
intranet-to-database
  integration, 114

intranet traffic
  encrypting all, 280
  prioritizing, 256
intranets, 1, 334
  accessibility of documents
    on, 23
  advanced technology, 61
  advertisements on, 261
  basic technology, 60
  building, 10–12
  as client/server systems,
    13–14
  as competitive weapons, 40
  cost of basic software for, 43
  database publishing with, 15
  delivering training over,
    142–146
  design of, 163–165
  designing for the screen, 310
  development speed of, 24–25
  distributing software over,
    124–129
  documenting, 240
  evolution of, 14
  explaining the use of on a
    Help Desk intranet,
    137–138
  flavors of, 15–16
  high uptime, 45
  impact on existing
    information systems,
    36–37
  infrastructure for, 46
  making web searchable, 131
  manageability of, 24
  medium technology, 60
  naming for ease of use,
    292–293
  navigability of, 25–26
  Network PCs and, 37–40
  open architecture of, 13
  optimizing for
    performance, 250
  physical security for, 269
  platform independence of, 13
  procedures for setting up
    SSL, 282
  publishing many document
    types, 32–33
  stateless nature of, 192
  supporting from central
    sites, 263
  system management, 48
  tools for tracking web server
    performance, 265–266
  tuning, 249–266
  versus traditional networks,
    12–13

inventory and configuration
  data, Help Desk access to,
  119–120
inventory programs, 120
IP address management
  products, industrial
  strength, 237
IP addresses, 11, 236, 238
  assigning to Internet
    servers, 11
  hiding intranet, 277
  maintaining and
    managing, 236
  registering, 167–168
IP (Internet Protocol), 236, 334
i publish, 357
IPX (Internet Packet
  eXchange), 11, 334. *See
  also* TCP/IP
IPX-to-IP gateway, 11
ISAPI (Information Server
  API), 94, 327, 334
ISDN (Integrated Services
  Digital Network), 334
  lines, cost of, 46
I-Server from PointCast, 206
ISP (Internet Service
  Provider), 9, 334

• *J* •

Java, 318, 335
  delivering documents with,
    179–181
  disabling content, 278
  drawbacks of, 221
  programming toolkits for, 221
  security features of, 221
Java applet buttons,
  printing, 52
Java applets, 52
  in IBT, 149
Java code, writing for web
  applets, 31
Java compilers, 318
Java DataBase Connectivity
  (JDBC) commands, 221
Java DataBase Connectivity.
  See JDBC
Java Development Kit, 362–363
Java forms, 95
Java home page, 362
Java programs
  configuring browsers to
    reject all, 276
  in IBT, 148–149
Java sandbox, 275
Java security versus ActiveX,
  275–276

Index

Java virtual machines, 318
JavaScript, 335. *See also* VBScript
  applications of, 223
  case sensitivity of, 223
  compared to VBScript, 224
  from Netscape, 223
JDBC (Java DataBase Connectivity), 95, 114, 335
job board, 82
JPEG file format, reducing the number of colors in, 260
JPEG files, creating, 213
JPEG format, 214
JPEG (Joint Photographic Experts Group), 335
jump, 335
Just-In-Time Java compilers, 221, 318

key frame, 219
key pair, generating for SSL, 282
key users
  cultivating, 301
  support of intranet projects, 160
knowledge bases, 121
  on a Help Desk intranet, 121–122
  publishing for users on an intranet, 134
Knowledge Builder from ServiceSoft, 122
Knowledge Network, 203, 204
KRNLUPD.EXE, 248

LAN (Local Area Network), 11, 335
LAN-based reporting tools, 247
LAN-based security, 269–271
LAN servers, remote management tools for, 247
landscape orientation, 174
learning organizations, building, 152
leased line connection, 9
Left hand-Right hand syndrome, 18, 49
legacy system, 335
lifetime batteries, 280
link. *See* hypertext link
link integrity, maintaining, 240, 241–242

link pages, versus content pages, 259
links
  on the CD-ROM with this book, 353
  posting pages of useful, 86
LINKS.HTM, 362
  on the CD-ROM with this book, 353
links page, 110
links to intranet publishing systems, placing everywhere, 295–297
LiveLink Intranet software, 99
LiveLink Search 64 from Open Text, 204
LiveWire Application Manager, 65
LiveWire server-side version of JavaScript, 223
LiveWire Site Manager, 65
LiveWire software bundle, 65
load balancing, 253–254
Local Area Network. *See* LAN
log file data, saving into a database format, 246
log files in web servers, 245–247
logins, encrypting on LAN-based web servers, 270
logon passwords, encrypting, 280
logon script, as a push system, 128
long pages, advantages of, 259
look-ahead caching, 258
loosely coupled software systems, 239
lossy compression technique, 214
Lotus Notes, 98–99
LView Pro v1.D2 from Leonardo Loureiro, 360

• *M* •

Macintosh PICT files, converting to GIF or JPEG, 227
macro virus, 286
Macromedia Authorware, 143
Macromedia Director, 219
Macromedia's Backstage Internet Studio Tryout, 362
Macromedia's Flash 2 Tryout, 361
Macromedia's Shockwave, 359

magazines, list of recommended, 352–353
mainframe systems, 14
maintenance
  designing for, 235–240
  of Network PCs, 37
manageability of intranets, 24
manager survey, 62
managers
  as a constituency, 157, 158
  promoting intranet systems to, 301–302
  support of intranet projects, 158–159
  surveying, 62
manuals, users and, 130–131
manufacturing tasks, streamlining with intranet publishing, 100–102
marketing bulletins, 113
Mastering HTML-Based Help, 357
matrix organizational structure, 77
MCI (Media Control Interface), 335
media flaws, 288
MediaServer from Vosaic, 220
medium technology intranets, 60
memory
  adding to servers, 252–253
  for client workstations, 256
Messenger e-mail module, 69
metering of software licenses, 244
mFactory mTropolis, 143
microprocessors, adding power to, 252
Microsoft Active Movie 1.0, 359
Microsoft backup program for Windows 95, 288
Microsoft browser, 68, 69
Microsoft FrontPage 97, 224–225
Microsoft Image Composer, 217
Microsoft Index Server, 201, 202, 203
Microsoft Internet Access Server, 278
Microsoft Internet Assistant for Access, 357
Microsoft Internet Assistant for Excel, 357–358
Microsoft Internet Assistant for PowerPoint 95, 358
Microsoft Internet Assistant for Schedule+, 358
Microsoft Internet Assistant for Word, 358

Microsoft Internet Explorer 3.0, 361
Microsoft Internet Explorer. *See* Internet Explorer
Microsoft Internet Information Server (IIS). *See* IIS
Microsoft Office, integration with FrontPage, 225
Microsoft Organizational Chart applet, 77–78, 79
Microsoft Personal Web Server (PWS), 67
Microsoft PowerPoint for IBT authoring, 145–146
Microsoft PowerPoint slide show of several organizational charts, 78
Microsoft Project, 162
  exporting HTML data from, 102
Microsoft Publisher 97, HTML export command, 184
Microsoft Site Server, 240, 241
  saving log file data into a database format, 246
Microsoft Viewer for Excel, 359
Microsoft Viewer for PowerPoint 97, 359
Microsoft Viewer for Word, 359
Microsoft Viewers, 359
Microsoft WinHelp format, 132
middleware, 335
MIDI (Musical Instrument Digital Interface) format, 215
MIME (Multipurpose Internet Mail Extension), 335
mirrored server, 285
mirroring, 285, 335. *See also* duplexing
mission-critical systems, 34
modular IBT course, 151
modular organization of IBT, 150–151
MOM software, 264
monitoring activities, effect on network speed, 264
monitoring utilities for operating systems, 265
movies, placing real-life on an intranet page, 219–220
MPEG (Motion Picture Experts Group) file format, 136, 220, 336. *See also* JPEG
msbatch.inf file, customizing, 296
multimedia, Web and, 212–220

multimedia design techniques for IBT, 151–152
multimedia publishing system, 58
multimedia utilities on the CD-ROM with this book, 360–361
multinet, 45, 72, 86
  firewalls with, 277
Multipurpose Internet Mail Extension, 335
multi-way, many-to-many system, 60

• N •

National Computer Security Association (NCSA), 278
navigability of intranets, 25–26
navigation, product-specific, 198–200
navigation design techniques for IBT, 147–148
Navigator 4.0, 68
NDS (NetWare Directory Services), 66, 336
Net PCs. *See* Network PCs
NetBIOS names, 237, 238, 336
NetCensus from Tally Systems, 120
NetHelp, 132, 133, 336
NetID from Isotro, 237
Net-Install from 20/20 Software, 125
Net-It Central, 180, 358
Net-It Now!, 180, 181, 358
Netscape, technical information site from, 118, 119
Netscape audio plug-in (npaudio.dll), 216
Netscape browser, 68–69
Netscape Catalog Server, 204
Netscape Enterprise Server, 65
Netscape FastTrack Server, 66
Netscape Navigator, 68–69, 361
  contents of a cache area, 257
  opening pages in a new window, 256
  plug-in for ActiveX, 222
  rejecting all Java programs, 276
  setting caching, 257, 258
Netscape Navigator Administration Kit, presetting browser options, 210
Netscape Server Application Program Interface. *See* NSAPI

NetShow, bundled with Internet Information Server, 64
NetSolve network monitoring services, 245
NetWare, 11
NetWare Directory Services. *See* NDS
network, 336. *See also* Local Area Network (LAN)
  effect of Network PCs on, 38
  maintaining, 243–245
  programming to enhance password security, 272
  segmenting, 253
  tuning up, 250–258
  upgrading for intranets, 46
network computers, 216, 336
network diagramming tools, 121
network drawings, saving in HTML format, 121
Network Interface Cards. *See* NICs
network load, balancing, 253–254
network logon script as a push system, 128
Network Management Systems. *See* NMSs
network management products, listing of, 244–245
network maps on a Help Desk intranet, 121
network operating systems, 336
  for Web servers, 9
Network PCs
  intranets and, 37–40
  keeping in sync, 37
  maintenance of, 37
  pros and cons of, 37–39
  user error and, 37
network software, tuning on clients, 256
network traffic, intranets and, 46
networks
  complete physical separation of, 276
  versus intranets, 12–13
new hire information, updating with an intranet form, 103
new-hire books, publicizing in, 295
newsletters
  posting on an intranet, 82–84
  publicizing in print and electronic, 294

Index

NIC drivers, updating, 253
NICs (Network Interface Cards), 336
  adding additional, 253
  adding faster on client workstations, 258
  capabilities of, 69–70
  replacing with combo cards, 255
  replacing with faster, 253
NMSs (Network Management Systems), 244
  identifying server problems, 245
  monitoring performance with, 263–264
nonphotographic images, compressing with JPEG, 215
nonreentrant quality of HTTP, 192–193
NovaSoft NovaManage, cost of, 44
Novell IntraNetware, using security features of NDS, 270
Novell NetWare, 11
Novell NetWare Web Server, 66
npaudio.dll, 216
NSAPI (Netscape Server Application Program Interface), 94, 336
NT, 336

• O •

Object Linking and Embedding (OLE). *See* ActiveX
object-oriented approach to web page design, 227
object-oriented graphics, 341
object-relational technology, 323
objects, HTML elements as, 227
OCR (Optical Character Recognition), 336
OCR scanning, 181–183
ODBC (Open DataBase Connectivity), 114, 336. *See also* JDBC
office procedures, streamlining routine, 87
office tasks, putting routine on an intranet, 96–104
OLE (Object Linking and Embedding), 336
OmniPage Pro, 182
one-way, one-to-many system, 58–59
ongoing intranet education, 299–300

online documents, embedding intranet links in, 297
online service, 9
open architecture of intranets, 13
Open DataBase Connectivity. *See* ODBC
Open Text, 204
Open Type font, 336
open-and-close model of CGI programs, 93
open-format document databases, 98–99
OpenType standard, 321–322
operating systems, 336
  maintaining on client workstations, 247
  monitoring utilities for, 265
  for Web servers, 9
Optical Character Recognition. *See* OCR
O'Reilly and Associates WebSite 1.1, 67
O'Reilly and Associates WebSite Professional, 66
organization charts, 77–78, 79
organization-wide intranet schedules, 84
outsourcing
  costs of, 47
  of intranet projects, 163–164
overcentralized development of intranet publishing, 51

• P •

P3 2.0 (Primavera Project Planner 2.0), 102
packet-filtering router, 277
packets, 11
page master (template) in PageMaker, 174
PageMaker 6.5, HTML conversion capabilities of, 184
PageMaker 6.5 Tryout, 356–357
PageMill, 227, 228
PageMill Inspector, 227, 228
page-on-demand capability, 179
page-on-demand in Acrobat 3.0, 189
pages, 337
  compared to screens, 208–209
  long versus new, 259
Paint Shop Pro from JASC, 360
palettes with GIF and JPEG formats, 214
paper, virtues of, 23

paper documents, converting into intranet documents, 181–183
paper publishing compared to intranet publishing, 33–34
paperwork, eliminating, 23
parametric searching, 201
parent style sheets, 316
partnering intranet projects, 164
password text in HTML forms, 88, 89
passwords, 272
patches, 124, 337
patent, 71
PCI (Peripheral Component interconnect), 337
PCs, slots in, 70
PDF documents, bookmarks in, 199, 200
PDF files, 188
PDF (Portable Document Format), 178, 188, 337, 358
PDFWriter, 188
people costs of intranet publishing, 46–48
people issues of intranet maintenance, 232–235
performance
  designing for, 258–263
  monitoring, 263–266
  optimizing an intranet for, 250
  planning for, 309
Performance Monitor in Windows NT Server, 265
periodicals, posting on an intranet, 82–84
Peripheral Component Interconnect. *See* PCI
PERL (Practical Extraction and Report Language), 337
personal search engines, 201
Personal Web Server, 224
personal Web server software, 9
Photoshop 4.0 Tryout, 360
Photoshop, reducing the color depth of an image in, 260
physical security for intranets, 269
pilot project, 161
pixels, 185, 213, 260
PKZIP, 124
plain text in HTML forms, 88, 89
plain text publishing system, 58
planning projects for success, 165
platform, 337
platform independence
  of intranets, 13
  of Java, 221

platform support of search engines, 202
plug-ins. *See also* helper programs
 for CBT programs, 144–145
 evaluating and testing new versions of, 248
plumbing, 34
 as a factor in intranet publishing, 70
Point-to-Point Protocol. *See* PPP
Point-to-Point Tunneling Protocol. *See* PPTP
policies and procedures manuals, publishing on intranets, 78–80
Policies Now! from KnowledgePoint, 79
pop-up windows, browsers and, 193
portability of web server programming, 238–239
Portable Document Format. *See* PDF
portable document format software for custom HTML, 177–178
porting software to different computers, 30–31
portrait orientation, 174
Post method, 92
PostScript files, creating PDF files from, 188
PostScript Level 3, 319–321
PostScript page description language, 337
power backup, 284–285
power conditioning, 337
power-on passwords, 280
PowerPoint 95, Internet Assistant for, 358
PowerPoint 97, viewer for, 359
PowerPoint for IBT authoring, 145–146
PowerPoint slide show of several organizational charts, 78
PPP (Point-to-Point Protocol), 337
PPTP (Point-to-Point Tunneling Protocol, 282–283, 337
Practical Extraction and Report Language. *See* PERL
predefined page element combinations and behaviors, 174
Premiere 4.2 Tryout, 360–361

PRI (Primary Rate Interface), 337
price lists on an intranet, 110
Primavera Project Planner 2.0 (P3 2.0), 102
printed pages, compared to intranet pages, 208–209
printing
 from framesets, 198
 Internet technologies and, 13
 pitfalls, 52
private Internets, 10–12
private key, 282
private key encryption, 337. *See also* encryption
problem management systems, supporting knowledge-base publishing via HTML, 122
problem reports, submitting on an intranet, 134–135
process reengineering, implementing with intranet projects, 105–106
processors, adding power to, 252
product design and manufacturing, streamlining with intranet publishing, 100–102
product diagrams and illustrations, providing, 109–110
product information, providing to sales people, 108–113
product pictures, links page for, 110
product-specific navigation, 198–200
product-specific security, 274–275
productivity
 as the goal for intranet systems, 310
 improving with Internet technology, 17–18
professionals, as a market for Information Technology (IT) education, 140
program code, embedding into HTML files, 223
programming, cost of custom, 44
programming language, compared to an interface, 91
programming toolkits
 for Java, 221
 weaknesses of, 51

progressive disclosure, 194
Progressive Networks, intranet video products from, 137
progressive rendering in Acrobat 3.0, 189
project leaders
 as a constituency, 157, 158
 support of intranet projects, 159
project management, intranet-enabled, 102
project management program, 162
projects
 planning the first, 161–165
 tracking the progress of, 162
proprietary standards, 13
protocols, 8–9, 24, 337
prototype model of a system, 161
proximity, searching by in Acrobat, 189
proximity statements, 201
proxy servers, 277–278, 279, 338
public key, 282
public key encryption, 338. *See also* encryption
publishing, 22
 strategies for, 172–174
publishing applications, costs of, 44–45
publishing on intranets, benefits of, 23–34
publishing policies for an intranet publishing system, 234
pull of content. *See* push publishing
pull software distribution, 124–128
pull software distribution system, starting with, 128
purchase requisition publishing system, 96–97
push downloads, limiting, 262
push publishing, 205–206
push software distribution systems, 128–129

QuarkXPress, HTML conversion capabilities of, 184
QuickTime video format, 136, 220, 338

Index

• R •

RA (RealAudio) format, 215
radio buttons in HTML forms, 89
RAID (Redundant Arrays of Inexpensive Disks), 285
RAM (Random Access Memory), 338
read-only access, 126
read-only database publishing applications, 15
read-only embedding, 322
read permissions, assigning in IIS, 271, 272, 273
Reader program, 189
real time, 40
RealAudio, playing, 216
RealAudio technology, 322–323
RealVideo from Progressive Networks, 220
Red Alert program, automatic downloading of Web pages, 245
red dot system, 244
redundancy, avoiding, 49
redundancy options, 288
redundant disk drives, 335
reengineering, 104
references, on an intranet, 111–112
regions, in image maps, 196
relational databases, 323
relative links, portability of, 239
remote access security, 276–280
remote administration of search engines, 203
repurposing, 173
requisitions. See purchase requisition
Reset form button in HTML forms, 89
resistance to change by users, 53–54
response time, effect on user productivity, 249–250
retirement plan data, posting on an intranet, 81
revenue enhancement with Internet technology, 17
rich text publishing system, 58
routers, 8, 11, 338
  packet-filtering, 277
RTF (Rich Text Format), 338

• S •

sales bulletins on an intranet, 113
sales leads, publishing, 114
sales support, providing general, 115
sales support data, supplying, 107–115
sales support home page, 107–108
Sandia Labs, intranet projects, 31
Save as HTML command in Word 97, 183
scalability of intranet projects, 51
scanners, cost of, 45
Schedule+, Interent Assistant for, 358
schedules, posting on an intranet, 84
score in Macromedia Director, 219
screen, designing for, 310
screens, compared to pages, 208–209
<SCRIPT> tag in HTML, 223
scripts, 92
SCSI disk drives, compared to EIDE, 253
SCSI (Small Computer Systems Interface), 338
Seagate Crystal Reports, bundled with Internet Information Server, 64
Search '97, 204
search engines, 200, 338
  as an alternative to hyperlink navigation, 200–201
  evaluation criteria for, 201–203
  in IBT, 148
  performance testing, 259
search method flexibility of search engines, 201–202
searchable documentation, publishing on an intranet, 130–134
secret intranet projects, 49
Secure HyperText Transfer Protocol. See SHTTP
Secure Sockets Layer (SSL), 281–282, 283
Securities and Exchange Commission (SEC) Web site, 113

security, 267
  application-level, 271–274
  communications, 280–283
  dial-up, 278–280
  Internet compared to traditional network, 13
  product-specific, 274–275
  remote access, 276–280
  uptime, 283–289
security features of Java, 221
segmentation, 338
segmenting, 253
selectivity of search engines, 202
self-extracting archives, 124
self-tests, 143
server, 8, 338
  dealing with problems remotely, 245
  maintaining, 245–247
  selecting for intranet projects, 63–67
  tuning, 250, 251–254
server computer, 13
server databases, 114
server logs, remote access to, 246
server redundancy, 45
server-side image maps, 196, 334
Server Side Includes. See SSIs
Service Manager, logging activity to a file or database, 246
service marks, 71
SGML (Standard Generalized Markup Language), 101, 225, 338
shareware, 355
shocked animations, 219
Shockwave, 339, 359
Shockwave plug-in, 186, 219
shttp:// prefix, 281
SHTTP (Secure HyperText Transfer Protocol), 281, 339
signature, 209
  linking to the home page in, 195
simple data, 58
simple data flows, 58–60
simple intranet systems, 57–58
Simple Mail Transfer Protocol (SMTP). See SMTP
Simple Network Management Protocol. See SNMP
simple technology, 60–61
single-spaces, replacing double-spaces after periods, 185

Site Analyst component of Site Server, 241, 242
site development tools, cost of, 43–44
site maps, 240–241, 339
SLED (Single Large Expensive Disks), 285
SM, 71
SMTP (Simple Mail Transfer Protocol), 8
SMTP (Simple Mail Transport Protocol), 339
SNMP (Simple Network Management Protocol), 244, 339
  effect on network speed, 264
software
  cost of specialized, 44
  distributing over an intranet, 124–129
  publishing documentation for commercial, 132–133
  publishing documentation for custom, 133–134
software distribution capability of NMS software, 244
software distribution on an intranet, 123–129
software for intranet publishing, costs of, 42–45
software guidelines for intranets, 235–236
software porting to different computers, 30–31
software toolkits, selecting for scalability, 51
sound
  adding to IBT, 151
  implementing on an intranet, 215–216
sound file editing utility, 361
Sound Forge, 216, 217
Sound Forge XP demo from Sonic Foundry, 361
sound formats, 215
sources of intranet documents, 181–188
specification sheets, providing over an intranet, 108–109
SQL (Structured Query Language), 114, 339
SSIs (Server Side Includes), 95, 238
SSL (Secure Sockets Layer), 281–282, 283. See also certificate
Standard Generalized Markup Language. See SGML

standard templates, posting, 263
standards for intranets, 313
start-up page. See home page
stateless nature of intranets, 192
static documents, 58
static HTML forms, 95
stock HTML, 175–177
stock purchase plan data, posting on an intranet, 81
streaming audio, 216, 322–323
streaming audio and video, firewalls and, 278
streaming audio file format, 215
streaming formats for sound or video, 151
Structured Query Language. See SQL
Stuffit Lite 3.6 from Aladdin Systems, 359–360
style sheets, 316, 339
Submit form button in HTML forms, 89
subnetting. See segmentation
success
  announcing, 300
  measuring for intranet publishing projects, 168–170
  planning for, 307–308
success stories, gathering, 170
suggestion box for users, 299
SuiteSpot, 65
SupportMagic from Magic Solutions, 122
surge protection, 285
switched Ethernet, 255
switching hub, 339
symmetric encryption, 337. See also private key encryption
Symmetric MultiProcessing (SMP), 252
system management of intranets, 48
system users. See users

● T ●

table of contents, dynamic, 101, 225, 317
table of contents window and document window, providing with frames, 198
tables, 339
  HTML, 73–75
  as positioning tools, 75
tabular data, HTML and, 73–75

tag, 339
TCO (Total Cost of Ownership), 339
TCP/IP communications, encrypting, 281
TCP/IP (Transmission Control Protocol/Internet Protocol), 8, 11, 340
  running the most efficient, 256
tech support intranet, 123
technical education. See training
technical staffs, cost of, 47
technical support
  intranet-based, 123
  obtaining on an intranet, 104
technical videos, publishing on an intranet, 135–137
technology
  fitting to an intranet project, 63–70
  simple, 60–61
technology briefings, 301
templates, 340
  for conversion to HTML, 177
  on the CD-ROM with this book, 361
  posting standard, 263
test results, scoring cumulatively for a session in IBT, 150
testimonials, posting, 111–112
text and graphics publishing system, 58
text area in HTML forms, 88, 89
text-based training materials, making available on an intranet, 142, 143
text colors, choosing in Netscape Navigator, 210, 211
text formatting of intranet pages, 210–211
Thadhani, Arvind, 249–250
thin client, 24, 340
thoroughness of search engines, 202
TIFF (Tagged Image File Format), 340
tightly coupled software systems, 239
tiled GIF images, 148
tiles, 340
tiling, 211
TM, 71
token generators, 272
Toolbook II Instructor 5.0, 145
top-down projects, 156

Index

Total Cost of Ownership. *See* TCO
tracking of software licenses, 244
trade secrets, 72
trademarks, 71–72
training
  costs of, 47–48
  delivery over an intranet, 142–146
training opportunities, posting on an intranet, 82
transaction processing applications, 40
Transit Central from InfoAccess, 177
Transmission Control Protocol/Internet Protocol. *See* TCP/IP
Transmitter server-side component of Castanet, 206
transparent GIF, 340
Transportation Work Station Net (TWSNet), 197
travel information, posting on an intranet, 100
trip expense reports. *See* expense reports
true color, 260, 340
TrueDoc, 321–322, 340
TrueType fonts in intranet pages, 210
trunk, 255
Tumbleweed Publishing Essentials software, 178
Tuner client-side software of Castanet, 206
TWAIN standard, 340
two-way intranet publishing system, designing, 87–88
two-way, one-to-many system, 59
TXT file suffix, 171

• U •

umbrella NMS, 264
Uniform Resource Locators. *See* URLs
Uninterruptible Power Supply (UPS). *See* UPS (Uninterruptible Power Supply)
universal servers, 323
UNIX operating system, 340
updates
  monitoring which pages need, 243
  setting regular schedules for, 243
uploading, 340
UPS (Uninterruptible Power Supply), 284–285, 340
  sizing of, 285
upsizing, intranet publishing systems, 32
uptime, 48
uptime security, 283–289
URLs (Uniform Resource Locators), 9, 195, 341
  embedding new into e-mail notification messages, 242
user error, Network PCs and, 37
user information on a Help Desk intranet, 120
user interface, 207
  importance of, 310
  inconsistent, 49–50
  of intranets, 28–30
user knowledge bases, 134
User Manager for Domains, 270
user productivity, effect of response time on, 249–250
user support for intranet systems, 234–235
user surveys, 61, 102–103
user workstations, names assigned to, 238
users
  as a constituency, 157, 158
  as a market for Information Technology (IT) education, 140
  cultivating key, 301
  needs and wants of, 61–63
  ongoing intranet education for, 299
  resistance to change, 53–54
  suggestion box for, 299
  support of intranet projects, 160
  surveying, 61
  tracking the number of, 169
utilities on the CD-ROM with this book, 358–360

• V •

values in HTML form check boxes, 88
VBScript
  applications of, 223
  compared to JavaScript, 224
  language, 341
  from Microsoft, 223
VDOLive from VDONet, 220
vector files, converting to GIF or JPEG format, 186
vector format, 110
vector graphics, 213, 341
vector images in Flash 2, 218
Verify Links command in FrontPage Explorer, 241
Verisign, applying to for digital certificates, 282
Verity, search technology products, 204
Verity Intelliserv, 206
Veronica, 8, 341
video
  adding to IBT, 151
  on an intranet page, 219–220
video clip utility program, 360–361
video clips, cost of capturing and compressing, 45
videos, publishing on an intranet, 135–137
videotape, capturing to a digital format, 136
View⇨Document Source command in Netscape Navigator, 26–27
View⇨Source command in Microsoft Internet Explorer, 26
Viewer for Excel, 359
Viewer for PowerPoint97, 359
Viewer for Word, 359
viewers, for displaying vector illustrations, 110
views, seeing intranet data in different, 225
virtual machine software, 179, 221
virtual printer, 178
  for creating PDF files, 188
virtual private networks, 9
Virtual Reality Modeling Language. *See* VRML
viruses. *See* computer viruses
Visio, building organization charts, 77
Visio Internet Assistant, converting organization charts to HTML, 77
Visio Professional, 121
visit, 341
VRML (Virtual Reality Modeling Language), 341
VXtreme Web Theater, 137

• W •

W3C. *See* World Wide Web Consortium
WAIS (Wide Area Information Server), 8, 341
wallpaper, 296
WAN links, 255
WANs, 9, 341
  monitoring, 264
warm standby, 285
watchdog programs, 271
WAV (Waveform Audio) format, 215
Web, 9, 341
  multimedia and, 212–220
Web Analyzer from InContext Systems, 240
web applets, writing Java code for, 31
web browser. *See* browser
web page design, object-oriented approach, 227
web page design programs on the CD-ROM with this book, 362
web page editing, tools designed for, 224–228
web page hyperlinks, embedding in mail messages, 296
Web Page Wizard in Word 97, 183, 184
web pages, 9
  interactive touches in, 221
  viewing the underlying HTML commands, 26–27
web searchable intranets, 131
web server applications, disabling unused, 273
web server performance, tools for tracking on intranets, 265–266
web server programming, portability of, 238–239
web server programs, security features of, 271–273
web servers, 9
  APIs in, 94–95
  log files in, 245–247
  selecting for intranet projects, 63–67
  splitting chores across multiple machines, 254
  tuning, 250, 251–254
Web Site API, 94
web site management software, 224, 225
web sites
  design principles for, 207–212
  on the CD-ROM with this book, 362
  standardizing key aspects of, 49–50
Web Theater from Vtreme, 220
WebBots, 224
webcasting. *See* push publishing
WebFIND! search utility, 203, 204
webmasters, 341
  costs of, 47
  hiring and training, 232–234
  ongoing education for, 233–234
WebMorsels from Image Club, 211
WebSite 1.1, 67
WebSite Professional, 66
WebWorks Lite from Quadralay, bundled with Adobe FrameMaker 5.1, 185
WebWorks Publisher, bundled with Adobe FrameMaker 5.1, 185
welcome page. *See* home page
wetware, 46–47
Whip plug-in software, 100, 213
Wide Area Information Server. *See* WAIS
Wide Area Networks. *See* WANs
widgets, 149, 150
Windows 95
  backing up, 288
  fix for premature memory loss from intranet links, 248
Windows BMP files, converting to GIF or JPEG, 227
Windows Media Player utility, 216
Windows NT, 336
Windows NT Server
  Performance Monitor, 265
  User Manager for Domains, 270
Windows Sound Recorder utility, 216
WinHelp format, 132
WINS (Windows Internet Naming Service), 237, 341
WinZip 95 v6.1, 360
WinZip compression utility, 124
Wizards, 66
Word 97, HTML conversion capabilities, 183
Word
  Internet Assistant for, 358
  viewer for, 359
Word Internet Assistant, 183
word processing programs, web publishing capabilities of, 183
workflow applications, 98
working prototype of a system, 161
World Wide Web Consortium, 314, 341
World Wide Web. *See* Web
WSAPI (Web Site API), 94
WWW (World Wide Web). *See* Web
WYSIWYG (What You See Is What You Get), 52, 341

• X •

XML (eXtensible Markup Language), 317, 342

• Z •

zip file, 342

Java™ Development Kit Version 1.1.3 Binary Code License

This binary code license ("License") contains rights and restrictions associated with use of the accompanying software and documentation ("Software"). Read the License carefully before installing the Software. By installing the Software you agree to the terms and conditions of this License.

1. **Limited License Grant.** Sun grants to you ("Licensee") a non-exclusive, non-transferable limited license to use the Software without fee for evaluation of the Software and for development of Java™ compatible applets and applications. Licensee may make one archival copy of the Software and may redistribute complete, unmodified copies of the Software to software developers within Licensee's organization to avoid unnecessary download time, provided that this License conspicuously appears with all copies of the Software. Except for the foregoing, Licensee may not redistribute the Software in whole or in part, either separately or included with a product. Refer to the Java Runtime Environment Version 1.1.1 binary code license (http://java.sun.com/products/JDK/1.1.1/index.html) for the availability of runtime code which may be distributed with Java compatible applets and applications.

2. **Java Platform Interface.** Licensee may not modify the Java Platform Interface ("JPI", identified as classes contained within the "java" package or any subpackages of the "java" package), by creating additional classes within the JPI or otherwise causing the addition to or modification of the classes in the JPI. In the event that Licensee creates any Java-related API and distributes such API to others for applet or application development, Licensee must promptly publish an accurate specification for such API for free use by all developers of Java-based software.

3. **Restrictions.** Software is confidential copyrighted information of Sun and title to all copies is retained by Sun and/or its licensors. Licensee shall not modify, decompile, disassemble, decrypt, extract, or otherwise reverse engineer Software. Software may not be leased, assigned, or sublicensed, in whole or in part. Software is not designed or intended for use in on-line control of aircraft, air traffic, aircraft navigation or aircraft communications; or in the design, construction, operation or maintenance of any nuclear facility. Licensee warrants that it will not use or redistribute the Software for such purposes.

4. **Trademarks and Logos.** This License does not authorize Licensee to use any Sun name, trademark or logo. Licensee acknowledges that Sun owns the Java trademark and all Java-related trademarks, logos and icons including the Coffee Cup and Duke ("Java Marks") and agrees to: (i) to comply with the Java Trademark Guidelines at http://java.sun.com/trademarks.html; (ii) not do anything harmful to or inconsistent with Sun's rights in the Java Marks; and (iii) assist Sun in protecting those rights, including assigning to Sun any rights acquired by Licensee in any Java Mark.

5. **Disclaimer of Warranty.** Software is provided "AS IS," without a warranty of any kind. ALL EXPRESS OR IMPLIED REPRESENTATIONS AND WARRANTIES, INCLUDING ANY IMPLIED WARRANTY OF MERCHANTABILITY, FITNESS FOR A PARTICULAR PURPOSE OR NON-INFRINGEMENT, ARE HEREBY EXCLUDED.

6. **Limitation of Liability.** SUN AND ITS LICENSORS SHALL NOT BE LIABLE FOR ANY DAMAGES SUFFERED BY LICENSEE OR ANY THIRD PARTY AS A RESULT OF USING OR DISTRIBUTING SOFTWARE. IN NO EVENT WILL SUN OR ITS LICENSORS BE LIABLE FOR ANY LOST REVENUE, PROFIT OR DATA, OR FOR DIRECT, INDIRECT, SPECIAL, CONSEQUENTIAL, INCIDENTAL OR PUNITIVE DAMAGES, HOWEVER CAUSED AND REGARDLESS OF THE THEORY OF LIABILITY, ARISING OUT OF THE USE OF OR INABILITY TO USE SOFTWARE, EVEN IF SUN HAS BEEN ADVISED OF THE POSSIBILITY OF SUCH DAMAGES.

7. **Termination. Licensee may terminate this License at any time by destroying all copies of Software.** This License will terminate immediately without notice from Sun if Licensee fails to comply with any provision of this License. Upon such termination, Licensee must destroy all copies of Software.

8. **Export Regulations.** Software, including technical data, is subject to U.S. export control laws, including the U.S. Export Administration Act and its associated regulations, and may be subject to export or import regulations in other countries. Licensee agrees to comply strictly with all such regulations and acknowledges that it has the responsibility to obtain licenses to export, re-export, or import Software. Software may not be downloaded, or otherwise exported or re-exported (i) into, or to a national or resident of, Cuba, Iraq, Iran, North Korea, Libya, Sudan, Syria or any country to which the U.S. has embargoed goods; or (ii) to anyone on the U.S. Treasury Department's list of Specially Designated Nations or the U.S. Commerce Department's Table of Denial Orders.

9. **Restricted Rights.** Use, duplication or disclosure by the United States government is subject to the restrictions as set forth in the Rights in Technical Data and Computer Software Clauses in DFARS 252.227-7013(c) (1) (ii) and FAR 52.227-19(c) (2) as applicable.

10. **Governing Law.** Any action related to this License will be governed by California law and controlling U.S. federal law. No choice of law rules of any jurisdiction will apply.

11. **Severability.** If any of the above provisions are held to be in violation of applicable law, void, or unenforceable in any jurisdiction, then such provisions are herewith waived to the extent necessary for the License to be otherwise enforceable in such jurisdiction. However, if in Sun's opinion deletion of any provisions of the License by operation of this paragraph unreasonably compromises the rights or increase the liabilities of Sun or its licensors, Sun reserves the right to terminate the License and refund the fee paid by Licensee, if any, as Licensee's sole and exclusive remedy.

IDG Books Worldwide, Inc., End-User License Agreement

READ THIS. You should carefully read these terms and conditions before opening the software packet(s) included with this book ("Book"). This is a license agreement ("Agreement") between you and IDG Books Worldwide, Inc. ("IDGB"). By opening the accompanying software packet(s), you acknowledge that you have read and accept the following terms and conditions. If you do not agree and do not want to be bound by such terms and conditions, promptly return the Book and the unopened software packet(s) to the place you obtained them for a full refund.

1. **License Grant.** IDGB grants to you (either an individual or entity) a nonexclusive license to use one copy of the enclosed software program(s) (collectively, the "Software") solely for your own personal or business purposes on a single computer (whether a standard computer or a workstation component of a multiuser network). The Software is in use on a computer when it is loaded into temporary memory (RAM) or installed into permanent memory (hard disk, CD-ROM, or other storage device). IDGB reserves all rights not expressly granted herein.

2. **Ownership.** IDGB is the owner of all right, title, and interest, including copyright, in and to the compilation of the Software recorded on the disk(s) or CD-ROM ("Software Media"). Copyright to the individual programs recorded on the Software Media is owned by the author or other authorized copyright owner of each program. Ownership of the Software and all proprietary rights relating thereto remain with IDGB and its licensers.

3. **Restrictions on Use and Transfer.**

    (a) You may only (i) make one copy of the Software for backup or archival purposes, or (ii) transfer the Software to a single hard disk, provided that you keep the original for backup or archival purposes. You may not (i) rent or lease the Software, (ii) copy or reproduce the Software through a LAN or other network system or through any computer subscriber system or bulletin-board system, or (iii) modify, adapt, or create derivative works based on the Software.

    (b) You may not reverse engineer, decompile, or disassemble the Software. You may transfer the Software and user documentation on a permanent basis, provided that the transferee agrees to accept the terms and conditions of this Agreement and you retain no copies. If the Software is an update or has been updated, any transfer must include the most recent update and all prior versions.

4. **Restrictions on Use of Individual Programs.** You must follow the individual requirements and restrictions detailed for each individual program in Appendix C ("About the CD-ROM") of this Book. These limitations are also contained in the individual license agreements recorded on the Software Media. These limitations may include a requirement that after using the program for a specified period of time, the user must pay a registration fee or discontinue use. By opening the Software packet(s), you will be agreeing to abide by the licenses and restrictions for these individual programs that are detailed in Appendix C ("About the CD-ROM") and on the Software Media. None of the material on this Software Media or listed in this Book may ever be redistributed, in original or modified form, for commercial purposes.

5. **Limited Warranty.**

    (a) IDGB warrants that the Software and Software Media are free from defects in materials and workmanship under normal use for a period of sixty (60) days from the date of purchase of this Book. If IDGB receives notification within the warranty period of defects in materials or workmanship, IDGB will replace the defective Software Media.

    (b) **IDGB AND THE AUTHOR OF THE BOOK DISCLAIM ALL OTHER WARRANTIES, EXPRESS OR IMPLIED, INCLUDING WITHOUT LIMITATION IMPLIED WARRANTIES OF MERCHANTABILITY AND FITNESS FOR A PARTICULAR PURPOSE, WITH RESPECT TO THE SOFTWARE, THE PROGRAMS, THE SOURCE CODE CONTAINED THEREIN, AND/OR THE TECHNIQUES DESCRIBED IN THIS BOOK. IDGB DOES NOT WARRANT THAT THE FUNCTIONS CONTAINED IN THE SOFTWARE WILL MEET YOUR REQUIREMENTS OR THAT THE OPERATION OF THE SOFTWARE WILL BE ERROR FREE.**

    (c) This limited warranty gives you specific legal rights, and you may have other rights that vary from jurisdiction to jurisdiction.

6. **Remedies.**

    (a) IDGB's entire liability and your exclusive remedy for defects in materials and workmanship shall be limited to replacement of the Software Media, which may be returned to IDGB with a copy of your receipt at the following address: Software Media Fulfillment Department, Attn.: *Intranet Publishing For Dummies*, IDG Books Worldwide, Inc., 7260 Shadeland Station, Ste. 100, Indianapolis, IN 46256, or call 800-762-2974. Please allow three to four weeks for delivery. This Limited Warranty is void if failure of the Software Media has resulted from accident, abuse, or misapplication. Any replacement Software Media will be warranted for the remainder of the original warranty period or thirty (30) days, whichever is longer.

    (b) In no event shall IDGB or the author be liable for any damages whatsoever (including without limitation damages for loss of business profits, business interruption, loss of business information, or any other pecuniary loss) arising from the use of or inability to use the Book or the Software, even if IDGB has been advised of the possibility of such damages.

    (c) Because some jurisdictions do not allow the exclusion or limitation of liability for consequential or incidental damages, the above limitation or exclusion may not apply to you.

7. **U.S. Government Restricted Rights.** Use, duplication, or disclosure of the Software by the U.S. Government is subject to restrictions stated in paragraph (c)(1)(ii) of the Rights in Technical Data and Computer Software clause of DFARS 252.227-7013, and in subparagraphs (a) through (d) of the Commercial Computer–Restricted Rights clause at FAR 52.227-19, and in similar clauses in the NASA FAR supplement, when applicable.

8. **General.** This Agreement constitutes the entire understanding of the parties and revokes and supersedes all prior agreements, oral or written, between them and may not be modified or amended except in a writing signed by both parties hereto that specifically refers to this Agreement. This Agreement shall take precedence over any other documents that may be in conflict herewith. If any one or more provisions contained in this Agreement are held by any court or tribunal to be invalid, illegal, or otherwise unenforceable, each and every other provision shall remain in full force and effect.

Installation Instructions

*F*or information on installing the software from the CD-ROM included with this book, see Appendix C. Use of the included Sun Microsystems Java™ Development Kit software is subject to the Binary Code License terms and conditions on page 382. Read the license carefully. By opening this package, you are agreeing to be bound by the terms and conditions of this license from Sun Microsystems, Inc.

IDG BOOKS WORLDWIDE REGISTRATION CARD

Visit our Web site at http://www.idgbooks.com

ISBN Number: 0-7645-0222-0
Title of this book: Intranet Publishing For Dummies®
My overall rating of this book: ❏ Very good [1] ❏ Good [2] ❏ Satisfactory [3] ❏ Fair [4] ❏ Poor [5]
How I first heard about this book:
❏ Found in bookstore; name: [6]   ❏ Book review: [7]
❏ Advertisement: [8]   ❏ Catalog: [9]
❏ Word of mouth; heard about book from friend, co-worker, etc.: [10]   ❏ Other: [11]

What I liked most about this book:

What I would change, add, delete, etc., in future editions of this book:

Other comments:

Number of computer books I purchase in a year: ❏ 1 [12] ❏ 2-5 [13] ❏ 6-10 [14] ❏ More than 10 [15]
I would characterize my computer skills as: ❏ Beginner [16] ❏ Intermediate [17] ❏ Advanced [18] ❏ Professional [19]
I use ❏ DOS [20] ❏ Windows [21] ❏ OS/2 [22] ❏ Unix [23] ❏ Macintosh [24] ❏ Other: [25]_____
(please specify)
I would be interested in new books on the following subjects:
(please check all that apply, and use the spaces provided to identify specific software)
❏ Word processing: [26]   ❏ Spreadsheets: [27]
❏ Data bases: [28]   ❏ Desktop publishing: [29]
❏ File Utilities: [30]   ❏ Money management: [31]
❏ Networking: [32]   ❏ Programming languages: [33]
❏ Other: [34]

I use a PC at (please check all that apply): ❏ home [35] ❏ work [36] ❏ school [37] ❏ other: [38]
The disks I prefer to use are ❏ 5.25 [39] ❏ 3.5 [40] ❏ other: [41]
I have a CD ROM: ❏ yes [42] ❏ no [43]
I plan to buy or upgrade computer hardware this year: ❏ yes [44] ❏ no [45]
I plan to buy or upgrade computer software this year: ❏ yes [46] ❏ no [47]

Name: **Business title:** [48]   **Type of Business:** [49]
Address (❏ home [50] ❏ work [51]/Company name:)
Street/Suite#
City [52]/**State** [53]/**Zip code** [54]:   **Country** [55]

❏ **I liked this book!** You may quote me by name in future
  IDG Books Worldwide promotional materials.

My daytime phone number is _____

IDG BOOKS WORLDWIDE™
THE WORLD OF COMPUTER KNOWLEDGE®

❏ **YES!**
Please keep me informed about IDG Books Worldwide's World of Computer Knowledge. Send me your latest catalog.

NO POSTAGE
NECESSARY
IF MAILED
IN THE
UNITED STATES

BUSINESS REPLY MAIL
FIRST CLASS MAIL   PERMIT NO. 2605   FOSTER CITY, CALIFORNIA

IDG Books Worldwide
919 E Hillsdale Blvd, Ste 400
Foster City, CA 94404-9691